# A
# Call to
# Character

Also by Colin Greer

*The Great School Legend*
*Choosing Equality* (co-author)
*After Reagan, What?* (co-author)
*What Nixon Is Doing to Us* (co-author)
*The Solution as Part of the Problem*
*After De-schooling, What?* (co-author)
*The Divided Society*
*Cobweb Attitudes*


Also by Herbert Kohl

*The Age of Complexity*
*Thirty-six Children*
*The Open Classroom*
*Reading How To*
*Golden Boy as Anthony Cool: A Photo Essay on Names and Graffiti*
*Half the House*
*View from the Oak* (with Judith Kohl)
*Growing with Your Children*
*A Book of Puzzlement*
*Basic Skills*
*Growing Minds: On Becoming a Teacher*
*Mathematical Puzzlements*
*Making Theater: Developing Plays with Young People*
*The Question Is College*
*From Archetype to Zeitgeist: An Essential Guide to Powerful Ideas*
*I Won't Learn from You*
*Should We Burn Babar?*

# A Call to Character

## A FAMILY TREASURY

*of stories, poems, plays, proverbs, and fables to guide the development of values for you and your children*

## Colin Greer &
## Herbert Kohl, *Editors*

HarperCollins*Publishers*

Permission acknowledgments appear on pages 441–450.

A CALL TO CHARACTER. Copyright © 1995 by Colin Greer and Herbert Kohl. All rights
reserved. Printed in the United States of America. No part of this book may be used or
reproduced in any manner whatsoever without written permission except in the case of
brief quotations embodied in critical articles and reviews. For information, address
HarperCollins Publishers, Inc., 10 East 53rd Street, New York, NY 10022.

HarperCollins books may be purchased for educational, business, or sales promotional
use. For information please write: Special Markets Department, HarperCollins
Publishers, Inc., 10 East 53rd Street, New York, NY 10022.

FIRST EDITION

*Designed by Nancy Singer*

Library of Congress Cataloging-in-Publication Data

Greer, Colin.
    A call to character : a family treasury / Colin Greer and Herbert Kohl. — 1st ed.
        p.   cm.
    Includes index.
    ISBN 0–06–017339–4
    1. Conduct of life—Literary collections.   2. Children's literature.   I. Kohl,
Herbert R.   II. Title.
PN6014.G72   1995
808.8'0353—dc20                                                        95-37302

95 96 97 98 99 ❖/RRD 10 9 8 7 6 5 4 3 2 1

*C.G.*
*To Franny—my love; and Olivia, Lucy, and Simon, our treasures*

———•••———

*H.K.*
*To a decent future for all children*

# Contents

PLAYFULNESS

Part 3: Values That Relate to People One Doesn't Know and
Nature (Idealism, Compassion, Responsibility, Balance,
and Fairness)

RESPONSIBILITY    332

PART 4: Values That Relate to Love

# Acknowledgments

---•◦•---

First, we want to thank each other for partnership in this venture. The making of the book has been as much a study group in moral philosophy as a literary voyage. Our families have been especially important in supporting our work and contributing selections and advice as the book developed. We especially appreciate their patience and indulgence, particularly when work on the book, coast to coast, meant very late nights and very early mornings.

In addition, lunches, meetings, and phone conversations with our editor, Hugh Van Dusen, and his associate, Katherine Boyle Ekrem, have been invaluable.

There are a few other people who made this book possible. Leon Chazanow, who magically traced down good ideas and typed and retyped the manuscript for us, worked through several nights. Keeping hundreds of selections organized through draft after draft was a major feat. His wife and family contributed to the making of the work and were patient when he put us first for a while. We thank them all.

No less an effort was demanded of Arthur Tobier on permissions. It required a thorough knowledge of the selections, several careful readings of the scanned material, and a cooperative family, ready to take numerous calls for Arthur from us and others at hours when any reasonable family might expect telephone calls to be personal, not work-related. Once again we thank them all.

We also acknowledge with gratitude the time and effort put in by Erick Ritchie, and his family, including his mom and dad, Lorie and Armand, and his brothers, Stevie and Tony, all of Point Arena, California. They scanned over a thousand pages of text and corrected the scanned material. Also helping with scanning were Wendy, Chad, and Lorraine Ruddick.

Thanks are due to Deborah Appleman, John Ramsey, and Herb's students at Carleton College. In addition, Daphne Muse was very helpful with ideas and selections and was a valuable source of moral support.

We also want to acknowledge the unfailing assistance of our agents, Elizabeth Kaplan and Wendy Weil, as well as Wendy's associate, Claire Needell.

As a final note about the construction of the book, all of the selections were read and agreed on by both of us. Herbert Kohl was primarily responsible for Part 1 and the sections on Balance, Compassion, and Fairness, and Colin Greer for Parts 2 and 4 and the sections on Idealism and Responsibility. We are both deeply indebted to the great literature collected here. The authors have given us—and we hope you, the reader—much for which to be thankful.

# A
# Call to
# Character

# General Introduction

———⋙◦⋘———

Children are wonderful and complicated. Understanding these simple things is the starting point of all good education—intellectual, social, and moral. It is sometimes difficult to keep this in mind as children grow and test out their strengths and values against the world. They do dangerous things, fall into and out of trouble, and invent preposterous schemes. But they also charm and move us by their unexpected insights into emotions and character and their passionate concern for others. Moral development takes place slowly. As parents and caring adults, we have to remember that our children's values are in the process of formation. And we have to acknowledge, when we look at their struggles to become decent people, that the waters around them are muddied. We have to avoid blaming children for their moral confusion in a world that adults have been unable to make nurturing or welcoming. What we owe them is time, love, and counsel as they move toward independence and autonomy.

A Call to Character is our attempt to provide a resource for parents and caring adults that can be used to encourage young people to read, talk, and think about moral issues. The "call" of the title is the call of a familiar dinner bell to a feast with good friends, not a strident trumpet call to attention and obedience.

Character develops and is tested throughout life; it is not fixed once and for all. Self-respect is tested during hard times, and there are moments when compassion conflicts with self-interest. It is not easy to be consistently honest if one feels deprived. Loyalty to family and friends can often contradict loyalty to ideas or principles. There is no simple formula, comparable to $2 + 2 = 4$, to be universally applied in the realm of morality. However, this does not mean that all moral decisions are relative and all actions equally valid. There are some fundamental principles of decent behavior, the behavior that distinguishes a person of good character, that stand out and can be used to weigh moral decisions, and these center on self-respect and a deep caring for others.

Public figures such as Helen Keller, Benjamin Spock, Rosa Parks, Elie

1

Wiesel, Marian Wright Edelman, Grace Paley, Nelson Mandela, and Dolores Huerta come to mind when we think of people who combine this delicate balance between regard for oneself and concern for humanity. Indeed, part of why they are so well-known is that they stand up for others and do so with great personal clarity. But, of course, we've all met people whose strength of character, though it will never be known in a public way, nevertheless compels our admiration and imitation. These famous and not-so-famous moral heroes strike our imaginations and call on us to be better and stronger ourselves. They assume responsibility for their own lives and within their families and at the same time find ways to help people in their communities and advocate for those who need to be protected.

Character, in the sense we use the word in this book, is the constellation of values that lead to self-respect, dignity, reverence, and concern for the lives of others. It emerges throughout life and is not a moral nature that is set once and for all in childhood.

The stories, fairy tales, fables, poems, and other literature in this anthology illustrate the moral challenges people face and portray the development of character. They are particularly valuable guides for young people during those years when moral principles are internalized and children begin to organize their actions and opinions on the basis of values.

A Call to Character is a family reader to share with your children during the sensitive preadolescent years when character and values emerge most forcefully. The book is divided into four sections, the first three of which focus on clusters of character values: The first addresses values that refer primarily to one's self; the second, those that emerge in relationships with family, friends, and neighbors; and the third, values that relate to people one doesn't know, to society, and to nature. The fourth section is about love, the joyous and harmonious ideal of the fullness of living.

In the first part of the book, our selections address values that contribute to the personal strengths of eight- to thirteen-year-olds. This is the time of life when young people begin to act independently and raise serious moral questions, such as, Where do I stand? How do I respond? What kind of a person am I? It is the time when children begin to form personal answers to questions of courage, integrity, and self-discipline. It is also the time when they begin to move into the world on their own and make decisions guided by principle rather than impulse or the wishes of peers or adults. It is a time when there is a voice growing inside which speaks and says, "This is the real me," a time when parents are acutely aware that their children's growth pains are not solely physical.

The awakening of a "real self" is beautifully described by Emily Dickinson as a convergence:

> Each life converges to some centre
> Expressed or still

Character first emerges in relation to children's feelings about themselves and evolves in relation to their immediate social world and then to the larger world beyond family and friends. To an important degree young people build their own characters and choose the kinds of people they become. The development of such values as courage and integrity occurs as they make personal choices when facing moral dilemmas, so adults have to be sensitive to their autonomy. Consequently, discussion and storytelling rather than preaching or didactic teaching are the appropriate ways to help children as they learn to make these choices.

The power and liberating force of the inner voice is conveyed by the poet Denise Levertov in her "Variation on a Theme by Rainer Maria Rilke":

> A certain day became a presence to me,
> there it was, confronting me, a sky, air, light:
> a being. And before it started to descend
> from the height of noon, it leaned over
> and struck my shoulder as if with
> the flat of a sword, granting me
> honor and a task. The day's blow
> rang out, metallic, or it was I, a bell awakened,
> and what I heard was my whole self
> saying and singing what it knew: I can.

But courage is often not enough to sustain our inner voice and our striving toward autonomy and integrity. We have to learn how to apply ourselves wholeheartedly and persevere in the face of difficulties. This self-discipline enriches and enlarges us, making it possible to do more than dream of and insist on opportunities and projects for ourselves, but to plan and carry them out creatively and with good humor. With creativity comes the ability to solve problems. With playfulness and good humor we can deal with frustration.

Personal choices and imperatives involving courage, self-discipline, integrity, creativity, and playfulness characterize all stages of life, but they are especially heightened and poignant during early adolescence. The challenges of school, the temptations of the media and the streets, the drives to test the limits of other people's love all demand that youngsters find out who they are and discover the essential rudiments of their characters even as they are molding them. When that doesn't happen, all too often an extended inability to deal with personal problems and cold insensitivity to other people's lives follow. The poet Jimmy Santiago Baca expresses this need to know and draw moral strength from one's emerging self:

> I cannot fly or make something appear in my hand,
> I cannot make the heavens open or the earth tremble,
> I can live with myself, and I am amazed at myself, my love, my beauty,
> I am taken by my failures, astounded by my fears,
> I am stubborn and childish,
> in the midst of this wreckage of life they incurred,
> I practice being myself,
> and I have found parts of myself never dreamed of by me
> —"Who Understands Me Best but Me"

In the second part of *A Call to Character*, our attention turns to how we learn to live with others. This is another major aspect of the development of character. How we live with others, our social development, is in fact the testing and training ground for character. As young people discover the effect that they have on the people they know—friends, family, teachers, acquaintances—they begin to develop their ability to be loyal, generous, empathetic, and honest social actors. But acquiring and applying these values is a gradual process, involving the interplay of experience and reflection. That's why adaptability is important; youngsters can, and will likely have to, change their minds, learn from mistakes, resist what comes most easily, and embrace new challenges as they make their way in an uncertain world.

It is through caring contacts with adults that young people can learn about strength of character without the rigidity which follows the punishment and forced feeding that once typified moral education. Released from rigidity, children and adults can change when they are faced with new challenges.

Youngsters need opportunities to think important things through in discussion with adults they respect in safe and nondidactic settings. A grounded understanding of social character values such as loyalty, honesty, and empathy can evolve through the conversations that reading stories makes possible. This is the province of proverbs and parables.

In Tomie de Paola's *The Clown of God*, a poor boy rises to become a celebrated juggler because he can bring joy and light into people's lives. But with age his skills diminish, and so does his popularity. In the end, poor once again, he hides in an old chapel and juggles for the "sad" figure of Jesus in his mother's arms. The juggler dies at the climax of his performance:

> "And now," said Giovanni, smiling at the face of the child, "first the red ball, then the orange. . .
> "Next the yellow. . . "
> "And the green, blue, and violet."
> Around and up they went until they looked like a rainbow.
> "And finally," cried Giovanni, "the Sun in the Heavens!"
> The gold ball flew up and around, higher and higher.
> Giovanni had never juggled so well in all his life.

At Giovanni's death, on the final page of the book, we see the impact of the clown's return to his earlier goal of simply bringing joy into people's lives in a clear and powerful way as he responded to the pain in the baby's face; the baby Jesus is smiling.

In the third part of the book, we look to the larger world of people we don't know and of our planet itself. Every youngster faces the challenge of learning about the needs and rights of people she or he doesn't know and about nature. This is a larger, universal, dimension to the development of character, one that relates to how we respect people we don't know well or at all and the natural world, on which we depend but which can all too easily remain invisible to us. Values such as idealism, compassion, responsibility, balance, and fairness come into play here.

As youngsters prepare to become citizens of a democratic society in the midst of a troubled world, they need to learn how to be sensitive and caring actors whose decisions make a difference. To do this they need to keep their dreams alive and be able to face reality with the hope that the poet Shirley Kaufman expresses in these simple and elegant lines:

> It's not what I wake up to
> but what I dream.

Literature, and especially children's literature, frequently reminds us of the power of the person of vision; no more so than in Brian Jacques's *The Bellmaker: A Tale from Redwall*:

Many warriors own the glory
But the saying in Redwall is
"This is the Bellmaker's story
Because the dream was his."

The fourth and last section of the book is on love. The capacity to dream, the genius to see the best in others and to imagine what's possible despite the odds requires the ability to love deeply. All other values are sharpened and illuminated by love. As a result, love sustains character. And love and the joy that can accompany it allow for the expression of the fullest sense of ourselves and our greatest appreciation for others and for the world we share.

Character cannot exist without love, yet when love is present character can flourish in the most unlikely places; in the most hopeless of circumstances it can nourish the richest possibility in a person, in a situation, in life.

An entry from Anne Frank's diary clearly illustrates this blossoming:

*Saturday, February 12, 1944:*

*Dear Kitty,*

*The sun is shining, the sky is deep blue, there is a magnificent breeze, and I'm longing, really longing, for everything: conversations, freedom, friends, being alone. I long . . . to cry! I feel as if I were about to explode. I know crying would help, but I can't cry. I'm restless. I walk from one room to another, breathe through the crack in the window frame, feel my heart beating as if to say, "Fulfill my longing at last . . . "*

*I think Spring is inside me. I feel Spring awakening, I feel it in my entire body and soul. I have to force myself to act normally. I'm in a state of utter confusion, don't know what to read, what to write, what to do. I only know that I'm longing for something . . .*

*Yours, Anne*

On the basis of her marvelous capacity for love, Anne could, despite the horrors she faced, take great responsibility for who she was:

I have one outstanding trait in my character, which must strike anyone who knows me for any length of time, and that is my knowledge of

myself. I can watch myself and my actions, just like an outsider. The
Anne of every day I can face entirely without prejudice, without making excuses for her, and watch what's good and what's bad about her.
This "self-consciousness" haunts me, and every time I open my mouth I
know as soon as I've spoken whether "that ought to have been different" or "that was right as it was." There are so many things about myself
that I condemn; I couldn't begin to name them all. I understand more
and more how true Daddy's words were when he said: "All children
must look after their own upbringing." Parents can only give good
advice or put them on the right paths, but the final forming of a person's character lies in their own hands.

> —Anne Frank, *Anne Frank: The Diary of*
> *a Young Girl*

The selections in *A Call to Character* have been chosen to stimulate you
and your children to discuss moral and character issues. They come from
contemporary and older children's literature as well as from the many
traditions of fiction and poetry that are readily available in English. We
have chosen a variety of voices from many cultures and drawn, when
possible, on folk wisdom and oral traditions. Although all the selections
can be read in the context of thinking and talking about issues of moral
development, they can also be read for the sheer delight and insight they
offer. They can become a common literary ground to bring adults and
young people together in serious conversation.

One way to begin using *A Call to Character* is to browse through it,
reading here and there, and getting familiar with the contents. Let children discover the book for themselves in the kitchen or living room, or
anyplace they are likely to find it. Letting your children choose portions
of this book that they wish to share can help open the way for them to
bring up issues of concern and to think about them through the book's
selections and themes.

Stories can be transformative for children and parents alike. And the
experience of reading is enriched when people share a text. When we
read together we can directly connect our own lives to those of others
and test our visions of right and wrong through different eyes and experiences. Literature helps us learn what we can expect from life and what
we can give to it. Our stories, myths, and legends are not simply fictions
about "Once upon a time." They are the "might be" out of which we
imagine the many ways the world can be conceived or constructed. This
imagining makes it possible for children to sort and determine what they
believe and how they choose to act. It helps children to think through

moral dilemmas and articulate challenges as they shape their characters, and it helps adults reaffirm their own values and convictions.

Although it certainly helps to discuss moral dilemmas during and after crises, a better time to discuss them is before crises develop. Yet many families don't find the time to sit down and read and talk with children, especially as they grow away from bedtime stories and the first few years of school. Too often TV commands the attention of children and parents, and threatens to overwhelm their imaginations.

Regular reading with your children when they are eight to thirteen years old is just as important as it was when they were younger. But often when it is done at this age there is a school assignment to complete. Reading and using a range of literature to discuss serious issues outside of school is new for many families. It may seem awkward at first, but that is true of the establishment of any new family ritual. It requires patience and a bit of planning. Careful choice of the first selections to read together is crucial. It might make sense to begin with short, provocative selections that relate to issues your family has discussed before. Another way to start might be to choose a familiar selection, one that you read as a child or one that you shared with your children when they were younger. As a general strategy it makes sense for each person in the family to have a chance to choose a selection for everyone to read.

Reading together provides a continuing opportunity for the family to stay close as children reach toward independence. Be careful, however, not to shape your conversations about literature in ways that demand definite conclusions for each session or lead to your children feeling manipulated. Trust is crucial for critical family reading. Children will use their own judgment, make up their own minds about the issues at stake, and often understand the messages of what they read in ways that are surprising to adults. The personal closeness provided by serious, non-judgmental discussion, based on shared stories, is as valuable as any specific conclusions you or your children come to.

We all need ways to discuss sensitive issues that do not irritate healing wounds or go over subjects which have caused tension and anger in the past. That's why we want this book to provide families with an occasion to reconnect and talk about questions of character. Sharing stories, plays, and poems that involve moral issues can be a wonderful way for adults and children to come together on neutral ground. From Jane Austen to Winnie the Pooh, and from Pippi Longstocking to James Baldwin, there are thoughts, insights, and intuitions that tease interest out of even the most reluctant readers or reticent children. In a story, valuable advice might come from the most unusual sources; as in the case of puppy training described by Albert Payson Terhune in his *Lad: A Dog*:

> Lad took his new duties very seriously indeed. He not only accepted the annoyance of Wolf's undivided teasing, but he assumed charge of the puppy's education as well, this to the amusement of everyone on the Place. But everyone's amusement was kept from Lad. The sensitive dog would rather have been whipped than laughed at. So both the mistress and master watched the educational process with straight faces.
>
> A puppy needs an unbelievable amount of educating. He's a task to wear threadbare the teacher's patience and does all kinds of things to the temper. Small wonder that many humans lose patience and temper during the process and idiotically resort to the whip, to the boot, toe and to bellowing, in which case the puppy is never decently educated, but emerges from the process with a proud and broken spirit or with an incurable streak of meanness that renders him worthless.
>
> Time, patience, firmness, wisdom, temper control, gentleness, these be the six absolute essentials for training a puppy. Happy the human who is blessed with any three of these qualities. Lad, being only a dog, was abundantly possessed of all six. And he had need of them.

This family treasury is designed to provoke conversation about moral decisions and actions, and provide support and nurturance for the intensity of children's complex inner lives.

We have been guided, in our choice of selections for this book, by our conviction that reading for and with children is a significant way of being with them. The stories present situations that dramatize issues of character. We hope you and your children enjoy them as literature and find them useful for family discussions of moral issues.

# PART 1

# Values That Relate to One's Self (Courage, Self-Discipline, Integrity, Creativity, and Playfulness)

# Introduction

In *The Prelude* (IV l. 354) William Wordsworth writes:

> When from our better selves we have too long
> Been parted by the hurrying world, and droop,
> Sick of its business, of its pleasures tired,
> How gracious, how benign, is Solitude.

Almost every one of us knows such quiet moments when we are alone with our better selves. In those solitary and reflective times, questions of personal identity often come to mind: Who am I? What resources do I bring to bear on the problems I face? How do I remain myself in the face of temptations to sell out or give in to social pressure? How can I deal with all of the problems that waylay me? And how can I keep my sense of humor and hope in a world that is often too sad to bear?

These questions are as urgent for preadolescent children as they are for adults. They are how we answer the question in Duke Ellington's song "What Am I Here For?" They refer to those personal dimensions of character explored in this section: *courage, self-discipline, integrity, creativity,* and *playfulness*—values at the heart of our ability to make moral decisions which shape the people we become as we deal with our experiences. These values give coherence to our feelings and expectations and lead us to act on our beliefs.

## COURAGE

The strength to face pain, act under pressure, and maintain one's values in the face of opposition is tested through confrontation with fear. However, courage can become foolish when it is out of proportion to actual danger. There are things to fear, and there are times when caution has to temper courage. The evolution of a sensible calculus of courage is one of the aspects of personal growth that can be enriched through liter-

13

ature, and in this section you will find many examples of how courage develops and contributes to the formation of a moral center.

## SELF-DISCIPLINE

The self-discipline to plan and pursue a project to a conclusion, as well as to persevere in the face of criticism and obstacles, is another dimension of character growth that is particularly important for eight- to thirteen-year-olds. This is the time when planning ahead and being able to carry through a difficult undertaking are crucial skills, necessary to becoming an independent, morally autonomous, and caring adult. This section contains many examples of the rewards of diligence and self-discipline as well as some cautionary tales about the dangers of being overindustrious and forgetting the goals that underlie effort.

## INTEGRITY

The sense of self as a person of moral worth and wholeness lies at the center of all the values that refer to one's self. Integrity implies the consistency of one's actions with one's values. It is perhaps the hardest value to realize consistently as a young person. There are so many temptations to be like someone else, to follow the lead of others, or to compromise values in order to avoid conflict that stories about such questions are valuable guides to growth.

## CREATIVITY

The willingness to explore unfamiliar ideas and to invent new ways to solve old problems is developed when young people are free to experiment and make mistakes. It is a character value that applies to all the varied challenges of life. While creativity is not to be found just in the arts, writers often focus on artistic expression to convey the excitement of taking on something new and breaking old boundaries. The ability to use one's experience and intelligence to solve problems is a fundamental strength of character, one worth reading and talking about.

## PLAYFULNESS

The ability to temper seriousness with a sense of playfulness and humor is a basic survival skill. Without the capacity to look at the world and oneself as slightly silly and out of joint, to make light of temporary setbacks or clumsiness, growth would be defeated at every point. In addition, the suspension of reality and the enjoyment of dancing, singing, or just being silly are fundamental and positive aspects of being alive. If you can't play, you stunt your own growth.

# Courage

───────✦───────

Eleanor Roosevelt described courage in the following way:

> *Courage* is the strength to face pain, act under pressure, and maintain one's values in the face of opposition You gain strength, courage and confidence by every experience in which you really stop to look fear in the face. You are able to say to yourself, "I lived through this horror. I can take the next thing that comes along."
> . . . You must do the thing you think you cannot do."
> —Eleanor Roosevelt, *You Learn by Living*

The selections in this section explore different aspects of courage. Stories of courage are both inspirational and cautionary. There are many aspects of this value that can be explored through stories and tales, and we have tried to provide a multifaceted portrait to encourage young people to think of themselves as courageous.

Some of the aspects of courage explored in this section are

- unexpected courage, the courage you did not know existed, discovered at the center of one's being under pressure. This kind of courage can be moral as well as physical. When a child defends another against bullies or prejudice, her or his courage is showing as much as when she or he rescues someone from physical danger.
- courage that maintains itself under threat of criticism from peers, family, or authority figures. This can be the courage to defend your values against people with more power, or the courage to pursue a dream when others call you foolish or incapable.
- lack of courage, facing cowardice and finding a way to come to turns with weaknesses you discover in yourself.
- fear and the way in which it tests courage. This includes fears that are perfectly reasonable and cannot be overcome, such as the fear of

being killed during a war, as well as fears arising from lack of self-confidence.

• foolish and dangerous courage, the sense of not knowing your limitations. This can consist of not knowing when to give up trying to solve a problem for yourself and ask for help or acting on the irrational but decent impulse to prevent someone from drowning when you can't swim.

• moral, social, and political courage at the risk of your life or health. This is the kind of courage that many children under age twelve manifested during the Civil Rights Movement and at other times of moral crisis.

Of course, reading and talking about courage can't, in and of themselves, create courage. But it can create a climate for the development of courageous behavior and an understanding of other people's fears and the courage they summon up despite those fears.

⇒•◦•⇐

*The physical world presented fearful challenges to Helen Keller, who was born without speech, hearing, or sight. In this selection she describes how confronting and overcoming terror can lead to deep personal enrichment. Encounters with nature can be fearful, and discussing real and imagined fears of the natural world can lead to a deeper understanding of how to call on courage.*

### Helen Keller, *The Story of My Life*

I recall many incidents of the summer of 1887 that followed my soul's sudden awakening. I did nothing but explore with my hands and learn the name of every object that I touched; and the more I handled things and learned their names and uses, the more joyous and confident grew my sense of kinship with the rest of the world.

When the time of daisies and buttercups came, Miss Sullivan took me by the hand across the fields, where men were preparing the earth for the seed, to the banks of the Tennessee River, and there, sitting on the warm grass, I had my first lessons in the beneficence of nature. I learned how the sun and the rain make to grow out of the ground every tree that is pleasant to the sight and good for food, how birds build their nests and live and thrive from land to land, how the squirrel, the deer, the lion and every other creature finds food and shelter. As my knowledge of things grew I felt more and more the delight of the world I was in. Long before I learned to do a sum in arithmetic or describe the shape of the earth, Miss Sullivan had taught me to find beauty in the fragrant woods, in every blade of grass, and in the curves and dimples of my baby sister's hand. She linked my earliest thoughts with nature and made me feel that "birds and flowers and I were happy peers."

But about this time I had an experience which taught me that nature is not always kind. One day my teacher and I were returning from a long ramble. The morning had been fine, but it was growing warm and sultry when at last we turned our faces homeward. Two or three times we stopped to rest under a tree by the wayside. Our last halt was under a wild cherry tree a short distance from the house. The shade was grateful and the tree was so easy to climb that with my teacher's assistance I was able to scramble to a seat in the branches. It was so cool up in the tree that Miss Sullivan proposed that we have our luncheon there. I promised to keep still while she went to the house to fetch it.

Suddenly a change passed over the tree. All the sun's warmth left the air. I knew the sky was black, because all the heat, which meant light to me, had died out of the atmosphere. A strange odor came up from the earth. I knew it, it was the odor that always precedes a thunderstorm, and a nameless fear clutched at my heart. I felt absolutely alone, cut off from my friends and the firm earth. The immense, the unknown, enfolded me. I remained still and expectant; a chilling terror crept over me. I longed for my teacher's return; but above all things I wanted to get down from that tree.

There was a moment of sinister silence, then a multitudinous stirring of the leaves. A shiver ran through the tree, and the wind sent forth a blast that would have knocked me off had I not clung to the branch with might and main. The tree swayed and strained. The small twigs snapped and fell about me in showers. A wild impulse to jump seized me, but terror held me fast. I crouched down in the fork of the tree. The branches lashed about me. I felt the intermittent jarring that came now and then, as if something heavy had fallen and the shock had traveled up till it reached the limb I sat on. It worked my suspense up to the highest point; and just as I was thinking the tree and I should fall together, my teacher seized my hand and helped me down. I clung to her, trembling with joy to feel the earth under my feet once more. I had learned a new lesson— that nature "wages open war against her children, and under softest touch hides treacherous claws."

After this experience, it was a long time before I climbed another tree. The mere thought filled me with terror. It was the sweet allurement of the mimosa tree in full bloom that finally overcame my fears. One beautiful spring morning when I was alone in the summerhouse, reading, I became aware of a wonderful subtle fragrance in the air. I started up and instinctively stretched out my hands. It seemed as if the spirit of spring had passed through the summerhouse. "What is it?" I asked, and the next minute I recognized the odor of the mimosa blossoms. I felt my way to the end of the garden, knowing that the mimosa tree was near the fence, at the turn of the path. Yes, there it was, all quivering in the warm sunshine, its blossom-laden branches almost touching the long grass. Was there ever anything so exquisitely beautiful in the world before! Its delicate blossoms shrank from the highest earthly touch; it seemed as if a tree of paradise had been transplanted to earth. I made my way through a shower of petals to the great trunk and for one minute stood irresolute; then, putting my foot in the broad space between the forked branches, I pulled myself up into the tree. I had some difficulty in holding on, for the branches were very large and the bark hurt my hands. But I had a delicious sense that I was doing something unusual and wonderful, so I kept on climbing higher and higher, until I reached a little seat which somebody had built there so long ago that it had grown part of the tree itself. I sat there for a long, long time, feeling like a fairy on a rosy cloud. After that I spent many happy hours in my tree of paradise, thinking fair thoughts and dreaming bright dreams.

---

*In* The Deliverers of Their Country, *young people act courageously when the adults around them are unable to overcome their fear. This funny fantasy by Edith Nesbit shows how courageous action can lead to the discovery of unexpected kindness and power. It illustrates how fear can be caused by accepting negative stereotypes and how social paralysis can develop. The selection raises the question of whether people can learn from childhood innocence how to have the courage to overcome adult prejudices.*

## E. Nesbit, "The Deliverers of Their Country," from *The Last of the Dragons*

It all began with Effie's getting something in her eye. It hurt very much indeed, and it felt something like a red-hot spark—only it seemed to have legs as well, and wings like a fly. Effie rubbed and cried—not real crying, but the kind your eye does all by itself without your being miserable inside your mind—and then she went to her father to have the thing in her eye taken out. Effie's father was a doctor, so of course he knew how to take things out of eyes—he did it very cleverly with a soft paintbrush dipped in castor-oil. When he had got the thing out, he said:

'This is very curious.' Effie had often got things in her eye before, and her father had always seemed to think it was natural—rather tiresome and naughty perhaps, but still natural. He had never before thought it curious. She stood holding her handkerchief to her eye, and said:

'I don't believe it's out.' People always say this when they have had something in their eyes.

'Oh, yes—it's *out*,' said the doctor—'here it is on the brush. This is very interesting.'

Effie had never heard her father say that about anything that she had any share in. She said '*What?*'

The doctor carried the brush very carefully across the room, and held the point of it under his microscope—then he twisted the brass screws of the microscope, and looked through the top with one eye.

'Dear me,' he said. 'Dear, *dear* me! Four well-developed limbs; a long caudal appendage; five toes, unequal in length, almost like one of the Lacertidae, yet there are traces of wings.' The creature under his eye wriggled a little in the castor-oil, and he went on: 'Yes; a bat-like wing. A new specimen, undoubtedly. Effie, run round to the professor and ask him to be kind enough to step in for a few minutes.'

'You might give me sixpence, daddy,' said Effie, 'because I did bring you the new specimen. I took great care of it inside my eye; and my eye *does* hurt.'

The doctor was so pleased with the new specimen that he gave Effie a shilling, and presently the professor stepped round. He stayed to lunch, and he and the doctor quarrelled very happily all the afternoon about the name and the family of the thing that had come out of Effie's eye.

But at tea-time another thing happened. Effie's brother Harry fished something out of his tea, which he thought at first was an earwig. He was just getting ready to drop it on the floor, and end its life in the usual way, when it shook itself in the spoon—spread two wet wings, and flopped on to the table-cloth. There it sat stroking itself with its feet and stretching its wings, and Harry said: 'Why, it's a tiny newt!'

The professor leaned forward before the doctor could say a word. 'I'll give you half a crown for it, Harry, my lad,' he said, speaking very fast; and then he picked it up carefully on his handkerchief.

'It is a new specimen,' he said, 'and finer than yours, doctor.'

It was a tiny lizard, about half an inch long—with scales and wings.

So now the doctor and the professor each had a specimen, and they were both very pleased. But before long these specimens began to seem less valuable. For the next morning, when the knife-boy was cleaning the doctor's boots, he suddenly dropped the brushes and the boot and the blacking, and screamed out that he was burnt.

And from inside the boot came crawling a lizard as big as a kitten, with large, shiny wings.

'Why,' said Effie, 'I know what it is. It is a dragon like St George killed.'

And Effie was right. That afternoon Towser was bitten in the garden by a dragon about the size of a rabbit, which he had tried to chase, and next morning, all the papers were full of the wonderful 'winged lizards' that were appearing all over the country. The papers would not call them dragons, because of course, no one believes in dragons nowadays—and at any rate the papers were not going to be so silly as to believe in fairy stories. At first there were only a few, but in a week or two the country was simply running alive with dragons of all sizes, and in the air you could sometimes see them as thick as a swarm of bees. They all looked alike except as to size. They were green with scales, and they had four legs and a long tail and great wings like bats' wings, only the wings were a pale, half-transparent yellow, like the gear-cases on bicycles.

And they breathed fire and smoke, as all proper dragons must, but still the newspapers went on pretending they were lizards, until the editor of 'The Standard' was picked up and carried away by a very large one, and then the other newspaper people had not anyone left to tell them what they ought not to believe. So that when the largest elephant in the Zoo was carried off by a dragon, the papers gave up pretending—and put: 'Alarming Plague of Dragons' at the top of the paper.

And you have no idea how alarming it was, and at the same time how aggravating. The large-sized dragons were terrible certainly, but when once you had found out that the dragons always went to bed early because they were afraid of the chill night air, you had only to stay indoors all day, and you were pretty safe from the big ones. But the small sizes were a perfect nuisance. The ones as big as earwigs got in the soap, and they got in the butter. The ones as big as dogs got in the bath, and the fire and smoke inside them made them steam like anything when the cold water tap was turned on, so that careless people were often scalded quite severely. The ones that were as large as pigeons would get into workbaskets or corner drawers, and bite you when you were in a hurry to get a needle or a handkerchief. The ones as big as sheep were easier to avoid, because you could see them coming; but when they flew in at the windows and curled up under your eiderdown, and you did not find them till you went to bed, it was always a shock. The ones this size did not eat people, only lettuces, but they always scorched the sheets and pillow-cases dreadfully.

Of course, the County Council and the police did everything that could be done: it was no use offering the hand of the Princess to anyone who killed a dragon. This way was all very well in olden times—when there was only one dragon and one Princess; but now there were far more dragons than Princesses—although the Royal Family was a large one. And besides, it would have been mere waste of Princesses to offer rewards for killing dragons, because everybody killed as many dragons as they could quite out of their own heads and without rewards at all, just to get the nasty things out of the way. The County Council undertook to cremate all dragons delivered at their offices between the hours of ten and two, and whole wagonloads and cart-loads and truck-loads of dead dragons could be seen any day of the week standing in a long line in the street where the County Council lived. Boys brought barrow-loads of dead dragons, and children on their way home from morning school would call in to leave the handful or two of little dragons they had brought in their satchels, or carried in their knotted pocket-handkerchiefs. And yet there seemed to be as many dragons as ever. Then the police stuck up great wood and canvas towers covered with patent glue. When the dragons flew against these towers, they stuck fast, as flies and wasps do on the sticky papers in the kitchen; and when the towers were covered all over with dragons, the police-inspector used to set light to the towers, and burnt them and dragons and all.

And yet there seemed to be more dragons than ever. The shops were full of patent dragon poison and anti-dragon soap, and dragon-proof curtains for the windows and, indeed, everything that could be done was done.

And yet there seemed to be more dragons than ever.

It was not very easy to know what would poison a dragon, because you see they ate such different things. The largest kind ate elephants as long as there were any, and then went on with horses and cows. Another size ate nothing but lilies of the valley, and a third size ate only Prime Ministers if they were to be had, and, if not, would feed freely on boys in buttons. Another size lived on bricks, and three of them ate two-thirds of the South Lambeth Infirmary in one afternoon.

But the size Effie was most afraid of was about as big as your dining-room, and that size ate *little girls and boys.*

At first Effie and her brother were quite pleased with the change in their lives. It was so amusing to sit out all night instead of going to sleep,

and to play in the garden lighted by electric lamps. And it sounded so
funny to hear mother say, when they were going to bed:

'Good night, my darlings, sleep sound all day, and don't get up too
soon. You must not get up before it's *quite* dark. You wouldn't like the
nasty dragons to catch you.'

But after a time they got very tired of it all: they wanted to see the
flowers and trees growing in the fields, and to see the pretty sunshine out
of doors, and not just through glass windows and patent dragon-proof
curtains. And they wanted to play on the grass, which they were not
allowed to do in the electric-lamp-lighted garden because of the nightdew.

And they wanted so much to get out, just for once, in the beautiful,
bright dangerous daylight, that they began to try and think of some reason why they *ought* to go out. Only they did not like to disobey their
mother.

But one morning their mother was busy preparing some new dragon
poison to lay down in the cellars, and their father was bandaging the
hand of the boot-boy which had been scratched by one of the dragons
who liked to eat Prime Ministers when they were to be had, so nobody
remembered to say to the children:

'Don't get up till it is quite dark!'

'Go now,' said Harry; 'it would not be disobedient to go. And I know
exactly what we ought to do, but I don't know how we ought to do it.'

'What ought we to do?' said Effie.

'*We* ought to wake St George, of course.' said Harry. 'He was the only
person in his town who knew how to manage dragons; the people in the
fairy tales don't count. But St George is a real person, and he is only
asleep, and he is waiting to be waked up. Only nobody believes in St
George now. I heard father say so.'

'*We* do,' said Effie.

'Of course we do. And don't you see, Ef, that's the very reason why
we could wake him? You can't wake people if you don't believe in them,
can you?'

Effie said no, but where could they find St George?

'We must go and look,' said Harry, boldly. 'You shall wear a dragon-
proof frock, made of stuff like the curtains. And I will smear myself all
over with the best dragon poison, and—'

Effie clasped her hands and skipped with joy, and cried:

'Oh, Harry! I know where we can find St George! In St George's
Church, of course.'

'Um,' said Harry, wishing he had thought of it for himself, 'you have
a little sense sometimes, for a girl.'

So next afternoon quite early, long before the beams of sunset announced the coming night, when everybody would be up and working, the two children got out of bed. Effie wrapped herself in a shawl of dragon-proof muslin—there was no time to make the frock—and Harry made a horrid mess of himself with the patent dragon poison. It was warranted harmless to infants and invalids, so he felt quite safe.

Then they took hands and set out to walk to St George's Church. As you know, there are many St George's churches, but, fortunately, they took the turning that leads to the right one, and went along in the bright sunlight, feeling very brave and adventurous.

There was no one about in the streets except dragons and the place was simply swarming with them. Fortunately none of the dragons were just the right size for eating little boys and girls, or perhaps this story might have had to end here. There were dragons on the pavement, and dragons on the road-way, dragons basking on the front-door steps of public buildings, and dragons preening their wings on the roofs in the hot afternoon sun. The town was quite green with them. Even when the children had got out of the town and were walking in the lanes, they noticed that the fields on each side were greener than usual with the scaly legs and tails; and some of the smaller sizes had made themselves asbestos nests in the flowering hawthorn hedges.

Effie held her brother's hand very tight, and once when a fat dragon flopped against her ear she screamed out, and a whole flight of green dragons rose from the field at the sound, and sprawled away across the sky. The children could hear the rattle of their wings as they flew.

'Oh, I want to go home,' said Effie.

'Don't be silly,' said Harry. 'Surely you haven't forgotten about the Seven Champions and all the princes. People who are going to be their country's deliverers never scream and say they want to go home.'

'And are we,' asked Effie—'deliverers, I mean?'

'You'll see,' said her brother, and on they went.

When they came to St George's Church they found the door open, and they walked right in—but St George was not there, so they walked round the churchyard outside, and presently they found the great stone tomb of St George, with the figure of him carved in marble outside, in his armour and helmet, and with his hands folded on his breast.

'How ever can we wake him?' they said.

Then Harry spoke to St George—but he would not answer; and he called, but St George did not seem to hear; and then he actually tried to waken the great dragon-slayer by shaking his marble shoulders. But St George took no notice.

Then Effie began to cry, and she put her arms round St George's neck as well as she could for the marble, which was very much in the way at the back, and she kissed the marble face and she said:

'Oh, dear, good, kind St George, please wake up and help us.'

And at that St George opened his eyes sleepily, and stretched himself and said: 'What's the matter, little girl?'

So the children told him all about it; he turned over in his marble and leaned on one elbow to listen. But when he heard that there were so many dragons he shook his head.

'It's no good,' he said, 'they would be one too many for poor old George. You should have waked me before. I was always for a fair fight— one man one dragon, was my motto.'

Just then a flight of dragons passed overhead, and St George half drew his sword.

But he shook his head again, and pushed the sword back as the flight of dragons grew small in the distance.

'I can't do anything,' he said; 'things have changed since my time. St Andrew told me about it. They woke him up over the engineers' strike, and he came to talk to me. He says everything is done by machinery now; there must be some way of settling these dragons. By the way, what sort of weather have you have having lately?'

This seemed so careless and unkind that Harry would not answer, but Effie said, patiently, 'It has been very fine. Father says it is the hottest weather there has ever been in this country.'

'Ah, I guessed as much,' said the Champion, thoughtfully. 'Well, the only thing would be . . . dragons can't stand wet and cold, that's the only thing. If you could find the taps.'

St George was beginning to settle down again on his stone slab.

'Good night, very sorry I can't help you,' he said, yawning behind his marble hand.

'Oh, but you can,' cried Effie. 'Tell us—what taps?'

'Oh, like in the bathroom,' said St George, still more sleepily; 'and there's a looking-glass, too; shows you all the world and what's going on. St Denis told me about it; said it was a very pretty thing. I'm sorry I can't—good night.'

And he fell back into his marble and was fast asleep again in a moment.

'We shall never find the taps,' said Harry. 'I say, wouldn't it be awful if St George woke up when there was a dragon near, the size that eats champions?'

Effie pulled off her dragon-proof veil. 'We didn't meet any the size of the dining-room as we came along,' she said; 'I daresay we shall be quite safe.'

So she covered St George with the veil, and Harry rubbed off as much as he could of the dragon poison on to St George's armour, so as to make everything quite safe for him.

'We might hide in the church till it is dark,' he said, 'and then—'

But at that moment a dark shadow fell on them, and they saw that it was a dragon exactly the size of the dining-room at home.

So then they knew that all was lost. The dragon swooped down and caught the two children in his claws; he caught Effie by her green silk sash, and Harry by the little point at the back of his Eton jacket—and then, spreading his great yellow wings, he rose into the air, rattling like a third-class carriage when the brake is hard on.

'Oh, Harry,' said Effie, 'I wonder when he will eat us!' The dragon was flying across woods and fields with great flaps of his wings that carried him a quarter of a mile at each flap.

Harry and Effie could see the country below, hedges and rivers and churches and farmhouses flowing away from under them, much faster than you see them running away from the sides of the fastest express train.

And still the dragon flew on. The children saw other dragons in the air as thy went, but the dragon who was as big as the dining-room never stopped to speak to any of them, but just flew on quite steadily.

'He knows where he wants to go,' said Harry. 'Oh, if he would only drop us before he gets there!'

But the dragon held on tight, and he flew and flew until at last, when the children were quite giddy, he settled down, with a rattling of all his scales, on the top of a mountain. And he lay there on his great green scaly side, panting, and very much out of breath, because he had come such a long way. But his claws were fast in Effie's sash and the little point at the back of Harry's Eton jacket.

Then Effie took out the knife Harry had given her on her birthday. It only cost sixpence to begin with, and she had had it a month, and it never could sharpen anything but slate-pencils; but somehow she managed to make that knife cut her sash in front, and crept out of it, leaving the dragon with only a green silk bow in one of his claws. That knife would never have cut Harry's jacket-tail off, though, and when Effie had tried for some time she saw that this was so, and gave it up. But with her help Harry managed to wriggle quietly out of his sleeves, so that the dragon had only an Eton jacket in his other claw. Then the children crept on tiptoe to a crack in the rocks and got in. It was much too narrow for the dragon to get in also, so they stayed in there and waited to make faces at the dragon when he felt rested enough to sit up and begin to think about eating them. He was very angry, indeed, when they made faces at him, and blew out fire and smoke at them, but they ran farther into the cave so that he could not reach them, and when he was tired of blowing he went away.

But they were afraid to come out of the cave, so they went farther in, and presently the cave opened out and grew bigger, and the floor was soft sand, and when they had come to the very end of the cave there was a door, and on it was written: *'Universal Tap-room. Private. No one allowed inside.'*

So they opened the door at once just to peep in, and then they remembered what St George had said.

'We can't be worse off than we are,' said Harry, 'with a dragon waiting for us outside. Let's go in.'

So they went boldly into the tap-room, and shut the door behind them.

And now they were in a sort of room cut out of the solid rock, and all along one side of the room were taps, and all the taps were labelled with china labels like you see to baths. And as they could both read words of two syllables or even three sometimes, they understood at once that they had got to the place where the weather is turned on from. There were six big taps labelled 'Sunshine', 'Wind', 'Rain', 'Snow,' 'Hail', 'Ice', and a lot of little ones, labeled 'Fair to moderate', 'Showery', 'South breeze', 'Nice growing weather for the crops', 'Skating', 'Good open weather', 'South wind', 'East wind', and so on. And the big tap labelled 'Sunshine' was turned full on. They could not see any sunshine—the cave was lighted by a skylight of blue glass—so they supposed the sunlight was pouring out by some other way, as it does with the tap that washes out the underneath parts of patent sinks in kitchens.

Then they saw that one side of the room was just a big looking-glass, and when you looked in it you could see everything that was going on in the world—and all at once, too, which is not like most looking-glasses. They saw the carts delivering the dead dragons at the County Council offices, and they saw St George asleep under the dragon-proof veil. And they saw their mother at home crying because her children had gone out in the dreadful, dangerous daylight, and she was afraid a dragon had eaten them. And they saw the whole of England, like a great puzzle-map—green in the field parts and brown in the towns, and black in the places where they make coal, and crockery, and cutlery, and chemicals. And all over it, on the black parts, and on the brown, and on the green, there was a network of green dragons. And they could see that it was still broad daylight, and no dragons had gone to bed yet.

So Effie said, 'Dragons do not like cold.' And she tried to turn off the sunshine, but the tap was out of order, and that was why there had been so much hot weather, and why the dragons had been able to be hatched. So they left the sunshine-tap alone, and they turned on the snow and left the tap full on while they went to look in the glass. There they saw the dragons running all sorts of ways like ants if you are cruel enough to pour water onto an ant-heap, which, of course, you never are. And the snow fell more and more.

Then Effie turned the rain-tap quite full on, and presently the dragons began to wriggle less, and by-and-by some of them lay quite still, so the children knew the water had put out the fires inside them, and they were dead. So then they turned on the hail—only half on, for fear of breaking people's windows—and after a while there were no more dragons to be seen moving.

Then the children knew that they were indeed the deliverers of their country.

'They will put up a monument to us,' said Harry; 'as high as Nelson's! All the dragons are dead.'

'I hope the one that was waiting outside for us is dead!' said Effie; 'and about the monument, Harry, I'm not so sure. What can they do with such a lot of dead dragons? It would take years and years to bury them, and they could never he burnt now they are so soaking wet. I wish the rain would wash them off into the sea.'

But this did not happen, and the children began to feel that they had not been so frightfully clever after all.

'I wonder what this old thing's for,' said Harry. He had found a rusty old tap, which seemed as though it had not been used for ages. Its china label was quite coated over with dirt and cobwebs. When Effie had cleaned it with a bit of her skirt—for curiously enough both the children had come out without pocket-handkerchiefs—she found that the label said 'Waste.'

'Let's turn it on,' she said; 'it might carry off the dragons.'

The tap was very stiff from not having been used for such a long time, but together they managed to turn it on, and then ran to the mirror to see what happened.

Already a great round, black hole had opened in the very middle of the map of England, and the sides of the map were tilting themselves up, so that the rain ran down towards the hole.

'Oh, hurrah, hurrah, hurrah!' cried Effie, and she hurried back to the taps and turned on everything that seemed wet. 'Showery', 'Good open weather', 'Nice growing weather for the crops', and even 'South' and 'South-West', because she had heard her father say that those winds brought rain.

And now the floods of rain were pouring down on the country, and great sheets of water poured into the great round hole in the middle of the map, and the dragons were being washed away and disappearing down the waste-pipe in great green masses and scattered green shoals—single dragons and dragons by the dozen; of all sizes, from the ones that carry off elephants down to the ones that get in your tea.

And presently there was not a dragon left. So then they turned off the tap named 'Waste', and they half-turned off the one labelled 'Sunshine'—it was broken, so that they could not turn it off altogether—and they turned on 'Fair to moderate' and 'Showery' and both taps stuck, so that they could not be turned off, which accounts for our climate.

How did they get home again? By the Snowdon railway—of course.

And was the nation grateful? Well—the nation was very wet. And by the time the nation had got dry again it was interested in the new invention for toasting muffins by electricity, and all the dragons were almost forgotten. Dragons do not seem so important when they are dead and gone, and, you know, there never was a reward offered.

And what did father and mother say when Effie and Harry got home?

My dear, that is the sort of silly question you children always will ask. However, just for this once I don't mind telling you.

Mother said: 'Oh, my darlings, my darlings, you're safe—you're safe! You naughty children—how could you be so disobedient? Go to bed at once!'

And their father the doctor said:

'I wish I had known what you were going to do! I should have liked to preserve a specimen. I threw away the one I got out of Effie's eye. I intended to get a more perfect specimen. I did not anticipate this immediate extinction of the species.'

The professor said nothing, but he rubbed his hands. He had kept his specimen—the one the size of an earwig that he gave Harry half a crown for—and he has it to this day.

You must get him to show it to you!

---

*This selection from Arnold Lobel's picture book* Dragons and Giants *shows his two heroes, Frog and Toad, learning to be courageous by pretending they are not afraid. In this case, making believe something is true leads to it becoming so. When does it make sense to pretend you are not afraid? When is fear justified and caution sensible?*

**Arnold Lobel, "Dragons and Giants," from *Frog and Toad Together***
Frog and Toad
were reading a book together.
"The people in this book
are brave," said Toad.
"They fight dragons and giants,
and they are never afraid."
"I wonder if we are brave,"
said Frog.
Frog and Toad looked into a mirror.
"We look brave," said Frog.
"Yes, but are we?"
asked Toad.
Frog and Toad went outside.
"We can try to climb this mountain,"
said Frog. "That should tell us
if we are brave."
Frog went leaping over rocks,
and Toad came puffing up
behind him.
They came to a dark cave.
A big snake came out of the cave.
"Hello lunch," said the snake
when he saw Frog and Toad.
He opened his wide mouth.
Frog and Toad jumped away.
Toad was shaking.
"I am not afraid!" he cried.
They climbed higher,
and they heard a loud noise.
Many large stones
were rolling down the mountain.
"It's an avalanche!" cried Toad.
Frog and Toad jumped away.
Frog was trembling.
"I am not afraid!" he shouted.

They came to the top
of the mountain.
The shadow of a hawk
fell over them.
Frog and Toad
jumped under a rock.
The hawk flew away.
"We are not afraid!"
screamed Frog and Toad
at the same time.
Then they ran down the mountain
very fast.
They ran past the place
where they saw the avalanche.
They ran past the place
where they saw the snake.
They ran all the way
to Toad's house.
"Frog, I am glad to have
a brave friend like you," said Toad.
He jumped into the bed
and pulled the covers
over his head.
"And I am happy to know
a brave person like you, Toad,"
said Frog.
He jumped into the closet
and shut the door.
Toad stayed in the bed,
and Frog stayed in the closet.
They stayed there
for a long time,
just feeling very brave together.

—————•◦◄—————

*In this selection from E. B. White's* Charlotte's Web, *Wilbur, a piglet, discovers that he is being fattened up for Christmas dinner; in an act of courage, and with the encouragement of the other farm animals, he tries to run away. The humans on the farm discover that Wilbur is no ordinary pig.*

*Special courage can be called up by all of us, and it's interesting to speculate on how you would act in extreme circumstances.*

## E. B. White, "Wilbur's Escape," from *Charlotte's Web*

"Ho-*mer*!" she cried. "Pig's out! Lurvy! Pig's out! Homer! Lurvy! Pig's out. He's down there under that apple tree."

"Now the trouble starts," thought Wilbur. "Now I'll catch it."

The goose heard the racket and she, too, started hollering. "Run-run-run downhill, make for the woods, the woods!" she shouted to Wilbur. "They'll never-never-never catch you in the woods."

The cocker spaniel heard the commotion, and he ran out from the barn to join in the chase. Mr. Zuckerman heard, and he came out of the machine shed where he was mending a tool. Lurvy, the hired man, heard the noise and came up from the asparagus patch where he was pulling weeds. Everybody walked toward Wilbur, and Wilbur didn't know what to do. The woods seemed a long way off, and anyway, he had never been down there in the woods and wasn't sure he would like it.

"Get around behind him, Lurvy," said Mr. Zuckerman, "and drive him toward the barn! And take it easy—don't rush him! I'll go and get a bucket of slops."

The news of Wilbur's escape spread rapidly among the animals on the place. Whenever any creature broke loose on Zuckerman's farm, the event was of great interest to the others. The goose shouted to the nearest cow that Wilbur was free, and soon all the cows knew. Then one of the cows told one of the sheep, and soon all the sheep knew. The lambs learned about it from their mothers. The horses, in their stalls in the barn, pricked up their ears when they heard the goose hollering; and soon the horses had caught on to what was happening. "Wilbur's out," they said. Every animal stirred its head and became excited to know that one of its friends had got free and was no longer penned up or tied fast.

Wilbur didn't know what to do or which way to run. It seemed as though everybody was after him. "If this is what it's like to be free," he thought, "I believe I'd rather be penned up in my own yard."

The cocker spaniel was sneaking up on him from one side, Lurvy the hired man was sneaking up on him from the other side. Mrs. Zuckerman stood ready to head him off if he started for the garden, and now Mr. Zuckerman was coming down toward him carrying a pail. "This is really awful," thought Wilbur. "Why doesn't Fern come?" He began to cry.

The goose took command and began to give orders.

"Don't just stand there, Wilbur! Dodge about, dodge about!" cried the goose. "Skip around, run toward me, slip in and out, in and out, in and out! Make for the woods! Twist and turn!"

The cocker spaniel sprang for Wilbur's hind leg. Wilbur jumped and ran. Lurvy reached out and grabbed. Mrs. Zuckerman screamed at Lurvy. The goose cheered for Wilbur. Wilbur dodged between Lurvy's legs. Lurvy missed Wilbur and grabbed the spaniel instead. "Nicely done, nicely done!" cried the goose. "Try it again, try it again."

"Run downhill!" suggested the cows.

"Run toward me!" yelled the gander.

"Run uphill!" cried the sheep.

"Turn and twist!" honked the goose.

"Jump and dance!" said the rooster.

"Look out for Lurvy!" called the cows.

"Look out for Zuckerman!" yelled the gander.

"Watch out for the dog!" cried the sheep.

"Listen to me, listen to me!" screamed the goose.

Poor Wilbur was dazed and frightened by this hullabaloo. He didn't like being the center of all this fuss. He tried to follow the instructions his friends were giving him, but he couldn't run downhill and uphill at the same time, and he couldn't turn and twist when he was jumping and dancing, and he was crying so hard he could barely see anything that was happening. After all, Wilbur was a very young pig—not much more than a baby, really. He wished Fern were here to take him in her arms and comfort him. When he looked up and saw Mr. Zuckerman standing quite close to him, holding a pail of warm slops, he felt relieved. He lifted his nose and sniffed. The smell was delicious—warm milk, potato skins, wheat middlings, Toasted Corn Flakes, and a popover left from the Zuckermans' breakfast.

"Come, pig!" said Mr. Zuckerman, tapping the pail. "Come, pig!"

Wilbur took a step toward the pail.

"No-no-no!" said the goose. "It's the old pail trick, Wilbur. Don't fall for it, don't fall for it! He's trying to lure you back into captivity-ivity. He's appealing to your stomach."

Wilbur didn't care. The food smelled appetizing. He took another step toward the pail.

"Pig, pig!" said Mr. Zuckerman in a kind voice and began walking slowly toward the barnyard, looking all about him innocently, as if he didn't know that a little white pig was following along behind him.

"You'll be sorry-sorry-sorry," called the goose.

Wilbur didn't care. He kept walking toward the pail of slops.

"You'll miss your freedom," honked the goose. "An hour of freedom is worth a barrel of slops."

Wilbur didn't care.

When Mr. Zuckerman reached the pigpen, he climbed over the fence and poured the slops into the trough. Then he pulled the loose board away from the fence, so that there was a wide hole for Wilbur to walk through.

"Reconsider, reconsider!" cried the goose.

Wilbur paid no attention. He stepped through the fence into his yard. He walked to the trough and took a long drink of slops, sucking in the milk hungrily and chewing the popover. It was good to be home again.

While Wilbur ate, Lurvy fetched a hammer and some eight-penny nails and nailed the board in place. Then he and Mr. Zuckerman leaned lazily on the fence, and Mr. Zuckerman scratched Wilbur's back with a stick.

"He's quite a pig," said Lurvy.

"Yes, he'll make a good pig," said Mr. Zuckerman.

Wilbur heard the words of praise. He felt the warm milk inside his stomach. He felt the pleasant rubbing of the stick along his itchy back. He felt peaceful and happy and sleepy. This had been a tiring afternoon. It was still only about four o' clock, but Wilbur was ready for bed.

"I'm really too young to go out into the world alone," he thought as he lay down.

---

*Here are some selected proverbs, sayings, and morals that provide a mini-portrait of the many faces of courage. They show how the same character value can assume a different role or weight according to larger circumstances: It's fun to think about the circumstances in which each might be appropriate.*

Here are two traditional Mexican proverbs:

Everyone can be master of their own fear.

Better to die on your feet than to live on your knees.

These three quotations approach courage with a broad view:

Courage is rightly esteemed the first of human qualities, because . . . it
is the quality that guarantees all others.
—Winston Churchill

Courage is the price that Life exacts for granting peace.
—Amelia Earhart

Life shrinks or expands in proportion to one's courage.
—Anaïs Nin

These selections of morals from student fables collected by Herbert
Kohl take a somewhat more skeptical view of unexamined courage:

Better to be old than bold!

It's better to run today and live another day.

He who hesitates is sometimes saved.

Finally, and by way of contrast, here are two literary quotations that
query courage in complex ways:

At times he regarded the wounded soldiers in an envious way. He conceived persons with torn bodies to be peculiarly happy. He wished that
he, too, had a wound, a red badge of courage.
—Stephen Crane, *The Red Badge of Courage*

Even when someone battles hard, there is an equal
portion for one who lingers behind, and in the same
honor are held both the coward and the brave man; the
idle and he who has done much meet death alike.
—Homer, *The Iliad* l. 318

---

*Sometimes an act of courage can put one's life in danger. This selection from
the archives of the Library of Congress brings up the question of how somebody develops the courage to make personal sacrifices for other people's freedom and dignity. It is a first-person account by one of the conductors on the*

*Underground Railroad, which led slaves out of the South to freedom before the Civil War.*

### Arnold Gragson, *The Underground Railroad*

It was 'cause he used to let me go around in the day and night so much that I came to be the one who carried the runnin'-away slaves over the river. It was funny the way I started it, too.

I didn't have no idea of ever gettin' mixed up in any sort of business like that, until one special night. I hadn't even thought of rowing across the river myself.

But one night I had gone on another plantation courtin', and the old woman whose house I went to told me she had a real pretty girl there who wanted to go across the river, and would I take her? I was scared and backed out in a hurry. But then I saw the girl, and she was such a pretty little thing—brown-skinned and kinda rosy, and looking as scared as I was feelin'—so it wasn't long before I was listenin' to the old woman tell me when to take her and where to leave her on the other side.

I didn't have nerve enough to do it that night, though, and I told them to wait for me until tomorrow night. All the next day I kept seeing Mr. Tabb laying a rawhide across my back or shooting me, and kept seeing that scared little brown girl back at the house, looking at me with her big eyes and asking me if I wouldn't just row her across to Ripley, Ohio. Me and Mr. Tabb lost, and soon as dusk settled that night, I was at the old lady's house.

I don't know how I ever rowed that boat across the river. The current was strong and I was trembling. I couldn't see a thing there in the dark, but I felt that girl's eyes. We didn't dare to whisper, so I couldn't tell her how sure I was that Mr. Tabb or some of the other owners would "tear me up" when they found our what I had done. I just knew they would find out.

I was worried, too, about where to put her out of the boat. I couldn't ride her across the river all night, and I didn't know a thing about the other side. I had heard a lot about it from other slaves, but I thought it was just about like Mason County, with slaves and masters, overseers and rawhides; and so, I just knew that if I pulled the boat up and went to asking people where to take her I would get a beating or get killed.

I don't know whether it seemed like a long time or a short time, now—it's so long ago. I know it was a long time rowing there in the cold and worryin', but it was short, too, 'cause as soon as I did get on the other side the big-eyed, brown skinned girl would be gone. Well, pretty soon I saw a tall light and I remembered what the old lady had told me about looking for that light and rowing to it. I did, and when I got up to it, two men reached down and grabbed her. I started tremblin' all over again, and prayin'. Then, one of the men took my arm and I just felt down inside of me that the Lord had got ready for me. "You hungry, boy?" is what he asked me, and if he hadn't been holdin' me I think I would have fell backward into the river.

That was my first trip. It took me a long time to get over my scared feelin', but I finally did, and I soon found myself goin' back across the river with two or three people, and sometimes a whole boatload. I got so I used to make three and four trips a month.

——»·◦·«——

*Many people are silenced. Some are victims of political or religious oppression; others are stigmatized because of their culture or sexual orientation. It takes courage for silenced people to learn to speak out on their own behalf. In* Unlearning to Not Speak, *the poet Marge Piercy urges women who have been silenced because of their gender to unlearn habits of silence and then take steps toward speaking out as women. The poem speaks to all silenced people. Many young people feel that they are silenced by the adult world, and reading this poem is a good way to open up a dialogue on learning to speak and listen across generations.*

*Following the poem is a short tale by Jade Snow Wong that describes the development of courage.*

**Marge Piercy, *Unlearning to Not Speak***
Blizzards of paper
in slow motion
sift through her.
In nightmares she suddenly recalls
a class she signed up for
but forgot to attend.
Now it is too late.
Now it is time for finals:
losers will be shot.
Phrases of men who lectured her
drift and rustle in piles:
Why don't you speak up?
Why are you shouting?

You have the wrong answer,
wrong line, wrong face.
They tell her she is womb-man,
babymachine, mirror image, toy,
earth mother and penis-poor,
a dish of synthetic strawberry icecream
rapidly melting.
She grunts to a halt.
She must learn again to speak
starting with I
starting with We ,
starting as the infant does
with her own true hunger
and pleasure
and rage.


**Jade Snow Wong,** *Fifth Chinese Daughter*

In Chinese school, Jade Snow had now passed beyond the vocabulary stage to the study of essays, which she was required to memorize by both oral recitation and writing. The correct spelling of a word could not be hazarded from the sound, but depended on one's remembering the exact look of a character, including the location of the tiniest dot.

The only subject which permitted students to exercise their imaginations and to demonstrate their knowledge of the language was composition. Once a week they were given a subject title, such as "The Value of Learning," or "The Necessity of Good Habits," and the class hummed with anticipation as the words were written on the blackboard. They worked first on a rough draft, and afterward copied the draft with fine brushes onto the squares of a tablet page, which they submitted for correction.

On Saturday mornings, an assembly was held in the chapel of the Chinese Presbyterian Church, where members of the advanced classes took turns in practicing public speaking before the student body. Their talks were usually moral clichés, many patterned after sermons heard from their minister. Patiently, the students suffered with the speakers through such subjects as "It Is Time for China to Unite," "The Little Boy Who Cried Wolf-Wolf and Betrayed Only Himself," or "You Can Trust Some Animals More Than You Can Trust Some People."

Sometimes at these assemblies, they heard sermons or guest speakers. But always the meeting began with prayer and hymns; Jade Snow and

Jade Precious Stone learned to sing in Chinese the words to such melodies as "Bringing in the Sheaves," "Day Is Dying in the West," "He Arose," and the stirring "Onward, Christian Soldiers."

Order, in the most uncompromising Chinese sense, was enforced strictly. Not a sound was tolerated from the rows of black-topped heads in the audience. A dean or disciplinarian preserved order and punished offenders for a multitude of infringements—from assembly misconduct to cheating in class. During assembly, this unpopular man paced up and down the aisles with a long rod held menacingly in his hand. At the slightest noise he was instantly there, and the guilty one was made to stand in the aisle to he shamed publicly for misbehavior. The boys were seated on the right side of the hall, with the girls on the left, arranged by grade. Several boys were notorious for disrupting the peace at almost any assembly. They seemed to enjoy their brief sojourn in the limelight as they stood in disgrace. Rarely was a girl stood out for punishment, but when she was, all heads turned toward her as if by signal.

One Saturday morning, Jade Snow's most humiliating Chinese school experience occurred in this setting. Simply for the pleasure of outwitting the disciplinarian, Mr. Dong, some of the girls had agreed upon the idea of passing notes surreptitiously from one aisle to the other. One assembly passed off successfully; another assembly found the girls still triumphant. The third week, Mr. Dong, who was conscious of a disturbance, decided that he must find a culprit or suffer a serious loss of face. Unfortunately he decided to pull out a culprit exactly at the moment when the note slid into Jade Snow's hand.

The next move was swift—the long rod tapped Jade Snow's shoulder. Shrinking, she looked up to find Mr. Dong, his face wreathed in triumph, motioning unmistakably for her to come out and stand in the aisle.

Jade Snow had never before been mortified so completely, suddenly, and publicly. Slowly she made her way from her seat to the aisle. She stood, perspiring and blushing, keeping her eyes down to screen her agony. She wished that her straight bangs were long enough to conceal her whole face from the curious eyes that she knew were turned to stare in surprise, disapproval, and sympathy. Her tears gathered, hung, and finally dropped unchecked. The green Victorian design on the faded red aisle carpet stamped itself indelibly on her memory during the interminable wait until the end of the assembly.

As usual, her first thought was "What would Daddy and Mama say?" Mostly it was "What would Daddy say?" Daddy probably would never have been party to passing notes. He would not mind refusing to cooperate in a project to which all others had agreed, if he thought it was not exactly right. But as just another little girl in a whole row of classmates with whom one had to get along every evening of the week, Jade Snow had not felt equal to resistance. It was her own fault, as usual.

Finally, the last hymn was sung, the students received the benediction, and as the assembly was dismissed, Mr. Dong announced, "All those who have been stood out at assembly will go to the principal's office immediately to receive their punishment."

"To receive punishment"—wasn't standing out enough? This aftermath had not occurred to Jade Snow. She picked up her books from her seat and trailed out after the dwindling crowd, turning off to enter the principal's office instead of going downstairs to the street as usual.

Guilty boys were waiting inside the office, which held two old-fashioned desks and a couple of old wooden chairs. Into this colorless, cluttered-looking place, Mr. Dong hustled with brisk anticipation. He went to his desk and found a long cane switch, heavier and tied more securely than Daddy's salvages from the bindings of the rice bundles. Evidently the boys were seasoned to this routine, for they quickly stepped up to Mr. Dong and held out their right palms. The switch cut the air and cracked down loudly three times on the open palms. The boys did not cry out, but stuck out their chests manfully before their lone female audience, and nonchalantly scampered off.

Mr. Dong began his treatment of Jade Snow more ceremoniously. "Wong Jade Snow, I am surprised at such misbehavior in a young lady, and you must be punished to teach you a lesson."

Jade Snow was terrified. Then indignation routed terror as it suddenly occurred to her that she need not necessarily submit. Nobody except her parents had ever whipped her. It was one thing to be stood out as a martyr for her friends, but nobody should whip her for it. According to Mama's and Daddy's instructions, she had never before argued with a teacher, but she needed no practice for the scornful words which she flung recklessly because she knew that they were righteous.

"Yes, I did pass a note, and for that perhaps I deserve to be stood out. But I am no more guilty than the girl who passed it to me, or the girl who had passed it to her, and even less at fault are we than the girl who started it. If you whip me, you should also have here all the girls from my row, with their palms outstretched. And I won't hold out my hand until I see theirs held out also!"

There was a stunned silence. Mr. Dong could not have been any more surprised than Jade Snow herself. From where had all those words tumbled, so suddenly and so forcefully?

Mr. Dong recovered somewhat and clutched his vanishing dignity. "So you dare to question me!"

The new Jade Snow spoke again, "I speak only for what is right, and I will always question wrong in the way my Daddy has taught me. I am willing to bring him here to submit this matter to his judgment. Until then, I hold out no hand."

There Mr. Dong was held. Obviously he did not wish to have a director of the school board brought in to arbitrate between the disciplinarian and his own daughter, Jade Snow. He generously waved his hand. "Very well, I shall let you off gently this time, but don't take advantage of my good nature to let this happen again!"

As Jade Snow went home that Saturday afternoon, her thoughts were not concerned with her victory, unprecedented as it was. She was struck with this new idea of speaking for what she knew was right. All the vague remarks which Mama and her older sisters had dropped from time to time, and the stories they had told about Daddy's well-known habit of speaking out forthrightly and fearlessly for what he believed was right, no matter what everyone else thought, had borne their first fruit in Jade Snow.

---

*Confronting fear calls upon self-knowledge and all the inner strength one can muster. In this selection from Madeleine L'Engle's* A Wrinkle in Time, *three children who have been chosen for a dangerous rescue mission are given hints about where to find the strengths that will sustain their courage. This selection raises two questions for readers: What are my resources? And how do I marshal them at times of crisis?*

### Madeleine L'Engle, *A Wrinkle in Time*

Her mouth was open and Meg could see the toothless gums and it seemed that she could almost hear her screaming at two small children who were standing by her. Then she grabbed a long wooden spoon from the sink and began whacking one of the children.

"Oh, dear—" the Medium murmured, and the picture began to dissolve. "I didn't really—"

"It's all right," Calvin said in a low voice. "I think I'd rather you knew."

Now instead of reaching out to Calvin for safety, Meg took his hand in hers, not saying anything in words but trying to tell him by the pressure of her fingers what she felt. If anyone had told her only the day before that she, Meg, the snaggle-toothed, the myopic, the clumsy, would be taking a boy's hand to offer him comfort and strength, particularly a popular and important boy like Calvin, the idea would have been beyond her comprehension. But now it seemed as natural to want to help and protect Calvin as it did Charles Wallace.

The shadows were swirling in the crystal again, and as they cleared Meg began to recognize her mother's lab at home. Mrs. Murry was sitting perched on her high stool, writing away at a sheet of paper on a clipboard on her lap. She's writing Father, Meg thought. The way she always does. Every night.

The tears that she could never learn to control swam to her eyes as she watched. Mrs. Murry looked up from her letter, almost as though she were looking toward the children, and then her head drooped and she put it down on the paper, and sat there, huddled up, letting herself relax into an unhappiness that she never allowed her children to see.

And now the desire for tears left Meg. The hot, protective anger she had felt for Calvin when she looked into his home she now felt turned toward her mother.

"Let's go!" she cried harshly. "Let's *do* something!"

"She's always so right," Mrs. Whatsit murmured, looking towards Mrs. Which. "Sometimes I wish she'd just say I told you so and have done with it."

"I only meant to help—" the Medium wailed.

"Oh, Medium, dear, *don't* feel badly," Mrs. Whatsit said swiftly. "Look at something cheerful, do. I can't bear to have you distressed!"

"It's all right," Meg assured the Medium earnestly. "Truly it is, Mrs. Medium, and we thank you very much."

"Are you sure?" the Medium asked, brightening.

"Of course! It really helped ever so much because it made me mad, and when I'm mad I don't have room to be scared."

"Well, kiss me good-by for good luck, then," the Medium said.

Meg went over to her and gave her a quick kiss, and so did Charles Wallace. The Medium looked smilingly at Calvin, and winked. "I want the young man to kiss me, too. I always did love red hair. And it'll give you good luck, Laddie-me-love."

Calvin bent down, blushing, and awkwardly kissed her cheek.

The Medium tweaked his nose. "You've got a lot to learn, my boy," she told him.

"Now, good-by, Medium dear, and many thanks," Mrs. Whatsit said. "I dare say we'll see you in an eon or two."

"Where are you going in case I want to tune in?" the Medium asked.

"Camazotz," Mrs. Whatsit told her. (Where and what was Camazotz? Meg did not like the sound of the word or the way in which Mrs. Whatsit pronounced it.) "But please don't distress yourself on our behalf. You know you don't like looking in on the dark planets, and it's very upsetting to us when you aren't happy."

"But I must know what happens to the children," the Medium said. "It's my worst trouble, getting fond. If I didn't get fond I could be happy all the time. *Oh*, well, *ho* hum, I manage to keep pretty jolly, and a little snooze will do wonders for me right now. Good-by, everyb—" and her word got lost in the general b-b-bz-z of a snore.

"Ccome," Mrs. Which ordered, and they followed her out of the darkness of the cave to the impersonal grayness of the Medium's planet.

"Nnoww, cchilldrenn, yyouu musstt nott bee frrightennedd att whatt iss ggoingg tto hhappenn," Mrs. Which warned.

"Stay angry, little Meg," Mrs. Whatsit whispered. "You will need all your anger now."

Without warning Meg was swept into nothingness again. This time the nothingness was interrupted by a feeling of clammy coldness such as she had never felt before. The coldness deepened and swirled all about her and through her, and was filled with a new and strange kind of darkness that was a completely tangible thing, a thing that wanted to eat and digest her like some enormous malignant beast of prey.

Then the darkness was gone. Had it been the shadow, the Black Thing? Had they had to travel through it to get to her father?

There was the by-now-familiar tingling in her hands and feet and the push through hardness, and she was on her feet, breathless but unharmed, standing beside Calvin and Charles Wallace.

"Is this Camazotz?" Charles Wallace asked as Mrs. Whatsit materialized in front of him.

"Yes," she answered. "Now let us just stand and get our breath and look around."

They were standing on a hill and as Meg looked about her she felt that it could easily be a hill on earth. There were the familiar trees she knew so well at home: birches, pines, maples. And though it was warmer than it had been when they so precipitously left the apple orchard, there was a faintly autumnal touch to the air; near them were several small trees with reddened leaves very like sumac, and a big patch of goldenrod-like flowers. As she looked down the hill she could see the smokestacks of a town, and it might have been one of any number of familiar towns. There seemed to be nothing strange, or different, or frightening, in the landscape.

But Mrs. Whatsit came to her and put an arm around her comfortingly. "I can't stay with you here, you know, love," she said. "You three children will be on your own. We will be near you; we will be watching you. But you will not be able to see us or to ask us for help, and we will not be able to come to you."

"But is Father here?" Meg asked tremblingly.

"Yes."

"But where? When will we see him?" She was poised for running, as though she were going to sprint off, immediately, to wherever her father was.

"That I cannot tell you. You will just have to wait until the propitious moment."

Charles Wallace looked steadily at Mrs. Whatsit. "Are you afraid for us?"

"A little."

"But if you weren't afraid to do what you did when you were a star, why should you be afraid for us now?"

"But I was afraid," Mrs. Whatsit said gently. She looked steadily at each of the three children in turn. "You will need help," she told them, "but all I am allowed to give you is a little talisman. Calvin, your great gift is your ability to communicate, to communicate with all kinds of people. So, for you, I will strengthen this gift. Meg, I give you your faults."

"My faults!" Meg cried.

"Your faults."

"But I'm always trying to get rid of my faults!"

"Yes," Mrs. Whatsit said. "However, I think you'll find they'll come in very handy on Camazotz. Charles Wallace, to you I can give only the resilience of your childhood."

From somewhere Mrs. Who's glasses glimmered and they heard her voice. "Calvin," she said, "a hint. For you a hint. Listen well:

. . . For that he was a spirit too delicate
To act their earthy and abhorr'd commands,
Refusing their grand hests, they did confine him
By help of their most potent ministers,
And in their most unmitigable rage,
Into a cloven pine; within which rift
Imprisoned, he didst painfully remain. . . .

Shakespeare. *The Tempest*."

"Where are you, Mrs. Who?" Charles Wallace asked. "Where is Mrs. Which?"

"We cannot come to you now," Mrs. Who's voice blew to them like the wind. *"Allwissend bin ich nicht; doch viel ist mir bewisst.* Goethe. *I do not know everything; still many things I understand.* That is for you, Charles. Remember that you do not know everything." Then the voice was directed to Meg. "To you I leave my glasses, little blind-as-a-bat. But do not use them except as a last resort. Save them for the final moment of peril." As she spoke there was another shimmer of spectacles, and then it was gone, and the voice faded out with it. The spectacles were in Meg's hand. She put them carefully into the breast pocket of her blazer, and the knowledge that they were there somehow made her a little less afraid.

"Tto alll tthreee off yyou I ggive mmy ccommandd," Mrs. Which said. "Ggo ddownn innttoo tthee ttownn. Ggo ttogetherr. Ddoo nnott llett tthemm ssepparate yyou. Bbee sstrongg." There was a flicker and then it vanished. Meg shivered.

Mrs. Whatsit must have seen the shiver, for she patted Meg on the shoulder. Then she turned to Calvin. "Take care of Meg."

"I can take care of Meg," Charles Wallace said rather sharply. "I always have."

Mrs. Whatsit looked at Charles Wallace, and the creaky voice seemed somehow both to soften and to deepen at the same time. "Charles Wallace, the danger here is greatest for you."

"Why?"

"Because of what you are. Just exactly because of what you are you will be by far the most vulnerable. You *must* stay with Meg and Calvin. You must *not* go off on your own. Beware of pride and arrogance, Charles, for they may betray you."

At the tone of Mrs. Whatsit's voice, both warning and frightening, Meg shivered again. And Charles Wallace butted up against Mrs. Whatsit in the way he often did with his mother, whispering, "Now I think I know what you meant about being afraid."

"Only a fool is not afraid," Mrs. Whatsit told him. "Now go." And where she had been there was only sky and grasses and a small rock.

"Come *on*," Meg said impatiently. "Come on, let's *go!*" She was completely unaware that her voice was trembling like an aspen leaf. She took Charles Wallace and Calvin each by the hand and started down the hill.

# Self-Discipline

An interviewer once said to the jazz saxophonist Charlie Parker, "You do amazing things on the saxophone, Mr. Parker." Parker replied, "I don't know about amazing—I practiced for fifteen hours a day for a few years."

It is often difficult to infer from the results of serious endeavor the time and effort it took to develop the skills that went into it. Yet achievement is as dependent upon patience, practice, and internal motivation as it is upon inspiration and talent. This is equally true for developing the moral dimensions of self and for developing intellectual or artistic sensibility. The abilities to control your temper, analyze your feelings, and articulate your beliefs before acting, as well as to understand the motives of others and weigh alternative forms of action, all require self-discipline.

In addition, self-discipline is a source of inner strength. It provides children with the conviction that they can overcome complex challenges and do difficult things. It gives them the confidence to explore new aspects of experience, make and overcome mistakes, and take chances challenging illegitimate authority in sensible ways. Above and beyond that, there is pleasure in being able to plan out a project, work hard on it, and see the results of one's own efforts. As the Jewish sage Ben Hei said:

Effort is its own reward.

We are here to do.
And through doing to learn;
and through learning to know;
and through knowing to experience wonder;
and through wonder to attain wisdom;
and through wisdom to find simplicity;
and through simplicity to give attention;

and through attention
to see what needs to be done.
                    —*The Wisdom of the Jewish Sages*

Some of the aspects of self-discipline explored in this section are persistence and patience, the ability to plan ahead, self-control, the value of hard work and the concomitant danger of working hard without knowing why or what you are doing, and the development of self-motivated behavior.

———⊷•⊶———

*Sometimes people achieve things despite all odds and expectations. The motive to overcome such challenges comes from within, from some conviction and strength that is as much moral as it is intellectual, scientific, or artistic. Reading about such amazing effort begs reflection and discussion about our own challenges and inner resources. It provides occasions for sharing those tales of success that give us pride in our inner selves.*

### Christy Brown, "The Letter 'A,'" from *My Left Foot*
At this time my mother had the five other children to look after besides the "difficult one," though as yet it was not by any means a full house. There were my brothers, Jim, Tony, and Paddy, and my two sisters, Lily and Mona, all of them very young, just a year or so between each of them, so that they were almost exactly like steps of stairs.

Four years rolled by and I was now five, and still as helpless as a newly-born baby. While my father was out at bricklaying earning our bread and butter for us, mother was slowly, patiently pulling down the wall, brick by brick, that seemed to thrust itself between me and the other children, slowly, patiently penetrating beyond the thick curtain that hung over my mind, separating it from theirs. It was hard, heartbreaking work, for often all she got from me in return was a vague smile and perhaps a faint gurgle. I could not speak or even mumble, nor could I sit up without support on my own, let alone take steps. But I wasn't inert or motionless. I seemed indeed to be convulsed with movement, wild, stiff, snakelike movement that never left me, except in sleep. My fingers twisted and twitched continually, my arms twined backwards and would often shoot out suddenly this way and that, and my head lolled and sagged sideways. I was a queer, crooked little fellow.

Mother tells me how one day she had been sitting with me for hours in an upstairs room, showing me pictures out of a great big storybook that I had got from Santa Claus last Christmas and telling me the names of the different animals and flowers that were in them, trying without success to get me to repeat them. This had gone on for hours while she talked and laughed with me. Then at the end of it she leaned over me and said gently into my ear:

"Did you like it, Chris? Did you like the bears and the monkeys and all the lovely flowers? Nod your head for yes, like a good boy."

But I could make no sign that I had understood her. Her face was bent over mine, hopefully. Suddenly, involuntarily, my queer hand reached up and grasped one of the dark curls that fell in a thick cluster about her neck. Gently she loosened the clenched fingers, though some dark strands were still clutched between them.

Then she turned away from my curious stare and left the room, crying. The door closed behind her. It all seemed hopeless. It looked as though there was some justification for my relatives' contention that I was an idiot and beyond help.

They now spoke of an institution.

"Never!" said my mother almost fiercely, when this was suggested to her. "I know my boy is not an idiot. It is his body that is shattered, not his mind. I'm sure of that."

Sure? Yet inwardly, she prayed God would give her some proof of her faith. She knew it was one thing to believe but quite another thing to prove.

I was now five, and still I showed no real sign of intelligence. I showed no apparent interest in things except with my toes—more especially those of my left foot. Although my natural habits were clean I could not aid myself, but in this respect my father took care of me. I used to lie on my back all the time in the kitchen or, on bright warm days, out in the garden, a little bundle of crooked muscles and twisted nerves, surrounded by a family that loved me and hoped for me and that made me part of their own warmth and humanity. I was lonely, imprisoned in a world of my own, unable to communicate with others, cut off, separated from them as though a glass wall stood between my existence and theirs, thrusting me beyond the sphere of their lives and activities. I longed to run about and play with the rest, but I was unable to break loose from my bondage.

Then, suddenly, it happened! In a moment everything was changed, my future life molded into a definite shape, my mother's faith in me rewarded and her secret fear changed into open triumph.

It happened so quickly, so simply after all the years of waiting and uncertainty that I can see and feel the whole scene as if it had happened last week. It was the afternoon of a cold, gray December day. The streets outside glistened with snow; the white sparkling flakes stuck and melted on the windowpanes and hung on the boughs of the trees like molten silver. The wind howled dismally, whipping up little whirling columns of snow that rose and fell at every fresh gust. And over all, the dull, murky sky stretched like a dark canopy, a vast infinity of grayness.

Inside, all the family were gathered around the big kitchen fire that lit up the little room with a warm glow and made giant shadows dance on the walls and ceiling.

In a corner Mona and Paddy were sitting huddled together, a few torn school primers before them. They were writing down little sums onto an old chipped slate, using a bright piece of yellow chalk. I was close to them, propped up by a few pillows against the wall, watching.

It was the chalk that attracted me so much. It was a long slender stick of vivid yellow. I had never seen anything like it before, and it showed up so well against the black surface of the slate that I was fascinated by it as much as if it had been a stick of gold.

Suddenly I wanted desperately to do what my sister was doing. Then—without thinking or knowing exactly what I was doing, I reached out and took the stick of chalk out of my sister's hand—*with my left foot.*

I do not know why I used my left foot to do this. It is a puzzle to many people as well as to myself, for, although I had displayed a curious interest in my toes at an early age, I had never attempted before this to use either of my feet in any way. They could have been as useless to me as were my hands. That day, however, my left foot, apparently on its own volition, reached out and very impolitely took the chalk out of my sister's hand.

I held it tightly between my toes, and, acting on an impulse, made a wild sort of scribble with it on the slate. Next moment I stopped, a bit dazed, surprised, looking down at the stick of yellow chalk stuck between my toes, not knowing what to do with it next, hardly knowing how it got there. Then I looked up and became aware that everyone had stopped talking and were staring at me silently. Nobody stirred. Mona, her black curls framing her chubby little face, stared at me with great big eyes and open mouth. Across the open hearth, his face lit by flames, sat my father, leaning forward, hands outspread on his knees, his shoulders tense. I felt the sweat break out on my forehead.

My mother came in from the pantry with a steaming pot in her hand. She stopped midway between the table and the fire, feeling the tension flowing through the room. She followed their stare and saw me, in the corner. Her eyes looked from my face down to my foot, with the chalk gripped between my toes. She put down the pot.

Then she crossed over to me and knelt down beside me, as she had done so many times before.

"I'll show you what do to with it, Chris," she said, very slowly and in a queer, jerky way, her face flushed as if with some inner excitement.

Taking another piece of chalk from Mona, she hesitated, then very deliberately drew, on the floor in front of me, *the single letter "A."*

"Copy that," she said, looking steadily at me. "Copy it, Christy."

I couldn't.

I looked about me, looked around at the faces that were turned toward me, tense, excited faces that were at that moment frozen, immobile, eager, waiting for a miracle in their midst.

The stillness was profound. The room was full of flame and shadow that danced before my eyes and lulled my taut nerves into a sort of waking sleep. I could hear the sound of the water tap dripping in the pantry, the loud ticking of the clock on the mantel shelf, and the soft hiss and crackle of the logs on the open hearth.

I tried again. I put out my foot and made a wild jerking stab with the chalk which produced a very crooked line and nothing more. Mother held the slate steady for me.

"Try again, Chris," she whispered in my ear. "Again."

I did. I stiffened my body and put my left foot out again, for the third time. I drew one side of the letter. I drew half the other side. Then the stick of chalk broke and I was left with a stump. I wanted to fling it away and give up. Then I felt my mother's hand on my shoulder. I tried once more. Out went my foot. I shook, I sweated and strained every muscle. My hands were so tightly clenched that my fingernails bit into the flesh. I set my teeth so hard that I nearly pierced my lower lip. Everything in the room swam till the faces around me were mere patches of white. But—I drew it—*the letter "A."* There it was on the floor before me. Shaky, with awkward, wobbly sides and a very uneven center line. But it *was* the letter "A." I looked up. I saw my mother's face for a moment, tears on her cheeks. Then my father stooped down and hoisted me onto his shoulder.

I had done it! It had started—the thing that was to give my mind its chance of expressing itself. True, I couldn't speak with my lips, but now I would speak through something more lasting than spoken words— written words.

That one letter, scrawled on the floor with a broken bit of yellow chalk gripped between my toes, was my road to a new world, my key to mental freedom. It was to provide a source of relaxation to the tense, taut thing that was me which panted for expression behind a twisted mouth.

**Langston Hughes, *Mother to Son***
Well, son, I'll tell you:
Life for me ain't been no crystal stair.
It's had tacks in it,
And splinters,
And boards torn up,
And places with no carpet on the floor—
Bare.
But all the time
I'se been a-climbin' on,
And reachin' lanbdin's,
And turnin' corners,
And sometimes goin' in the dark
Where there ain't been no light.
So boy, don't you turn back.
Don't you set down on the steps
'Cause you finds it kiner hard.
Don't you fall now—
For I'se still goin', honey,
I's still climbin',
And life for me ain't been no crystal stair.

*Persistence and patience are virtues that are sometimes hard to come by. Yet working simply, continuously, and patiently can produce wonderful results. These two selections raise the questions: How do you know when to persist in trying to accomplish something difficult and when to ask for help or quit? What inner resources lead to the development of patience? And how can other people's stories strengthen your own resolve to do complex and caring things with your life?*

**Jean Giono, *The Man Who Planted Trees***
For a human character to reveal truly exceptional qualities, one must have the good fortune to be able to observe its performance over many

years. If this performance is devoid of all egoism, if its guiding motive is unparalleled generosity, if it is absolutely certain that there is no thought of recompense and that, in addition, it has left its visible mark upon the earth, then there can be no mistake.

About forty years ago I was taking a long trip on foot over mountain heights quite unknown to tourists, in that ancient region where the Alps thrust down into Provence. All this, at the time I embarked upon my long walk through these deserted regions, was barren and colorless land. Nothing grew there but wild lavender.

I was crossing the area at its widest point, and after three days' walking, found myself in the midst of unparalleled desolation. I camped near the vestiges of an abandoned village. I had run out of water the day before, and had to find some. These clustered houses, although in ruins, like an old wasps' nest, suggested that there must once have been a spring or well here. There was indeed a spring, but it was dry. The five or six houses, roofless, gnawed by wind and rain, the tiny chapel with its crumbling steeple, stood about like the houses and chapels in living villages, but all life had vanished.

It was a fine June day, brilliant with sunlight, but over this unsheltered land, high in the sky, the wind blew with unendurable ferocity. It growled over the carcasses of the houses like a lion disturbed at its meal. I had to move my camp.

After five hours' walking I had still not found water and there was nothing to give me any hope of finding any. All about me was the same dryness, the same coarse grasses. I thought I glimpsed in the distance a small black silhouette, upright, and took it for the trunk of a solitary tree. In any case I started toward it. It was a shepherd. Thirty sheep were lying about him on the baking earth.

He gave me a drink from his water-gourd and, a little later, took me to his cottage in a fold of the plain. He drew his water—excellent water—from a very deep natural well above which he had constructed a primitive winch.

The man spoke little. This is the way of those who live alone, but one felt that he was sure of himself, and confident in his assurance. That was unexpected in this barren country. He lived, not in a cabin, but in a real house built of stone that bore plain evidence of how his own efforts had reclaimed the ruin he had found there on his arrival. His roof was strong and sound. The wind on its tiles made the sound of the sea upon its shore.

The place was in order, the dishes washed, the floor swept, his rifle oiled; his soup was boiling over the fire. I noticed then that he was cleanly shaved, that all his buttons were firmly sewed on, that his clothing had been mended with the meticulous care that makes the mending invisible. He shared his soup with me and afterwards, when I offered my tobacco pouch, he told me that he did not smoke. His dog, as silent as himself, was friendly without being servile.

It was understood from the first that I should spend the night there; the nearest village was still more than a day and a half away. And besides I was perfectly familiar with the nature of the rare villages in that region. There were four or five of them scattered well apart from each other on these mountain slopes, among white oak thickets, at the extreme end of the wagon roads. They were inhabited by charcoalburners, and the living was bad. Families, crowded together in a climate that is excessively harsh both in winter and in summer, found no escape from the unceasing conflict of personalities. Irrational ambition reached inordinate proportions in the continual desire for escape. The men took their wagonloads of charcoal to the town, then returned. The soundest characters broke under the perpetual grind. The women nursed their grievances. There was rivalry in everything, over the price of charcoal as over a pew in the church, over warring virtues as over warring vices as well as over the ceaseless combat between virtue and vice. And over all there was the wind, also ceaseless, to rasp upon the nerves. There were epidemics of suicide and frequent cases of insanity, usually homicidal.

The shepherd went to fetch a small sack and poured out a heap of acorns on the table. He began to inspect them, one by one, with great concentration, separating the good from the bad. I smoked my pipe. I did offer to help him. He told me that it was his job. And in fact, seeing the care he devoted to the task, I did not insist. That was the whole of our conversation. When he had set aside a large enough pile of good acorns he counted them out by tens, meanwhile eliminating the small ones or those which were slightly cracked, for now he examined them more closely. When he had thus selected one hundred perfect acorns he stopped and we went to bed.

There was peace in being with this man. The next day I asked if I might rest here for a day. He found it quite natural—or, to be more exact, he gave me the impression that nothing could startle him. The rest was not absolutely necessary, but I was interested and wished to know more about him. He opened the pen and led his flock to pasture. Before leaving, he plunged his sack of carefully selected and counted acorns into a pail of water.

I noticed that he carried for a stick an iron rod as thick as my thumb and about a yard and a half long. Resting myself by walking, I followed a path parallel to his. His pasture was in a valley. He left the dog in charge of the little flock and climbed toward where I stood. I was afraid that he was about to rebuke me for my indiscretion, but it was not that at all: this was the way he was going, and he invited me to go along if I had nothing better to do. He climbed to the top of the ridge, about a hundred yards away.

There he began thrusting his iron rod into the earth, making a hole in which he planted an acorn; then he refilled the hole. He was planting oak trees. I asked him if the land belonged to him. He answered no. Did he know whose it was? He did not. He supposed it was community property, or perhaps belonged to people who cared nothing about it. He was not interested in finding out whose it was. He planted his hundred acorns with the greatest care.

After the midday meal he resumed his planting. I suppose I must have been fairly insistent in my questioning, for he answered me. For three years he had been planting trees in this wilderness. He had planted one hundred thousand. Of the hundred thousand, twenty thousand had sprouted. Of the twenty thousand he still expected to lose about half, to rodents or to the unpredictable designs of Providence. There remained ten thousand oak trees to grow where nothing had grown before.

That was when I began to wonder about the age of this man. He was obviously over fifty. Fifty-five, he told me. His name was Elzéard Bouffier. He had once had a farm in the lowlands. There he had had his life. He had lost his only son, then his wife. He had withdrawn into this solitude where his pleasure was to live leisurely with his lambs and his dog. It was his opinion that this land was dying for want of trees. He added that, having no very pressing business of his own, he had resolved to remedy this state of affairs.

Since I was at that time, in spite of my youth, leading a solitary life, I understood how to deal gently with solitary spirits. But my very youth forced me to consider the future in relation to myself and to a certain quest for happiness. I told him that in thirty years his ten thousand oaks would be magnificent. He answered quite simply that if God granted him life, in thirty years he would have planted so many more that these ten thousand would be like a drop of water in the ocean.

Besides, he was now studying the reproduction of beech trees and had a nursery of seedlings grown from beechnuts near his cottage. The seedlings, which he had protected from his sheep with a wire fence, were very beautiful. He was also considering birches for the valleys where, he told me, there was a certain amount of moisture a few yards below the surface of the soil.

The next day, we parted.

*       *       *

The following year came the War of 1914, in which I was involved for the next five years. An infantryman hardly had time for reflecting upon trees. To tell the truth, the thing itself had made no impression upon me; I had considered it as a hobby, a stamp collection, and forgotten it.

The war over, I found myself possessed of a tiny demobilization bonus and a huge desire to breathe fresh air for a while. It was with no other objective that I again took the road to the barren lands.

The countryside had not changed. However, beyond the deserted village I glimpsed in the distance a sort of greyish mist that covered the mountaintops like a carpet. Since the day before, I had begun to think again of the shepherd tree planter. "Ten thousand oaks," I reflected, "really take up quite a bit of space."

I had seen too many men die during those five years not to imagine easily that Elzéard Bouffier was dead, especially since, at twenty, one regards men of fifty as old men with nothing left to do but die. He was not dead. As a matter of fact, he was extremely spry. He had changed jobs. Now he had only four sheep but, instead, a hundred beehives. He had got rid of the sheep because they threatened his young trees. For, he told me (and I saw for myself), the war had disturbed him not at all. He had imperturbably continued to plant.

The oaks of 1910 were then ten years old and taller than either of us. It was an impressive spectacle. I was literally speechless and, as he did not talk, we spent the whole day walking in silence through his forest. In three sections, it measured eleven kilometers in length and three kilometers at its greatest width. When you remembered that all this had sprung from the hands and the soul of this one man, without technical resources, you understood that men could be as effectual as God in other realms than that of destruction.

He had pursued his plan, and beech trees as high as my shoulder, spreading out as far as the eye could reach, confirmed it. He showed me handsome clumps of birch planted five years before—that is, in 1915, when I had been fighting at Verdun. He had set them out in all the valleys where he had guessed—and rightly—that there was moisture almost at the surface of the ground. They were as delicate as young girls, and very well established.

Creation seemed to come about in a sort of chain reaction. He did not worry about it; he was determinedly pursuing his task in all its simplicity; but as we went back toward the village I saw water flowing in brooks that had been dry since the memory of man. This was the most impressive result of chain reaction that I had seen. These dry streams had once, long ago, run with water. Some of the dreary villages I mentioned before had been built on the sites of ancient Roman settlements, traces of which still remained; and archaeologists, exploring there, had found fishhooks where, in the twentieth century, cisterns were needed to assure a small supply of water.

The wind, too, scattered seeds. As the water reappeared, so there reappeared willows, rushes, meadows, gardens, flowers, and a certain purpose in being alive. But the transformation took place so gradually that it became part of the pattern without causing any astonishment. Hunters, climbing into the wilderness in pursuit of hares or wild boar, had of course noticed the sudden growth of little trees, but had attributed it to some natural caprice of the earth. That is why no one meddled with Elzéard Bouffier's work. If he had been detected he would have had opposition. He was indetectable. Who in the villages or in the administration could have dreamed of such perseverance in a magnificent generosity?

To have anything like a precise idea of this exceptional character one must not forget that he worked in total solitude: so total that, toward the end of his life, he lost the habit of speech. Or perhaps it was that he saw no need for it.

In 1933 he received a visit from a forest ranger who notified him of an order against lighting fires out of doors for fear of endangering the growth of this *natural* forest. It was the first time, the man told him naively, that he had ever heard of a forest growing of its own accord. At that time Bouffier was about to plant beeches at a spot some twelve kilometers from his cottage. In order to avoid traveling back and forth—for he was then seventy-five—he planned to build a stone cabin right at the plantation. The next year he did so.

In 1935 a whole delegation came from the Government to examine the "natural forest." There was a high official from the Forest Service, a deputy, technicians. There was a great deal of ineffectual talk. It was decided that something must be done and, fortunately, nothing was done except the only helpful thing: the whole forest was placed under the protection of the State, and charcoal burning prohibited. For it was impossible not to be captivated by the beauty of those young trees in the fullness of health, and they cast their spell over the deputy himself.

A friend of mine was among the forestry owners of the delegation. To him I explained the mystery. One day the following week we went together to see Elzéard Bouffier. We found him hard at work, some ten kilometers from the spot where the inspection had taken place.

This forester was not my friend for nothing. He was aware of values. He knew how to keep silent. I delivered the eggs I had brought as a present. We shared our lunch among the three of us and spent several hours in wordless contemplation of the countryside.

In the direction from which we had come the slopes were covered with trees twenty to twenty-five feet tall. I remembered how the land had looked in 1913: a desert. . . . Peaceful, regular toil, the vigorous mountain air, frugality and, above all, serenity of spirit had endowed this old man with awe-inspiring health. He was one of God's athletes. I wondered how many more acres he was going to cover with trees.

Before leaving, my friend simply made a brief suggestion about certain species of trees that the soil here seemed particularly suited for. He did not force the point. "For the very good reason," he told me later, "that Bouffier knows more about it than I do." At the end of an hour's walking—having turned it over in his mind—he added, "He knows a lot more about it than anybody. He's discovered a wonderful way to be happy!"

It was thanks to this officer that not only the forest but also the happiness of the man was protected. He delegated three rangers to the task, and so terrorized them that they remained proof against all the bottles of wine the charcoalburners could offer.

The only serious danger to the work occurred during the war of 1939. As cars were being run on gazogenes (wood-burning generators), there was never enough wood. Cutting was started among the oaks of 1910, but the area was so far from any railroads that the enterprise turned out to be financially unsound. It was abandoned. The shepherd had seen nothing of it. He was thirty kilometers away, peacefully continuing his work, ignoring the war of '39 as he had ignored that of '14.

I saw Elzéard Bouffier for the last time in June of 1945. He was then eighty-seven. I had started back along the route through the wastelands; but now, in spite of the disorder in which the war had left the country, there was a bus running between the Durance Valley and the mountain. I attributed the fact that I no longer recognized the scenes of my earlier journeys to this relatively speedy transportation. It seemed to me, too, that the route took me through new territory. It took the name of a village to convince me that I was actually in that region that had been all ruins and desolation.

The bus put me down at Vergons. In 1913 this hamlet of ten or twelve houses had three inhabitants. They had been savage creatures, hating one another, living by trapping game, little removed, both physically and morally, from the conditions of prehistoric man. All about them nettles were feeding upon the remains of abandoned houses. Their condition had been beyond hope. For them, nothing but to await death—a situation which rarely predisposes to virtue.

Everything was changed. Even the air. Instead of the harsh dry winds that used to attack me, a gentle breeze was blowing, laden with scents. A sound like water came from the mountains: it was the wind in the forest. Most amazing of all, I heard the actual sound of water falling into a pool. I saw that a fountain had been built, that it flowed freely and—what touched me most—that someone had planted a linden beside it, a linden that must have been four years old, already in full leaf, the incontestable symbol of resurrection.

Besides, Vergons bore evidence of labor at the sort of undertaking for which hope is required. Hope, then, had returned. Ruins had been cleared away, dilapidated walls torn down and five houses restored. Now there were twenty-eight inhabitants, four of them young married couples. The new houses, freshly plastered, were surrounded by gardens where vegetables and flowers grew in orderly confusion, cabbages and roses, leeks and snapdragons, celery and anemones. It was now a village where one would like to live.

From that point on I went on foot. The war just finished had not yet allowed the full blooming of life, but Lazarus was out of the tomb. On the lower slopes of the mountain I saw little fields of barley and of rye; deep in the narrow valleys the meadows were turning green.

It has taken only the eight years since then for the whole countryside to glow with health and prosperity. On the site of ruins I had seen in 1913 now stand neat farms, cleanly plastered, testifying to a happy and comfortable life. The old streams, fed by the rains and snows that the forest conserves, are flowing again. Their waters have been channeled. On each farm, in groves of maples, fountain pools overflow on to carpets of fresh mint. Little by little the villages have been rebuilt. People from the plains, where land is costly, have settled here, bringing youth, motion, the spirit of adventure. Along the roads you meet hearty men and women, boys and girls who understand laughter and have recovered a taste for picnics. Counting the former population, unrecognizable now that they live in comfort, more than ten thousand people owe their happiness to Elzéard Bouffier.

When I reflect that one man, armed only with his own physical and moral resources, was able to cause this land of Canaan to spring from the wasteland, I am convinced that in spite of everything, humanity is admirable. But when I compute the unfailing greatness of spirit and the tenacity of benevolence that it must have taken to achieve this result, I am taken with an immense respect for that old and unlearned peasant who was able to complete a work worthy of God.

Elzéard Bouffier died peacefully in 1947 at the hospice in Banon.

### Dorothy Canfield Fisher, *Understood Betsy*

Molly trotted at her heels, quite comforted, now that Betsy was talking so competently to grownups. She did not hear what they said, nor try to. Now that Betsy's voice sounded all right she had no more fears. Betsy would manage somehow. She heard Betsy's voice again talking to the other man, but she was busy looking at an exhibit of beautiful jelly glasses, and paid no attention. Then Betsy led her away again out of doors, where everybody was walking back and forth under the bright September sky, blowing on horns, waving plumes of brilliant tissue paper, tickling each other with peacock feathers, and eating popcorn and candy out of paper bags.

That reminded Molly that they had ten cents yet. "Oh, Betsy," she proposed, "let's take a nickel of our money for some popcorn."

She was startled by Betsy's fierce sudden clutch at their little purse and by the quaver in her voice as she answered: "No, no, Molly. We've got to save every cent of that. I've found out it costs thirty cents for us both to go home to Hillsboro on the train. The last one goes at six o'clock."

"We haven't got but ten," said Molly.

Betsy looked at her silently for a moment and then burst out, "I'll earn the rest! I'll earn it somehow! I'll have to! There isn't any other way!"

"All right," said Molly quaintly, not seeing anything unusual in this. "You can, if you want to. I'll wait for you here."

"No, you won't!" cried Betsy, who had quite enough of trying to meet people in a crowd. "No, you won't! You just follow me every minute! I don't want you out of my sight!"

They began to move forward now, Betsy's eyes wildly roving from one place to another. How *could* a little girl earn money at a county fair! She was horribly afraid to go up and speak to a stranger, and yet how else could she begin?

"Here, Molly, you wait here," she said. "Don't you budge till I come back."

But alas! Molly had only a moment to wait that time, for the man who was selling lemonade answered Betsy's shy question with a stare and a curt, "Lord, no! What could a young one like you do for me?"

The little girls wandered on, Molly calm and expectant, confident in

Betsy; Betsy with a dry mouth and a gone feeling. They were passing by a big shed-like building now, where a large sign proclaimed that the Woodford Ladies' Aid Society would serve a hot chicken dinner for thirty-five cents. Of course the sign was not accurate, for at half-past three, almost four, the chicken dinner had long ago been all eaten and in place of the diners was a group of weary women moving languidly about or standing saggingly by a great table piled with dirty dishes. Betsy paused here, meditated a moment, and went in rapidly so that her courage would not evaporate.

The woman with gray hair looked down at her a little impatiently and said, "Dinner's all over."

"I didn't come for dinner," said Betsy, swallowing hard. "I came to see if you wouldn't hire me to wash your dishes. I'll do them for twenty-five cents."

The woman laughed, looked from little Betsy to the great pile of dishes, and said, turning away, "Mercy, child, if you washed from now till morning, you wouldn't make a hole in what we've got to do."

Betsy heard her say to the other women, "Some young one wanting more money for the sideshows."

Now, now was the moment to remember what Cousin Ann would have done. She would certainly not have shaken all over with hurt feelings nor have allowed the tears to come stingingly to her eyes. So Betsy sternly made herself stop doing these things. And Cousin Ann wouldn't have given way to the dreadful sinking feeling of discouragement, but would have gone right on to the next place. So, although Betsy felt like nothing so much as crooking her elbow over her face and crying as hard as she could cry, she stiffened her back, took Molly's hand again, and stepped out, heartsick within but very steady (although rather pale) without.

She and Molly walked along in the crowd again, Molly laughing and pointing out the pranks and antics of the young people, who were feeling livelier than ever as the afternoon wore on. Betsy looked at them grimly with unseeing eyes. It was four o'clock. The last train for Hillsboro left in two hours and she was no nearer having the price of the tickets. She stopped for a moment to get her breath; for, although they were walking slowly, she kept feeling breathless and choked. It occurred to her that if ever a little girl had had a more horrible birthday she never heard of one!

"Oh, I wish I could, Dan!" said a young voice near her. "But honest! Momma'd just eat me up alive if I left the booth for a minute!"

Betsy turned quickly. A very pretty girl with yellow hair and blue eyes (she looked as Molly might when she was grown up) was leaning over the edge of a little canvas-covered booth, the sign of which announced that home-made doughnuts and soft drinks were for sale there. A young man, very flushed and gay, was pulling at the girl's blue gingham sleeve. "Oh, come on, Annie. Just one turn! The floor's just right. You can keep an eye on the booth from the hall! Nobody's going to run away with the old thing anyhow!"

"Honest, I'd love to! But I got a great lot of dishes to wash, too! You know Momma!" She looked longingly toward the open-air dancing floor, out from which just then floated a burst of brassy music.

"Oh, *please!*" said a small voice. "I'll do it for twenty cents."

Betsy stood by the girl's elbow, quivering earnestness.

"Do what, kiddie?" asked the girl in good-natured surprise.

"Everything!" said Betsy, compendiously. "Everything! Wash the dishes, tend the booth; *you* can go dance! I'll do it for twenty cents."

The eyes of the girl and the man met. "My! Aren't we up and coming!" said the man. "You're 'most as big as a pint cup, aren't you?" he said to Betsy.

The little girl flushed—she detested being laughed at, but she looked straight into the laughing eyes. "I'm ten years old today," she said, "and I can wash dishes as well as anybody." She spoke with dignity.

The young man burst out into a great laugh.

"Great kid, what?" he said to the girl, and then, "Say, Annie, why not? Your mother won't be here for an hour. The kid can keep folks from walking off with the stuff and . . . "

"I'll do the dishes, too," repeated Betsy, trying hard not to mind being laughed at, and keeping her eyes fixed steadily on the tickets to Hillsboro.

"Well, by gosh," said the young man, laughing. "Here's our chance, Annie, for fair! Come along!"

---

*Sometimes after disciplined work, amazing personal fulfillment comes. At times the work itself keeps one alive in very trying circumstances. Here are three selections that illustrate these aspects of work and self-discipline. They prompt reflection on the rewards you get from effort and are occasions to consider the quality of your efforts and the pleasure they provide.*

### Mike Spino, *Running as a Spiritual Experience*

Weather is different every day; running has its shades of sunshine and rain. At Syracuse I ran daily in the worst weather imaginable. Because of the hard winter, my running mate and I had an agreement that we would never talk while running. Snow covered many of the roads, so out of convenience, with only slight variation, we ran the same course morning and afternoon. After classes we would return to our rooms and prepare to run. To watch us get ready, you would have thought us looney. First, there was long underwear, shorts and hood. Next socks for hands and feet and navy caps. The run back was always better because you could think of a warm shower, and know that the nervous feeling preceding the daily task of running would be gone.

Eastern winters linger into spring, but one day the sun shone in a different way. Snow still curbed the road, but the inside of the pavement, where the black-brown dirt met cement, looked almost bounceable. Earlier in the day the spirit of approaching spring made us—my unofficial coach, my running mate, and I—decide on a formidable venture. At a place beginning in the mountains and ending in a valley near the city, we had a six-mile stretch which was part of a longer, twenty-mile course. We decided to run the six miles as fast as possible. The plan was for Jack, our coach, to trail us with his car, and sound his horn as we passed each mile. Marty, my running mate, was to run the first three miles, jump in the car for the next two, and finish the last mile with me. We traveled to the starting point which was out of the sunshine into the late afternoon mist. Jack suggested a time schedule he thought we could run. I was sure I couldn't keep the pace; Marty said nothing, taking an "if you think you can do it I'll try, since I'm not running the whole way" attitude.

Almost even before we started, cars began to back up behind Jack's car, but he continued to drive directly behind us, and the cars soon tired of sounding horns and drove around all three of us. From my first step I felt lighter and looser than ever before. My thin shirt clung to me, and I felt like a skeleton flying down a wind tunnel. My times at the mile and two-mile were so fast that I almost felt I was cheating, or had taken some unfair advantage. It was like getting a new body that no one else had heard about. My mind was so crystal clear I could have held a conversation. The only sensation was the rhythm and the beat; all perfectly natural, all and everything part of everything else. Marty told me later that he could feel the power I was radiating. He said I was frightening.

Marty jumped back into the car. There were three miles to go; it was still pure pleasure. A car darted from a side street, I had to decide how to react, and do it, both at the same time. I decided to outrun the car to the end of the intersection. The car skidded and almost hit Jack's car, but somehow we got out of danger and had two miles to run. The end of the fourth and the start of the fifth mile was the beginning of crisis. My legs lost their bounce: I struggled to keep my arms low, so they wouldn't swing across my chest and cut off the free passage of air. My mind concentrated on only one thing: to keep the rhythm. If I could just flick my legs at the same cadence for a few more minutes I would run a fast time.

Slowly I realized I was getting loose again. I knew then I could run the last mile strongly. Perhaps, there is such a thing as second wind. Whatever, Marty jumped from the car when a mile remained, but after a few hundred yards he couldn't keep the pace, so he jumped back in.

In the last half-mile something happened which may have occurred only one or two times before or since. Furiously I ran; time lost all semblance of meaning. Distance, time, motion were all one. There were myself, the cement, a vague feeling of legs, and the coming dusk. I tore on. Jack had planned to sound the horn first when a quarter mile remained, and then again at the completion of the six miles. The first sound barely reached my consciousness. My running was a pouring feeling. The final horn sounded. I kept on running. I could have run and run. Perhaps I had experienced a physiological change, but whatever, it was magic. I came to the side of the road and gazed, with a sort of bewilderment, at my friends. I sat on the side of the road and cried tears of joy and sorrow. Joy at being alive; sorrow for a vague feeling of temporalness, and a knowledge of the impossibility of giving this experience to anyone.

We got back into the car and drove. Everyone knew something special, strange, and mystically wonderful had happened. At first no one spoke. Jack reminded us that the time I had run was phenomenal compared to my previous times. At first we thought Jack's odometer might be incorrect, so we drove to a local track and measured a quarter mile. It measured correctly. On the way home, I asked Jack if he would stop at a grass field, near our house. I wanted to savor the night air; I wanted to see if the feeling remained. It did, and it didn't. I have never understood what occurred that late afternoon: whether it was just a fine run, combined with dusk, as winter was finally breaking, or finding out who and what I was through a perfect expression of my own art form. It still remains a mystery.

**Nazim Hikmet, *Some Advice to Those Who Will Serve Time in Prison*, translated by Randy Blessing and Mutlu Konuk**
. . . To wait for letters inside,
to sing sad songs,
or to lie awake all night staring at the ceiling
is sweet but dangerous.

Look at your face from shave to shave,
forget your age,
watch out for lice
and for spring nights,
and always remember
to eat every last piece of bread—
also don't forget to laugh heartily.
And who knows,
the woman you love may stop loving you.
Don't say it's no big thing:
it's like the snapping of a green branch to the man inside.
To think of roses and gardens inside is bad,
to think of seas and mountains is good.
Read and write without rest,
and I also advise weaving
and making mirrors.
I mean, it's not that you can't pass
ten or fifteen years inside
and more—
you can,
as long as the jewel
on the left side of your chest doesn't
lost its luster!

## Beryl Markham, *West with the Night*

I have seldom dreamed a dream worth dreaming again, or at least none worth recording. Mine are not enigmatic dreams; they are peopled with characters who are plausible and who do plausible things, and I am the most plausible amongst them. All the characters in my dreams have quiet voices like the voice of the man who telephoned me at Elstree one morning in September of nineteen-thirty-six and told me that there was rain and strong head winds over the west of England and over the Irish sea, and that there were variable winds and clear skies in midAtlantic and fog off the coast of Newfoundland.

'If you are still determined to fly the Atlantic this late in the year,' the voice said, 'the Air Ministry suggests that the weather it is able to forecast for tonight, and for tomorrow morning, will be about the best you can expect.'

The voice had a few other things to say, but not many, and then it was gone, and I lay in bed half-suspecting that the telephone call and the man who made it were only parts of the mediocre dream I had been dreaming. I felt that if I closed my eyes the unreal quality of the message would be re-established, and that, when I opened them again, this would be another ordinary day with its usual beginning and its usual routine.

But of course I could not close my eyes, nor my mind, nor my memory. I could lie there for a few moments—remembering how it had begun, and telling myself, with senseless repetition, that by tomorrow morning I should either have flown the Atlantic to America—or I should not have flown it. In either case this was the day I would try.

I could stare up at the ceiling of my bedroom in Aldenham House, which was a ceiling undistinguished as ceilings go, and feel less resolute than anxious, much less brave than foolhardy. I could say to myself, 'You needn't do it, of course,' knowing at the same time that nothing is so inexorable as a promise to your pride.

I could ask, 'Why risk it?' as I have been asked since, and I could answer, 'Each to his element.' By his nature a sailor must sail, by his nature a flyer must fly. I could compute that I had flown a quarter of a million miles; and I could foresee that, so long as I had a plane and the sky was there, I should go on flying more miles.

There was nothing extraordinary in this. I had learned a craft and had worked hard learning it. My hands had been taught to seek the controls of a plane. Usage had taught them. They were at ease clinging to a stick, as a cobbler's fingers are in repose grasping an awl. No human pursuit achieves dignity until it can be called work, and when you can experience a physical loneliness for the tools of your trade, you see that the other things—the experiments, the irrelevant vocations, the vanities you used to hold—were false to you.

---

*Harriet Tubman was a remarkable woman, and in these recollections of her life by Mariline Wilkins, her great-grandniece, we see her through extraordinary self-discipline successfully taking advantage of other people's misjudgments about her physical limitations.*

### Mariline Wilkins, *Harriet Tubman Is in My Blood*

I am Mariline Wilkins, great-grandniece of Harriet Tubman. Most of the information that I have is information given to me by my mother when she would talk to people and answer questions about Harriet Tubman. My mother was raised by her, lived with her throughout her childhood and most of her young adult life. A lot of the things she told my mother were of her experiences during the Civil War, before the Civil War, and what went on prior to her wanting to free the slaves from bondage.

Harriet Tubman was the youngest of twelve children. She started out working when she was but five years old. She was small in stature. I always thought of her as big because of the things that she did; I just visualized her as being real tall and big, but this was not true. My mother was shorter than I am, and Harriet Tubman was about five feet one inch or five feet one and a half inches tall. She was small but she was strong physically.

Of course, you know that she did not read or write, but she had implicit confidence and trusted in God for everything that she did.

The family had been bought by the Brodess family, which was considered one of the wealthiest slaveowners on the Eastern Shore, and Harriet Tubman worked for them from the time she was five until she left to work for Mr. Cook, another slaveowner. Mr. Cook's wife was pregnant, and he wanted someone to come to his place to look after the baby when it was born and to help him with his muskrat trappings. So she was lent to Mr. Cook while still a child. Some of the stories say that she was sold to him, but she was not. She was lent to him, and Mr. Cook told Mr. Brodess that his wife would teach her how to weave cloth and this weaving would help clothe his family.

However, Harriet didn't like indoor work. She preferred to be outdoors. When the baby came, Harriet was so small that she would have to sit on the floor, and they would put the baby in her lap in order for her to take care of it. She also helped Mr. Cook with his muskrat trappings. While she was doing this, over two or three years, I think, she caught cold. When her mother heard about it, she asked Mr. Brodess to get her child and bring her back to her so she could nurse her back to health. She heard that she had been sick for a long time. This was because of this trapping through the swamp in the wintertime. Mr. Brodess did go and get her and, after she got better, she went back to the Cook house.

Eventually Harriet left the Cook household and returned to the Brodesses again, working in the fields. It was at that time, while working in the fields at the Brodesses, that a worker in the field left the field and one of the field supervisors followed him. Harriet decided, after the field supervisor had gone, to follow the worker in the field who had left; she would see what was going on. When she did, she went to the little store, and there the field supervisor was after the field hand who had gone away. When she appeared at the door, the field supervisor told her to stop him. She refused to stop him. When she refused to stop him, he picked up a tool, iron weights, threw it, and cut her. Some storybooks say she was hit in the back of the head, but the scar is on her forehead. She carried that until death, and she developed sleeping seizures.

They thought she was a nitwit after that. They said she wasn't capable of work and all that sort of thing, so she let them believe that because it was to her advantage. She continued to work wherever she was available, but she preferred working out of doors. And it was when she was working at the Cook house again that she heard them discussing, at one of the evening meals, that they were going to sell some of her family, her sisters and brothers, to another slaveowner farther south. She decided then that this business of slavery was terrible, and she didn't like it. She said, "Dear God, help me get rid of this terrible thing and these terrible people." She listened some more and heard some more information, and she decided that that was what she was going to do, try to free them. The first time she tried to go free or leave, she wanted her brothers to go with her, but they didn't want to go. They started out but got scared, so she decided not to continue because, if they didn't go, she was sure they would come back and tell what she was trying to do. For a long time, she told my mother, they thought that this person who was freeing the slaves was a man.

She did not dress like a man. When she started freeing the slaves, she would put on old clothes and act decrepit like an old woman. Because she was considered a nitwit, they never suspected her. They never suspected this little black woman and it was to her advantage. She had many little tricks, and they never suspected this person who had gotten hit in the head and had these sleeping seizures.

She could be sitting here talking to you just like I am, and all of a sudden one of those spells would come over her and she'd go to sleep. And when she woke up, she would start right where she left off. I don't think you could consider her a nitwit, not in any way, shape, or form. Several times she would get caught in one of those things, and people would say, "Oh, just wake her up, wake her up." You couldn't wake her up, Mama said. She just had to sleep it off. Once she was lying on a park bench with her face to the back of the park bench, and somebody put this poster up offering a reward for her, dead or alive. When the man finished, she woke up and saw the poster, and she just looked at it and went on. She knew who it was, she recognized her face.

She used to tell many stories of things that had happened to her and to other people. For example, there had been a man in Washington whose name was Eally, I think; she freed him. They were going to hang him up there in Albany. She heard about it and got the people in the community together, and she said, "When I give you the high sign, you holler 'Fire!'" They were having a meeting like a court, I guess, and she eased her way in like an old woman. By being small she was able to do a lot of this. That's why she wore dark clothes so she wouldn't be conspicuous. She went in and stuck her head out of the window, and the people she had alerted started hollering "Fire!" When they brought Eally down the stairs, she wrestled him away from the guards. She had somebody waiting with a boat. She rushed him through the crowd and into the boat and pushed him off, and they were still trying to get him, but he went on to Canada.

# Integrity

The actress Ethel Barrymore was reported to have said, when she was
seventy-six years old,

> You must learn day by day, year by year, to broaden your horizon. The
> more things you love, the more you are interested in, the more you
> enjoy, the more you are indignant about—the more you have left when
> anything happens.

It is not easy to simply and consistently be oneself. Integrity, the
thorough integration of decent values and actions, is an ideal that few
people achieve. As the preceding quotation indicates, there is never point
at which a person is completed or her or his values set in concrete.
Integrity is not a matter of dogmatic adherence to a rigid code of behavior so much as an ongoing challenge to remain consistent and caring. For
young people who are still articulating values for themselves, there is a
particular paradox in integrity. They are expected to be true to values
they have just begun to understand. For them, developing integrity is a
matter of discovery, a definition of their center, a testing of internal
strength.

A number of aspects of the complex route to integrity are illustrated
in this section. One central aspect of integrity is the articulation of the
central unifying values of your life. Metaphorically this can be understood as learning to be at home with yourself. But the metaphor is true
in another sense: Learning to be at home with yourself also has to do
with learning to come home and honor what you have been given, culturally and personally, in childhood. It also has to do with understanding
those forms of alienation that you have to face in a society in which stable communities are so rare.

This leads to two other central aspects of integrity: self-respect and
resistance to the betrayal of values. You have to have inner strength in
order to care for others and take risks for them. Integrity is rooted in the
comfort you feel within. The ability to maintain integrity under pressure

and to resist betraying others or giving in to negative values such as greed or jealousy is developed throughout life, and this is certainly an area where sharing stories with others can be a source of inner strength.

Among the rewards of living with integrity are a clear mind and a free conscience. This freedom is as rare as it is precious. Literature celebrates this gift of spirit which many young people hold precious despite all the social pressures for them to adjust to "the real world" and allow compromise and conformity to insinuate themselves into their lives.

---

*Perhaps the hardest thing in life is to be simple and consistent. This wonderful Shaker hymn celebrates simplicity and raises the question: What simple things can we say to ourselves and others about goodness and decency?*

### Shaker Hymn, *Simple Gifts*
'Tis the gift to be simple, 'tis the gift to be free,
'Tis the gift to come down where we ought to be,
And when we find ourselves in the place just right,
'Twill be in the valley of love and delight.
When true simplicity is gain'd,
To bow and to bend we shan't be asham'd,
To turn, turn will be our delight
'Till by turning, turning we come round right.

---

*Here are three selections about discontent and the effort it sometimes takes to like oneself. They beg conversation about who we are and why we sometimes feel unhappy about ourselves, about the journeys we all take to our own selves and therefore to the sources of our integrity.*

### Sandra Cisneros, *Eleven*
What they don't understand about birthdays and what they never tell you is that when you're eleven, you're also ten, and nine, and eight, and seven, and six, and five, and four, and three, and two, and one. And when you wake up on your eleventh birthday you expect to feel eleven, but you don't. You open your eyes and everything's just like yesterday, only it's

today. And you don't feel eleven at all. You feel like you're still ten. And you are—underneath the year that makes you eleven.

Like some days you might say something stupid, and that's the part of you that's still ten. Or maybe some days you might need to sit on your mama's lap because you're scared, and that's the part of you that's five. And maybe one day when you're all grown up maybe you will need to cry like if you're three, and that's okay. That's what I tell Mama when she's sad and needs to cry. Maybe she's feeling three.

Because the way you grow old is kind of like an onion or like the rings inside a tree trunk or like my little wooden dolls that fit one inside the other, each year inside the next one. That's how being eleven years old is.

You don't feel eleven. Not right away. It takes a few days, weeks even, sometimes even months before you say Eleven when they ask you. And you don't feel smart eleven, not until you're almost twelve. That's the way it is.

Only today I wish I didn't have only eleven years rattling inside me like pennies in a tin Band-Aid box. Today I wish I was one hundred and two instead of eleven because if I was one hundred and two I'd have known what to say when Mrs. Price put the red sweater on my desk. I would've known how to tell her it wasn't mine instead of just sitting there with that look on my face and nothing coming out of my mouth.

"Whose is this?" Mrs. Price says, and she holds the red sweater up in the air for all the class to see. "Whose? It's been sitting in the coatroom for a month."

"Not mine," says everybody. "Not me."

"It has to belong to somebody," Mrs. Price keeps saying, but nobody can remember. It's an ugly sweater with red plastic buttons and a collar and sleeves all stretched out like you could use it for a jump rope. It's maybe a thousand years old and even if it belonged to me I wouldn't say so.

Maybe because I'm skinny, maybe because she doesn't like me, that stupid Sylvia Saldivar says, "I think it belongs to Rachel." An ugly sweater like that, all raggedy and old, but Mrs. Price believes her. Mrs. Price takes the sweater and puts it right on my desk, but when I open my mouth nothing comes out.

"That's not, I don't, you're not . . . Not mine," I finally say in a little voice that was maybe me when I was four.

"Of course it's yours," Mrs. Price says. "I remember you wearing it once." Because she's older and the teacher, she's right and I'm not. Not mine, not mine, not mine, but Mrs. Price is already turning to page thirty-two, and math problem number four. I don't know why but all of a sudden I'm feeling sick inside, like the part of me that's three wants to come out of my eyes, only I squeeze them shut tight and bite down on my teeth real hard and try to remember today I am eleven, eleven. Mama is making a cake for me for tonight, and when Papa comes home everybody will sing Happy birthday, happy birthday to you.

But when the sick feeling goes away and I open my eyes, the red sweater's still sitting there like a big red mountain. I move the red sweater to the corner of my desk with my ruler. I move my pencil and books and eraser as far from it as possible. I even move my chair a little to the right. Not mine, not mine, not mine.

In my head I'm thinking how long till lunch time, how long till I can take the red sweater and throw it over the schoolyard fence, or leave it hanging on a parking meter, or bunch it up into a little ball and toss it in the alley. Except when math period ends Mrs. Price says loud and in front of everybody, "Now, Rachel, that's enough," because she sees I've shoved the red sweater to the tippy-tip corner of my desk and it's hanging all over the edge like a waterfall, but I don't care.

"Rachel," Mrs. Price says. She says it like she's getting mad. "You put that sweater on right now and no more nonsense."

"But it's not—"

"Now!" Mrs. Price says.

This is when I wish I wasn't eleven, because all the years inside of me—ten, nine, eight, seven, six, five, four, three, two, and one—are pushing at the back of my eyes when I put one arm through one sleeve of the sweater that smells like cottage cheese, and then the other arm through the other and stand there with my arms apart like if the sweater hurts me and it does, all itchy and full of germs that aren't even mine.

That's when everything I've been holding in since this morning, since when Mrs. Price put the sweater on my desk, finally lets go, and all of a sudden I'm crying in front of everybody. I wish I was invisible but I'm not. I'm eleven and it's my birthday today and I'm crying like I'm three in front of everybody. I put my head down on the desk and bury my face in my stupid clown-sweater arms. My face all hot and spit coming out of my mouth because I can't stop the little animal noises from coming out of me, until there aren't any more tears left in my eyes, and it's just my body shaking like when you have the hiccups, and my whole head hurts like when you drink milk too fast.

But the worst part is right before the bell rings for lunch. That stupid Phyllis Lopez, who is even dumber than Sylvia Saldivar, says she remembers the red sweater is hers! I take it off right away and give it to her, only Mrs. Price pretends like everything's okay.

Today I'm eleven. There's a cake Mama's making for tonight, and when Papa comes home from work we'll eat it. There'll be candles and presents and everybody will sing Happy birthday, happy birthday to you, Rachel, only it's too late.

I'm eleven today. I'm eleven, ten, nine, eight, seven, six, five, four, three, two, and one, but I wish I was one hundred and two. I wish I was anything but eleven, because I want today to be far away already, far away like a runaway balloon, like a tiny *o* in the sky, so tiny-tiny you have to close your eyes to see it.

### Mark Vecchoise, *The Head Man,* a fable

This guy was born, but he was just a head. So he went to a witchdoctor and he said, "I don't want to be just a head."

The witchdoctor put up his hands and went *puff* and turned him into a hand.

Then the guy ran around hollering, "I don't want to be a hand!"

Moral: "You should have quit while you were a head."

By Mark Vecchoise, eighth grade

### Gertrude Stein, *The World Is Round*

Once upon a time the world was round and you could go on it around and around.

Everywhere there was somewhere and everywhere there they were men women children dogs cows wild pigs little rabbits cats lizards and animals. That is the way it was. And everybody dogs cats sheep rabbits and lizards and children all wanted to tell everybody all about it and they wanted to tell all about themselves.

And then there was Rose.

Rose was her name and would she have been Rose if her name had not been Rose. She used to think and then she used to think again.

Would she have been Rose if her name had not been Rose and would she have been Rose if she had been a twin.

Rose was her name all the same and her father's name was Bob and her mother's name was Kate and her uncle's name was William and her aunt's name was Gloria and her grandmother's name was Lucy. They all had names and her name was Rose, but would she have been she used to cry about it would she have been Rose if her name had not been Rose.

I tell you at this time the world was all round and you could go on it around and around.

\*        \*        \*

Rose had two dogs a big white one called Love, and a little black one called Pepe, the little black one was not hers but she said it was, it belonged to a neighbor and it never did like Rose and there was a reason why, when Rose was young, she was nine now and nine is not young no Rose was not young, well anyway when she was young she one day had little Pepe and she told him to do something, Rose liked telling everybody what to do, at least she liked to do it when she was young, now she was almost ten so now she did not tell every one what they should do but then she did and she told Pepe, and Pepe did not want to, he did not know what she wanted him to do but even if he had he would not have wanted to, nobody does want to do what anybody tells them to do, so Pepe did not do it, and Rose shut him up in a room. Poor little Pepe he had been taught never to do in a room what should be done outside but he was so nervous being left all alone he just did, poor little Pepe. And then he was let out and there were a great many people about but little Pepe made no mistake he went straight among all the legs until he found those of Rose and then he went up and he bit her on the leg and then he ran away and nobody could blame him now could they. It was the only time he ever bit any one. And he never would say how do you do to Rose again and Rose always said Pepe was her dog although he was not, so that she could forget that he never wanted to say how do you do to her. If he was her dog that was alright he did not have to say how do you do but Rose knew and Pepe knew oh yes they both knew.

Rose and her big white dog Love were pleasant together they sang songs together, these were the songs they sang.

Love drank his water and as he drank, it just goes like that like a song a nice song and while he was doing that Rose sang her song. This was her song

I am a little girl and my name is Rose
Rose is my name.
Why am I a little girl
And why is my name Rose
And when am I a little girl
And when is my name Rose
And where am I a little girl
And where is my name Rose
And which little girl am I
Am I the little girl named Rose
Which little girl named Rose.

And as she sang this song and she sang it while Love did his drinking

Why am I a little girl
Where am I a little girl
When am I a little girl
Which little girl am I

And singing that made her so sad she began to cry.

And when she cried Love cried he lifted up his head and looked up at the sky and he began to cry and he and Rose and Rose and he cried and cried and cried until she stopped and at last her eyes were dried.

And all this time the world just continued to be round.

———※◇※———

*The discovery of one's deepest self is often accompanied by a discovery of one's roots and the unexpected inner strengths that one can draw upon from family and culture. This can take place under the harsh conditions of slavery or during a personal moment of revelation. It is such moments that give us a sense of our wholeness and establish a commitment to live with integrity. These four selections give us pause to reflect on our own commitments to culture, family, and most of all to leading a consistent, whole, and decent life.*

## Frederick Douglass, *Narrative of the Life of Frederick Douglass, an American Slave*

My new mistress proved to be all she appeared when I first met her at the door—a woman of the kindest heart and finest feelings. She had never had a slave under her control previously to myself, and prior to her marriage she had been dependent upon her own industry for a living. She was by trade a weaver; and by constant application to her business, she had been in a good degree preserved from the blighting and dehumanizing effects of slavery. I was utterly astonished at her goodness. I scarcely knew how to behave towards her. She was entirely unlike any other white woman I had ever seen. I could not approach her as I was accustomed to approach other white ladies. My early instruction was all out of place. The crouching servility, usually so acceptable a quality in a slave, did not answer when manifested toward her. Her favor was not gained by it; she seemed to be disturbed by it. She did not deem it impudent or unmannerly for a slave to look her in the face. The meanest slave was put fully at ease in her presence, and none left without feeling better for having seen her. Her face was made of heavenly smiles, and her voice of tranquil music.

But, alas! this kind heart had but a short time to remain such. The fatal poison of irresponsible power was already in her hands, and soon commenced its infernal work. That cheerful eye, under the influence of slavery, soon became red with rage; that voice, made all of sweet accord, changed to one of harsh and horrid discord; and that angelic face gave place to that of a demon.

Very soon after I went to live with Mr. and Mrs. Auld, she very kindly commenced to teach me the A, B, C. After I had learned this, she assisted me in learning to spell words of three or four letters. Just at this point of my progress, Mr. Auld found out what was going on, and at once forbade Mrs. Auld to instruct me further, telling her, among other things, that it was unlawful, as well as unsafe, to teach a slave to read. To use his own words, further, he said, "If you give a nigger an inch, he will take an ell. A nigger should know nothing but to obey his master—to do as he is told to do. Learning would *spoil* the best nigger in the world. Now," said he, "if you teach that nigger (speaking of myself) how to read, there would be no keeping him. It would forever unfit him to be a slave. He would at once become unmanageable, and of no value to his master. As to himself, it could do him no good, but a great deal of harm. It would make him discontented and unhappy." These words sank deep into my heart, stirred up sentiments within that lay slumbering, and called into existence an entirely new train of thought. It was a new and special revelation, explaining dark and mysterious things, with which my youthful understanding had struggled, but struggled in vain. I now understood what had been to me a most perplexing difficulty—to wit, the white man's power to enslave the black man. It was a grand achievement, and I prized it highly. From that moment, I understood the pathway from slavery to freedom. It was just what I wanted, and I got it at a time when I the least expected it. Whilst I was saddened by the thought of losing the aid of my kind mistress, I was gladdened by the invaluable instruction which, by the merest accident, I had gained from my master. Though conscious of the difficulty of learning without a teacher, I set out with high hope, and a fixed purpose, at whatever cost of trouble, to learn how to read. The very decided manner with which he spoke, and strove to impress his wife with the evil consequences of giving me instruction, served to convince me that he was deeply sensible of the truths he was uttering. It gave me the best assurance that I might rely with the utmost confidence on the results which, he said, would flow from teaching me to read. What he most dreaded, that I most desired. What he most loved, that I most hated. That which to him was a great evil, to be carefully shunned, was to me a great good, to be diligently sought; and the argument which he so warmly urged, against my learning to read, only served to inspire me with a desire and determination to learn. In learning to read, I owe almost as much to the bitter opposition of my master, as to the kindly aid of my mistress. I acknowledge the benefit of both.

**Yehuda Amichai, *Half the People in the World*,**
**translated by Stephen Mitchell**

Half the people in the world
love the other half,
half the people
hate the other half.
Must I because of this half and that half
go wandering and changing ceaselessly
like rain in its cycle,
must I sleep among rocks,
and grow rugged like the trunks of olive trees,
and hear the moon barking at me,
and camouflage my love with worries,
and sprout like frightened grass between the railroad tracks,
and live underground like a mole,
and remain with roots and not with branches,
and not feel my cheek against the cheek of angels,
and love in the first cave,
and marry my wife beneath a canopy
of beams that support the earth,
and act out my death, always
till the last breath and the last
words and without ever understanding,
and put flagpoles on top of my house
and a bomb shelter underneath. And go out on roads
made only for returning and go through
all the appalling stations—
cat, stick, fire, water, butcher,
between the kid and the angel of death?
Half the people love,
half the people hate.
And where is my place between such well-matched halves,
and through what crack will I see

the white housing projects of my dreams
and the barefoot runners on the sands
or, at least, the waving
of a girl's kerchief, beside the mound?

**Martín Espada, *Tony Went to the Bodega but He Didn't Buy Anything***
*Para Angel Guadalupe*
Tony's father left the family
and the Long Island city projects,
leaving a mongrel-skinny puertorriqueño boy
nine years old
who had to find work.

Makengo the Cuban
let him work at the bodega.
In grocery aisles
he learned the steps of the dry-mop mambo,
banging the cash register
like piano percussion
in the spotlight of Machito's orchestra,
polite with the abuelas who bought on credit,
practicing the grin on customers
he'd seen Makengo grin
with his bad yellow teeth.

Tony left the projects too,
with a scholarship for law school.
But he cursed the cold primavera
in Boston;
the cooking of his neighbors
left no smell in the hallway,
and no one spoke Spanish
(not even the radio).

So Tony walked without a map
through the city,
a landscape of hostile condominiums
and the darkness of white faces,
sidewalk-searcher lost
till he discovered the projects.

Tony went to the bodega
but he didn't buy anything:
he sat by the doorway satisfied
to watch la gente (people
island-brown as him)
crowd in and out,
hablando español,
thought: this is beautiful,
and grinned
his bodega grin.

This is a rice and beans
success story:
today Tony lives on Tremont Street,
above the bodega.


**Louise Erdrich, *Indian Boarding School: The Runaways***
Home's the place we head for in our sleep.
Boxcars stumbling north in dreams
don't wait for us. We catch them on the run.
The rails, old lacerations that we love,
shoot parallel across the face and break
just under Turtle Mountains. Riding scars
you can't get lost. Home is the place they cross.

The lame guard strikes a match and makes the dark
less tolerant. We watch through cracks in boards
as the land starts rolling, rolling till it hurts
to be here, cold in regulation clothes.
We know the sheriff's waiting at midrun
to take us back. His car is dumb and warm.
The highway doesn't rock, it only hums
like a wing of long insults. The worn-down welts
of ancient punishments lead back and forth.

All runaways wear dresses, long green ones,
the color you would think shame was. We scrub
the sidewalks down because it's shameful work.
Our brushes cut the stone in watered arcs
and in the soak frail outlines shiver clear

a moment, things us kids pressed on the dark
face before it hardened, pale, remembering
delicate old injuries, the spines of names and leaves.

<hr />

*Integrity can be tested in many ways. Sometimes the test will be dramatic, as under conditions of war, during the Civil Rights Movement, or in other circumstances where life and death are at stake. Other times the tests of one's integrity come over small issues, like stealing or telling on friends. This selections raises questions relating to how integrity stands up under pressure: What worth is integrity when I can gain from giving in? What strengths do I have to draw upon when pressure is exerted on me? And finally, how do I learn how my integrity or lack of it affects the lives of others?*

## Ossie Davis, *Just Like Martin*

"I'm sorry, Daddy. I know I should have told you. But—but—"

"But you were scared, right? Right?"

I had to think a moment. I hadn't thought about it before, but honestly, I had to tell him yes.

He looked up the road awhile before he spoke. "My son, my own flesh and blood, not scared of the sheriff and his deputies with their billy clubs; of the police with their dogs and water hoses; marching in the streets with people screaming and cussing and throwing things—not scared of that, but scared to death of his own father. I wonder what Lucy would say to me about that." He sighed hard, and looked up the road again.

"This children's march thing is like a red flag to a bull. And you right there in the middle of it. That's hard, mighty hard, for me to swallow. I said to myself that I was going to tell you no. But I couldn't. I asked myself, over and over again: What would Lucy do if she was here? That wasn't the answer either. So you and me, we got to settle this whole nonviolent thing—man to man—once and for all. And we got to settle it now."

What did he mean by that? I had taken a vow to be nonviolent just like Dr. King. What would I do if Daddy ordered me to change my mind?

"You ain't but almost fourteen, but that don't mean you still a baby. You old enough to have your own way of doing things, even if it is nonviolent—which certainly ain't my way. I think it's wrong; I think it's weak; I think it's for cowards and sissies. It's already got them two girls killed. I mean, if I was to say to you right now, I admire what you all are trying to do, but you stay home, not get mixed up in it. Would you do it?"

"I wouldn't want to disobey you, Daddy."

"Dammit, son. This ain't baby talk. If I asked you, man to man, not to get mixed up in this children's march, what would you say? What would you do?"

"Man to man?"

"Yeah, man to man."

"I'd tell you how sorry I was, and then I think . . . I'd go. I think I'd have to."

"Even though you might get hurt or even killed, you'd still have to go?"

"Yes, sir." That was all I could say.

"Well, like I said . . . a man has got to do what he's got to do."

My daddy was calling me a man. I couldn't believe it!

"You got your way, and I got mine. You children will be putting yourselves in harm's way, and since I can't stop you, I'll have to go with you."

"What's that, sir?"

"I said, I'll have to go with you."

---

*Sometimes acting with integrity is very painful, as these two selections, one from* King Lear *and one from a young woman in Britain, illustrate. Acting with integrity can demand all of one's strength and yet preserve one's wholeness and dignity.*

## William Shakespeare, *King Lear*

LEAR:          Meantime we shall express our darker purpose.
               Give me the map there. Know that we have divided
               In three our kingdom; and 'tis our fast intent
               To shake all cares and business from our age,
               Conferring them on younger strengths while we
               Unburdened crawl toward death. Our son of Cornwall,
               And you, our no less loving son of Albany,
               We have this hour a constant will to publish
               Our daughters' several dowers, that future strife
               May be prevented now. The princes, France and Burgundy,
               Great rivals in our youngest daughter's love,
               Long in our court have made their amorous sojourn

And here are to be answered. Tell me, my daughters—
Since now we will divest us both of rule,
Interest of territory, cares of state—
Which of you shall we say doth love us most,
That we our largest bounty may extend
Where nature doth with merit challenge. Goneril,
Our eldest born, speak first.

GONERIL: Sir, I love you more than words can wield the matter,
Dearer than eyesight, space, and liberty,
Beyond what can be valued, rich or rare,
No less than life, with grace, health, beauty, honor;
As much as child e'er loved, or father found;
A love that makes breath poor and speech unable.
Beyond all manner of so much I love you.

CORDELIA [Aside]: What shall Cordelia speak? Love and be silent.

LEAR: Of all these bounds, even from this line to this,
With shadowy forests and with champains riched,
With plenteous rivers and wide-skirted meads,
We make thee lady. To thine and Albany's issue
Be this perpetual.—What says our second daughter,
Our dearest Regan, wife to Cornwall? Speak.

REGAN: I am made of that self metal as my sister,
And prize me at her worth. In my true heart
I find she names my very deed of love;
Only she comes too short, that I profess
Myself an enemy to all other joys
Which the most precious square of sense possesses,
And find I am alone felicitate
In your dear Highness' love.

CORDELIA [Aside]: Then poor Cordelia!
And yet not so, since I am sure my love's
More ponderous than my tongue.

LEAR: To thee and thine hereditary ever
Remain this ample third of our fair kingdom
No less in space, validity, and pleasure
Than that conferred on Goneril.—Now, our joy,
Although our last and least, to whose young love
The vines of France and milk of Burgundy
Strive to be interessed, what can you say to draw
A third more opulent than your sisters? Speak.

CORDELIA: Nothing, my lord.

| | |
|---|---|
| LEAR: | Nothing? |
| CORDELIA: | Nothing. |
| LEAR: | Nothing will come of nothing. Speak again. |
| CORDELIA: | Unhappy that I am, I cannot heave<br>My heart into my mouth. I love Your Majesty<br>According to my bond, no more nor less. |
| LEAR: | How, how, Cordelia? Mend your speech a little,<br>Lest you may mar your fortunes. |
| CORDELIA: | Good my lord,<br>You have begot me, bred me, loved me. I<br>Return those duties back as are right fit,<br>Obey you, love you, and most honor you.<br>Why have my sisters husbands if they say<br>They loved you all? Haply, when I shall wed,<br>That lord whose hand must take my plight shall carry<br>Half my love with him, half my care and duty.<br>Sure I shall never marry like my sisters,<br>To love my father all. |
| LEAR: | But goes thy heart with this? |
| CORDELIA: | Ay, my good lord. |
| LEAR: | So young, and so untender? |
| CORDELIA: | So young, my lord, and true. |
| LEAR: | Let it be so! Thy truth then be thy dower!<br>For, by the sacred radiance of the sun,<br>The mysteries of Hecate and the night,<br>By all the operation of the orbs<br>From whom we do exist and cease to be,<br>Here I disclaim all my paternal care,<br>Propinquity and property of blood,<br>And as a stranger to my heart and me<br>Hold thee from this forever. The barbarous Scythian,<br>Or he that makes his generation messes<br>To gorge his appetite, shall to my bosom<br>Be as well neighbored, pitied, and relieved<br>As thou my sometime daughter. |
| KENT: | Good my liege— |
| LEAR: | Peace, Kent!<br>Come not between the dragon and his wrath.<br>I loved her most, and thought to set my rest<br>On her kind nursery. [*To Cordelia*] Hence, and avoid my<br>    sight!— |

So be my grave my peace, as here I give
Her father's heart from her!


**Liza Rymer,** *Mam's Gone*
Age Nine
walking home from school,
nothing's altered
nothing new.
In the house
big sister crying,
arms outstretched
and reaching, reaching.
Mam's gone, she said,
go get your things
a clean nightie
and anything else
you want to bring.
Age Nine,
and life goes on the same
for friends
and others
too numerous to name
We caught the bus
I had no choice.
The whims of adults,
I had no voice.
Fait accompli
that's what it was.
No time to feel
a sense of loss
Or think of Dad
after a hard day's work
in the empty house
where shadows lurk.
Age Nine
strange bed
laying down to sleep,
thinking
don't make promises
you can't keep.

---

*Here is an example of lack of integrity or integrity unraveled through subtle social pressure. It gives rise to the questions: How do society and in particular the media and the pressure to buy things affect our integrity? What is to prevent us from turning into the kind of person we don't respect?*

## Luisa Valenzuela, *The Censors*, translated by David Unger

Poor Juan! One day they caught him with his guard down before he could even realize that what he had taken as a stroke of luck was really one of fate's dirty tricks. These things happen the minute you're careless and you let down your guard, as one often does. Juancito let happiness— a feeling you can't trust—get the better of him when he received from a confidential source Mariana's new address in Paris and he knew that she hadn't forgotten him. Without thinking twice, he sat down at his table and wrote her a letter. *The* letter that keeps his mind off his job during the day and won't let him sleep at night (what had he scrawled, what had he put on that sheet of paper he sent to Mariana?).

Juan knows there won't be a problem with the letter's contents, that it's irreproachable, harmless. But what about the rest? He knows that they examine, sniff, feel, and read between the lines of each and every letter, and check its tiniest comma and most accidental stain. He knows that all letters pass from hand to hand and go through all sorts of tests in the huge censorship offices and that, in the end, very few continue on their way. Usually it takes months, even years, if there aren't any snags; all this time the freedom, maybe even the life, of both sender and receiver is in jeopardy. And that's why Juan's so down in the dumps: thinking that something might happen to Mariana because of his letters. Of all people, Mariana, who must finally feel safe there where she always dreamed she'd live. But he knows that the *Censor's Secret Command* operates all over the world and cashes in on the discount in air rates; there's nothing to stop them from going as far as that hidden Paris neighborhood, kidnapping Mariana, and returning to their cozy homes, certain of having fulfilled their noble mission. Well, you've got to beat them to the punch, do what everyone tries to do: sabotage the machinery, throw sand in its gears, get to the bottom of the problem so as to stop it.

This was Juan's sound plan when he, like many others, applied for a censor's job—not because he had a calling or needed a job: no, he applied simply to intercept his own letter, a consoling but unoriginal idea. He was hired immediately, for each day more and more censors are needed and no one would bother to check on his references.

Ulterior motives couldn't be overlooked by the *Censorship Division,* but they needn't be too strict with those who applied. They knew how hard it would be for those poor guys to find the letter they wanted and even if they did, what's a letter or two when the new censor would snap up so many others? That's how Juan managed to join the *Post Office's Censorship Division,* with a certain goal in mind.

The building had a festive air on the outside which contrasted with its inner staidness. Little by little, Juan was absorbed by his job and he felt at peace since he was doing everything he could to get his letter for Mariana. He didn't even worry when, in his first month, he was sent to *Section K* where envelopes are very carefully screened for explosives.

It's true that on the third day, a fellow worker had his right hand blown off by a letter, but the division chief claimed it was sheer negligence on the victim's part. Juan and the other employees were allowed to go back to their work, albeit feeling less secure. After work, one of them tried to organize a strike to demand higher wages for unhealthy work, but Juan didn't join in; after thinking it over, he reported him to his superiors and thus got promoted.

You don't form a habit by doing something once, he told himself as he left his boss's office. And when he was transferred to *Section J,* where letters are carefully checked for poison dust, he felt he had climbed a rung in the ladder.

By working hard, he quickly reached *Section E* where the work was more interesting, for he could now read and analyze the letters' contents. Here he could even hope to get hold of his letter which, judging by the time that had elapsed, had gone through the other sections and was probably floating around in this one.

Soon his work became so absorbing that his noble mission blurred in his mind. Day after day he crossed out whole paragraphs in red ink, pitilessly chucking many letters into the censored basket. These were horrible days when he was shocked by the subtle and conniving ways employed by people to pass on subversive messages; his instincts were so sharp that he found behind a simple 'the weather's unsettled' or 'prices continue to soar' the wavering hand of someone secretly scheming to overthrow the Government.

His zeal brought him swift promotion. We don't know if this made him happy. Very few letters reached him in *Section B*—only a handful passed the other hurdles—so he read them over and over again, passed them under a magnifying glass, searched for microprint with an electronic microscope, and tuned his sense of smell so that he was beat by the time he made it home. He'd barely managed to warm up his soup, eat some fruit, and fall into bed, satisfied with having done his duty. Only his darling mother worried, but she couldn't get him back on the right road. She'd say, though it wasn't always true: Lola called, she's at the bar with the girls, they miss you, they're waiting for you. Or else she'd leave a bottle of red wine on the table. But Juan wouldn't overdo it: any distraction could make him lose his edge and the perfect censor had to be alert, keen, attentive, and sharp to nab cheats. He had a truly patriotic task, both self-denying and uplifting.

His basket for censored letters became the best fed as well as the most cunning basket in the whole *Censorship Division*. He was about to congratulate himself for having finally discovered his true mission, when his letter to Mariana reached his hands. Naturally, he censored it without regret. And just as naturally, he couldn't stop them from executing him the following morning, another victim of his devotion to his work.

———•◦•———

*A person who acts on the basis of conscience is guided by a strong sense of what is morally right and will speak out for justice even if doing so threatens her or his life. Integrity is bound up with conscience; for instance, when a person refuses to act on the basis of conscience, her or his integrity is compromised. This poem about the republic of conscience suggests the following questions: If you believe something is morally wrong, do you have to act to correct it? What moral risks are worth taking? What are the rewards of acting with a good conscience and the problems caused by betraying your conscience?*

## Seamus Heaney, *The Republic of Conscience*

### I

When I landed in the republic of conscience
it was so noiseless when the engines stopped
I could hear a curlew high above the runway.

At immigration, the clerk was an old man
who produced a wallet from his homespun coat
and showed me a photograph of his grandfather.

The woman in customs asked me to declare
the words of our traditional cures and charms
to cure dumbness and heal the evil eye.

No porters. No interpreters. No taxi.
You carried your own burden and very soon
your symptoms of creeping privilege disappeared.

## II

Fog is a dreaded omen there but lightning
spells universal good and parents hang
swaddled infants in trees during thunderstorms.

Salt is their precious mineral. And seashells
are held to the ear during births and funerals.
The base of all inks and pigments is seawater.

The sacred symbol is a stylized boat.
The sail is an ear, the mast a sloping pen,
The hull a mouth-shape, the keel an open eye.

At their inauguration, public leaders
must swear to uphold unwritten law and weep
to atone for their presumption to hold office—

and to affirm their faith that all life sprang
from salt in tears which the sky-god wept
after he dreamt his solitude was endless.

## III

I came back from that frugal republic
with my two arms the one length, the customs woman
having insisted my allowance was myself.

The old man rose and gazed into my face
and said that was official recognition
that I was now a dual citizen.

He therefore desired me when I got home
to consider myself a representative
and to speak on their behalf in my own tongue

Their embassies, he said, were everywhere
but operated independently
and no ambassador would ever be relieved.

# Creativity

In *The Art of Writing* the Chinese sage Wen-Fu said:

> The pleasure a writer knows is the pleasure all sages enjoy. Out of non-being, being is born; out of silence, the writer produces a song.
>
> In a single yard of silk, infinite space is found; language is a deluge from one small corner of the heart.
>
> The net of images is cast wider and wider; thought searches more and more deeply.
>
> The writer spreads the fragrance of new flowers, an abundance of sprouting buds.
>
> Laughing winds lift up the metaphor; clouds rise from a forest of writing brushes.

The ability to be creative, to raise new questions and develop new ideas and solutions, to make something out of nothing, is a gift humans have. At the core of this gift is the imagination, the capacity to think and dream of things that never were or will be. The imagination is a problem-posing as well as a problem-solving tool, which can be developed or stifled in childhood. As character develops, the imagination can be a companion to other values and help in moral as well as artistic creation. Though it can be distorted and serve destructive purposes, it is a central guide to decent action. The moral imagination is what keeps hope alive and makes it possible for people to find ways to solve even the most painful and delicate moral dilemmas.

Creative use of the imagination develops when young people are not afraid to experiment and make mistakes. The arts and sciences depend upon the free exercise of the imagination for their development. There is a lot for everyone to learn about creative living from how the imagination functions in these areas. Creativity, however, need not be restricted to the arts. Creativity applied to everyday life, to the budgeting of our time and talents and the ways in which friendship and love are nurtured, is a source of positive energy much needed in difficult times.

The selections in this part of the book examine various aspects of the creative imagination and creative lives. We hope they will lead beyond themselves to family discussions of creativity and to projects and programs that involved development of the imagination. The poet Marianne Moore, in this short poem, illustrates the reach of the imagination, and the pleasures imagining can bring:

> If I, like Solomon,
> could have my wish—
> my wish . . . O to be a dragon
> a symbol of the power of Heaven, of silkworm
> size or immense; at times invisible.
> Felicitous phenomenon!
> —"O, To Be a Dragon"

---

*Sometimes profound truths can be found in a simple line of verse or in the expression on a face in a painting or a photograph. Music can lead to a revelation of character or inspire hope. Denise Levertov, in this poem, speaks of the importance of creative insight and of its elusive nature. After reading the poem, think of lines, stories, performances, or melodies that have had major effects on the way you think, feel, or live. Share them with your family.*

**Denise Levertov, *The Secret***
Two girls discover
the secret of life
in a sudden line of
poetry.

I who don't know the
secret wrote
the line. They
told me

(through a third person)
they had found it

but not what it was
not even

what line it was. No doubt
by now, more than a week
later, they have forgotten
the secret,

the line, the name of
the poem. I love them
for finding what
I can't find,

and for loving me
for the line I wrote,
and for forgetting it
so that

a thousand times, till death
finds them, they may
discover it again, in other
lines

in other
happenings. And for
wanting to know it,
for

assuming there is
such a secret, yes,
for that
most of all.

———><•><———

*Questioning is central to the development of creativity. The way you ask and answer questions determines the kinds of solutions you develop to problems. When questions are closed, require only a yes or no, have only one right answer, they can shut down creativity. But when they are raised in what Lewis Carroll called the spirit of "puzzlement," that is, of a genuine desire to learn, they open up the mind and often lead to powerful solutions. In the following selection the physicist Richard Feynman describes how he learned to question from his father. The second selection is a delightful dialogue created by Gregory Bateson, between a father and daughter, on knowledge and questioning. The third selection, from Frances Hodgson Burnett's* The Lost Prince, *shows how creativity can be called upon under duress.*

*When reading these selections, reflect on the kinds of questions and answers used in your family and the kinds of inquiry young people are encouraged to make.*

### Richard P. Feynman, *Fathers*

My father taught me to notice things. One day, I was playing with an "express wagon," a little wagon with a railing around it. It had a ball in it, and when I pulled the wagon, I noticed something about the way the ball moved. I went to my father and said, "Say, Pop, I noticed something. When I pull the wagon, the ball rolls to the back of the wagon. And when I'm pulling it along and I suddenly stop, the ball rolls to the front of the wagon. Why is that?"

"That nobody knows," he said. "The general principle is that things which are moving tend to keep on moving, and things which are standing still tend to stand still, unless you push them hard. This tendency is called 'inertia,' but nobody knows why it's true." Now, that's a deep understanding. He didn't just give me the name.

He went on to say, "If you look from the side, you'll see that it's the back of the wagon that you're pulling against the ball, and the ball stands still. As a matter of fact, from the friction it starts to move forward a little bit in relation to the ground. It doesn't move back."

I ran back to the little wagon and set the ball up again and pulled the wagon. Looking sideways, I saw that indeed he was right. Relative to the sidewalk, it moved forward a little bit.

That's the way I was educated by my father, with those kinds of examples and discussions: no pressure—just lovely, interesting discussions. It has motivated me for the rest of my life, and makes me interested in *all* the sciences. (It just happens I do like physics better.)

### Gregory Bateson, *Metalogue: How Much Do You Know?*

DAUGHTER:    Daddy, how much do you know?
FATHER:      Me? Hmm—I have about a pound of knowledge.
D:           Don't be silly. Is it a pound sterling or a pound weight?
             I mean *really* how much do you know?

F:    Well, my brain weighs about two pounds and I suppose I use about a quarter of it—or use it at about a quarter efficiency. So let's say half a pound.

D:    But do you know more than Johnny's daddy? Do you know more than I do?

F:    Hmm—I once knew a little boy in England who asked his father, "Do fathers always know more than sons?" and the father said, "Yes." The next question was, "Daddy, who invented the steam engine?" and the father said, "James Watt." And then the son came back with "—but why didn't James Watt's father invent it?"

D:    I know. I know more than that boy because I know why James Watt's father didn't. It was because somebody else had to think of something else before *anybody* could make a steam engine. I mean something like—I don't know—but there was somebody else who had to discover oil before anybody could make an engine.

F:    Yes—that makes a difference. I mean, it means that knowledge is all sort of knitted together, or woven, like cloth, and each piece of knowledge is only meaningful or useful because of the other pieces—and . . .

D:    Do you think we ought to measure it by the yard?

F:    No. I don't.

D:    But that's how we buy cloth.

F:    Yes. But I didn't mean that it *is* cloth. Only it's like it—and certainly would not be flat like cloth—but in three dimensions—perhaps four dimensions.

D:    What do you mean, Daddy?

F:    I really don't know, my dear. I was just trying to think.

F:    I don't think we are doing very well this morning. Suppose we start out on another tack. What we have to think about is how the pieces of knowledge are woven together. How they help each other.

D:    How do they?

F:    Well—it's as if sometimes two facts get added together and all you have is just two facts. But sometimes instead of just adding they multiply—and you get *four* facts.

D:    You cannot multiply one by one and get four. You know you can't.

F:    Oh.

*       *       *

F: But yes I can, too. If the things to be multiplied are pieces of knowledge or facts or something like that. Because every one of them is a double something.

D: I don't understand.

F: Well—at least a double something.

D: Daddy!

F: Yes—take the game of Twenty Questions. You think of something. Say you think of "tomorrow." All right. Now I ask "Is it abstract?" and you say "Yes." Now from your "yes" I have got a double bit of information. I know that it *is* abstract and I know that it isn't concrete. Or say it this way—from your "yes" I can *halve* the number of possibilities of what the thing can be. And that's a multiplying by one over two.

D: Isn't it a division?

F: Yes—it's the same thing. I mean—all right—it's a multiplication by .5. The important thing is that it's not just a subtraction or an addition.

D: How do you *know* it isn't?

F: How do I know it?—Well, suppose I ask another question which will halve the possibilities among the abstractions. And then another. That will have brought down the total possibilities to an eighth of what they were at the beginning. And two times two times two is eight.

D: And two and two and two is only six.

F: That's right.

D: But, Daddy, I don't see—what happens with Twenty Questions?

F: The point is that if I pick my questions properly I can decide between two times two times two times two twenty times over things—[20] things. That's over a million things that you might have thought of. One question is enough to decide between two things; and two questions will decide between four things—and so on.

D: I don't like arithmetic, Daddy.

F: Yes, I know. The working it out is dull, but some of the ideas in it are amusing. Anyhow, you wanted to know how to measure knowledge, and if you start measuring things that always leads to arithmetic.

D: We haven't measured any knowledge yet.

F:    No. I know. But we have made a step or two toward knowing how we would measure it if we wanted to. And that
means we are a little nearer to knowing what knowledge is.

D:    That would be a funny sort of knowledge, Daddy. I mean
knowing *about* knowledge—would we measure that sort of
knowing the same way?

F:    Wait a minute—I don't know—that's really the $64
Question on this subject. Because—well, let's go back to the
game of Twenty Questions. The point that we never mentioned is that those questions have to be in a certain order.
First the wide general question and then the detailed question. And it's only from answers to the wide questions that I
know which detailed questions to ask. But we counted
them all alike. I don't know. But now you ask me if knowing about knowledge would be measured the same way as
other knowledge. And the answer must surely be no. You
see, if the early questions in the game tell me what questions to ask later, then they must be partly questions about
knowing. They're exploring the business of knowing.

D:    Daddy—has anybody ever measured how much anybody
knew.

F:    Oh yes. Often. But I don't quite know what the answers
meant. They do it with examinations and tests and quizzes,
but it's like trying to find out how big a piece of paper is by
throwing stones at it.

D:    How do you mean?

F:    I mean—if you throw stones at two pieces of paper from
the same distance and you find that you hit one piece more
often than the other, then probably the one that you hit
most will be bigger than the other. In the same way, in an
examination you throw a lot of questions at the students,
and if you find that you hit more pieces of knowledge in
one student than in the others, then you think that student
must know more. That's the idea.

D:    But could one measure a piece of paper that way?

F:    Surely one could. It might even be quite a good way of doing
it. We do measure a lot of things that way. For example, we
judge how strong a cup of coffee is by looking to see how
black it is—that is, we look to see how much light is stopped.
We throw light waves at it instead of stones, it's the same idea.

D:    Oh.

\*    \*    \*

D:  But then—why shouldn't we measure knowledge that way?

F:  How? By quizzes? No—God forbid. The trouble is that sort of measuring leaves out your point—that there are different sorts of knowledge—and that there's knowing about knowledge. And ought one to give higher marks to the student who can answer the widest question? Or perhaps there should be a different *sort* of marks for each different sort of question.

D:  Well, all right. Let's do that and then add the marks together and then . . .

F:  No, we couldn't add them together. We might multiply or divide one sort of marks by another sort but we couldn't add them.

D:  Why not, Daddy?

F:  Because—because we couldn't. No wonder you don't like arithmetic if they don't tell you that sort of thing at school. What do they tell you? Golly—I wonder what the teachers think arithmetic is about.

D:  What is it about, Daddy?

F:  No. Let's stick to the question of how to measure knowledge—Arithmetic is a set of tricks for thinking clearly and the only fun in it is just its clarity. And the first thing about being clear is not to mix up ideas which are really different from each other. The idea of two oranges is really different from the idea of two miles. Because if you add them together you only get fog in your head.

D:  But, Daddy, I can't keep ideas separate. Ought I to do that?

F:  No—No—Of course not. Combine them. But don't add them. That's all. I mean—if the ideas are numbers and you want to combine two different sorts, the thing to do is to multiply them by each other. Or divide them by each other. And then you'll get some new sort of idea, a new sort of quantity. If you have miles in your head, and you have hours in your head, and you divide the miles by the hours, you get "miles per hour"—that's a speed.

D:  Yes, Daddy. What would I get if I multiplied them?

F:  Oh—er—I suppose you'd get mile-hours. Yes. I know what they are. I mean, what a mile-hour is. It's what you pay a taxi driver. His meter measures miles and he has a clock which measures hours, and the meter and the clock work together and multiply the hours by the miles and then it multiplies the mile-hours by something else which makes mile-hours into dollars.

D: I did an experiment once.

F: Yes?

D: I wanted to find out if I could think two thoughts at the same time. So I thought "It's summer." and I thought "It's winter." And then I tried to think the two thoughts together.

F: Yes?

D: But I found I wasn't having two thoughts. I was only having one thought *about* having two thoughts.

F: Sure, that's just it. You can't mix thoughts, you can only combine them. And in the end, that means you can't count them. Because counting is really only adding things together. And you mostly can't do that.

D: Then *really* do we only have one big thought which has lots of branches—lots and lots and lots of branches?

F: Yes. I think so. I don't know. Anyhow I think that is a clearer way of saying it. I mean it's clearer than talking about bits of knowledge and trying to count them.

D: Daddy, why don't you use the other three-quarters of your brain?

F: Oh, yes—that—you see the trouble is that I had school-teachers too. And they filled up about a quarter of my brain with fog. And then I read newspapers and I listened to what other people said, and that filled up another quarter with fog.

D: And the other quarter, Daddy?

F: Oh—that's fog that I made for myself when I was trying to think.

## Frances Hodgson Burnett, *The Lost Prince*

One of the most fascinating things he and his father talked about together was the power of the thoughts which human beings allowed to pass through their minds—the strange strength of them. When they talked of this, Marco felt as if he were listening to some marvelous Eastern story of magic which was true. In Loristan's travels, he had visited the far Oriental countries, and he had seen and learned many things which seemed marvels. He had known, and reasoned through days with men who believed that when they desired a thing, clear and exalted thought would bring it to them.

What he himself believed, he had taught Marco quite simply from his childhood. It was this: he himself Marco, with the strong boy-body, the thick mat of black hair, and the patched clothes—was the magician. He held and waved his wand himself—and his wand was his own Thought. When special privation or anxiety beset them, it was their rule to say, 'What will it be best to think about first?' which was Marco's reason for saying it to himself now as he stood in the darkness which was like black velvet.

He waited a few minutes for the right thing to come to him.

'I am not afraid,' Marco said aloud. 'I shall not be afraid. In some way I shall get out.'

This was the image he wanted most to keep steadily in his mind— that nothing could make him afraid, and that in some way he could get out of the wine-cellar.

He thought of this for some minutes, and said the words over several times. He felt more like himself when he had done it.

'When my eyes are accustomed to the darkness, I shall see if there is any little glimmer of light anywhere,' he said next.

He waited with patience, and it seemed for some time that he saw no glimmer at all. He put out his hands on either side of him, and found that, on the side of the wall against which he stood, there seemed to be no shelves. Perhaps the cellar had been used for other purposes than the storing of wine, and, if that was true, there might be somewhere some opening for ventilation. The air was not bad, but then the door had not been shut tightly when the man opened it.

'I am not afraid,' he repeated, 'I shall not be afraid. In some way I shall get out.'

He would not allow himself to stop and think about his father waiting for his return. He knew that would only arouse his emotions and weaken his courage. He began to feel his way carefully along the wall. It reached farther than he had thought it would. The cellar was not so very small. He crept round it gradually, and then he made his way across it, keeping his hands extended below him and setting down each foot cautiously. Then he sat down on the stone floor and thought again, and what he thought was that there was a way out of this place for him, and he should somehow find it, and, before too long a time had passed, be walking in the street again.

It was while he was thinking in this way that he felt a startling thing. It seemed almost as if something touched him. It made him jump, though the touch was so light and soft that it was scarcely a touch at all, in fact he could not be sure that he had not imagined it. He stood up and leaned against the wall again. Perhaps the suddenness of his movement placed him at some angle he had not reached before, or perhaps his eyes had become more completely accustomed to the darkness, for, as he turned his head to listen, he made a discovery: above the door there was a place where the velvet blackness was not so dense. There was something like a slit in the wall, though, as it did not open upon daylight but upon the dark passage, it was not light it admitted so much as a lesser shade of darkness. But even that was better than nothing, and Marco drew another long breath.

'That is only the beginning. I shall find a way out,' he said. 'I *shall*.'

He remembered reading a story of a man who, being shut by accident in a safety vault, passed through such terrors before his release that he believed he had spent two days and nights in the place when he had been there only a few hours.

'His thoughts did that. I must remember. I will sit down again and begin thinking of all the pictures in the cabinet rooms of the Art History Museum in Vienna. It will take some time, and then there are the others,' he said.

It was a good plan. While he could keep his mind upon the game, he could think of nothing else, as it required close attention—and perhaps, as the day went on, his captors would begin to feel that it was not safe to run the risk of doing a thing as desperate as this would be. They might think better of it before they left the house at least.

He had walked in imagination through three of the cabinet rooms and was turning mentally into a fourth, when he found himself starting again quite violently. This time it was not at a touch but at a sound. Surely it was a sound. And it was in the cellar with him. But it was the tiniest possible noise, a ghost of a squeak and a suggestion of a movement. It came from the opposite side of the cellar, the side where the shelves were. He looked across in the darkness, and in the darkness saw a light which there could be no mistake about. It *was* a light, two lights indeed, two round phosphorescent greenish balls. They were two eyes staring at him. And then he heard another sound. Not a squeak this time, but something so homely and comfortable that he actually burst out laughing. It was a cat purring, a nice warm cat! And she was curled up on one of the lower shelves purring to some newborn kittens. He knew there were kittens because it was plain now what the tiny squeak had been, and it was made plainer by the fact that he heard another much more distinct one and then another. They had all been asleep when he had come into the cellar. If the mother had been awake, she had probably been very much afraid. Afterwards she had perhaps come down from her shelf to investigate, and had passed close to him. The feeling of relief which came upon him at this simple discovery was wonderful. It was so natural and comfortable an everyday thing that it seemed to make spies and criminals unreal, and only natural things possible. With a mother cat purring away among her kittens, even a dark wine-cellar was not so black. He got up and kneeled by the shelf. The greenish eyes did not shine in an unfriendly way. He could feel that the owner of them was a nice big cat, and he counted four round little balls of kittens. It was a curious delight to stroke the soft fur and talk to the mother cat. She answered with purring as if she liked the sense of friendly human nearness. Marco laughed to himself.

'It's queer what a difference it makes!' he said. 'It is almost like finding a window.'

The presence of these harmless living things was companionship. He sat down close to the low shelf and listened to the motherly purring, now and then speaking and putting out his hand to touch the warm fur. The phosphorescent light in the green eyes was a comfort in itself.

'We shall get out of this—both of us,' he said. 'We shall not be here very long, Puss-cat.'

He was not troubled by the fear of being really hungry for some time. He was so used to eating scantily from necessity, and to passing long hours without food during his journeys, that he had proved to himself that fasting is not, after all, such a desperate ordeal as most people imagine. If you begin by expecting to feel famished and by counting the hours between your meals, you will begin to be ravenous. But he knew better.

The time passed slowly; but he had known it would pass slowly, and he had made up his mind not to watch it nor ask himself questions about it. He was not a restless boy, but, like his father, could stand or sit or lie still. Now and then he could hear distant rumblings of carts and vans passing in the street. There was a certain degree of companionship in these also. He kept his place near the cat and his hand where he could occasionally touch her. He could lift his eyes now and then to the place where the dim glimmer of something like light showed itself.

Perhaps the stillness, perhaps the darkness, perhaps the purring of the mother cat, probably all three, caused his thoughts to begin to travel through his mind slowly and more slowly. At last they ceased and he fell asleep. The mother cat purred for some time, and then fell asleep herself.

*Here are a number of tales about the reality that can be created by the imagination. Think of how your own life has been shaped at times by other people's imaginative work. Sometimes, even the most ordinary experience, like marveling at the beauty of flowers, is given a new freshness by the author's fantasy.*

## Colin Greer, *The Boy Who Drew Cats*, adapted from a fifteenth-century Japanese legend

In ancient Japan the time came when farmers and their families were close to starvation, because there was a terrible drought. The land was dry and little grew.

Kenji's mother and brothers worked hard to eke out food for the family. Kenji was not strong enough to work, he tired quickly.

His mother was never harsh with him. She and his brothers loved his drawing—and oh how he loved to draw. So he spent his days drawing. He drew cats and flowers. He drew plates filled to overflowing with rice.

But conditions worsened, and food was even more scare. Kenji's mother decided to place him in a monastery where he could be cared for and do light work.

The priests took him in. He swept the floors of the monastery and cleaned the kitchen. And so he ate enough and still he drew. Above all else, he loved to draw.

The priests taught Kenji to help with copying their scrolls, but his mind would wander and in his daydreams he would add pictures to his writing, usually of cats and birds. One priest, Takada, befriended him. The older priest, Joshida, grew more and more angry with Kenji's drawing. He did not like the pictures on the monastery scrolls. At first he warned Kenji to stop and finally grew impatient with Kenji's daydreaming and sent him away. As Kenji sadly left the monastery Takada gave him a wonderful set of brushes and ink. "Go." Takada said, "you are to be an artist, not a priest."

Kenji wandered off. Not wanting to burden his family, he walked in the opposite direction. He wandered through many poor farmlands until he found a deserted temple at the top of a mountain. People living nearby avoided the temple because a terrible Goblin Rat with a magic sword lived in the temple. The rat was so ferocious that it had been many years since anyone had dared enter the temple. But Kenji did not know all this.

He climbed to the mountaintop and entered the temple. He could hear scratching all around him. Before him he saw large, white screens.

To quiet his fears he decided to draw on the screens. Quickly he took out Takada's gift and began to draw marvelous cats. He filled the empty screens with pictures of imperial cats with fiery eyes, smaller cats chasing each other and smiling toward him. Soon every screen was filled with Kenji's drawings.

By now he was very tired. But he was too lonely and too afraid to sleep. He could still hear scratching all around him. As he turned to leave he could hear scratching ahead of him toward the front door. He pulled back, he couldn't get to the door. He was too afraid to move any further toward it.

He lay down behind a small cabinet for safety. Soon, tired out, he was fast asleep. He was awakened close to sunrise by scratching, screeching and growling on the other side of his cabinet. He clenched his fists and squinted his eyes. He was about to scream, he was so afraid. Then suddenly he felt a fresh breeze blowing through the temple and a strange wonderful silence seemed to comfort him. Soon he took courage enough to peek out from behind his cabinet.

What he saw was a great wonder. Only one screen still stood. All the others were broken and tattered. On the single standing screen was one of his imperial cats, truly the King of Cats. In front of the screen lay a sword, the sword of the Goblin Rat.

Kenji ran through the temple door. But before he had gone but a few steps, the villagers were running up the mountainside toward him. They had felt the breeze too. It had come from the temple across the nearby farmlands. They all yelled, "The Goblin Rat is dead! the Goblin Rat is dead!"

The priests returned to the temple, and they were so grateful to Kenji that they invited him to live in the temple with them. For many, many years he drew his pictures. His drawings were famous far and wide, and most famous of all were Kenji's drawings of cats.

**Brian Patten,** *You'd Better Believe Him: A Fable*
He discovered an old rocking-horse in Woolworth's,
He tried to feed it but without much luck.
So he stroked it, had a long conversation about
The trees it came from, the attics it had visited.
Tried to take it out then
But the store detective he
Called the store manager who
Called the police who in court next morning said
'He acted strangely when arrested,

His statement read simply "I believe in rocking-horses".
We have reason to believe him mad.'
'Quite so,' said the prosecution,
'Bring in the rocking-horse as evidence.'
'I'm afraid it's escaped, sir,' said the store manager,
'Left a hoof-print as evidence
On the skull of the store detective.'
'Quite so,' said the prosecution, fearful
Of the neighing
Out in the corridor.


## Lewis Carroll, *Alice in Wonderland*

For a few minutes all went on well, and she was just saying, 'I really *shall* do it this time—' when the path gave a sudden twist and shook itself (as she described it afterwards), and the next moment she found herself actually walking in at the door.

'Oh, it's too bad!' she cried. 'I never saw such a house for getting in the way! Never! '

However, there was the hill full in sight, so there was nothing to be done but start again. This time she came upon a large flower-bed, with a border of daisies, and a willow-tree growing in the middle.

'O Tiger-lily,' said Alice, addressing herself to one that was waving gracefully about in the wind, 'I *wish* you could talk!'

'We *can* talk,' said the Tiger-lily: 'when there's anybody worth talking to.'

Alice was so astonished that she could not speak for a minute: it quite seemed to take her breath away. At length, as the Tiger-lily only went on waving about, she spoke again, in a timid voice—almost in a whisper. 'And can *all* the flowers talk?'

'As well as *you* can,' said the Tiger-lily. 'And a great deal louder.'

'It isn't manners for us to begin, you know,' said the Rose, 'and I really was wondering when you'd speak! Said I to myself "Her face has got *some* sense in it, though it's not a clever one!" Still, you're the right colour, and that goes a long way.'

'I don't care about the colour,' the Tiger-lily remarked. 'If only her petals curled up a little more, she'd be all right.'

Alice didn't like being criticised, so she began asking questions. 'Aren't you sometimes frightened at being planted out here, with nobody to take care of you? '

'There's the tree in the middle,' said the Rose: 'what else is it good for?'

'But what could it do, if any danger came? ' Alice asked.

'It could bark,' said the Rose.

'It says "Bough-wough!"' cried a Daisy: 'that's why its branches are called boughs!'

'Didn't you know *that*?' cried another Daisy, and here they all began shouting together, till the air seemed quite full of little shrill voices. 'Silence, every one of you!' cried the Tiger-lily, waving itself passionately from side to side, and trembling with excitement. 'They know I can't get at them!' it panted, bending its quivering head towards Alice, 'or they wouldn't dare to do it!'

'Never mind!' Alice said in a soothing tone, and stooping down to the daisies, who were just beginning again, she whispered, 'If you don't hold your tongues, I'll pick you!'

There was silence in a moment, and several of the pink daisies turned white.

'That's right!' said the Tiger-lily. 'The daisies are worst of all. When one speaks, they all begin together, and it's enough to make one wither to hear the way they go on!'

'How is it you can all talk so nicely?' Alice said, hoping to get it into a better temper by a compliment. 'I've been in many gardens before, but none of the flowers could talk.'

'Put your hand down, and feel the ground,' said the Tiger-lily. 'Then you'll know why.'

Alice did so. 'It's very hard,' she said, 'but I don't see what that has to do with it.'

'In most gardens,' the Tiger-lily said, 'they make the beds too soft— so that the flowers are always asleep.'

This sounded a very good reason, and Alice was quite pleased to know it. 'I never thought of that before!' she said.

'It's my opinion that you never think *at all*,' the Rose said in a rather severe tone.

'I never saw anybody looked stupider,' a Violet said, so suddenly, that Alice quite jumped; for it hadn't spoken before.

'Hold *your* tongue! ' cried the Tiger-lily. 'As if *you* ever saw anybody! You keep your head under the leaves, and snore away there, till you know no more what's going on in the world, than if you were a bud!'

'Are there any more people in the garden besides me?' Alice said, not choosing to notice the Rose's last remark.

'There's one other flower in the garden that can move about like you,' said the Rose. 'I wonder how you do it—' ('You're always wondering,' said the Tiger-lily), 'but she's more bushy than you are.'

'Is she like me?' Alice asked eagerly, for the thought crossed her mind, 'There's another little girl in the garden, somewhere!'

'Well, she has the same awkward shape as you,' the Rose said, 'but she's redder—and her petals are shorter, I think.'

'Her petals are done up close, almost like a dahlia,' the Tiger-lily interrupted: 'not tumbled about anyhow, like yours.'

'But that's not *your* fault,' the Rose added kindly: 'you're beginning to fade, you know—and then one can't help one's petals getting a little untidy.'

Alice didn't like this idea at all: so, to change the subject, she asked 'Does she ever come out here?'

'I daresay you'll see her soon,' said the Rose. 'She's one of the thorny kind.'

'Where does she wear the thorns?' Alice asked with some curiosity.

'Why, all round her head, of course,' the Rose replied. 'I was wondering *you* hadn't got some too. I thought it was the regular rule.'

'She's coming!' cried the Larkspur. 'I hear her footstep, thump, thump, along the gravel-walk!'

Alice looked round eagerly, and found that it was the Red Queen. 'She's grown a good deal!' was her first remark. She had indeed: when Alice first found her in the ashes, she had been only three inches high— and here she was, half a head taller than Alice herself!

'It's the fresh air that does it,' said the Rose: 'wonderfully fine air it is, out here.'

'I think I'll go and meet her,' said Alice, for, though the flowers were interesting enough, she felt that it would be far grander to have a talk with a real Queen.

'You can't possibly do that,' said the Rose: '*I* should advise you to walk the other way.'

This sounded nonsense to Alice, so she said nothing, but set off at once towards the Red Queen. To her surprise, she lost sight of her in a moment, and found herself walking in at the front-door again.

---

*These two selections provide insight into what could be called the life history and struggles of the imagination. They are cautionary and encouraging at the same time and reaffirm that creative and imaginative effort is its own reward.*

## Langston Hughes, *The Genius Child*

This is a song for the genius child.
Sing it softly, for the song is wild.
Sing it softly as ever you can—
Lest the song get out of hand.

*Nobody loves a genius child.*

Can you love an eagle,
Tame or wild?

Wild or tame,
Can you love a monster
Of frightening name?

*Nobody loves a genius child.*

*Kill him*—and let his soul run wild!

## Bruce Brooks, *Midnight Hour Encores*

In 1947, exactly thirty-six years before I won the same two prizes at the same age, a thirteen-year-old Russian boy known only by the single name Dzyga swept through the revered Brussels concours and beat the crap out of everybody by winning both the cello first prize and the festival's grand prize as the top instrumentalist among all competitors on all instruments.

. . .

I went to a couple of libraries and music bookstores, and searched everywhere for mention of Dzyga. Nothing.

. . .

Then one day I found him.

. . .

When I heard his first notes, I stopped being a musician. I stopped being smart. I stopped being tall and lonesome. My outlines and edges faded away and spread out everywhere like light and water. There was nothing but this sound worth my notice.

Then his playing *pulled* on me, deep in my chest and legs and eyes, and I felt as if I knew nothing, as if my body was just being made. I sat there and shivered and blinked, like a baby hearing a voice it loves before it knows words.

His playing was so good it was almost wild, as if boundaries of music were stretching. Yet finally, he was in perfect control of himself. Lots of people have very precise pitch. Dzyga's was better—almost original. He found the notes by some secret path. His sense of rhythm was free, almost improvisatory, emphasized by what I first thought was a hotdog thing: an almost complete lack of vibrato. *Hey, I don't need to feel my way into the notes, folks—I nail them and hold them.* The sustained notes were kind of eerie.

The most difficult thing to pin down in terms of technique was a way he had of making it clear that every note was coming out of silence, a surprise. Not one tumbled logically from the note before it. He went back to the nothingness before every stroke.

---

*There is an artist in everybody. Some people spend the bulk of their time working to develop that creative impulse into a lifelong craft. Others of us become artists once in a while or take pleasure in being the audience for the arts—the willing witnesses of other people's imaginative efforts. As you read these five descriptions of the inspiration and meaning of the arts in people's lives, think of yourself as an artist and the treasures your imagination holds. And imagine ways in which the arts and the play of imagination can be shared within your family and across generations.*

**Siegfried Sassoon, *Everyone Sang***
Everyone suddenly burst out singing;
And I was fill'd with such delight
As prison'd birds must find in freedom
Winging wildly across the white
Orchards and dark-green fields; on; on; and out of sight.

Everyone's voice was suddenly lifted,
And beauty came like the setting sun.
My heart was shaken with tears; and horror
Drifted away . . . O but every one
Was a bird; and the song was wordless; the singing will never be done.

**Langston Hughes, *Daybreak in Alabama***
When I get to be a composer
I'm gonna write me some music about

Daybreak in Alabama
And I'm gonna put the purtiest songs in it
Rising out of the ground like a swamp mist
And falling out of heaven like soft dew.
I'm gonna put some tall tall trees in it
And the scent of pine needles
And the smell of red clay after rain
And long red necks
And poppy colored faces
And big brown arms
And the field daisy eyes
Of black and white black white black people
And I'm gonna put white hands
And black hands and brown and yellow hands
And red clay earth hands in it
Touching everybody with kind fingers
And touching each other natural as dew
In that dawn of music when I
Get to be a composer
And write about daybreak
In Alabama


**Dylan Thomas, *In My Craft or Sullen Art***
In my craft or sullen art
Exercised in the still night
When only the moon rages
And the lovers lie abed
With all their griefs in their arms,
I labor by singing light
Not for ambition or bread
Or the strut and trade of charms
On the ivory stages
But for the common wages
Of their most secret heart.

Not for the proud man apart
From the raging moon I write
On these spindrift pages
Nor for the towering dead
With their nightingales and psalms

But for the lovers, their arms
Round the griefs of the ages,
Who pay no praise or wages
Nor heed my craft or art.

### Leo Lionni, *Frederick*

But little by little they had nibbled up most of the nuts and berries, the straw was gone. and the corn was only a memory. It was cold in the wall and no one felt like chatting.

Then they remembered what Frederick had said about sun rays and colors and words. "What about *your* supplies, Frederick"? they asked.

"Close your eyes," said Frederick, as he climbed on a big stone. "Now I send you the rays of the sun. Do you feel how their golden glow . . ." And as Frederick spoke of the sun the four little mice began to feel warmer. Was it Frederick's voice? Was it magic?

"And how about the colors, Frederick?" they asked anxiously. "Close your eyes again," Frederick said. And when he told them of the blue periwinkles, the red poppies in the yellow wheat, and the green leaves of the berry bush, they saw the colors as clearly as if they had been painted in their minds.

### Miguel Algarín, Prologue, from *Angelitos Negros: A Salsa Ballet*

Good Vibrations Sound Studio,
the date is for three
but we arrive at 2:30 P.M.,
the occasion: the first recording
of Willie Colon's score of "A Salsa Ballet":
the studio is refrigerator cool,
the vibes are mellow,
the rhythm is sleepy slow,
the set is slowly pulling together,
musicians arrive, slapping hands
talking through months of absence
into hugs and tightly held hands,
they are coming together
                    to invent
the sound that Willie
has in his head,
musicians are Willie's brush,
musicians are Willie's sound partners,

today's the day for an orgy of sounds,
today is the day for the birth
of a new latin perception of sound,
Willie walks around,
four months into his pregnancy,
I see prenatal rhythmic juices pour
out of his pores as notes shoot
pitches of sounds high into the atmosphere,
musicians come together in a holy
trust, the bond of marriage for
a trumpet and a saxophone
is the listening
that they do to one another,
there in the listening,
there is hope.

⇒•⇐

*It can be dangerous to sit back and let other people solve problems and exercise their imaginations for you. Not only do you have to take the consequences of their choices and ideas but you become smaller, less open to all of the magical and interesting things experience can provide. These two tales offer insights into the dangers of passivity as well as encouragement for the active engagement of the imagination with everyday problems. Given the quick fix of TV and the seeming intractability of large problems in our society, passivity can become a way of life. Sharing literature and the arts is a way to become active and alive to the possibilities of an engaged communal life.*

### Idries Shah, "Dry in the Rain," from *The Pleasantries of the Incredible Mulla Nasrudin*

A Man invited Nasrudin to go hunting with him, but mounted him on a horse which was too slow. The Mulla said nothing. Soon the hunt outpaced him and was out of sight. It began to rain heavily, and there was no shelter. All the members of the hunt got soaked through. Nasrudin, however, as soon as the rain started, took off all his clothes and folded them. Then he sat down on the pile. As soon as the rain stopped, he dressed himself and went back to his host's house for lunch. Nobody could work out why he was dry. With all the speed of their horses they had not been able to reach shelter on that plain.

'It was the horse you gave me,' said Nasrudin.

The next day he was given a fast horse and his host took the slow one. Rain fell again. The horse was so slow that the host got wetter than ever, riding at a snail's pace to his house. Nasrudin carried out the same procedure as before.

When he got back to the house he was dry.

'It is your fault!' shouted his host. 'You made me ride this terrible horse.'

'Perhaps', said Nasrudin, 'you did not contribute anything of your own to the problem of keeping dry?'

### E. Nesbit, *The Last of the Dragons*

Of course you know that dragons were once as common as motor-omnibuses are now, and almost as dangerous. But as every well-brought-up prince was expected to kill a dragon, and rescue a princess, the dragons grew fewer and fewer till it was often quite hard for a princess to find a dragon to be rescued from. And at last there were no more dragons in France and no more dragons in Germany, or Spain, or Italy, or Russia. There were some left in China, and are still, but they are cold and bronzy, and there were never any, of course, in America. But the last real live dragon left was in England, and of course that was a very long time ago, before what you call English History began. This dragon lived in Cornwall in the big caves amidst the rocks, and a very fine dragon it was, quite seventy feet long from the tip of its fearful snout to the end of its terrible tail. It breathed fire and smoke, and rattled when it walked, because its scales were made of iron. Its wings were like half-umbrellas— or like bat's wings, only several thousand times bigger. Everyone was very frightened of it, and well they might be.

Now the King of Cornwall had one daughter, and when she was sixteen, of course she would have to go and face the dragon: such tales are always told in royal nurseries at twilight, so the Princess knew what she had to expect. The dragon would not eat her, of course—because the prince would come and rescue her. But the Princess could not help thinking it would be much pleasanter to have nothing to do with the dragon at all—not even to be rescued from him. 'All the princes I know are such, very silly little boys,' she told her father. 'Why must I be rescued by a prince?'

'It's always done, my dear,' said the King, taking his crown off and putting it on the grass, for they were alone in the garden, and even kings must unbend sometimes.

'Father, darling,' said the Princess presently, when she had made a daisy chain and put it on the King's head, where the crown ought to have been. 'Father, darling, couldn't we tie up one of the silly little princes for the dragon to look at—and then *I* could go and kill the dragon and rescue the prince? I fence much better than any of the princes we know.'

'What an unladylike idea!' said the King, and put his crown on again, for he saw the Prime Minister coming with a basket of new-laid Bills for him to sign. 'Dismiss the thought, my child. I rescued your mother from a dragon, and you don't want to set yourself up above her, I should hope?'

'But this is the *last* dragon. It is different from all other dragons.'

'How?' asked the King.

'Because he *is* the last,' said the Princess, and went off to her fencing lessons, with which she took great pains. She took great pains with all her lessons—for she could not give up the idea of fighting the dragon. She took such pains that she became the strongest and boldest and most skillful and most sensible princess in Europe. She had always been the prettiest and nicest.

And the days and years went on, till at last the day came which was the day before the Princess was to be rescued from the dragon. The Prince who was to do this deed of valour was a pale prince, with large eyes and a head full of mathematics and philosophy, but he had unfortunately neglected his fencing lessons. He was to stay the night at the palace, and there was a banquet.

After supper the Princess sent her pet parrot to the Prince with a note. It said:

> Please, Prince, come on to the terrace. I want to talk to you without anybody else hearing. –The Princess.

So, of course, he went—and he saw her gown of silver a long way off shining among the shadows of the trees like water in starlight. And when he came quite close to her he said: 'Princess, at your service,' and bent his cloth-of-gold-covered knee and put his hand on his cloth-of-gold-covered heart.

'Do you think,' said the Princess earnestly, 'that you will be able to kill the dragon?'

'I will kill the dragon,' said the Prince firmly, 'or perish in the attempt.'

'It's no use your perishing,' said the Princess.

'It's the least I can do,' said the Prince.

'What I'm afraid of is that it'll be the most you can do,' said the Princess.

'It's the only thing I can do,' said he, 'unless I kill the dragon.'

'Why you should do anything for me is what I can't see,' said she.

'But I want to,' he said. 'You must know that I love you better than anything in the world.'

When he said that he looked so kind that the Princess began to like him a little.

'Look here,' she said, 'no one else will go out tomorrow. You know they tie me to a rock and leave me—and then everybody scurries home and puts up the shutters and keeps them shut till you ride through the town in triumph shouting that you've killed the dragon, and I ride on the horse behind you weeping for joy.'

'I've heard that that is how it is done,' said he.

'Well, do you love me well enough to come very quickly and set me free—and we'll fight the dragon together?'

'It wouldn't be safe for you.'

'Much safer for both of us for me to be free, with a sword in my hand, than tied up and helpless. *Do* agree.'

He could refuse her nothing. So he agreed. And next day everything happened as she had said.

When he had cut the cords that tied her to the rock they stood on the lonely mountain-side looking at each other.

'It seems to me,' said the Prince, 'that this ceremony could have been arranged without the dragon.'

'Yes,' said the Princess, 'but since it had been arranged with the dragon—'

'It seems such a pity to kill the dragon—the last in the world,' said the Prince.

'Well then, don't let's,' said the Princess; 'let's tame it not to eat Princesses but to eat out of their hands. They say everything can be tamed by kindness.'

'Taming by kindness means giving them things to eat,' said the Prince. 'Have you got anything to eat?'

She hadn't, but the Prince owned that he had a few biscuits. 'Breakfast was so very early,' said he, 'and I thought you might have felt faint after the fight.'

'How clever,' said the Princess, and they took a biscuit in each hand. And they looked here, and they looked there, but never a dragon could they see.

'But here's its trail,' said the Prince, and pointed to where the rock was scarred and scratched so as to make a track leading to a dark cave. It was like cart-ruts in a Sussex road, mixed with the marks of sea-gull's feet on the sea-sand. 'Look, that's where it's dragged its brass tail and planted its steel claws.'

'Don't let's think how hard its tail and its claws are,' said the Princess, 'or I shall begin to be frightened—and I know you can't tame anything, even by kindness, if you're frightened of it. Now or never.'

She caught the Prince's hand in hers and they ran along the path towards the dark mouth of the cave. But they did not run into it. It really was so very *dark*.

So they stood outside, and the Prince shouted: 'What ho! Dragon there! What ho within!' And from the cave they heard an answering voice and great clattering and creaking. It sounded as though a rather large cotton-mill were stretching itself and waking up out of its sleep.

The Prince and the Princess trembled, but they stood firm.

'Dragon—I say, dragon!' said the Princess, 'do come out and talk to us. We've brought you a present.'

'Oh yes—I know your presents,' growled the dragon in a huge rumbling voice. 'One of those precious princesses, I suppose? And I've got to come out and fight for her. Well, I tell you straight, I'm not going to do it. A fair fight I wouldn't say no to—a fair fight and no favour—but one of these put-up fights where you've got to lose—no! So I tell you. If I wanted a princess I'd come and take her, in my own time—but I don't. What do you suppose I'd do with her, if I'd got her?'

'Eat her, wouldn't you?' said the Princess, in a voice that trembled a little.

'Eat a fiddle-stick end,' said the dragon very rudely. 'I wouldn't touch the horrid thing.'

The Princess's voice grew firmer.

'Do you like biscuits?' she said.

'No,' growled the dragon.

'Not the nice little expensive ones with sugar on the top?'

'*No*,' growled the dragon.

'Then what *do* you like?' asked the Prince.

'You go away and don't bother me,' growled the dragon, and they could hear it turn over, and the clang and clatter of its turning echoed in the cave like the sound of the steam-hammers in the Arsenal at Woolwich.

The Prince and Princess looked at each other. What *were* they to do? Of course it was no use going home and telling the King that the dragon didn't want princesses—because His Majesty vas very old-fashioned and would never have believed that a new-fashioned dragon could ever be at all different from an old-fashioned dragon. They could not go into the cave and kill the dragon. Indeed, unless he attacked the Princess it did not seem fair to kill him at all.

'He must like something,' whispered the Princess, and she called out in a voice as sweet as honey and sugar-cane:

'Dragon! Dragon dear!'

'WHAT?' shouted the dragon. 'Say that again!' and they could hear the dragon coming towards them through the darkness of the cave. The Princess shivered, and said in a very small voice:

'Dragon—Dragon dear!'

And then the dragon came out. The Prince drew his sword, and the Princess drew hers—the beautiful silver-handled one that the Prince had brought in his motor-car. But they did not attack; they moved slowly back as the dragon came out, all the vast scaly length of him, and lay along the rock—his great wings halfspread and his silvery sheen gleaming like diamonds in the sun. At last they could retreat no further—the dark rock behind them stopped their way—and with their backs to the rock they stood swords in hand and waited.

The dragon drew nearer and nearer—and now they could see that he was not breathing fire and smoke as they had expected—he came crawling slowly towards them wriggling a little as a puppy does when it wants to play and isn't quite sure whether you're not cross with it

And then they saw that great tears were coursing down its brazen cheek.

'Whatever's the matter?' said the Prince.

'Nobody,' sobbed the dragon, 'ever called me "dear" before!'

Don't cry, dragon dear,' said the Princess. 'We'll call you "dear" as often as you like. We want to tame you.'

'I *am* tame,' said the dragon—'that's just it. That's what nobody but you has ever found out. I'm so tame that I'd eat out of your hands.'

'Eat what, dragon dear?' said the Princess. 'Not biscuits?' The dragon slowly shook his heavy head.

'Not biscuits?' said the Princess tenderly, 'What, then, dragon dear?'

'Your kindness quite undragons me,' it said. 'No one has ever asked any of us what we like to eat—always offering us princesses, and then rescuing them—and never once, "What'll you take to drink the King's health in?" Cruel hard I call it,' and it wept again.

'But what would you like to drink our health in?' said the Prince. 'We're going to be married today, aren't we, Princess?'

She said that she supposed so.

'What'll I take to drink your health in?' asked the dragon. 'Ah, you're something like a gentleman, you are, sir. I don't mind if I do, sir. I'll be proud to drink your and your good lady's health in a tiny drop of'—its voice faltered—'to think of you asking me so friendly like,' it said. 'Yes, sir, just a tiny drop of puppuppuppuppupetrol—tha-that's what does a dragon good, sir—'

'I've lots in the car,' said the Prince, and was off down the mountain like a flash. He was a good judge of character and knew that with this dragon the Princess would be safe.

'If I might make so bold,' said the dragon, 'while the gentleman's away—p'raps just to pass the time you'd be so kind as to call me Dear again, and if you'd shake claws with a poor old dragon that's never been anybody's enemy but his own—well, the last of the dragons'll be the proudest dragon that's ever been since the first of them.'

It held out an enormous paw, and the great steel hooks that were its claws closed over the Princess's hand as softly as the claws of the Himalayan bear will close over the bit of bun you hand it through the bars at the Zoo.

And so the Prince and Princess went back to the palace in triumph, the dragon following them like a pet dog. And all through the wedding festivities no one drank more earnestly to the happiness of the bride and bridegroom than the Princess's pet dragon—whom she had at once named Fido.

And when the happy pair were settled in their own kingdom, Fido came to them and begged to be allowed to make himself useful.

'There must be some little thing I can do,' he said, rattling his wings and stretching his claws. 'My wings and claws and so on ought to be turned to some account—to say nothing of my grateful heart.'

So the Prince had a special saddle or howdah made for him—very long it was—like the tops of many tramcars fitted together. One hundred and fifty seats were fitted to this, and the dragon, whose greatest pleasure was now to give pleasure to others, delighted in taking parties of children to the sea-side. It flew through the air quite easily with its hundred and fifty little passengers—and would lie on the land patiently waiting till they were ready to return. The children were very fond of it, and used to call it Dear, a word which never failed to bring tears of affection and gratitude to its eyes. So it lived, useful and respected, till quite the other day—when someone happened to say, in his hearing, that dragons were out-of-date, now so much new machinery had come in. This so distressed him that he asked the King to change him into something less old-fashioned, and the kindly monarch at once changed him into a mechanical contrivance. The dragon, indeed, became the first aeroplane.

———❧———

*Finally, here are two selections about the demands and unexpected rewards of creativity that invite you to celebrate your own creativity and exercise your imagination with joy.*

**Arnold Lobel, "Tear-Water Tea," from *Owl at Home***

Owl took the kettle out of the cupboard. "Tonight I will make tear-water tea," he said.

He put the kettle on his lap. "Now," said Owl, "I will begin."

Owl sat very still. He began to think of things that were sad. "Chairs with broken legs." said Owl. His eyes began to water. "Songs that cannot be sung," said Owl, "because the words have been forgotten."

Owl began to cry. A large tear rolled down and dropped into the kettle.

"Spoons that have fallen behind the stove and are never seen again," said Owl. More tears dropped down into the kettle.

"Books that cannot be read," said Owl, "because some of the pages have been torn out."

"Clocks that have stopped," said Owl, "with no one near to wind them up." Owl was crying. Many large tears dropped into the kettle. "Mornings that nobody saw because everybody was sleeping," sobbed Owl.

"Mashed potatoes left on a plate," he cried, "because no one wanted to eat them. And pencils that are too short to use."

Owl thought about many other sad things. He cried and cried. Soon the kettle was all filled up with tears.

"There," said Owl. "That does it!" Owl stopped crying. He put the kettle on the stove to boil for tea.

Owl felt happy as he filled his cup. "It tastes a little bit salty," he said, "but tear-water tea is always very good."

**John Guare, *Six Degrees of Separation***

The imagination. That's our out. Our imagination teaches us our limits and then how to grow beyond those limits. The imagination says "Listen to me. I am your darkest voice. I am your 4 A.M. voice. I am the voice that wakes you up and says, 'This is what I'm afraid of. Do not listen to me at your peril.'" The imagination is the noon voice that sees clearly and says, "Yes, this is what I want for my life." It's there to sort out your nightmare, to show you the exits from the maze of your nightmare, to transform the nightmare into dreams to become your bedrock. . . . The imagination is not our escape. On the contrary, the imagination is the place we are all trying to get to.

# Playfulness

---

Bernard de Koven, a game inventor and central force in the New
Games movement, describes play as

> the enactment of anything that is not for real. Play is intended to be
> without consequence. We can play fight, and nobody gets hurt. We can
> play, in fact, with anything—ideas, emotions, challenges, principles. We
> can play with fear, getting as close as possible to sheer terror, without
> ever really being afraid. We can play with being other than we are—
> being famous, being mean, being a role, being a world.
>
> When we are playing, we are *only* playing. We do not mean any-
> thing else by it.
>
> —from *The Well-Played Game*

Through play we carve out safe zones for ourselves and explore the
"might be" and the "what if." Though we may not "mean anything else by
it," we can learn through play and prepare ourselves for serious challenges. We can also simply have fun. The capacity to have fun even when
life seems very difficult is a basic survival skill.

In addition, without the ability to look at the world and oneself as
slightly silly and out of joint, it would be impossible to live through the
horrors and absurdities we encounter every day. The wisdom of the joker
and the power of the trickster have to do with this ability to use one's
mind and one's sense of humor to level the playing field and deflate people who think that brute force can triumph over intelligence. Playfulness
thus contributes to cultural and personal survival, as some of the selections here illustrate. The ability of laughter to sustain energy and hope is
quite amazing and, for young people, a powerful aid to dealing with the
continuing challenges of growth and mastery that they face. It is also difficult for adults to teach and nurture children without a sense of humor
and a sense of play. Finally, remembering the happy moments of childhood and those times throughout life when you were able to play and

laugh without fear or anxiety is a constant reminder that life can indeed be wonderful.

The best way to end this brief introduction is with a quotation from Shakespeare's *Midsummer Night's Dream* (V, i, 363):

> No epilogue, I pray you, for your play needs no excuse.
> Never excuse.

---

*There is perhaps no more playful character in all of children's literature than Pippi Longstocking. In this selection thieves try to take advantage of her, and she plays with them in more than one sense. This selection raises the questions: Can conflict be defused through play? How can people turn aggression into play without loss of face? Can we find ways to use Pippi's example and our strengths to defuse problems?*

**Astrid Lindgren, *Pippi Longstocking*, translated by Florence Lamborn**
After Pippi's performance at the circus there was not a single person in all the little town who did not know how strong she was. There was even a piece about her in the paper. But people who lived in other places, of course, didn't know who Pippi was.

One dark autumn evening two tramps came walking down the road past Villa Villekulla. They were two bad thieves wandering about the country to see what they could steal. They saw that there was a light in the windows of Villa Villekulla and decided to go in to ask for a sandwich.

That evening Pippi had poured out all her gold pieces on the kitchen floor and sat there counting them. To be sure, she couldn't count very well, but she did it now and then anyway, just to keep everything in order.

"... sixty-five, sixty-six, sixty-seven, sixty-eight, sixty-nine, sixty-ten, sixty-eleven, sixty-twelve, sixty-thirteen, sixty-sixteen—whew, it makes my throat feel like sixty! Goodness, there must be some more numbers in the arithmetic, yes, now I remember—one hundred four, one thousand. That certainly is a lot of money," said Pippi.

There was a loud knock on the door.

"Walk in or stay out, whichever you choose!" shouted Pippi. "I never force anyone against his will."

The door opened and the two tramps came in. You can imagine that they opened their eyes when they saw a little red-headed girl sitting all alone on the floor, counting money.

"Are you all alone at home?" they asked craftily.

"Of course not," said Pippi. "Mr. Nilsson is at home too."

The thieves couldn't very well know that Mr. Nilsson was a monkey sleeping in a little green bed with a doll's quilt around his stomach. They thought the man of the house must be named Mr. Nilsson and they winked at each other. "We can come back a little later" is what they meant, but to Pippi they said, "We just came in to ask what your clock is."

They were so excited that they had forgotten all about the sandwich.

"Great, strong men who don't know what a clock is!" said Pippi. "Where in the world were you brought up? The clock is a little round thingamajig that says 'tick tack, tick tack,' and that goes and goes but never gets to the door. Do you know any more riddles? Out with them if you do," said Pippi encouragingly.

The tramps thought Pippi was too little to tell time, so without another word they went out again.

"I don't demand that you say 'tack' " [thanks in Swedish], shouted Pippi after them, "but you could at least make an effort and say 'tick.' You haven't even as much sense as a clock has. But by all means go in peace." And Pippi went back to her counting.

No sooner were the tramps outside than they began to rub their hands with delight. "Did you see all that money? Heavenly day!" said one of them.

"Yes, once in a while luck is with us," said the other. "All we need to do is wait until the kid and that Nilsson are asleep. Then we'll sneak in and grab the dough."

They sat down under an oak tree in the garden to wait. A drizzling rain was falling; they were very hungry, so they were quite uncomfortable, but the thought of all that money kept their spirits up.

From time to time lights went out in other houses, but in Villa Villekulla they shone on. It so happened that Pippi was learning to dance the shottische, and she didn't want to go to bed until she was sure she could do it. At last, however, the lights went out in the windows of Villa Villekulla too.

The tramps waited quite a while until they were sure Mr. Nilsson would have gone to sleep. At last they crept quietly up to the kitchen door and prepared to open it with their burglar tools. Meanwhile one of them his name, as a matter of fact, was Bloom just happened to feel the doorknob. The door was not locked!

"Well, some people *are* smart," he whispered to his companion. "The door is open!"

"So much the better for us," answered his companion, a black-haired man called Thunder-Karlsson by those who knew him. Thunder-Karlsson turned on his pocket flashlight, and they crept into the kitchen. There was no one there. In the next room was Pippi's bed, and there also stood Mr. Nilsson's little doll bed.

Thunder-Karlsson opened the door and looked around carefully. Everything was quiet as he played his flashlight around the room. When the light touched Pippi's bed the two tramps were amazed to see nothing but a pair of feet on the pillow. Pippi, as usual, had her head under the covers at the foot of the bed.

"That must be the girl," whispered Thunder-Karlsson to Bloom. "And no doubt she sleeps soundly. But where in the world is Nilsson, do you suppose?"

"*Mr.* Nilsson, if you please," came Pippi's calm voice from under the covers. "*Mr.* Nilsson is in the little green doll bed."

The tramps were so startled that they almost rushed out at once, but then it suddenly dawned on them what Pippi had said. That Mr. Nilsson was lying in a doll's *bed*. And now in the light of the flashlight they could see the little bed and the tiny monkey lying in it.

Thunder-Karlsson couldn't help laughing. "Bloom," he said, "Mr. Nilsson is a monkey. Can you beat that?"

"Well, what did you think he was?" came Pippi's calm voice from under the covers again. "A lawnmower?

"Aren't your mother and father at home?" asked Bloom.

"No," said Pippi. "They're gone. Completely gone."

Thunder-Karlsson and Bloom chuckled with delight.

"Listen, little girl," said Thunder-Karlsson, "come out so we can talk to you."

"No, I'm sleeping," said Pippi. "Is it more riddles you want? If so, answer this one. What is it that goes and goes and never gets to the door?"

Now Bloom went over and pulled the covers off Pippi.

"Can you dance the schottische?" asked Pippi, looking at him gravely in the eye. "I can."

"You ask too many questions," said Thunder-Karlsson. "Can we ask a few too? Where, for instance, is the money you had on the floor a little while ago?"

"In the suitcase on top of the wardrobe," answered Pippi truthfully.

Thunder-Karlsson and Bloom grinned.

"I hope you don't have anything against our taking it, little friend," said Thunder-Karlsson.

"Certainly not," said Pippi. "Of course I don't."

Whereupon Bloom lifted down the suitcase.

"I hope you don't have anything against my taking it back, little friend," said Pippi, getting out of bed and stepping over to Bloom.

Bloom had no idea how it all happened, but suddenly the suitcase was in Pippi's hand.

"Here, quit your fooling!" said Thunder-Karlsson angrily. "Hand over the suitcase." He took Pippi firmly by the hand and tried to snatch back the booty.

"Fooling, fooling, too much fooling," said Pippi and lifted Thunder-Karlsson up on the wardrobe. A moment later she had Bloom up there too. Then the tramps were frightened; they began to see that Pippi was no ordinary girl. However, the suitcase tempted them so much they forgot their fright.

"Come on now, both together," she yelled, and they jumped down from the wardrobe and threw themselves on Pippi, who had the suitcase in her hand. Pippi gave each one a little poke with her finger, and they shrank away into a corner. Before they had a chance to get up again, Pippi had fetched a rope and quick as a flash had bound the arms and legs of both burglars. Now they sang a different tune.

"Please, please, miss," Bloom begged, "forgive us. We were only joking. Don't hurt us. We are just two tramps who came in to ask for food."

Bloom even began to cry a bit.

Pippi put the suitcase neatly back on the wardrobe. Then she turned to her prisoners. "Can either of you dance the schottische?"

"Why, yes," said Thunder-Karlsson, "I guess we both can."

"Oh, what fun!" cried Pippi, clapping her hands. "Can't we dance a little? I've just learned, you know."

"Well, certainly, by all means," said Thunder-Karlsson, a bit confused.

Pippi took some large scissors and cut the ropes that bound her guests.

"But we don't have any music," she said in a worried voice. Then she had an idea. "Can't you blow on a comb?" she said to Bloom. "And I'll dance with him." She pointed to Thunder-Karlsson.

Oh, yes, Bloom could blow on a comb, all right. And blow he did, so that you could hear it all through the house. Mr. Nilsson sat up in bed, wide awake, just in time to see Pippi whirling around with Thunder-Karlsson. She was dead serious and danced as if her life depended on it.

At last Bloom said he couldn't blow on the comb any longer because it tickled his mouth unmercifully. And Thunder-Karlsson, who had tramped the roads all day, began to feel tired.

"Oh, please, just a little longer," begged Pippi, dancing on, and Bloom and Thunder-Karlsson could do nothing but continue.

At three in the morning Pippi said, "I could keep on dancing until Thursday, but maybe you're tired and hungry."

That was exactly what they were, though they hardly dared to say so. Pippi went to the pantry and took out bread and cheese and butter, ham and cold roast and milk; and they sat around the kitchen table Bloom and Thunder-Karlsson, and Pippi and ate until they were almost four-cornered.

Pippi poured a little milk into her ear. "That's good for earache," she said.

"Poor thing, have you got an earache?" asked Bloom.

"No," said Pippi, "but I might get one."

Finally the two tramps got up, thanked Pippi for the food, and begged to be allowed to say goodby.

"It was awfully jolly that you came. Do you really have to go so soon?" said Pippi regretfully.

"Never have I seen anyone who can dance the schottische the way you do, my sugar pig," she said to Thunder-Karlsson. And to Bloom, "If you keep on practicing on the comb, you won't notice the tickling."

As they were going out of the door Pippi came running after them and gave them each a gold piece. "These you have honestly earned," she said.

---

*Here are three selections about the joy of play for its own sake. After you read them, it may be fun to talk about the things you enjoy doing.*

### Robert Frost, *Birches*

When I see birches bend to left and right
Across the lines of straighter darker trees,
I like to think some boy's been swinging them.
But swinging doesn't bend them down to stay
As ice-storms do. Often you must have seen them
Loaded with ice a sunny winter morning
After a rain. They click upon themselves

As the breeze rises, and turn many-colored
As the stir cracks and crazes their enamel.
Soon the sun's warmth makes them shed crystal shells
Shattering and avalanching on the snow-crust—
Such heaps of broken glass to sweep away
You'd think the inner dome of heaven had fallen.
They are dragged to the withered bracken by the load,
And they seem not to break; though once they are bowed
So low for long, they never right themselves:
You may see their trunks arching in the woods
Years afterwards, trailing their leaves on the ground
Like girls on hands and knees that throw their hair
Before them over their heads to dry in the sun.
But I was going to say when Truth broke in
With all her matter-of-fact about the ice-storm
I should prefer to have some boy bend them
As he went out and in to fetch the cows—
Some boy too far from town to learn baseball,
Whose only play was what he found himself,
Summer or winter, and could play alone.
One by one he subdued his father's trees
By riding them down over and over again
Until he took the stiffness out of them,
And not one but hung limp, not one was left
For him to conquer. He learned all there was
To learn about not launching out too soon
And so not carrying the tree away
Clear to the ground. He always kept his poise
To the top branches, climbing carefully
With the same pains you use to fill a cup
Up to the brim, and even above the brim.
Then he flung outward, feet first, with a swish,
Kicking his way down through the air to the ground.
So was I once myself a swinger of birches.
And so I dream of going back to be.
It's when I'm weary of considerations,
And life is too much like a pathless wood
Where your face burns and tickles with the cobwebs
Broken across it, and one eye is weeping
From a twig's having lashed across it open.
I'd like to get away from earth awhile

And then come back to it and begin over.
May no fate willfully misunderstand me
And half grant what I wish and snatch me away
Not to return. Earth's the right place for love:
I don't know where it's likely to go better.
I'd like to go by climbing a birch tree,
And climb black branches up a snow-white trunk
*Toward* heaven, till the tree could bear no more,
But dipped its top and set me down again.
That would be good both going and coming back.
One could do worse than be a swinger of birches.

**Victor Hernandez Cruz, *Listening to the Music of Arsenio Rodriguez Is Moving Closer to Knowledge***
The researchers will come to
research the puddles of water
that we have turned into
all over your room

Doña Flores
who is next door
is not innocent
She too begins
to *liquidarse*

Warm water so good
Listen to the box
It is damaging
everybody

Opening like a curtain
the air in front of us
whistles
in the thousands of afternoons
that everybody is
nervously plucking
transformationally swimming
to where it is safe to dance
like flowers in the wind
who know no *bossordomos*

Inside your brains
each cell stands up
to *dance el son*
as the explorers come in
to research
yelling:
Where is everybody?
Are the windows opened?
Has it rained?

## Doug Lipman, *The Sword of Wood*

There was once a king who loved nothing better than to go out alone at night in the clothes of a commoner. He wanted to meet the ordinary people of his kingdom—to learn their way of life and especially their way of thinking about the world.

One night this king found himself walking in the poorest, narrowest street of the city. This was the street of the Jews. He heard a song in the distance. The king thought, *A song sung in this place of poverty must be a lament.* But as he got closer, he could hear the true character of the song: it was a song of pride! "Bai-yum-dum, bai-yum-bai, yum-bai, bai . . ."

The king was drawn to the source of the song: the smallest, humblest shack on the street. He knocked on the door. "Is a stranger welcome here?"

The voice from within said, "A stranger is God's gift. Come in."

In the dim light inside. the king saw a man sitting on his only piece of furniture, a wooden box. Then the king came in, the man stood up and sat on the floor, offering the king the crate for a seat.

"Well, my friend," the king asked, "what do you do to earn a living?

"Oh, I am a cobbler. "

"You have a shop where you make shoes?"

"Oh, no, I could not afford a shop. I take my box of tools—you are sitting on it—to the side of the road. There I repair shoes for people as they need them."

"You cobble shoes by the side of the road? Can you make enough money that way?"

The cobbler spoke with both humility and pride, "Every day I make just enough money to buy food for that day."

"Just enough for one day? Aren't you afraid that one day you won't make enough and then you'll go hungry?"

"Blessed be the One who carries us day by day."

The next day the king determined to put this man's philosophy to the test. He issued a proclamation that anyone wishing to cobble shoes by the side of the read must purchase a license for 50 pieces of gold.

That night the king returned to the street of the Jews. Again he heard a song in the distance, and thought, *This time, the cobbler will be singing a different tune.* But when the king neared the house, he heard the cobbler sing the same song. In fact, it was even longer, with a new phrase that soared joyfully: "Ah, ha-ah-ah, ah-ha, ah-ha, ah-yai."

The king knocked on the door. "Oh, my friend, I heard about that wicked king and his proclamation. I was so worried about you. Were you able to eat today?"

"Oh, I was angry when I heard I could not make my living in the way I always have. But I knew: I am entitled to make a living, and I will find a way. As I stood there, saying those very words to myself, a group of people passed me by. When I asked them where they were going, they told me: into the forest to gather firewood. Every day they bring back wood to sell as kindling. When I asked if I could join them, they said, 'There is a whole forest out there. Come along!'

"So I gathered firewood. At the end of the day I was able to sell it for just enough money to buy food for today."

The king sputtered, "Just enough for one day? What about tomorrow? What about next week?"

"Blessed be the One who carries us day by day."

The next day the king again returned to his throne and issued a new proclamation that anyone caught gathering firewood in the royal forest would be inducted into the royal guard. For good measure he issued another: No new members of the royal guard would be paid for 40 days.

That night the king returned to the street of the Jews. Amazed, he heard the same song! But now it had a third part that was militant and determined: "Dee, dee, dee, dee-dee, dee-dee, da . . . "

The king knocked on the door, "Cobbler, what happened to you today?"

"They made me stand at attention all day in the royal guard. They issued me a sword and a scabbard. But then they told me I wouldn't be paid for 40 days!"

"Oh, my friend, I bet you wish now that you had saved some money."

"Well, let me tell you what I did. At the end of the day I looked at that metal sword blade. I thought to myself, *That must be valuable.* So I removed the blade from the handle and fashioned another blade of wood. When the sword is in the scabbard, no one can tell the difference. I took the metal blade to a pawnbroker, and I pawned it for just enough money to buy food for one day."

The king was stunned. "But what if there's a sword inspection tomorrow?"

"Blessed be the One who carries us day by day."

The next day the cobbler was pulled out of line in the king's guard and was presented with a prisoner in chains.

"Cobbler, this man has committed a horrible crime. You are to take him to the square. Using your sword, you are to behead him."

"Behead him? I'm an observant Jew. I couldn't take another human life."

"If you do not, we'll kill both of you."

The cobbler led the trembling man into the square, where a crowd had gathered to watch the execution, and put the prisoner's head on the chopping block. He stood tall, his hand on the handle of his sword. Facing the crowd, he spoke.

"Let God be my witness: I am no murderer! If this man is guilty as charged, let my sword be as always. But if he is innocent, let my sword turn to wood!"

He pulled his sword. The people gasped when they saw the wooden blade, and they bowed down at the great miracle that had taken place there.

The king, who had been watching all of this, came over to the cobbler. He took him by the hand and looked him deep in the eyes. "I am the king. And I am also your friend who has visited you these last several nights. I want you to come live with me in the palace and be my advisor. Please teach me how to live as you do—one day at a time."

Then, in front of everyone, the two of them danced and sang: "Bai-yum-dum, bai-yum-bai, yum-bai, bai . . . "

---

*Laughter can be a genuine expression of joy or a mask for sadness, as in the opera* Pagliacci. *It can also be canned—insincere and nothing but a stimulus to get other people laughing. Here are two selections that introduce the anatomy of laughter and raise the questions: What causes me to laugh? When is my laughter sincere and when is it insincere, embarrassed, or mocking? What is funny?*

### P. L. Travers, *Mary Poppins*

"Oh, Uncle Albert—not *again?* It's not your birthday, is it?"

And as she spoke she looked up at the ceiling. Jane and Michael looked up too and to their surprise saw a round, fat, bald man who was hanging in the air without holding on to anything. Indeed, he appeared to be *sitting* on the air, for his legs were crossed and he had just put down the newspaper which he had been reading when they came in.

"My dear," said Mr. Wigg, smiling down at the children, and looking apologetically at Mary Poppins, "I'm very sorry, but I'm afraid it is my birthday."

"Tch, tch, tch!" said Mary Poppins.

"I only remembered last night and there was no time then to send you a postcard asking you to come another day. Very distressing, isn't it?" he said, looking down at Jane and Michael.

"I can see you're rather surprised," said Mr. Wigg. And, indeed, their mouths were so wide open with astonishment that Mr. Wigg, if he had been a little smaller, might almost have fallen into one of them.

"I'd better explain, I think," Mr. Wigg went on calmly. "You see, it's this way. I'm a cheerful sort of man and very disposed to laughter. You wouldn't believe, either of you, the number of things that strike me as being funny. I can laugh at pretty nearly everything, I can."

And with that Mr. Wigg began to bob up and down, shaking with laughter at the thought of his own cheerfulness.

"Uncle Albert!" said Mary Poppins, and Mr. Wigg stopped laughing with a jerk.

"Oh, beg pardon, my dear. Where was I? Oh, yes. Well, the funny thing about me is all right, Mary, I won't laugh if I can help it!—that whenever my birthday falls on a Friday, well, it's all up with me. Absolutely U.P.," said Mr. Wigg.

"But why?" began Jane.

"But how—?" began Michael.

"Well, you see, if I laugh on that particular day I become so filled with Laughing Gas that I simply can't keep on the ground. Even if I smile it happens. The first funny thought, and I'm up like a balloon. And until I can think of something serious I can't get down again." Mr. Wigg began to chuckle at that, but he caught sight of Mary Poppins's face and stopped the chuckle, and continued:

"It's awkward, of course, but not unpleasant. Never happens to either of you, I suppose?"

Jane and Michael shook their heads.

"No, I thought not. It seems to be my own special habit. Once, after I'd been to the Circus the night before, I laughed so much that—would you believe it?—I was up here for a whole twelve hours, and couldn't get down till the last stroke of midnight. Then, of course, I came down with a flop because it was Saturday and not my birthday any more. It's rather odd, isn't it? Not to say funny?

"And now here it is Friday again and my birthday, and you two and Mary P. to visit me. Oh, Lordy, Lordy, don't make me laugh, I beg of you—" But although Jane and Michael had done nothing very amusing, except to stare at him in astonishment, Mr. Wigg began to laugh again loudly, and as he laughed he went bouncing and bobbing about in the air, with the newspaper rattling in his hand and his spectacles half on and half off his nose.

He looked so comic, floundering in the air like a great human bubble, clutching at the ceiling sometimes and sometimes at the gas-bracket as he passed it, that Jane and Michael, though they were trying hard to be polite, just couldn't help doing what they did. They laughed. And they laughed. They shut their mouths tight to prevent the laughter escaping, but that didn't do any good. And presently they were rolling over and over on the floor, squealing and shrieking with laughter.

"Really!" said Mary Poppins. "Really, such behaviour!"

"I can't help it, I can't help it!" shrieked Michael as he rolled into the fender. "It's so terribly funny. Oh, Jane, isn't it funny?"

Jane did not reply, for a curious thing was happening to her. As she laughed she felt herself growing lighter and lighter, just as though she were being pumped full of air. It was a curious and delicious feeling and it made her want to laugh all the more. And then suddenly, with a bouncing bound, she felt herself jumping through the air. Michael, to his astonishment, saw her go soaring up through the room. With a little bump her head touched the ceiling and then she went bouncing along it till she reached Mr. Wigg.

"*Well!*" said Mr. Wigg, looking very surprised indeed. "Don't tell me it's your birthday, too?" Jane shook her head.

"It's not? Then this Laughing Gas must be catching! Hi—whoa there, look out for the mantelpiece." This was to Michael, who had suddenly risen from the floor and was swooping through the air, roaring with laughter, and just grazing the china ornaments on the mantelpiece as he passed. He landed with a bounce right on Mr. Wigg's knee.

"How do you do," said Mr. Wigg, heartily shaking Michael by the hand. "I call this really friendly of you—bless my soul, I do! To come up to me since I couldn't come down to you—eh?" And then he and Michael looked at each other and flung back their heads and simply howled with laughter.

"I say," said Mr. Wigg to Jane, as he wiped his eyes. "You'll be thinking I have the worst manners in the world. You're standing and you ought to be sitting—a nice young lady like you. I'm afraid I can't offer you a chair up here, but I think you'll find the air quite comfortable to sit on. I do."

Jane tried it and found she could sit down quite comfortably on the air. She took off her hat and laid it down beside her and it hung there in space without any support at all.

"That's right," said Mr. Wigg. Then he turned and looked down at Mary Poppins.

"Well, Mary, we're fixed. And now I can enquire about you, my dear. I must say, I am very glad to welcome you and my two young friends here today—why, Mary, you're frowning. I'm afraid you don't approve of—er—all this."

He waved his hand at Jane and Michael, and said hurriedly:

"I apologize, Mary, my dear. But you know how it is with me. Still, I must say I never thought my two young friends here would catch it, really I didn't, Mary! I suppose I should have asked them for another day or tried to think of something sad or something."

"Well, I must say," said Mary Poppins primly, "that I have never in my life seen such a sight. And at your age, Uncle—"

"Mary Poppins, Mary Poppins, do come up!" interrupted Michael. "Think of something funny and you'll find it's quite easy."

"Ah, now do, Mary!" said Mr. Wigg persuasively.

"We're lonely up here without you!" said Jane, and held out her arms towards Mary Poppins. "*Do* think of something funny!"

"Ah, *she* doesn't need to," said Mr. Wigg sighing. "She can come up if she wants to, even without laughing—and she knows it." And he looked mysteriously and secretly at Mary Poppins as she stood down there on the hearth-rug.

"Well," said Mary Poppins, "it's all very silly and undignified, but, since you're all up there and don't seem able to get down, I suppose I'd better come up, too."

With that, to the surprise of Jane and Michael, she put her hands down at her sides and without a laugh, without even the faintest glimmer of a smile, she shot up through the air and sat down beside Jane.

"How many times, I should like to know," she said snappily, "have I told you to take off your coat when you come into a hot room?" And she unbuttoned Jane's coat and laid it neatly on the air beside the hat.

"That's right, Mary, that's right," said Mr. Wigg contentedly, as he leant down and put his spectacles on the mantelpiece. "Now we're all comfortable—"

"There's comfort *and* comfort," sniffed Mary Poppins.

"And we can have tea," Mr. Wigg went on, apparently not noticing her remark. And then a startled look came over his face.

"My goodness!" he said. "How dreadful! I've just realized—that table's down there and we're up here. What *are* we going to do? We're here and it's there. It's an awful tragedy—awful! But oh, it's terribly comic!" And he hid his face in his handkerchief and laughed loudly into it. Jane and Michael, though they did not want to miss the crumpets and the cake, couldn't help laughing too, because Mr. Wigg's mirth was so infectious.

Mr. Wigg dried his eyes.

"There's only one thing for it," he said. "We must think of something serious. Something sad, very sad. And then we shall be able to get down. Now—one, two, three! Something *very* sad, mind you!"

They thought and thought, with their chins on their hands. Michael thought of school, and that one day he would have to go there. But even that seemed funny today and he had to laugh. Jane thought: "I shall be grown up in another fourteen years!" But that didn't sound sad at all but quite nice and rather funny. She could not help smiling at the thought of herself grown up, with long skirts and a hand-bag.

"There was my poor old Aunt Emily," thought Mr. Wigg out loud. "She was run over by an omnibus. Sad. Very sad. Unbearably sad. Poor Aunt Emily. But they saved her umbrella. That was funny, wasn't it?" And before he knew where he was, he was heaving and trembling and bursting with laughter at the thought of Aunt Emily's umbrella.

"It's no good," he said, blowing his nose. "I give it up. And my young friends here seem to be no better at sadness than I am. Mary, can't you do something? We want our tea."

To this day Jane and Michael cannot be sure of what happened then. All they know for certain is that, as soon as Mr. Wigg had appealed to Mary Poppins, the table below began to wriggle on its legs. Presently it was swaying dangerously, and then with a rattle of china and with cakes lurching off their plates on to the cloth, the table came soaring through the room, gave one graceful turn, and landed beside them so that Mr. Wigg was at its head.

"Good girl!" said Mr. Wigg, smiling proudly upon her. "I knew you'd fix something. Now, will you take the foot of the table and pour out, Mary? And the guests on either side of me. That's the idea," he said, as Michael ran bobbing through the air and sat down on Mr. Wigg's right. Jane was at his left hand. There they were, all together, up in the air and the table between them. Not a single piece of bread-and-butter or a lump of sugar had been left behind.

Mr. Wigg smiled contentedly.

"It is usual, I think, to begin with bread-and-butter," he said to Jane and Michael, "but as it's my birthday we will begin the wrong way, which I always think is the right way—with the Cake!"

And he cut a large slice for everybody.

"More tea?" he said to Jane. But before he had time to reply there was a quick, sharp knock at the door.

## Heinrich Böll, *The Laugher,* translated by Leila Vennewitz

When someone asks me what business I am in, I am seized with embarrassment: I blush and stammer, I who am otherwise known as a man of poise. I envy people who can say: I am a bricklayer. I envy barbers, bookkeepers and writers the simplicity of their avowal, for all these professions speak for themselves and need no lengthy explanation, while I am constrained to reply to such questions: I am a laugher. An admission of this kind demands another, since I have to answer the second question: 'Is that how you make your living?' truthfully with 'Yes.' I actually do make a living at my laughing, and a good one too, for my laughing is—commercially speaking—much in demand. I am a good laugher, experienced, no one else laughs as well as I do, no one else has such command of the fine points of my art. For a long time, in order to avoid tiresome explanations, I called myself an actor, but my talents in the field of mime and elocution are so meager that I felt this designation to be too far from the truth: I love the truth, and the truth is: I am a laugher. I am neither a clown nor a comedian. I do not make people gay, I portray gaiety: I laugh like a Roman emperor, or like a sensitive schoolboy, I am as much at home in the laughter of the seventeenth century as in that of the nineteenth, and when occasion demands I laugh my way through all the centuries, all classes of society, all categories of age: it is simply a skill which I have acquired, like the skill of being able to repair shoes. In my breast I harbor the laughter of America, the laughter of Africa, white, red, yellow laughter—and for the right fee I let it peal out in accordance with the director's requirements.

I have become indispensable; I laugh on records, I laugh on tape, and television directors treat me with respect. I laugh mournfully, moderately, hysterically; I laugh like a streetcar conductor or like a helper in the grocery business; laughter in the morning, laughter in the evening, nocturnal laughter and the laughter of twilight. In short: wherever and however laughter is required—I do it.

It need hardly be pointed out that a profession of this kind is tiring, especially as I have also—this is my specialty—mastered the art of infectious laughter; this has also made me indispensable to third- and fourth-rate comedians, who are scared—and with good reason—that their audiences will miss their punch lines, so I spend most evenings in night clubs as a kind of discreet claque, my job being to laugh infectiously during the weaker parts of the program. It has to be carefully timed: my hearty, boisterous laughter must not come too soon, but neither must it come too late, it must come just at the right spot: at the pre-arranged moment I burst out laughing, the whole audience roars with me, and the joke is saved.

But as for me, I drag myself exhausted to the checkroom, put on my overcoat, happy that I can go off duty at last. At home I usually find telegrams waiting for me: 'Urgently require your laughter. Recording Tuesday,' and a few hours later I am sitting in an overheated express train bemoaning my fate.

I need scarcely say that when I am off duty or on vacation I have little inclination to laugh: the cowhand is glad when he can forget the cow, the bricklayer when he can forget the mortar, and carpenters usually have doors at home which don't work or drawers which are hard to open. Confectioners like sour pickles, butchers like marzipan, and the baker prefers sausage to bread; bullfighters raise pigeons for a hobby, boxers turn pale when their children have nosebleeds: I find all this quite natural, for I never laugh off duty. I am a very solemn person, and people consider me—perhaps rightly so—a pessimist.

During the first years of our married life, my wife would often say to me: 'Do laugh!' but since then she has come to realize that I cannot grant her this wish. I am happy when I am free to relax my tense face muscles, my frayed spirit, in profound solemnity. Indeed, even other people's laughter gets on my nerves, since it reminds me too much of my profession. So our marriage is a quiet, peaceful one, because my wife has also forgotten how to laugh: now and again I catch her smiling, and I smile too. We converse in low tones, for I detest the noise of the night clubs, the noise that sometimes fills the recording studios. People who do not know me think I am taciturn. Perhaps I am, because I have to open my mouth so often to laugh.

I go through life with an impassive expression, from time to time permitting myself a gentle smile, and I often wonder whether I have ever laughed. I think not. My brothers and sisters have always known me for a serious boy.

So I laugh in many different ways, but my own laughter I have never heard.

*Sometimes play can be used as an indirect approach to solving problems. This kind of play requires a sensitivity to the nature of conflict and confidence that affectionate, joking relationships can be a source of growth. The selections here suggest that it is important to think and talk about the different ways adults try to teach children outside of school, and the ways learning often takes place without books or formal instruction.*

## John Fire/Lame Deer and Richard Erdoes, *Lame Deer's Vision*

*Nonge Pahloka*—the Piercing of Her Ears—is a big event in a little girl's life. By this ceremony her parents, and especially her grandmother, want to show how much they love and honor her. They ask a man who is respected for his bravery or wisdom to pierce the ears of their daughter. The grandmother puts on a big feed. The little girl is placed on a blanket surrounded by the many gifts her family will give away in her name. The man who does the piercing is much admired and gets the most valuable gift. Afterward they get down to the really important part—the eating.

Well, one day I watched somebody pierce a girl's ears. I saw the fuss they made over it, the presents he got and all that. I thought I should do this to my little sister. She was about four years old at the time and I was nine. I don't know anymore what made me want to do this. Maybe I wanted to feel big and important like the man whom I had watched perform the ceremony. Maybe I wanted to get a big present. Maybe I wanted to make my sister cry. I don't remember what was in my little boy's mind then. I found some wire and made a pair of "ear rings" out of it. Then I asked my sister, "Would you like me to put these on you?" She smiled. "*Ohan*—yes." I didn't have the sharp bone one uses for the ear-piercing, and I didn't know the prayer that goes with it. I just had an old awl but thought it would do fine. Oh, how my sister yelled. I had to hold her down, but I got that awl through her earlobes and managed to put the "ear rings" in. I was proud of the neat job I had done.

When my mother came home and saw those wire loops in my sister's ears she gasped. But she recovered soon enough to go and tell my father. That was one of the few occasions he talked to me. He said, "I should punish you and whip you, but I won't. That's not my way. You'll get your punishment later." Well, some time passed and I forgot all about it. One morning my father announced that we were going to a powwow. He had hitched up the wagon and it was heaped high with boxes and bundles. At that powwow my father let it be known that he was doing a big *otuhan*—

a give-away. He put my sister on a rug, a pretty Navajo blanket, and laid out things to give away—quilts, food, blankets, a fine shotgun, his own new pair of cowboy boots, a sheepskin coat, enough to fit out a whole family. Dad was telling the people, "I want to honor my daughter for her ear-piercing. This should have been done openly, but my son did it at home. I guess he's too small. He didn't know any better." This was a long speech for Dad. He motioned me to come closer. I was sitting on my pretty gray horse. I thought we were both cutting a very fine figure. Well, before I knew it, Dad had given my horse away, together with its beautiful saddle and blanket. I had to ride home in the wagon and I cried all the way. The old man said, "You have your punishment now, but you will feel better later on. All her life your sister will tell about how you pierced her ears. She'll brag about you. I bet you are the only small boy who ever did this big ceremony."

That was no consolation to me. My beautiful gray was gone. I was heart-broken for three days. On the fourth morning I looked out the door and there stood a little white stallion with a new saddle and a silver-plated bit. "It's yours," my father told me. "Get on it." I was happy again.

### Carl Sandburg, *How the Hat Ashes Shovel Helped Snoo Foo*

If you want to remember the names of all six of the Sniggers children, remember that the three biggest were named Blink, Swink and Jink but the three littlest ones were named Blunk, Swunk and Junk. One day last January the three biggest had a fuss with the three littlest. The fuss was about a new hat for Snoo Foo, the snow man, about what kind of a hat he should wear and how he should wear it. Blink, Swink and Jink said, "He wants a crooked hat put on straight." Blunk, Swunk and Junk said, "He wants a straight hat put on crooked." They fussed and fussed. Blink fussed with Blunk, Swink fussed with Swunk, and Jink fussed with Junk. The first ones to make up after the fuss were Jink and Junk. They decided the best way to settle the fuss. "Let's put a crooked hat on crooked," said Jink. "No, let's put a straight hat on straight," said Junk. Then they stood looking and looking into each other's shiny laughing eyes and then both of them exploded to each other at the same time, "Let's put on two hats, a crooked hat crooked and a straight hat straight."

Well, they looked around for hats. But there were not any hats anywhere, that is, no hats big enough for a snow man with a big head like Snoo Foo. So they went in the house and asked their mother for *the hat ashes shovel*. Of course, in most any other house, the mother would be all worried if six children came tramping and clomping in, banging the door and all six ejaculating to their mother at once, "Where is the hat ashes shovel?" But Missus Sniggers wasn't worried at all. She rubbed her chin with her finger and said softly, "Oh lah de dab, oh la de dah, where is that hat ashes shovel, last week I had it when I was making a hat for Mister Sniggers; I remember I had that hat ashes shovel right up here over the clock, oh lah de dah, oh lah de dah. Go out and ring the front door bell," she said to Jink Sniggers. Jink ran away to the front door. And Missus Sniggers and the five children waited. Bling-bling the bell began ringing and—listen—the door of the clock opened and the hat ashes shovel fell out. "Oh lah de dah, get out of here in a hurry," said Missus Sniggers.

Well, the children ran out and dug a big pail of hat ashes with the hat ashes shovel. And they made two hats for Snoo Foo. One was a crooked hat. The other was a straight hat. And they put the crooked hat on crooked and the straight hat on straight. And there stood Snoo Foo in the front yard and everybody who came by on the street, he would take off his hat to them, the crooked hat with his arm crooked and the straight hat with his arm straight. That was the end of the fuss between the Sniggers children and it was Jink, the littlest one of the biggest, and Junk, the littlest one of the littlest, who settled the fuss by looking clean into each other's eyes and laughing. If you ever get into a fuss try this way of settling it.

*Here are some dialogues between a father and daughter by Gregory Bateson. They are delightful conversations that explicitly raise dozens of questions and illustrate how rewarding playful relationships between parents and children can be.*

## Gregory Bateson, Metalogue: About Games and Being Serious

DAUGHTER:  Daddy, are these conversations serous?
FATHER:    Certainly they are.
D:         They're not a sort of game that you play with me?
F:         God forbid . . . but they are a sort of game that we play together.
D:         Then they're *not* serious!

F:         Suppose you tell me what you would understand by the words "serious" and "game".
D:         Well . . . if you're . . . I don't know.

F:      If I am what?

D:      I mean . . . the conversations are serious for me, but if you are only playing a game . . .

F:      Steady now. Let's look at what is good and what is bad about "playing" and "games". First of all, I don't mind—not much—about winning or losing. When your questions put me in a tight spot, sure, I try a little harder to think straight and to say clearly what I mean. But I don't bluff and I don't set traps. There is no temptation to cheat.

D:      That's just it. It's not serious to you. It's a game. People who cheat just don't know how to *play*. They treat the game as though it were serious.

F:      But it *is* serious.

D:      No, it isn't—not for you it isn't.

F:      Because I don't even want to cheat?

D:      Yes—partly that.

F:      But do you want to cheat and bluff all the time?

D:      No—of course not.

F:      Well then?

D:      Oh—Daddy—you'll *never* understand.

F:      I guess I never will.

F:      Look, I scored a sort of debating point just now by forcing you to admit that you don't want to cheat—and then I tied onto that admission the conclusion that therefore the conversations are not "serious" for you either. Was that a sort of cheating?

D:      Yes—sort of.

F:      I agree—I think it was. I'm sorry.

D:      You see, Daddy—if I cheated or wanted to cheat, that would mean that I was not serious about the things we talk about. It would mean that I was only playing a game with you.

F:      Yes, that makes sense.

D:      But it doesn't make sense, Daddy. It's an awful muddle.

F:      Yes—a muddle—but still a sort of sense.

D:      How, Daddy?

F:      Wait a minute. This is difficult to say. First of all—I think that we get somewhere with these conversations. I enjoy them very much and I think you do. But also, apart from that, I think that we get some ideas straight and I think that the muddles help. I mean—that if we both spoke logically all the time, we would never get anywhere. We would only parrot all the old clichés that everybody has repeated for hundreds of years.

D: What is a cliché, Daddy?

F: A cliché? It's a French word, and I think it was originally a printer's word. When they print a sentence they have to take the separate letters and put them one by one into a sort of grooved stick to spell out the sentence. But for words and sentences which people use often, the printer keeps little sticks of letters ready made up. And these ready-made sentences are called clichés.

D: But I've forgotten now what you were saying about clichés, Daddy.

F: Yes—it was about the muddles that we get into in these talks and how getting into muddles makes a sort of sense. If we didn't get into muddles, our talks would be like playing rummy without first shuffling the cards.

D: Yes, Daddy—but what about those things—the ready-made sticks of letters?

F. The clichés? Yes—it's the same thing. We all have lots of ready-made phrases and ideas, and the printer has ready-made sticks of letters, all sorted out into phrases. But if the printer wants to print something new—say, something in a new language, he will have to break up all that old sorting of the letters. In the same way, in order to think new thoughts or to say new things, we have to break up all our ready-made ideas and shuffle the pieces.

D: But, Daddy, the printer would not shuffle all the letters? Would he? He wouldn't shake them all up in a bag. He would put them one by one in their places—all the *a*'s in one box and all the *b*'s in another, and all the commas in another, and so on.

F: Yes—that's right. Otherwise he would go mad trying to find an *a* when he wanted it.

F: What are you thinking?

D: No, it's only that there are so many questions.

F: For example?—

D: Well, I see what you mean about our getting into muddles.

That that makes us say new sorts of things. But I am thinking about the printer. He has to keep all his little letters
sorted out even though he breaks up all the ready-made
phrases. And I am wondering about our muddles. Do we
have to keep the little pieces of our thought in some sort of
order—to keep from going mad?

F:    I think so—yes—but I don't know *what* sort of order. That
would be a terribly hard question to answer. I don't think
we could get an answer to that question today.

F:    You said there were "so many questions." Do you have
another?

D:    Yes—about games and being serious. That's what we
started from, and I don't know how or why that led us to
talk about our muddles. The way you confuse everything—it's a sort of cheating.

F:    No, absolutely not.

F:    You brought up two questions. And really there are a lot
more . . . We started from the question about these conversations—are they serious? Or are they a sort of game?
And you felt hurt that I might be playing a game, while
you were serious. It looks as though a conversation is a
game if a person takes part in it with one set of emotions
or ideas—but not a "game" if his ideas or emotions are
different.

D:    Yes, it's if your ideas about the conversation are different
from mine . . .

F:    If we *both* had the game idea, it would be all right?

D:    Yes—of course.

F:    Then it seems to be up to me to make clear what I mean by
the game idea. I know that I am serious—whatever that
means—about the things that we talk about. We talk about
ideas. And I know that I play with the ideas in order to
understand them and fit them together. It's "play" in the
same sense that a small child "plays" with blocks . . . And a
child with building blocks is mostly very serious about his
"play."

D:    But is it a *game*, Daddy? Do you play *against* me?

F:    No. I think of it as you and I playing together against the
building blocks—the ideas. Sometimes competing a bit—

but competing as to who can get the next idea into place. And sometimes we attack each other's bit of building, or I will try to defend my built-up ideas from your criticism. But always in the end we are working together to build the ideas up so that they will stand.

D:   Daddy, do our talks have *rules?* The difference between a game and just playing is that a game has rules.

F:   Yes. Let me think about that. I think do have a sort of rules . . . and I think a child playing with blocks has rules. The blocks themselves make a sort of rules. They will balance in certain positions and thev will not balance in other positions. And it would be a sort of cheating if the child used glue to make the blocks stand up in a position from which they would otherwise fall.

D:   But what rules do *we* have?

F:   Well, the ideas that we play with bring in a sort of rules. There are rules about how ideas will stand up and support each other. And if they are wrongly put together the whole building falls down.

D:   No glue, Daddy?

F:   No—no glue. Only logic.

D:   But you said that if we always talked logically and did not get into muddles, we could never say anything new. We could only say ready-made things. What did you call those things?

F:   Clichés. Yes. Glue is what clichés are stuck together with.

D:   But you said "logic," Daddy.

F:   Yes, I know. We're in a muddle again. Only I don't see a way out of this particular muddle.

D:   How did we get into it, Daddy?

F:   All right, let's see if we can retrace our steps. We were talking about the "rules" of these conversations. And said that the ideas that we play with have rules of logic . . .

D:   Daddy! Wouldn't it be a good thing if we had a few more rules and obeyed them more carefully? Then we might not get into these dreadful muddles.

F:   Yes. But wait. You mean that I get us into these muddles because I cheat against rules which we don't have. Or put it this way. That we might have rules which would stop us from getting into muddles—as long as we obeyed them.

D: Yes, Daddy, that's what the rules of a game are for.

F: Yes, but do you want to turn these conversations into *that* sort of a game? I'd rather play canasta—which is fun too.

D: Yes, that's right. We can play canasta whenever we want to. But at the moment I would rather play this game. Only I don't know what sort of a game this is. Nor what sort of rules it has.

F: And yet we have been playing for some time.

D: Yes. And it's been fun.

F: Yes.

F: Let's go back to the question which you asked and which I said was too difficult to answer today. We were talking about the printer breaking up his clichés, snd you said that he would still keep some sort of order among his letters—to keep from going mad. And then you asked "What sort of order should we cling to so that when we get into a muddle we do not go mad?" It seems to me that the "rules" of the game is only another name for that sort of order.

D: Yes—and cheating is what gets us into muddles.

F: In a sense, yes. That's right. Except that the whole point of the game is that we do get into muddles, and do come out on the other side, and if there were no muddles our "game" would be like canasta or chess—and that is not how we want it to be.

D: Is it *you* that make the rules, Daddy? Is that fair?

F: That, daughter, is a dirty crack. And probably an unfair one. But let me accept it at face value. Yes, it is I who make the rules—after all, I do not want us to go mad.

D: All right. But, Daddy, do you also change the rules? Sometimes?

F: Hmm, another dirty crack. Yes, daughter, I change them constantly. Not all of them, but some of them.

D: I wish you'd tell me when you're going to change them!

F: Hmm—yes—again. I wish I could. But it isn't like that. If it were like chess or canasta, I could tell you the rules, and we could, if we wanted to, stop playing and discuss the rules. And then we could start a new game with the new rules. But what rules would hold us between the two games? While we were discussing the rules?

D:     I don't understand.

F:     Yes. The point is that the purpose of these conversations is to discover the "rules." It's like life—a game whose purpose is to discover the rules, which rules are always changing and always undiscoverable.

D:     But I don't call that a *game*, Daddy.

F:     Perhaps not. I would call it a game, or at any rate "play." But it certainly is not like chess or canasta. It's more like what kittens and puppies do. Perhaps. I don't know.

D:     Daddy, what do kittens and puppies play?

F:     I don't know—I don't know.

---

*The idea of the innocence and joy of childhood is common to many people, and it arises very early in life. Perhaps the sorrows and difficulties we all face lead to reveries of an earlier, happier time as well as to hopes for a better future. Reflecting on early childhood, as these selections do, and sharing first memories is a wonderful and playful way to come close to somebody. The memories of eight-year-olds can be as interesting as the memories of forty-year-olds. There can be nothing more playful than indulging in nostalgia with children.*

## Lewis Carroll, *Alice in Wonderland*

"No, no!" said the Queen. "Sentence first—verdict afterwards."

"Stuff and nonsense!" said Alice loudly. "The idea of having the sentence first!"

"Hold your tongue!" said the Queen, turning purple.

"I won't!" said Alice.

"Off with her head!" the Queen shouted at the top of her voice. Nobody moved.

"Who cares for *you?*" said Alice (she had grown to her full size by this time). "You're nothing but a pack of cards!"

At this the whole pack rose up into the air, and came flying down upon her; she gave a little scream, half of fright and half of anger, and tried to beat them off, and found herself lying on the bank, with her head in the lap of her sister, who was gently brushing away some dead leaves that had fluttered down, from the trees upon her face.

"Wake up, Alice dear!" said her sister. "Why, what a long sleep you've had!"

"Oh, I've had such a curious dream!" said Alice. And she told her sister, as well as she could remember them, all these strange Adventures of hers that you have just been reading about; and, when she had finished, her sister kissed her, and said "It *was* a curious dream, dear, certainly; but now run in to your tea: it's getting late." So Alice got up and ran off, thinking while she ran, as well she might, what a wonderful dream it had been.

But her sister sat still just as she left her, leaning her head on her hand, watching the setting sun, and thinking of little Alice and all her wonderful Adventures, till she too began dreaming after a fashion, and this was her dream:

First, she dreamed about little Alice herself: once again the tiny hands were clasped upon her knee, and the bright eager eyes were looking up into hers—she could hear the very tones of her voice, and see that queer little toss of her head to keep back the wandering hair that *would* always get into her eyes—and still as she listened, or seemed to listen, the whole place around her became alive with the strange creatures of her little sister's dream.

The long grass rustled at her feet as the White Rabbit hurried by—the frightened Mouse splashed his way through the neighbouring pool—she could hear the rattle of the teacups as the March Hare and his friends shared their never-ending meal, and the shrill voice of the Queen ordering off her unfortunate guests to execution—once more the pig-baby was sneezing on the Duchess's knee, while plates and dishes crashed around it—once more the shriek of the Gryphon, the squeaking of the Lizard's slate-pencil, and the choking of the suppressed guinea pigs, filled the air, mixed up with the distant sob of the miserable Mock Turtle.

So she sat on, with closed eyes, and half believed herself in Wonderland, though she knew she had but to open them again, and all would change to dull reality—the grass would be only rustling in the wind, and the pool rippling to the waving of the reeds—the rattling teacups would change to tinkling sheep-bells, and the Queen's shrill cries to the voice of the shepherd-boy—and the sneeze of the baby, the shriek of the Gryphon, and all the other queer noises, would change (she knew) to the confused clamour of the busy farm-yard—while the lowing of the cattle in the distance would take the place of the Mock Turtle's heavy sobs.

Lastly, she pictured to herself how this same little sister of hers would, in the after-time, be herself a grown woman; and how she would keep, through all her riper years, the simple and loving heart of her childhood; and how she would gather about her other little children, and make *their* eyes bright and eager with many a strange tale, perhaps even with the dream of Wonderland of long ago; and how she would feel with all their simple sorrows, and find a pleasure in all their simple joys, remembering her own childlife, and the happy summer days.

### James M. Barrie, *Peter Pan*

Mrs. Darling first heard of Peter when she was tidying up her children's minds. It is the nightly custom of every good mother after her children are asleep to rummage in their minds and put things straight for next morning, repacking into their proper places the many articles that have wandered during the day. If you could keep awake (but of course you can't) you would see your own mother doing this, and you would find it very interesting to watch her. It is quite like tidying up drawers. You would see her on her knees, I expect, lingering humorously over some of your contents, wondering where on earth you had picked this thing up, making discoveries sweet and not so sweet, pressing this to her cheek as if it were as nice as a kitten, and hurriedly stowing that out of sight. When you wake in the morning, the naughtinesses and evil passions with which you went to bed have been folded up small and placed at the bottom of your mind, and on the top, beautifully aired, are spread out your prettier thoughts, ready for you to put on.

I don't know whether you have ever seen a map of a person's mind. Doctors sometimes draw maps of other parts of you, and your own map can become intensely interesting, but catch them trying to draw a map of a child's mind, which is not only confused, but keeps going round all the time. There are zigzag lines on it, just like your temperature on a card, and these are probably roads in the island, for the Neverland is always more or less an island, with astonishing splashes of colour here and there, and coral reefs and rakish-looking craft in the offing, and savages and lonely lairs, and gnomes who are mostly tailors, and caves through which a river runs, and princes with six elder brothers, and a hut fast going to decay, and one very small old lady with a hooked nose. It would be an easy map if that were all, but there is also first day at school, religion, fathers, the round pond, needle-work, murders, hangings, verbs that take the dative, chocolate pudding day, getting into braces, say ninety-nine, threepence for pulling out your tooth yourself, and so on, and either these are part of the island or they are another map showing through, and it is all rather confusing, especially as nothing will stand still.

Of course the Neverlands vary a good deal. John's, for instance, had a lagoon with flamingoes flying over it at which John was shooting, while

Michael, who was very small, had a flamingo with lagoons flying over it. John lived in a boat turned upside down on the sands, Michael in a wigwam, Wendy in a house of leaves deftly sewn together. John had no friends, Michael had friends at night, Wendy had a pet wolf forsaken by its parents. But on the whole the Neverlands have a family resemblance, and if they stood still in a row you could say of them that they have each other's nose, and so forth. On these magic shores children at play are for ever beaching their coracles. We too have been there; we can still hear the sound of the surf, though we shall land no more.

Of all delectable islands the Neverland is the snuggest and most compact, not large and sprawly, you know, with tedious distances between one adventure and another, but nicely crammed. When you play at it by day with the chairs and tablecloth, it is not in the least alarming, but in the two minutes before you go to sleep it becomes very nearly real. That is why there are night-lights.

Occasionally in her travels through her children's minds Mrs. Darling found things she could not understand, and of these quite the most perplexing was the word Peter. She knew of no Peter, and yet he was here and there in John and Michael's minds, while Wendy's began to be scrawled all over with him. The name stood out in bolder letters than any of the other words, and as Mrs. Darling gazed she felt that it had an oddly cocky appearance.

"Yes, he is rather cocky," Wendy admitted with regret. Her mother had been questioning her.

"But who is he, my pet?"

"He is Peter Pan, you know, mother."

At first Mrs. Darling did not know, but after thinking back into her childhood she just remembered a Peter Pan who was said to live with the fairies. There were odd stories about him, as that when children died he went part of the way with them, so that they should not be frightened. She had believed in him at the time, but now that she was married and full of sense she quite doubted whether there was any such person.

"Besides," she said to Wendy, "he would be grown up by this time."

"Oh no, he isn't grown up," Wendy assured her confidently, "and he is just my size." She meant that he was her size in both mind and body; she didn't know how she knew it, she just knew it.

Mrs. Darling consulted Mr. Darling, but he smiled pooh-pooh. "Mark my words," he said, "it is some nonsense Nana has been putting into their heads; just the sort of idea a dog would have. Leave it alone, and it will blow over."

But it would not blow over, and soon the troublesome boy gave Mrs. Darling quite a shock.

Children have the strangest adventures without being troubled by them. For instance, they may remember to mention, a week after the event happened, that when they were in the wood they met their dead father and had a game with him. It was in this casual way that Wendy one morning made a disquieting revelation. Some leaves of a tree had been found on the nursery floor, which certainly were not there when the children went to bed, and Mrs. Darling was puzzling over them when Wendy said with a tolerant smile:

"I do believe it is that Peter again!"

"Whatever do you mean, Wendy!"

"It is so naughty of him not to wipe," Wendy said, sighing. She was a tidy child.

She explained in quite a matter-of-fact way that she thought Peter sometimes came to the nursery in the night and sat on the foot of her bed and played on his pipes to her. Unfortunately she never woke, so she didn't know how she knew, she just knew.

"What nonsense you talk, precious! No one can get into the house without knocking."

"I think he comes in by the window," she said.

"My love, it is three floors up."

"Weren't the leaves at the foot of the window, mother?"

It was quite true; the leaves had been found very near the window.

Mrs. Darling did not know what to think, for it all seemed so natural to Wendy that you could not dismiss it by saying she had been dreaming.

"My child," the mother cried, "why did you not tell me of this before?"

"I forgot," said Wendy lightly. She was in a hurry to get her breakfast.

Oh, surely she must have been dreaming;

But, on the other hand, there were the leaves. Mrs. Darling examined them carefully; they were skeleton leaves, but she was sure did not come from any tree that grew in England. She crawled about the floor, peering at it with a candle for marks of a strange foot. She rattled the poker up the chimney and tapped the walls. She let down a tape from the window to the pavement, and it was a sheer drop of thirty feet, without so much as a spout to climb up by.

Certainly Wendy had been dreaming.

But Wendy had not been dreaming as the very next night showed, the night on which the extraordinary adventures of these children may be said to have begun.

On the night we speak of all the children were once more in bed. It happened to be Nana's evening off, and Mrs. Darling had bathed them and sung to them till one by one they had let go her hand and slid away into the land of sleep.

All were looking so safe and cosy that she smiled at her fears now and sat down tranquilly by the fire to sew.

It was something for Michael, who on his birthday was getting into shirts. The fire was warm, however, and the nursery dimly lit by three nightlights, and presently the sewing lay on Mrs. Darling's lap. Then her head nodded, oh, so gracefully. She was asleep. Look at the four of them, Wendy and Michael over there, John here, and Mrs. Darling by the fire. There should have been a fourth night-light.

While she slept she had a dream. She dreamt that the Neverland had come too near and that a strange boy had broken through from it. He did not alarm her, for she thought she had seen him before in the faces of many women who have no children. Perhaps he is to be found in the faces of some mothers also. But in her dream he had rent the film that obscures the Neverland, and she saw Wendy and John and Michael peeping through the gap.

The dream by itself would have been a trifle, but while she was dreaming the window of the nursery blew open, and a boy did drop on the floor. He was accompanied by a strange light, no bigger than your fist, which darted about the room like a living thing, and I think it must have been this light that wakened Mrs. Darling.

She started up with a cry, and saw the boy, and somehow she knew at once that he was Peter Pan. If you or I or Wendy had been there we should have seen that he was very like Mrs. Darling's kiss. He was a lovely boy, clad in skeleton leaves and the juices that ooze out of trees, but the most entrancing thing about him was that he had all his first teeth. When he saw she was a grown-up, he gnashed the little pearls at her.

# PART 2

# Values That Relate to People One Knows (Loyalty, Generosity, Empathy, Honesty, and Adaptability)

# Introduction

———⊷∘⊰———

Walt Whitman's *Song of Myself* begins:

I celebrate myself, and sing myself,
And what I assume you shall assume,
For every atom belonging to me as good as belongs to you.

People are inextricably connected to one another. That connection can be strong or weak, salutary or damaging. As a consequence, certain values relate to the development of positive social relationships. When people respect one another and see themselves as neighbors with much in common, they can cooperate in making their social world. But if people consider only their own security and pleasure, then intimacy and friendship are compromised.

During the preadolescent years, close bonds within the family and with friends and neighbors evolve, and children make choices in relationships which previously were taken for granted. That is the stage of life when we become aware that other people don't always make the same choices we do. One person's values can produce conflicts that challenge our own—and test our character.

It's not possible to avoid this challenge; we can only succeed or fail in meeting it. Our lives have to be lived with others—that's a fact we can't run away from. In time we learn that to live in total solitude, to be entirely alone, is to be lost. Safety from the risks of relationship is fantasy, but there is no safe place without it; there is no "where" there. And if there is no "where," as Stephen Sondheim warns in his song *No More*, "You'll only be wandering blind."

For preadolescents some of the specific character values evolving in relation to others close to home, in their families, and in their communities are *loyalty, generosity, empathy, honesty,* and *adaptability.*

## LOYALTY

Faithfulness to people or ideas is tested time and again during childhood. Do you stick up for friends when they are ridiculed or rejected by a group? What do you do if people make fun of your family or culture? What makes sticking to your guns more important than popularity? And what do you do when loyalties are in conflict—when friends' or family ideas differ from your own? As the protagonists in our selections make clear, none of these questions has a simple answer.

## GENEROSITY

An open and giving attitude toward others is one of the gifts of childhood, one that can disappear in encounters with the hostile or indifferent faces that the world often confronts us with. It takes strength and intelligence to resist becoming suspicious and guarded, especially since innocent generosity can easily be taken advantage of. Tutoring and nurturing generous impulses are essential challenges of raising children, and through stories and tales that delicate aspect of character can be preserved.

## EMPATHY

Fellow feeling, the ability to reach out and understand someone else on her or his own terms, is central to the development of personal relationships. It is easy to misunderstand other people or to be afraid of them. But it is also possible to be sensitive to other people's concerns and experience. Doing that requires developing the imaginative ability to share in their feelings and ideas almost as if they were your own; being almost at one with them while being, at the same time, your own person. Poetry and fiction are full of empathy, which is so much a part of how young people root themselves in the world of others. The success of that connection is the foundation of social cohesion.

## HONESTY

A personal commitment to telling the truth and taking the consequences does not magically emerge in childhood. Nor does a sensitivity to the dangers of a brutal honesty which seeks to wound. The kind of honest person we prize maintains an open and giving attitude toward others. A consistently honest though sensitive person has an underlying sense of what is necessary and what is appropriate.

## ADAPTABILITY

Developing and maintaining the ability to change ideas or habits when they become dysfunctional and to deal with unexpected encounters in life is a lifelong challenge. It is important for youngsters to understand when to adapt and when to remain firm. Old habits can be the worst of friends in new circumstances, especially when situations threaten to spin out of control. Children's recognition that they can adapt themselves without undermining the core of their being, perhaps even enhancing it, is an important lesson as they become independent and are expected to take control of their own lives.

# Loyalty

———❦———

To be faithful to people close to you and to be true to your beliefs means that you can be depended on for support when needed—for a helping hand, for friendly counsel, and for solidarity with colleagues and allies.

In *Ecclesiasticus* 27:17–18, we are reminded,

> Love thy friend, and be faithful: but if you betrayest a friend's secrets, follow no more after. For as you might destroy an enemy, so hath thou lost the love of thy neighbor.

People will recognize you as faithful if they can safely confide in you, if you honor them even in their absence, and if you protect their best interests when it is in your power to do so. Do not forget the people and ideas you've been close to. There is great comfort for those who know you, if they can be sure of you even during long periods of separation. W. B. Yeats said it elegantly in *The Lover Pleads with His Friends for Old Friends*:

> Though you are in your shining days,
> Voices among the crowd
> And new friends busy with your praise,
> Be not unkind or proud,
> But think about old friends the most:
> Time's bitter flood will rise,
> Your beauty perish and be lost
> For all eyes but these eyes.

Loyalty is tested in the face of need and crisis, but it is forged in small acts of consideration and dependability. It is no good to regret later what you could have done when you were called on. This conversation in Laurence Sterne's *A Sentimental Journey* opens the curtain on the difference between actions and good intentions:

> Thou hast one comfort, friend said I, at least in the loss of thy poor beast; I'm sure thou hast been a merciful master to him.—Alas, said the mourner, I thought so, when he was alive—but now that he is dead, I think otherwise.—I fear the weight of myself and my afflictions together have been too much for him, and I fear I have them to answer for.

But, as William Steig recalls in *Amos and Boris*, even the smallest of us can befriend and remain critically loyal to those who are as big as giants. Boris is a huge whale, and Amos is a little mouse. Boris saves Amos's life and they become friends—but their lives must be lived in very different ways and in different places.

> The time came to say goodbye. They were at the shore. "I wish we could be friends forever," said Amos. "We will be friends forever, but we can't be together. You must live on land, and I must live at sea. I'll never forget you though."
>
> "And you can be sure I'll never forget you," said Amos.

They do remember each other—and years later Boris is washed up on a beach in a hurricane and can't move. He will die, but Amos comes along, recognizes Boris, and, despite his own small size, figures out a way to return Boris to the water by getting two elephants to help. Once Boris is back in the water, they bid each other farewell, with tears in their eyes. Even though they are not likely to see each other again, they know for sure now they will never forget each other.

Friends, parents, and children, allies in a great cause, have big enough hearts to hold a mess of troubles for one another—as if a piece of one person's heart were always available to suffer with others.

---

*Geoffrey Canada's* Grandma *reminds us that we first know loyalty, and perhaps we know it best, in our families. Despite disputes or great distances, family members will very often be able to depend on one another for help in troubled times. Sara, in* A Little Princess, *uses the memory of her father's love to strengthen her in the face of hardship. Even across generations, we can find support and dependability either from the actual help we are given or from memories to call on and to learn from when the need arises.*

**Frances Hodgson Burnett, *A Little Princess***

"My mamma has a diamond ring which cost forty pounds," she said. "And it is not a big one, either. If there were mines full of diamonds, people would be so rich it would be ridiculous,"

"Perhaps Sara will be so rich that she will be ridiculous," giggled Jessie.

"She's ridiculous without being rich," Lavinia sniffed

"I believe you hate her," said Jessie.

"No, I don't," snapped Lavinia. "But I don't believe in mines full of diamonds."

"Well, people have to get them from somewhere," said Jessie. "Lavinia"—with a new giggle—"what do you think Gertrude says?"

"I don't know, I'm sure; and I don't care if it's something more about that everlasting Sara."

"Well, it is. One of her 'pretends' is that she is a princess. She plays it all the time—even in school. She says it makes her learn her lessons better. She wants Ermengarde to be one, too, but Ermengarde says she is too fat."

"She *is* too fat," said Lavinia. "And Sara is too thin."

Naturally, Jessie giggled again.

"She says it has nothing to do with what you look like, or what you have. It has only to do with what you *think* of, and what you *do*."

"I suppose she thinks she could be a princess if she was a beggar," said Lavinia.

. . .

It seemed a strange thing to remember that she—the drudge whom the cook had said insulting things to an hour ago—had only a few years ago been surrounded by people who all treated her as Ram Dass had treated her; who salaamed when she went by, whose foreheads almost touched the ground when she spoke to them, who were her servants and her slaves. It was like a sort of dream. It was all over, and it could never come back. It certainly seemed that there was no way in which any change could take place. She knew what Miss Minchin intended that her future should be. So long as she was too young to be used as a regular teacher, she would be used as an errand girl and servant and yet expected to remember what she had learned and in some mysterious way to learn more. The greater number of her evenings she was supposed to spend at study, and at various indefinite intervals she was examined and knew she would have been severely admonished if she had not advanced as was expected of her. The truth, indeed, was that Miss Minchin knew that she was too anxious to learn to require teachers. Give her books, and she would devour them and end by knowing them by heart. She might be trusted to be equal to teaching a good deal in the course of a few years. This was what would happen: when she was older she would be expected to drudge in the school-room as she drudged now in various parts of the house; they would be obliged to give her more respectable clothes, but they would be sure to be plain and ugly and to make her look somehow like a servant. That was all there seemed to be to look forward to, and Sara stood quite still for several minutes and thought it over.

Then a thought came back to her which made the color rise in her cheek and a spark light itself in her eyes. She straightened her thin little body and lifted her head.

"Whatever comes," she said, "cannot alter one thing. If I am a princess in rags and tatters, I can be a princess inside. It would be easy to be a princess if I were dressed in cloth of gold, but it is a great deal more of a triumph to be one all the time when no one knows it. There was Marie Antoinette when she was in prison and her throne was gone and she had only a black gown on, and her hair was white, and they insulted her and called her Widow Capet. She was a great deal more like a queen then than when she was so gay and everything was so grand. I like her best then. Those howling mobs of people did not frighten her. She was stronger than they were, even when they cut her head off."

This was not a new thought, but quite an old one, by this time. It had consoled her through many a bitter day, and she had gone about the house with an expression on her face which Miss Minchin could not understand and which was a source of great annoyance to her, as it seemed as if the child were mentally living a life which held her above the rest of the world. It was as if she scarcely heard the rude and acid things said to her; or, if she heard them, did not care for them at all. Sometimes, when she was in the midst of some harsh, domineering speech, Miss Minchin would find the still, unchildish eyes fixed upon her with something like a proud smile in them. At such times she did not know that Sara was saying to herself:

"You don't know that you are saying these things to a princess, and that if I chose I could wave my hand and order you to execution. I only spare you because I *am* a princess, and you are a poor, stupid, unkind, vulgar old thing, and don't know any better."

This used to interest and amuse her more than anything else; and queer and fanciful as it was, she found comfort in it and it was a good thing for her. While the thought held possession of her, she could not be made rude and malicious by the rudeness and malice of those about her.

"A princess must be polite," she said to herself.

## Geoffrey Canada, *Grandma's Cherries*

America has won a great victory as the Soviet Union has turned toward democracy and turned its nuclear missiles away from our shores. But we have shown little of the grace and compassion at home that this victory should have produced. We have turned from a cold war with the Soviet Union to a cold war with poor Americans, mostly poor women and children. I have heard much debate about the poor, much of it threatening and angry. There is so much this country needs to understand and to do about poverty.

I grew up in the Bronx. My mother raised my three brothers and me by herself. When she couldn't find work, we went on welfare. When she could find work, it was jobs that paid women—especially black women—so little money that we couldn't tell the difference between welfare and work except that our mother wasn't home when she was working.

People talk about poverty and the poor like it's so easy not to be poor. But I know a different story. It takes great sacrifice and talent to work your way out of poverty. My mother used to make all of her own clothes. You couldn't raise four boys on her salary and afford to buy dresses to wear to work. When we were young, she used to make our clothes, cut our hair and make toys for us out of cereal boxes. All her life she sacrificed for us. She put off getting her college degree and her master's degree until we were grown and on our own.

And you know what? We hated being poor. We loved our mother but we ruined her Christmas every year with our tears of disappointment at not getting exactly what we wanted. I couldn't help but be angry when my shoes had holes in them and there was no money to buy new ones. And I couldn't help but to stare angrily when I needed money to go on a school trip and there wasn't any money to be had.

And while there was much love in our family, being poor strained our loving bonds. We had to blame someone, and my mother was the only target. And here she was giving up all she had for us, going without lunch, without movies and nights out, walking 10 blocks to the train because she couldn't afford to pay the 15 cents extra to take the bus. And she would come home to four boys with their hands out, angry because we wanted something, needed something she could not give.

There are some Americans who think poverty stems from a lack of values and determination. But you can work hard all your life, have impeccable values and still be poor. My grandfather was the pastor of Mount Pleasant Baptist Church in Harlem. My grandmother was a Christian woman. They were hard-working, moral people. They were poor.

I lived with my grandparents during my high school years. My grandmother worked all her life: caring for other people's children, selling baked goods or Avon products, doing whatever she could do to help bring money into the house. She was a beautiful woman, kind and intelligent. She was determined to save my soul.

I was a wild and reckless adolescent whose soul was indeed in peril. And I fell in love with my grandmother. A deep love that any of us would develop if an angel came into of our lives. The more time I spent with her, the more I loved her. She cooled my hot temper and anger over being poor, and she showed me there was dignity even in poverty.

In all the years I knew her, she was never able to afford material things that others took for granted. She worked very hard but never could afford anything of luxury. She taught me how one could enjoy a deep spiritual love of life that was not tied to material things. This is a tough lesson to teach in a country that places so much value on materialism.

But each summer my grandmother and I would conspire to indulge her one vice: cherries. She loved cherries. Two or three times a week when my grandfather was at work we would walk the mile to the supermarket and buy half a pound of cherries. My grandmother and I would eat them secretly because grandfather would have had a fit if he'd known we spent an extra dollar a week on them.

My summers with my grandmother were measured by how good the cherries were that year. It was our little secret. And I was amazed by how much she loved cherries, and how expensive cherries were. Later when I went off to Bowdoin College in Brunswick, Me., I would sit in my room and think how much grandmother and grandfather had sacrificed for me to be in college.

I would fantasize about how when I graduated and got a good job, the first thing I would buy with my first check in August would be a whole crate of cherries. It would have to be August because our cherry summers taught us that August cherries were the sweetest. I would dream of wrapping the crate up in gift paper, putting a bow on it and presenting it to Grandma. And many a night I would go to sleep in the cold winter Maine night warmed by the vision of my grandmother's excitement when I brought her this small treasure.

Grandma died during my sophomore year. I never got to give her the cherries she would eat. And if you want my opinion, the summer of 1971, the last summer she was alive, was really the last great summer for cherries.

Poverty is tough on families in many ways. It's not quite as simple to get out of as people make out. We must be careful to make sure we build ladders so children and their families can climb out of poverty. It's not an easy climb. You can climb all your life and never make it out.

Grandma, who sacrificed so much for all of us, I just want to say I know that in all I've been acknowledged for, I still haven't reached the level of love and compassion that you tried to teach me. I think you accomplished your goal: you saved my soul. And I hope they let me bring gifts to Heaven. You'll know what's in the box.

———————

*But it is not simply what you get out of being loyal that counts, it's what you must contribute to mutually loyal relationships. In the following stories we see how the expression of love by a parent for a child can take various forms, sometimes requiring great restraint.*

### Beverly Cleary, *Ramona Quimby, Age 8*

During the night Ramona was half awakened when her mother wiped her face with a cool washcloth and lifted her head from the pillow to help her sip something cold. Later, as the shadows of the room were fading, Ramona had to hold a thermometer under her tongue for what seemed like a long time. She felt safe, knowing her mother was watching over her. Safe but sick. No sooner did she find a cool place on her pillow than it became too hot for comfort, and Ramona turned again.

As her room grew light, Ramona dozed off, faintly aware that her family was moving quietly so they would not disturb her. One tiny corner of her mind was pleased by this consideration. She heard breakfast sounds, and then she must have fallen completely asleep, because the next thing she knew she was awake and the house was silent. Had they all gone off and left her? No, someone was moving quietly in the kitchen. Howie's grandmother must have come to stay with her.

Ramona's eyes blurred. Her family had all gone off and left her when she was sick. She blinked away the tears and discovered on her bedside table a cartoon her father had drawn for her. It showed Ramona leaning against one tree and the family car leaning against another. He had drawn her with crossed eyes and a turned-down mouth. The car's headlights were crossed and its front bumper turned down like Ramona's mouth. They both looked sick. Ramona discovered she remembered how to smile. She also discovered she felt hot and sweaty instead of hot and dry. For a moment she struggled to sit up and then fell back on her pillow. Sitting up was too much work. She longed for her mother, and suddenly, as if her wish were granted, her mother was entering the bedroom with a basin of water and a towel.

"Mother!" croaked Ramona. "Why aren't you at work?"

"Because I stayed home to take care of you," Mrs. Quimby answered, as she gently washed Ramona's face and hands. "Feeling better?"

"Sort of." In some ways Ramona felt better, but she also felt sweaty, weak, and worried. "Are you going to lose your job?" she asked, remembering the time her father had been out of work.

"No. The receptionist who retired was glad to come in for a few days to take my place." Mrs. Quimby gave Ramona a sponge bath and helped her into cool, dry pajamas. "There," she said. "How about some tea and toast?"

"Grown-up tea?" asked Ramona, relieved that her mother's job was safe so that her father wouldn't have to drop out of school.

### Carlo Collodi, *Pinocchio*

As Pinocchio swam with all his might toward the shore, he noticed that his father, who was riding on his shoulders with his legs trailing in the water, was trembling violently as if he had a terrible chill and fever. Was he trembling because he was cold, or because he was afraid? It was hard to tell; perhaps it was a little of both. But Pinocchio, thinking that the poor old man was shivering from fear, tried to comfort him: "Don't be afraid, Daddy! In just a few minutes we'll reach land all safe and sound."

"But, for heaven's sake, where is the land?" asked the old man, becoming even more nervous and squinting like an old tailor threading a needle. "I've been looking all around and all I can see is the sea and the sky!"

"But I can see land, too," said the puppet. "Don't forget, I have eyes like a cat. I can see better at night than I can in the daytime."

However, poor Pinocchio was only pretending to be cheerful, but instead . . . instead, he was beginning to be very discouraged. He became weaker and weaker and he had begun to gasp for breath. In fact, he just couldn't swim any farther, and the shore was still a long way off! At last he turned to Geppetto and stammered brokenly, "Oh, Daddy . . . ! help me . . . I'm dying!"

Father and son were about to drown when suddenly they heard a voice in the darkness that sounded like a guitar out of tune. "Who's dying?" said the voice.

"Me—me and my poor old father!"

"It seems to me I know that voice! Sure, you're Pinocchio!"

"That's right, but who are you?"

"Me? I'm the Tuna, your old friend from the belly of the Shark."

"But how did you ever get away from there?"

"Well, I did just what you did. You showed me the way out, so I followed you and escaped the same way."

"Dear old friend, you've come just in time! Now, for the love of all your own little Tuna children, please help us, or we'll drown!"

"Of course, I'll be glad to help! Just grab my tail and I'll tow the two of you behind me. In four minutes I'll put you on shore."

As you can easily guess, Pinocchio and Geppetto quickly accepted the big Tuna's invitation, but instead of holding onto his tail, they decided that it would be better if they climbed right up and sat on his back.

"Are we too heavy for you?" asked Pinocchio

"Heavy—? Oh, no, you're light as a feather. It feels as if I have two empty snail shells on my back," answered the Tuna who was as big and strong as a two-year-old ox.

As soon as they reached land, Pinocchio jumped off the Tuna's back and then helped his father down. Then he turned to the Tuna and said in a voice filled with emotion, "Dear old friend, you have saved my Daddy's life and I just don't know how to thank you! At least, let me give you a big kiss as a token of my eternal gratitude."

The Tuna stuck his nose out of the water and Pinocchio, getting down on his knees, gave him an affectionate kiss right on the mouth. The poor Tuna, who was not really accustomed to such expression of warm affection, began to cry like a baby, and to hide his embarrassment, he suddenly plunged under the water and disappeared.

By this time the sun had risen and it was no longer dark. Pinocchio put out his arm to Geppetto who, by now, was so weak he could hardly stand. "Here Daddy, lean on my arm and let's go. We'll walk along very, very slowly, and when we get tired, we'll just stop and rest ourselves along the way."

"But where can we go?" asked Geppetto.

"We'll look for a house or a cottage where we can ask for a little bread and some straw to sleep on."

They had hardly walked a hundred steps along the way when they saw a pair of ugly beggars sitting beside the road. And just who do you suppose those two beggars turned out to be? You're absolutely right! They were none other than the Fox and the Cat, but they had changed so much you would hardly have recognized them. Imagine! The Cat had pretended to be blind for so long that by now he was really blind. And the Fox—he had grown so old that his fur was completely moth-eaten on one side, and he no longer had a tail. In fact, that poor old thief had become so miserable that he had been forced to sell his tail to a peddler who used it for a whisk to keep the flies off him.

"Hey there, Pinocchio!" shouted the Fox with his voice full of tears, "Give a little something to two poor souls !"

". . . two poor souls!" repeated the Cat.

"Keep away from me, you thieves!" answered the puppet, "You stole my money once, but you'll never get anything from me again!"

"Oh, but believe us this time, Pinocchio! We're really poor and sick now!"

". . . really poor and sick now!" repeated the Cat.

"Well, if you're poor and sick, it serves you right. Just remember the old saying, 'Stolen money doesn't bear interest.' So long, you thieves!"

"Please, have pity on us!"

". . . pity on us!"

"So long, you crooks. Remember the proverb, 'The devil's flour all turns to bran.'"

"Oh, don't abandon us!"

". . . abandon us!"

"Good-bye, robbers! Just remember the old saying, 'Whoever steals his neighbor's coat, usually dies without a shirt!' "

With this, Pinocchio and Geppetto went quietly on their way. But they had hardly gone another hundred steps, when at the end of a country lane, they saw a nice little cottage built of straw with a roof of red tile.

"Now, someone must be living in that cottage," said Pinocchio. "Let's knock at the door."

"Who's there?" asked a little voice from inside the cottage.

"It's only a poor old man and his son who have nothing to eat, and no roof over our heads," answered the puppet.

"Well, just turn the handle and the door'll open," said the same tiny voice.

Pinocchio turned the door handle and, sure enough, the door opened wide. They went into the cottage and they looked here, and they looked there, but they couldn't find anyone.

"Is there really anybody home?" asked Pinocchio in a loud voice.

"Here I am, up here!"

Father and son both quickly looked up toward the roof and there, sitting on a rafter, was—*Talking Cricket!*

"Oh, dear little Cricket!" cried Pinocchio with a deep bow.

"Aha! so now I'm your 'dear little Cricket,' am I? It seems to me I can remember a time when you wanted to get rid of me so bad you threw a wooden mallet at me to kill me!"

"Yes, you're right, Cricket! You should do the same to me—throw a wooden mallet at me ! But, please have pity on my poor old father."

"Well, for that matter, I'll have pity on both of you—father and son— but I just wanted to remind you of the cruel and heartless way you treated me. I just wanted to teach you a very important lesson. I wanted you to learn finally that in this world you should treat everyone with as much kindness and compassion as you possibly can because, some day, you too may need that same sort of kindness and compassion from others."

"Yes, you're right about that, Talking Cricket! You've been right about that all along, and I've really learned my lesson at last. But, tell me, how do you happen to be living in a pretty little cottage like this?"

"Well, it happens that this cottage was given to me only yesterday by a lovely goat with blue hair."

"Really? And now what has happened to this pretty goat?" asked Pinocchio anxiously.

"I really don't know."

"Will she ever come back?"

"No, she'll never come back again. She went away yesterday bleating mournfully in a voice that seemed to say, 'Poor little Pinocchio, I'll never see him again, ever . . . by this time that terrible Shark must have swallowed him up, and he's gone forever'!"

"Did that little blue-haired goat really say that? Then— then it must have been—oh! it must surely have been—yes, it was—it was my dear little Fairy!" and Pinocchio began to cry and sob piteously.

After he had cried a long time, Pinocchio finally dried his eyes and went about making a warm bed of straw for old Geppetto to sleep in. Then he turned to Talking Cricket and asked, "Tell me, where can I find a cup of milk for my poor old Daddy?"

"Well, about three miles from here there's a farmer—Giangio is his name. He keeps milk cows and you could try there if you want milk."

Pinocchio ran off at once to Giangio's farm and, when he got there, the farmer asked him, "How much milk do you want?"

"Oh, I only want a cupful," said Pinocchio.

"Well," said Giangio, "a cupful of milk'll cost you one *soldo*, so, first let's see your money. . . ."

"One soldo! Well, you see I don't even have—I thought—" and Pinocchio lowered his eyes and stammered in embarrassment.

"Look, puppet," said Giangio, "if you don't even have one soldo, why should I give you any milk?"

"Yes, I guess you're right," said Pinocchio, and he turned sadly away.

"Now, just a minute," said Giangio. "Maybe we can make a little deal. How'd you like to turn my *bindolo* for a while?"

"Turn your bindolo! What in the world is that?"

"That's a waterwheel that carries water up from the pond to water the fields."

"Well, I can try."

"All right, then, if you draw up a hundred buckets of water, I'll give you a cup of milk."

"I'll do it!"

Giangio led the puppet to the pond and harnessed him to the bindolo. Pinocchio went to work at once, but long before he was able to draw a hundred buckets of water, he found himself drenched with sweat from head to foot. He had never worked so hard before in his whole life!

"You understand," said Giangio, "that up to now, this work was done by my donkey. But now the poor animal is sick and dying."

"Oh, how awful!" said Pinocchio, "May I see him?"

"Of course."

When Pinocchio went into the farmer's stable, he saw a beautiful little donkey stretched out on a bed of straw. The poor little animal was worn out from hunger and ill-treatment. The puppet took one look at him and said to himself, "I've seen that little donkey before—I'm sure I know that face! " Then, in donkey language, he said, "Who are you?"

At this, the poor dying donkey opened his eyes and said—also in donkey language—"I'm . . . I'm Lamp . . . I'm Lampwick!" and with this he closed his eyes and died.

"Oh, poor Lampwick!" murmured Pinocchio, and he took a bit of straw and wiped away the tears that were streaming down his face.

"It seems to me," said Giangio, "you feel awfully sorry for a donkey that didn't cost you anything! What about me? I paid a lot of money for him in hard cash!"

"Sorry about that, but he was my friend."

"What do you mean, your friend?"

"Well, you see, he happened to be a schoolmate of mine."

"A schoolmate!" shouted Giangio in a burst of laughter. "You mean you had a *jackass* for a schoolmate? Just what kind of a school did you go to?"

The poor puppet was so embarrassed by these questions that he didn't answer. Instead, he just took his cup of milk and walked sadly back to the little cottage.

Then, from that day, for more than five months, Pinocchio got up every morning before dawn to go to Giangio's farm to draw water for his fields just to earn that daily cup of milk for Geppetto.

**Annette Kennerly,** *My Mother's Mother*
A small, strong woman,
Proud and plain.
Some would call her face hard . . .
But I see only strength and wisdom there.
A dark, plain overcoat,
A small-brimmed hat, no smile.
Annie Matthews.
My grandmother.
My mother's mother.
I never knew her.
At 52, hard work cut short her life—
Seventeen years before I came into this world.
And yet, through my mother's tales,
She lives with me.
My mother was forbidden to read books—
Only the idle could indulge in pastimes such as that.
So she read by candlelight in bed at night, secretly.
Annie Matthews—
Working to feed four children,
With an invalid husband, shell-shocked from the 14/18 War;
She was a fustian-cutter in a local factory.
Long hours, low pay,
Women's work.
Treading the boards in her wooden clogs and starched white apron,
Cutting the loops of a velvet pile with a thin, sharp blade—
Up and down the long benches with a steady hand.
When my mother was small, she would often be taken to the mill with
    her.
Curled up to sleep under the benches,
She would sometimes wake and see,
By flickering candlelight,
Vague female figures, dressed in white,
Gliding silently along the room,
And she'd think she were in heaven in her dreams.
Annie Matthews—
She threw a clog at my mother's brother when he told her, at 26, that he
    wanted to get married.

She threw my mother's first dance dress on the fire—because it had a
    low-cut back.
She reared my mother's sister's illegitimate son as if her own.
She believed in the after-life and feared God.
She took my mother with her to the Spiritualist Church.
One day, the minister said he could see a small, grey-haired woman on
    the other side,
Feeding some white hens in a yard.
'That was my mother . . . ' said my mother's mother.
My mother was the youngest of the family.
She was just 20 when her mother died,
The year the Second World War began.
That's all I know of her.
One faded photograph, these handed-down memories.
And yet I know her well,
And feel her with me now,
As I prepare to be a mother, too.


**Victor Hugo, *The Last Day of a Condemned Man,* translated by
Geoff Woollen**

She is young, she is rosy-cheeked, she has big eyes, she is just beautiful!

She is wearing a little dress that suits her so well.

I took her and swung her up in my arms, sat her on my knee, and
kissed her hair.

But why did her mother not come? Mother is ill, and so is grandmother. Just as I thought.

She looked at me with some surprise, allowing herself to be stroked,
hugged, and smothered with kisses, but looking anxiously from time to
time towards her maid, who sat weeping in the corner.

At last I managed to speak. 'Marie,' I said, 'my little Marie.'

I clasped her fiercely to my sobbing breast. She gave a faint cry. 'Oh,
sir, you are hurting me,' she said.

*Sir!* It is nearly a year since she saw me, poor child. She has forgotten
my face, my speech, and my tone of voice; and who else would recognize
me with this beard, these clothes, and this pallid complexion? Have I
already been wiped clean from her memory, the only one in which I had
wished to live on! And am I no longer a father! no longer worthy to be
called *daddy*, that child's word too pretty for the adult to use!

Yet I would have gladly given the forty years of life I am losing to
hear it once more from her mouth, just one more time.

'Now Marie,' I said to her, clasping her tiny hands in mine, 'don't you know who I am?'

She looked at me with her pretty eyes, and replied: 'Why, no.'

'Look carefully,' I repeated. 'Don't tell me you don't know who I am?'

'Oh, yes,' she said. 'A gentleman.'

Alas! how tragic it is to love but one person in the whole world, with all your heart, and for her to be there, seeing and looking at you, speaking and replying to you, yet not knowing you! To seek consolation from her alone, yet she is the only one not to know that it is because you are going to die!

'Marie,' I went on, 'do you have a daddy?'

'Yes, sir,' the child said.

'Well, where is he?'

She looked up, blinking wide in astonishment. 'Why, don't you know? He is dead.'

Then she cried out, for I had almost dropped her.

'Dead!' I said. 'Marie, do you know what it means to be dead?'

'Yes, sir,' she replied. 'He is in the ground and also in heaven.' She went on, unprompted: 'Every morning and evening, I sit on mummy's knee and pray for him.'

I kissed her on the forehead. 'Marie, let me hear you pray.'

'Oh no, sir. You can't say prayers during the day. Come to my house this evening, and you can hear me.'

That was quite enough, and I broke in: 'Marie, I am your daddy.'

'Oh!' she said.

I added: 'Do you want me for your daddy?'

The child turned away. 'No, my daddy was much more handsome.'

I showered her with tears and with kisses. She tried to wriggle free from my arms, crying: 'You're scratching me with your beard.'

Then I sat her back on my knee, staring tenderly at her, and asked her: 'Marie, can you read?'

'Yes,' she replied. 'I'm a good reader. Mummy helps me with my spelling.'

<hr />

*If we are too self-involved to respond to other people's needs for recognition and dignity, if, like those of Willy Loman's sons in* Death of a Salesman, *our unexamined prejudices get in the way, we can end up disconnected from others.*

**Yamanoue Okura, from *Man'Yoshu*, translated by Donald Keene**
I find no solace in my heart;
Like the bird flying behind the clouds
I weep aloud.

Helpless and in pain,
I would run out and vanish,
But the thought of my children holds me.

No children to wear them in wealthy homes,
They are thrown away as waste,
Those silks and quilted clothes!

With no sackcloth for my children to wear,
Must I thus grieve,
For ever at a loss!

Though vanishing like a bubble,
I live, praying that my life be long
Like a rope of a thousand fathoms.

Humble as I am,
Like an armband of coarse twill,
How I crave a thousand years of life!

**Arthur Miller, *Death of a Salesman***

LINDA:      I don't say he's a great man. Willy Loman never made a lot
            of money. His name was never in the paper. He's not the
            finest character that ever lived. But he's a human being, and
            a terrible thing is happening to him. So attention must be
            paid. He's not to be allowed to fall into his grave like an old
            dog. Attention, attention must be finally paid to such a per-
            son. . . .

WILLY:      (*Angrily*) Business is definitely business, but just listen for a
            minute. You don't understand this. When I was a boy—
            eighteen, nineteen—I was already on the road. And there
            was a question in my mind as to whether selling had a
            future for me. Because in those days I had a yearning to go
            to Alaska. See, there were three gold strikes in one month in

Alaska, and I felt like going out. Just for the ride, you might say.

HOWARD: (*Barely interested*) Don't say.

WILLY: Oh, yeah, my father lived many years in Alaska. He was an adventurous man. We've got quite a little streak of self-reliance in our family. I thought I'd go out with my older brother and try to locate him, and maybe settle in the North with the old man. And I was almost decided to go, when I met a salesman in the Parker House. His name was Dave Singleman. And he was eighty-four years old, and he'd drummed merchandise in thirty-one states. And old Dave, he'd go up to his room, y'understand, put on his green velvet slippers—I'll never forget—and pick up his phone and call the buyers, and without ever leaving his room, at the age of eighty-four, he made his living. And when I saw that, I realized that selling was the greatest career a man could want. 'Cause what could be more satisfying than to be able to go, at the age of eighty-four, into twenty or thirty different cities, and pick up a phone, and be remembered and loved and helped by so many different people? Do you know? when he died—and by the way he died the death of a salesman, in his green velvet slippers in the smoker of the New York, New Haven and Hartford, going into Boston—when he died, hundreds of salesmen and buyers were at his funeral. Things were sad on a lotta trains for months after that. (*He stands up. Howard has not looked at him.*) In those days there was personality in it, Howard. There was respect, and comradeship, and gratitude in it. Today, it's all cut and dried, and there's no chance for bringing friendship to bear—or personality. You see what I mean? They don't know me any more.

HOWARD: (*Moving away, toward the right*) That's just the thing, Willy.

WILLY: If I had forty dollars a week—that's all I'd need. Forty dollars, Howard.

HOWARD: Kid, I can't take blood from a stone, I—

WILLY: (*Desperation is on him now*) Howard, the year Al Smith was nominated, your father came to me and—

HOWARD: (*Starting to go off*) I've got to see some people, kid.

WILLY: (*Stopping him*) I'm talking about your father! There were promises made across this desk! You mustn't tell me you've got people to see—I put thirty-four years into this firm,

Howard, and now I can't pay my insurance! You can't eat the orange and throw the peel away—a man is not a piece of fruit! (*After a pause*) Now pay attention.

———◆———

*Friendship is built on loyalty. Friends are, first and foremost, people who can count on each other even when they learn they have limitations.*

## Lynne Reid Banks, *The Return of the Indian*

"... I just kept Boone in my pocket all the time, like ... well, sort of for good luck."

Omri had picked up the figure of Boone tenderly and was examining it. The horse's legs had become a bit bent, and Boone's beloved hat was looking decidedly the worse for wear. But it was still, unmistakably, even in plastic, Boone. It was the way they had last seen him, sitting on his horse, in his ten-gallon hat, his hand holding a big red bandanna to his nose, blowing a trumpet blast of farewell.

"*Ah cain't stand sayin' 'good-bye. Ah jest re-fuse t'say it, that's all! Ah'll only bust out cryin' if Ah do . . .*"

"Come on, Boone!" whispered Omri. And he put him, without more ado, into the cupboard and turned the key.

He and Patrick bent over eagerly, bumping heads. Neither of them brought to the surface of his mind the deep fear they shared. Boone, too, had lived in dangerous times. Omri knew now that time worked the same at both ends, so to speak. A year had passed for him, and, in another place and time, a year had passed for his little men. And an awful lot (and a lot of it awful!) could happen in a year.

But almost at once their fears were laid to rest. There was a split second's silence, and then, on the other side of the cupboard door, Boone began battering and kicking it, and a faint stream of swear words issued through the metal.

"Ah ain't puttin' up with it! No, sir, it ain't fair, it ain't dawggone well right! Ah ain't bin drinkin', Ah ain't bin fightin', Ah ain't cheated at poker in over a week! Ain't no law kin sling a man in jail when he's inny-cint as a noo-born babe, never mind keepin' him shut in a cell so dark he cain't see his own mus-tash!"

The boys were too fascinated to do anything at first, even open the door. They just crouched there, grinning imbecilically at each other.

"It's Boone! It's really him!" breathed Patrick.

But Boone, all unaware, and getting no response to his yells and blows, now decided no one was listening, and his voice began to quaver.

"They done up and left me," he muttered. "Gone plumb away and left ol' Boone alone in the dark . . ." There was a pause, followed by a long nose-blow that shook the cupboard. "T'ain't fu-funny," he went on, his voice now definitely shaking with sobs. "Don't they know a man kin be brave as a lion and still skeered o' the dark? Ain't they got no 'magination, leavin' a fella ter rot in this pitch-black hell-hole? . . . " His voice rose on a shrill tide of tearful complaint.

Omri could not bear it a second longer. He opened the door. The light struck through and Boone instantly looked up, his red bandanna dropping to the floor between his knees. He jumped to his feet, staring, his mouth agape, his battered old hat askew on his ginger head. The horse backed off and snorted.

"Well, Ah'll be e-ternally hornswoggled!" Boone got out at last. "If it ain't you-all!"

### Charlotte Brontë, *Jane Eyre*

"St. John, I am unhappy, because you are still angry with me. Let us be friends."

"I hope we are friends," was the unmoved reply; while he still watched the rising of the moon, which he had been contemplating as I approached.

"No, St. John, we are not friends as we were. You know that."

"Are we not? That is wrong. For my part, I wish you no ill and all good."

"I believe you, St. John; for I am sure you are incapable of wishing any one ill: but, as I am your kinswoman, I should desire somewhat more of affection than that sort of general philanthropy you extend to mere strangers."

"Of course," he said. "Your wish is reasonable; and I am far from regarding you as a stranger."

This, spoken in a cool, tranquil tone, was mortifying and baffling enough. Had I attended to the suggestions of pride and ire, I should immediately have left him: but something worked within me more strongly than those feelings could. I deeply venerated my cousin's talent and principle. His friendship was of value to me: to lose it tried me severely. I would not so soon relinquish the attempt to reconquer it.

"Must we part in this way, St. John? And when you go to India, will you leave me so, without a kinder word than you have yet spoken?"

He now turned quite from the moon, and faced me.

"When I go to India, Jane, will I leave you? What! do you not go to India?"

"You said I could not, unless I married you."

"And you will not marry me? You adhere to that resolution?"

Reader, do you know, as I do, what terror those cold people can put into the ice of their questions? How much of the fall of the avalanche is in their anger? of the breaking up of the frozen sea in their displeasure?

"No, St. John, I will not marry you. I adhere to my resolution."

The avalanche had shaken and slid a little forward; but it did not yet crash down.

"Once more, why this refusal?" he asked.

"Formerly," I answered, "because you did not love me; now, I reply, because you almost hate me. If I were to marry you, you would kill me. You are killing me now."

His lips and cheeks turned white, quite white.

"*I should kill you—I am killing you?* Your words are such as ought not to be used: violent, unfeminine, and untrue. They betray an unfortunate state of mind: they merit severe reproof: they would seem inexcusable; but that it is the duty of man to forgive his fellow, even until seventy-and-seven times."

I had finished the business now. While earnestly wishing to erase from his mind the trace of my former offence, I had stamped on that tenacious surface, another and far deeper impression: I had burnt it in.

"Now, you will indeed hate me," I said. "It is useless to attempt to conciliate you: I see I have made an eternal enemy of you."

A fresh wrong did these words inflict: the worse, because they touched on the truth. That bloodless lip quivered to a temporary spasm. I knew the steely ire I had whetted. I was heart-wrung.

"You utterly misinterpret my words," I said, at once seizing his hand: "I have no intention to grieve or pain you—indeed, I have not."

Most bitterly he smiled—most decidedly he withdrew his hand from mine. "And now you recall your promise, and will not go to India at all, I presume?" said he, after a considerable pause.

"Yes, I will, as your assistant," I answered.

A very long silence succeeded. What struggle there was in him between Nature and Grace in this interval, I cannot tell: only singular gleams scintillated in his eyes, and strange shadows passed over his face.

*Loyalty to ideals and convictions—both one's personal commitments and those one holds with others in pursuit of shared goals—is worthy of high esteem. As Isabel in* My Children! My Africa! *tells us, this kind of loyalty is what calls us to value people we might think of as not like ourselves. Mr. M. is a black teacher who, until she got to know and respect him, seemed almost a nonperson in her segregated South African life. Denise Levertov emphasizes this point in her poem* Complicity.

### Athol Fugard, *My Children! My Africa!*

ISABEL        (Alone. SHE stands quietly, examining the silence. After a few seconds SHE nods her head slowly.): Yes! Thami was right, Mr. M. He said I'd feel near you up here.

He's out there somewhere, Mr. M. . . . travelling north. He didn't say where exactly he was going, but I think we can guess, can't we?

I'm here for a very "old-fashioned" reason, so I know you'll approve. I've come to pay my last respects to Anela Myalatya. I know the old-fashioned way of doing that is to bring flowers, lay them on the grave, say a quiet prayer and then go back to your life. But that seemed sort of silly this time. You'll have enough flowers around here when the spring comes . . . which it will. So instead I've brought you something which I know will mean more to you than flowers or prayers ever could. A promise. I am going to make Anela Myalatya a promise.

You gave me a little lecture once about wasted lives . . . how much of it you'd seen, how much you hated it, how much you didn't want that to happen to Thami and me. I sort of understood what you meant at the time. Now, I most certainly do. Your death has seen to that.

My promise to you is that I am going to try as hard as I can, in every way that I can, to see that it doesn't happen to me. I am going to try my best to make my life useful in the way yours was. I want you to be proud of me. After all, I am one of your children you know. You did welcome me to your family. (A pause.) The future is still ours, Mr. M. (The ACTRESS leaves the stage.)

### Denise Levertov, *Complicity*

On the young tree's highest twig,
a dark leaf, dry solitary, left over

from winter, among the small new buds.
But it turns its head!
                         It's a hummingbird,
tranquil, at rest, taking time off
from the hummingbird world of swift intensities—
yet no less attentive. Taking
a long and secret look at the day,
like a child whose hiding-place
has not been discovered, who hasn't even
been missed. No hue and cry.
                         I saw
a leaf: I shall not betray you.

*Loyalty can also be a call to a sense of faithfulness to all humanity. Through countless generations, people like Joe Hill who are the victims of terrible injustice have found ways to recognize the value of working together, regardless of their personal and social differences. And America, as Emma Lazarus has immortalized the ideal, has striven to open itself up to the world's needy and terrified.*

**Alfred Hayes, *Joe Hill***
I dreamed I saw Joe Hill last night alive as you and me.
"But Joe, you're ten years dead."
"I never died," says he.

"In Salt Lake, Joe," I said to him, standing by my bed,
"They framed you on a murder charge,"
Joe. "But I ain't dead."

"The Copper Bosses shot you Joe, they killed you Joe," says I.
"Takes more than guns to kill a man," says Joe, "I didn't die."

And standing there as big as life and smiling with his eyes,
Joe says, "What they could never kill/went on to organize."
From San Diego up to Maine in every mine and mill
Where workers stand up for their rights
It's there you'll find Joe Hill.

I dreamed I saw Joe Hill last night alive as you and me.
"But Joe, you're ten years dead."
"I never died," says he.


**Emma Lazarus,** *The New Colossus*
Not like the brazen giant of Greek fame,
With conquering limbs astride from land to land;
Here at our sea-washed, sunset gates shall stand
A mighty woman with a torch, whose flame
Is the imprisoned lightning, and her name
Mother of Exiles. From her beacon-hand
Glows world-wide welcome; her mild eyes command
The air-bridged harbor that twin cities frame.
"Keep, ancient lands, your storied pomp!" cries she
With silent lips. "Give me your tired, your poor,
Your huddled masses yearning to breathe free,
The wretched refuse of your teeming shore.
Send these, the homeless, tempest-tost to me,
I lift my lamp beside the golden door!"

# Generosity

———⊱◦⊰———

Generosity is frequently present in quite complex ways. Thinking about someone else's well-being and doing something about it is clearly generous. Being open to the possibility of someone else's generosity is also a form of generosity. So is being open enough to clear up misunderstandings for friendship's sake. Another kind of generosity is when we try to make sure that friends benefit from opportunities we and they know will make a big difference to them. And if you are the recipient of such kindness, it's important to be sure that you want it, that it's right for you—and, if it is, to be sure to make the most of it. Lucinda and Corry in Bianca Bradbury's *Lots of Love, Lucinda* struggle with questions like these:

Corry would try to think of something to change the subject when Lucinda continued, "Mama's had it real hard, with five of us to feed. She owns our home, so that helps. It's a little, four-room house near a busy road. Mama used to work in the laundry in town, but then an all-night diner was opened up near where we live, she got a job doing their short order cooking. She works all night, seven in the evening until seven in the morning."

. . .

Lucinda seemed to have something else on her mind, and finally she got it out. "When your mother came up to my room that night and spoke about my clothes, I felt terrible, because I thought you folks suspected I'd done it on purpose. I mean that I'd come up here with an empty suitcase, hoping I'd be given things. I should have known you people aren't so mean-minded, you'd think any such thing. "I'd like to make something clear, Corry, my mother doesn't have two cents to rub together. What your mother puts on the table for a day would just about feed my family for a week. I mean, we don't see a piece of meat more than once in a blue moon."

"Mama wanted me to buy clothes with the money I'd saved while I was working, but I couldn't. I made her take it. She'll miss my wages;

she'll have a real rough year, I hate to think how rough. But learning means an awful lot to her. When the principal of our high school came and told her he'd recommended me for the education project, she thought this chance came straight from heaven."

Distressed, Corry insisted, "Lucinda, you don't owe me any exclamation!"

But there are other times when generosity is more like an extension of the happiness in people's lives. That is the case in Maureen's family in *Misty of Chincoteague*, by Marguerite Henry:

Grandpa was in the kitchen, standing before the mirror, trimming the bristles in his ears when Maureen and Paul came in with the groceries.

"Consarn it all!" he fussed. "Do you got to rustle them bags like cows trompin' through a cornfield? A fella can't hear hisself think, let alone hold his hand steady. This here's a mighty ticklish job."

"Why, Clarence!" exclaimed Grandma, "I've never seed you so twittery."

"Ef'n you had whisk brooms in your ears, maybe you'd be twittery too."

Grandma stopped basting the marsh hen she had just taken out of the oven and burst out in helpless laughter. "Whisk brooms in my ears!" she chortled. And soon Maureen and Paul and even Grandpa were laughing with her.

"All right now," said Grandma, recovering her breath. "Maureen, you can set the potatoes to boil and lay the table. Lay an extra place like allus. Never know when some human straggler is goin' to stop."

In the selections that follow we have family, friends, and the straggler who might stop by in mind.

---

*Stories like* Pollyanna *and* Heidi *remind us that to be an open and kind person is to know and embody the splendor of making life better for others.*

## Eleanor Porter, *Pollyanna*

"Well, Miss Pollyanna, may I have the pleasure of seeing you home?" asked the doctor, smilingly. I started to drive on a few minutes ago: then it occurred to me that I'd wait for you."

"Thank you, sir. I'm glad you did. I just love to ride," beamed Pollyanna, as he reached out his hand to help her in.

"Do you?" smiled the doctor, nodding his head in farewell to the young man on the steps. "Well, as near as I can judge, there are a good many things that you 'love' to do—eh?" he added, as they drove briskly away.

Pollyanna laughed.

"Why, I don't know. I reckon perhaps there are," she admitted. "I like to do 'most everything that's living. Of course I don't like the other things very well—sewing, and reading out loud, and all that. But they aren't living."

"No? What are they, then?"

"Aunt Polly says they're 'learning to live," sighed Pollyanna with a rueful smile.

The doctor smiled now—a little queerly.

"Does she? Well, I should think she might say—just that."

"Yes," responded Pollyanna. "But I don't see it that way at all. I don't think you have to learn how to live. I didn't anyhow."

The doctor drew a long sigh.

"After all, I'm afraid some of us—do have to, little girl," he said.

Then, for a time he was silent. Pollyanna, stealing a glance at his face, felt vaguely sorrow for him. He looked so sad. She wished, uneasily, that she could "do something." It was this, perhaps, that caused her to say in a timid voice: "Doctor Clinton, I should think being a doctor would be the very gladdest kind of business there was." The doctor turned in surprise.

"'Gladdest'!—when I see so much suffering always, everywhere I go?" he cried.

She nodded.

"I know; but you're helping it—don't you see?—and of course you're glad to help it! And so that makes you the gladdest of any of us all the time."

The doctor's eyes filled with sudden tears. The doctor's life was a singularly lonely one. He had no wife and no home save his two-room office in a boarding house. His profession was very dear to him. Looking now into Pollyanna's shining eyes, he felt as if a loving hand had been suddenly laid on his head in blessing. He knew, too, that never again would a long day's work or a long night's weariness be quiet without that new-found exultation that came to him through Pollyanna's eyes.

### Johanna Spyri, *Heidi*

"But if you go out into the bright snow, surely it is bright for you, then. Come with me, Grandmother, I'll show it to you!" Heidi took the old hand to draw her out, for suddenly she began to be terribly afraid that it could never be light again for her, either.

"No. Let me be, you good child. It will always remain dark for me, no matter if it's snow or sunshine."

"Even in summer," Heidi began, searching more and more anxiously for some comfort. "In summer, when the sun gets hot, and then says good night to the mountains, until they glow as if they were on fire, then it will be light again for you."

"Ah, child," the old woman shook her head. "It will never be light for me in this world. Never again."

At this, Heidi burst into floods of tears and loud sobs. "Who can make it light for you again? Can anybody? Is there nobody who can?"

Now the grandmother had to comfort the child, but it was not easy. Heidi seldom cried, but when she once started, it was almost impossible for her to stop. Although the grandmother tried everything she could think of to distract Heidi from her grief, it was of no avail. It pained the old woman to hear the child sobbing so, as if her heart would break.

At last she said, "Come here, dear Heidi, and I will tell you something. When one can't see, then listening can be most pleasant. Come, sit by me, and talk to me. Tell me what you do way up there on the Alm. Tell me what your grandfather does. Long ago I used to know him, but I have heard nothing about him for many years now except what Peter tells me—and that is not too much."

Heidi wiped away her tears and said consolingly: "Just wait a bit, Grandmother, and I will tell my grandfather all about you. He can surely make it light for you again. And he can fix your cottage so it will not fall to pieces. He can make everything right."

The old woman smiled gently but said nothing. Heidi began to tell her about her life up on the mountain, and about the days spent in the pasture, and the winter life indoors. She told how her grandfather could make anything out of wood—three-legged stools, benches and chairs and mangers into which hay could be put for Schwanli and Barli. He had just finished a big new tub for summer bathing, and a new porringer and some spoons. Heidi became quite excited as she recounted the wonderful things his skillful hands fashioned from the wood.

The old lady listened to all this with great interest, calling out to Brigitte now and then, "Do you hear what the child tells me about the Alm-Uncle? Is it not remarkable?"

Suddenly there was a great stamping at the door and Peter burst into the room. He stood stock still with his big round eyes and mouth open when he saw Heidi and she cried, "Good evening, Peter."

"Are you out of school already, Peterkin?" the grandmother said. "The afternoon has not passed so quickly for me for many a year. How is the reading going?"

"About the same," Peter replied, making a face.

"Well now, I thought there might be a little change by this time. Remember! You will be twelve years old come February," the old woman reminded him, sighing a little.

"Why should there be a change then?" asked Heidi, curiously.

"I thought perhaps he might have learned to read a little," the grandmother said wistfully, "I have an old prayer book on the shelf full of beautiful hymns. I haven't heard them for a long time, and I can't remember them any more. I hoped when Peterkin had learned to read, he would sometimes read me a hymn. But it is no use. He can't learn. It is too hard for him."

"I think I'd better light the lamp," said Brigitte, who had been working all this time at her mending. "The afternoon has flown away without my knowing it, and now it's quite dark."

"Oh!" Heidi sprang from her chair and stretched out her hand to the old lady, saying, "Good night, Grandmother, I must go straight home now." She shook hands with Peter's mother, and hurried toward the door.

"Wait, child, wait!" cried the grandmother anxiously. "You cannot go alone. Peterkin must go with you. Take care of the child, Peter, and do not let her stand still, lest she be frostbitten. Has she a warm shawl?"

"I haven't any shawl, but my coat is warm. I shan't be cold," Heidi assured her and she was out of the house in an instant, running so nimbly that Peter could not overtake her for a while.

The children had not gone far up the mountain when they saw the Alm-Uncle coming toward them. In a few great strides he was beside them.

His white head nodded as he looked down at Heidi. "You have kept your promise," he said, "that is good," and wrapping her carefully again in the coverlet, he took her in his arms and turned back toward his hut.

Brigitte, who had run out of the house to watch the children, went back in with Peter, to tell her mother what they had seen. The old woman threw up her hands in surprise. "Thank God that the Alm-Uncle is so kind to Heidi! I hope he will permit the little one to come to me again. It has done me a world of good. What a kind heart she has, and how she can talk!"

Even when the grandmother went to bed, she kept talking about Heidi. "If only she would come again! I would have something to look forward to. She is such a dear and happy child."

Brigitte agreed heartily with this, and Peter grinned and nodded vigorously.

All this time while Heidi went up the mountain in her grandfather's arms, she chattered without ceasing, but as nothing could get through the coverlet so closely wrapped about her, Alm-Uncle could not understand a single word. "Wait a bit," he said at last. "Wait until we reach home, child. Then you can tell me everything."

So just as soon as they reached the hut, and Heidi was free of her warm wrappings, she began, "Tomorrow we must take your hammer and the nails and go down to Peter's house, Grandfather. The shutters shake so. We must make them fast, and make everything else fast, too, for the whole place creaks and rattles dreadfully."

"Must we, indeed? Who says we must?" demanded the old man.

"I do," Heidi replied stoutly. "Everything is so loose there, that it makes the grandmother so afraid. Sometimes she cannot sleep because she fears the house will fall to pieces on top of them all. And oh, Grandfather, she says that no one can make it light for her again, but surely you can! Think how sad it must be for her always to sit in the dark. Tomorrow we will help her, won't we?"

The old man looked at her for a long time in silence, then he said, "Yes, Heidi, tomorrow we will make things fast for the grandmother, just as you say."

———◆———

*The work it takes at times to be generous, to give of yourself to benefit others can bring a good feeling to you and those you help. There are a number of rewards when you share yourself and what you own: Sometimes you will receive gifts and kindness in return; sometimes you will discover new parts of yourself.*

### A. A. Milne, *The House at Pooh Corner*

"Pooh," he said solemnly, "it isn't the *toes* so much as the *ears*."

By this time they were getting near Eeyore's Gloomy Place, which was where he lived, and as it was still very snowy behind Piglet's ears, and he was getting tired of it, they turned into a little pine wood, and sat down on the gate which led into it. They were out of the snow now, but it was very cold, and to keep themselves warm they sang Pooh's song right through six times, Piglet doing the tiddely-poms and Pooh doing the rest of it, and both of them thumping on the top of the gate with pieces of stick at the proper places. And in a little while they felt much warmer, and were able to talk again.

"I've been thinking," said Pooh, "and what I've been thinking is this. I've been thinking about Eeyore."

"What about Eeyore?"

"Well, poor Eeyore has nowhere to live."

"Nor he has," said Piglet.

"You have a house, Piglet, and I have a house, and they are very good houses. And Christopher Robin has a house, and Owl and Kanga and Rabbit have houses, and even Rabbit's friends and relations have houses or somethings, but poor Eeyore has nothing. So what I've been thinking is: Let's build him a house."

"That," said Piglet, "is a Grand Idea. Where shall we build it?"

"We will build it here," said Pooh, "just by this wood, out of the wind, because this is where I thought of it. And we will call this Pooh Corner. And we will build an Eeyore House with sticks at Pooh Corner for Eeyore."

"There was a heap of sticks on the other side of the wood," said Piglet. "I saw them. Lots and lots. All piled up."

"Thank you, Piglet," said Pooh. "What you have just said will be a Great Help to us, and because of it I could call this place Poohanpiglet Corner if Pooh Corner didn't sound better, which it does, being smaller and more like a corner. Come along."

So they got down off the gate and went around to the other side of the wood to fetch the sticks.

Christopher Robin had spent the morning indoors going to Africa and back, and he had just got off the boat and was wondering what it was like outside, when who should come knocking at the door but Eeyore.

"Hallo, Eeyore," said Christopher Robin, as he opened the door and came out. "How are *you?*"

"It's snowing still," said Eeyore gloomily.

"So it is."

*"And* freezing."

"Is it?"

"Yes," said Eeyore. "However," he said, brightening up a little, "we haven't had an earthquake lately."

"What's the matter, Eeyore?"

"Nothing, Christopher Robin. Nothing important. I suppose you haven't seen a house or whatnot anywhere about?"

"What sort of a house?"

"Just a house."

"Who lives there?"

"I do. At least I thought I did. But I suppose I don't. After all, we can't all have houses."

"But, Eeyore, I didn't know, I always thought—"

"I don't know how it is, Christopher Robin, but what with all this snow and one thing and another, not to mention icicles and such-like, it isn't so Hot in my field about three o'clock in the morning as some people think it is. It isn't Close, if you know what I mean—not so as to be uncomfortable. It isn't Stuffy. In fact, Christopher Robin," he went on in a loud whisper, "quite-between-ourselves-and-don't-tell-anybody, it's Cold."

"Oh, Eeyore!"

"And I said to myself: The others will be sorry if I'm getting myself all cold. They haven't got Brains, any of them, only grey fluff that's blown into their heads by mistake, and they don't Think, but if it goes on snowing for another six weeks or so, one of them will begin to say to himself: 'Eeyore can't be so very much too Hot about three o'clock in the morning.' And then it will Get About. And they'll be Sorry."

"Oh, Eeyore!" said Christopher Robin, feeling very sorry already.

"I don't mean you, Christopher Robin. You're different. So what it all comes to is that I built myself a house down by my little wood."

"Did you really? How exciting!"

"The really exciting part," said Eeyore in his most melancholy voice, "is that when I left it this morning it was there, and when I came back it wasn't. Not at all, very natural, and it was only Eeyore's house. But still I just wondered."

Christopher Robin didn't stop to wonder. He was already back in *his* house, putting on his waterproof hat, his waterproof boots and his waterproof macintosh as fast as he could.

"We'll go and look for it at once," he called out to Eeyore.

"Sometimes," said Eeyore, "when people have quite finished taking a person's house, there are one or two bits which they don't want and are rather glad for the person to take back, if you know what I mean. So I thought if we just went."

"Come on," said Christopher Robin, and off they hurried, and in a very little time they got to the corner of the field by the side of the pine-wood, where Eeyore's house wasn't any longer.

"There!" said Eeyore. "Not a stick of it left! Of course, I've still got all this snow to do what I like with. One mustn't complain."

But Christopher Robin wasn't listening to Eeyore, he was listening to something else.

"Can't you hear it?" he asked.

"What is it? Somebody laughing?"

"Listen."

They both listened . . . and they heard a deep gruff voice saying in a singing voice that the more it snowed the more it went on snowing and a small high voice tiddely-pomming in between.

"It's Pooh," said Christopher Robin excitedly. . . .

"Possibly," said Eeyore.

"*And* Piglet!" said Christopher Robin excitedly.

"Probably," said Eeyore. "What we *want* is a Trained Bloodhound."

The words of the song changed suddenly.

"*We've finished our HOUSE!*" sang the gruff voice.

"*Tiddely pom!*" sang the squeaky one.

"*It's a beautiful HOUSE . . .* "

"*Tiddely pom . . .* "

"*I wish it were MINE. . . .*"

"*Tiddely pom. . . .*"

"Pooh!" shouted Christopher Robin. . . .

The singers on the gate stopped suddenly.

"It's Christopher Robin!" said Pooh eagerly.

"He's round by the place where we got all those sticks from," said Piglet.

"Come on," said Pooh.

They climbed down their gate and hurried round the corner of the wood, Pooh making welcoming noises all the way.

"Why, here is Eeyore," said Pooh, when he had finished hugging Christopher Robin, and he nudged Piglet, and Piglet nudged him, and they thought to themselves what a lovely surprise they had got ready.

"Hallo, Eeyore."

"Same to you, Pooh Bear, and twice on Thursdays," said Eeyore gloomily.

Before Pooh could say: "Why Thursdays?" Christopher Robin began to explain the sad story of Eeyore's Lost House. And Pooh and Piglet listened, and their eyes seemed to get bigger and bigger.

"*Where* did you say it was?" asked Pooh.

"Just here," said Eeyore.

"Made of sticks?"

"Yes."

"Oh!" said Piglet.

"What?" said Eeyore.

"I just said 'Oh!'" said Piglet nervously. And so as to seem quite at ease he hummed Tiddely-pom once or twice in a what-shall-we-do-now kind of way.

"You're sure it *was* a house?" said Pooh. "I mean, you're sure the house was just here?"

"Of course I am," said Eeyore. And he murmured to himself, "No brain at all some of them."

"Why, what's the matter, Pooh?" asked Christopher Robin.

"Well," said Pooh. . . . "The fact is," said Pooh . . . "Well, the fact is," said Pooh . . . "You see," said Pooh. . . . "It's like this," said Pooh, and something seemed to tell him that he wasn't explaining very well, and he nudged Piglet again.

"It's like this," said Piglet quickly. . . . "Only warmer," he added after deep thought.

"What's warmer?"

"The other side of the wood, where Eeyore's house is."

"My house?" said Eeyore. "My house was here."

"No," said Piglet firmly. "The other side of the wood."

"Because of being warmer," said Pooh.

"But I ought to *know*—"

"Come and look," said Piglet simply, and he led the way.

"There wouldn't be two houses," said Pooh. "Not so close together."

They came round the corner, and there was Eeyore's house, looking as comfy as anything. "There you are," said Piglet.

"Inside as well as outside," said Pooh proudly. Eeyore went inside . . . and came out again. "It's a remarkable thing," he said. "It is my house, and I built it where I said I did, so the wind must have blown it here. And the wind blew it right over the wood, and blew it down here, and here it is as good as ever. In fact, better in places."

"Much better," said Pooh and Piglet together.

"It just shows what can be done by taking a little trouble," said Eeyore. "Do you see, Pooh? Do you see, Piglet? Brains first and then Hard Work. Look at it! *That's* the way to build a house," said Eeyore proudly.

So they left him in it; and Christopher Robin went back to lunch with his friends Pooh and Piglet, and on the way they told him of the Awful Mistake they had made. And when he had finished laughing, they all sang the Outdoor Song for Snowy Weather the rest of the way home, Piglet, who was still not quite sure of his voice, putting in the tiddely-poms again.

"And I know it *seems* easy," said Piglet to himself, "but it isn't every *one* who could do it."

*We shouldn't forget that sometimes our own circumstances will improve as a result of what we've helped to make possible.*

### Louisa May Alcott, *Little Women*

The big house did prove a Palace Beautiful, though took some time for all to get in, and Beth found it very hard to pass the lions. Old Mr. Laurence was the biggest one; but after he had called, said something funny or kind to each one of the girls, and talked over old times with their mother, nobody felt much afraid of him, except timid Beth. The other lion was the fact that they were poor and Laurie rich; for this made them shy of accepting favors which they could not return. But, after a while, they found that he considered them the benefactors, and could not do enough to show how grateful he was for Mrs. March's motherly welcome, their cheerful society, and the comfort he took in that humble home of theirs. So they soon forgot their pride, and interchanged kindnesses without stopping to think which was the greater.

All sorts of pleasant things happened about that time, for the new friendship flourished like grass in spring. Everyone liked Laurie, and he privately informed his tutor that the Marches were "regularly splendid girls." With the delightful enthusiasm of youth, they took the solitary boy into their midst, and made much of him, and he found something very charming in the innocent companionship of these simple hearted girls. Never having known mother or sisters, he was quick to feel the influences they brought about him; and their busy, lively ways made him ashamed of the indolent life he led. He was tired of books, and found people so interesting now that Mr. Brooke was obliged to make very unsatisfactory reports; for Laurie was always playing truant, and running over to the Marches'.

"Never mind; let him take a holiday, and make it up afterwards," said the old gentleman. "The good lady next door says he is studying too hard, and needs young society, amusement, and exercise. I suspect she IS right, and that I've been coddling the fellow as if I'd been his grandmother. Let him do what he likes, so long as he is happy. He can't get into mischief in that little nunnery over there; and Mrs. March is doing more for him than we can."

What good times they had, to be sure! Such plays and tableaux, such sleigh rides and skating frolics, such pleasant evenings in the old parlor, and now and then such gay little parties at the great house. Meg could walk in the conservatory whenever she liked, and revel in bouquets; Jo browsed over the new library voraciously, and convulsed the old gentleman with her criticisms; Amy copied pictures, and enjoyed beauty to her heart's content; and Laurie played "lord of the manor" in the most delightful style.

But Beth, though yearning for the grand piano, could not pluck up courage to go to the "Mansion of Bliss," as Meg called it. She went once with Jo; but the old gentleman, not being aware of her infirmity, stared at her so hard from under his heavy eyebrows, and said "Hey!" so loud, that he frightened her so much her "feet chattered on the floor," she told her mother; and she ran away, declaring she would never go there any more, not even for the dear piano. No persuasions or enticements could overcome her fear, till the fact coming to Mr. Laurence's ears in some mysterious way, he set about mending matters. During one of the brief calls he made, he artfully led the conversation to music, and talked away about great singers whom he had seen, fine organs he had heard, and told such charming anecdotes that Beth found it impossible to stay in her distant corner, but crept nearer and nearer, as if fascinated. At the back of his chair she stopped, and stood listening, with her great eyes wide open, and her cheeks red with the excitement of this unusual performance. Taking no more notice of her than if she had been a fly, Mr. Laurence talked on about Laurie's lessons and teachers; and presently, as if the idea had just occurred to him, he said to Mrs. March:

"The boy neglects his music now, and I'm glad of it, for he was getting too fond of it. But the piano suffers for want of use. Wouldn't some of your girls like to run over, and practice on it now and then, just to keep it in tune, you know, ma'am?"

Beth took a step forward, and pressed her hands tightly together to keep from clapping them, for this was an irresistible temptation; and the thought of practicing on that splendid instrument quite took her breath away. Before Mrs. March could reply, Mr. Laurence went on with an odd little nod and smile:

"They needn't see or speak to anyone, but run in at any time; for I'm shut up in my study at the other end of the house, Laurie is out a great deal, and the servants are never near the drawing room after nine o'clock."

Here he rose, as if going, and Beth made up her mind to speak, for that last arrangement left nothing to be desired. "Please tell the young ladies what I say; and if they don't care to come, why, never mind." Here a little hand slipped into his, and Beth looked up at him with a face full of gratitude, as she said, in her earnest yet timid way:

"Oh, sir, they do care, very, very much!"

"Are you the musical girl?" he asked, without any startling "Hey!" as he looked down at her kindly.

"I'm Beth. I love it dearly, and I'll come, if you are quite sure nobody will hear me, and be disturbed," she added, fearing to be rude, and trembling at her own boldness as she spoke.

"Not a soul, my dear. The house is empty half the day; so come, and drum away as much as you like, and I shall be obliged to you."

"How kind you are, sir!"

Beth blushed like a rose under the friendly look he wore; but she was not frightened now, and gave the big hand a grateful squeeze, because she had no words to thank him for the precious gift he had given her. The old gentleman softly stroked the hair off her forehead, and, stooping down, he kissed her, saying, in a tone few people ever heard:

"I had a little girl once, with eyes like these. God bless you, my dear! Good day, madam," and away he went, in a great hurry.

Beth had a rapture with her mother, and then rushed up to impart the glorious news to her family of invalids, as the girls were not at home. How blithely she sung that evening, and how they all laughed at her because she woke Amy in the night by playing the piano on her face in her sleep. Next day, having seen both the old and young gentleman out of the house, Beth, after two or three retreats, fairly got in at the side door, and made her way, as noiselessly as any mouse, to the drawing room, where her idol stood. Quite by accident, of course, some pretty, easy music lay on the piano; and, with trembling fingers, and frequent stops to listen and look about, Beth at last touched the great instrument, and straightway forgot her fear, herself, and everything else but the unspeakable delight which the music gave her, for it was like the voice of a beloved friend.

She stayed till Hannah came to take her home to dinner but she had no appetite, and could only sit and smile upon everyone in a general state of beatitude.

After that, the little brown hood slipped through the hedge nearly every day, and the great drawing room was haunted by a tuneful spirit that came and went unseen. She never knew that Mr. Laurence often opened his study door to hear the old-fashioned airs he liked; she never saw Laurie mount guard in the hall to warn the servants away; she never suspected that the exercise books and new songs which she found in the rack were put there for her especial benefit; and when he talked to her about music at home, she only thought how kind he was to tell things that helped her so much. So she enjoyed herself heartily, and found, what isn't always the case, that her granted wish was all she had hoped. Perhaps it was because she was so grateful for this blessing that a greater was given her; at any rate, she deserved both.

"Mother, I'm going to work Mr. Laurence a pair of slippers. He is so kind to me, I must thank him, and I don't know any other way. Can I do it?" asked Beth, a few weeks after that eventful call of his.

"Yes, dear. It will please him very much, and be a nice way of thanking him. The girls will help you about them, and I will pay for the making up," replied Mrs. March, who took peculiar pleasure in granting Beth's requests, because she so seldom asked anything for herself.

After many serious discussions with Meg and Jo, the pattern was chosen, the materials bought, and the slippers begun. A cluster of grave yet cheerful pansies, on a deeper purple ground, was pronounced very appropriate and pretty; and Beth worked away early and late, with occasional lifts over hard parts. She was a nimble little needlewoman, and they were finished before anyone got tired of them. Then she wrote a very short, simple note, and, with Laurie's help, got them smuggled onto the study table one morning before the old gentleman was up.

When this excitement was over, Beth waited to see what would happen. All that day passed, and a part of the next, before any acknowledgment arrived, and she was beginning to fear she had offended her crotchety friend. On the afternoon of the second day, she went out to do an errand, and give poor Joanna, the invalid doll, her daily exercise. As she came up the street, on her return, she saw three, yes, four, heads popping in and out of the parlor windows, and the moment they saw her, several hands were waved, and several joyful voices screamed:

"Here's a letter from the old gentleman! Come quick, and read it!"

"Oh, Beth, he's sent you—" began Amy, gesticulating with unseemly energy; but she got no further, for Jo quenched her by slamming down the window.

Beth hurried on in a flutter of suspense. At the door, her sisters seized and bore her to the parlor in a triumphal procession, all pointing, and all saying at once, "Look there! look there!" Beth did look, and turned pale with delight and surprise; for there stood a little cabinet piano, with a letter lying on the glossy lid, directed, like a signboard, to "Miss Elizabeth March."

"For me?" gasped Beth, holding on to Jo, and feeling as if she should tumble down, it was such an overwhelming thing altogether.

"Yes; all for you, my precious! Isn't it splendid of him? Don't you think he's the dearest old man in the world? Here's the key in the letter.

We didn't open it, but we are dying to know what he says," cried Jo, hugging her sister, and offering the note.

"You read it! I can't, I feel so queer! Oh, it is too lovely!" and Beth hid her face in Jo's apron, quite upset by her present.

Jo opened the paper, and began to laugh, for the first words she saw were:

*MISS MARCH:*

*Dear Madam—*

"*How nice it sounds! I wish someone would write to me so!*" said Amy, who thought the old-fashioned address very elegant.

"*I have had many pairs of slippers in my life, but I never had any that suited me so well as yours,*" continued Jo. "*Heart'sease is my favorite flower, and these will always remind me of the gentle giver. I like to pay my debts; so I know you will allow 'the old gentleman' to send you something which once belonged to the little granddaughter he lost. With hearty thanks and best wishes, I remain*

"*Your grateful friend and humble servant,*
*JAMES LAURENCE.*

"There, Beth, that's an honor to be proud of, I'm sure! Laurie told me how fond Mr. Laurence used to be of the child who died, and how he kept her little things carefully. Just think, he's given you her piano. That comes of having big blue eyes, and loving music," said Jo, trying to soothe Beth, who trembled and looked more excited than she had ever been before.

"See the cunning brackets to hold candles, and the nice green silk, puckered up, with a gold rose in the middle, and the pretty rack and stool, all complete," added Meg, opening the instrument and displaying its beauties.

"'Your humble servant, James Laurence'—only think of his writing that to you. I'll tell the girls. They'll think it's splendid," said Amy, much impressed by the note.

"Try it, honey. Let's hear the sound of the baby pianny," said Hannah, who always took a share in the family joys and sorrows.

So Beth tried it; and everyone pronounced it the most remarkable piano ever heard. It had evidently been newly tuned and put in apple-pie order; but, perfect as it was, I think the real charm of it lay in the happiest of all happy faces which leaned over it, as Beth lovingly touched the beautiful black and white keys and pressed the bright pedals.

"You'll have to go and thank him," said Jo, by way of a joke; for the idea of the child's really going never entered her head.

"Yes, I mean to. I guess I'll go now, before I get frightened thinking about it." And, to the utter amazement of the assembled family, Beth walked deliberately down the garden, through the hedge, and in at the Laurences' door.

"Well, I wish I may die if it ain't the queerest thing I ever see! The pianny has turned her head! She'd never have gone in her right mind," cried Hannah, staring after her, while the girls were rendered quite speechless by the miracle.

They would have been still more amazed if they had seen what Beth did afterward. If you will believe me, she went and knocked at the study door before she gave herself time to think; and when a gruff voice called out, "Come in!" she did go in, right up to Mr. Laurence, who looked quite taken aback, and held out her hand, saying, with only a small quaver in her voice, "I came to thank you, sir, for—" But she didn't finish; for he looked so friendly that she forgot her speech, and, only remembering that he had lost the little girl he loved, she put both her arms round his neck, and kissed him.

If the roof of the house had suddenly flown off, the old gentleman wouldn't have been more astonished; but he liked it—oh, dear, yes, he liked it amazingly!—and was so touched and pleased by that confiding little kiss that all his crustiness vanished; and he just set her on his knee, and laid his wrinkled cheek against her rosy one, feeling as if he had got his own little granddaughter back again. Beth ceased to fear him from that moment, and sat there talking to him as cozily as if she had known him all her life; for love casts out fear, and gratitude can conquer pride. When she went home, he walked with her to her own gate, shook hands cordially, and touched his hat as he marched back again, looking very stately and erect, like a handsome, soldierly old gentleman, as he was.

When the girls saw that performance, Jo began to dance a jig, by way of expressing her satisfaction; Amy nearly fell out of the window in her surprise; and Meg exclaimed, with uplifted hands, "Well, I do believe the world is coming to an end!"

### Guy A. Zona, *Soul Would Have No Rainbow If the Eyes Had No Tears*, from *Native American Proverbs*

Always assume your guest is tired, cold, and hungry, and act accordingly. Even as you desire good treatment, so render it.

Who serves his fellows is of all the greatest.
If you see no reason for giving thanks, the fault lies in yourself.

**Guy A. Zona,** *The House of the Heart Is Never Full,* **from**
*Proverbs of Africa*
One tree receiving all the wind, breaks.
A descent for the sake of a friend is an ascent.
Every ambitious man is a captive and every covetous one a pauper.
If spending your money gives you pain, you will go hungry.

————◦◦◦————

*It's not always easy to give generously, as A. A. Milne shows in "The King's
Breakfast." You might find you have to give up something you very much
want or find a way, as Malcolm X's aunt does, to use your own achieve-
ments and rewards for the benefit of others. You might, like the cob in* The
Trumpet of the Swans, *have to risk your reputation and undertake new
ways of behaving, even at the risk of offending old friends and acquaintances.*

**A. A. Milne, "The King's Breakfast," from** *When We Were Very Young*
The King asked
The Queen, and
The Queen asked
The Dairymaid:
"Could we have some butter for
The Royal slice of bread?"
The Queen asked
The Dairymaid,
The Dairymaid
Said, "Certainly,
I'll go and tell
The cow
Now
Before she goes to bed."

The Dairymaid
She curtsied,

And went and told
The Alderney:
"Don't forget the butter for
The Royal slice of bread."
The Alderney
Said sleepily:
"You'd better tell
His Majesty
That many people nowadays
Like marmalade
Instead."

The Dairymaid
Said, "Fancy!"
And went to
Her Majesty.
She curtsied to the Queen, and
She turned a little red:
"Excuse me,
Your Majesty,
For taking of
The liberty,
But marmalade is tasty, if
It's very
Thickly
Spread."

The Queen said
"Oh!"
And went to
His Majesty:
"Talking of the butter for
The Royal slice of bread,
Many people
Think that
Marmalade
Is nicer.
Would you like to try a little
Marmalade
Instead?"

The King said,
"Bother!"
And then he said,
"Oh, dear me!"
The King sobbed,
"Oh, deary me!"
And went back to bed.
"Nobody,"
He whimpered,
"Could call me
A fussy man;
I *only* want
A little bit
Of butter for
My bread!"

The Queen said,
"There, there!"
And went to
The Dairymaid.
The Dairymaid
Said, "There, there!"
And went to the shed.
The cow said,
"There, there!

I didn't really
Mean it;
Here's milk for his porringer
And butter for his bread."
The Queen took
The butter
And brought it to
His Majesty;
The King said,
"Butter, eh?"
And bounced out of bed.
"Nobody," he said,
As he kissed her
Tenderly,
"Nobody," he said,

As he slid down
The banisters,
"Nobody,
My darling,
Could call me
A fussy man—
BUT
*I do like a little bit of butter to my bread!"*


### Malcolm X, *The Autobiography of Malcolm X*

None of us talked much about our mother. And we never mentioned our father. I guess none of us knew what to say. We didn't want anybody else to mention our mother either, I think. From time to time, though, we would all go over to Kalamazoo to visit her. Most often we older ones went singly, for it was something you didn't want to have to experience with anyone else present, even your brother or sister.

During this period, the visit to my mother that I most remember was toward the end of that seventh-grade year, when our father's grown daughter by his first marriage, Ella, came from Boston to visit us. Wilfred and Hilda had exchanged some letters with Ella, and I, at Hilda's suggestion, had written to her from the Swerlins'. We were all excited and happy when her letter told us that she was coming to Lansing.

I think the major impact of Ella's arrival, at least upon me, was that she was the first really proud black woman I had ever seen in my life. She was plainly proud of her very dark skin. This was unheard of among Negroes in those days, especially in Lansing.

I hadn't been sure just what day she would come. And then one afternoon I got home from school and there she was. She hugged me, stood me away, looked me up and down. A commanding woman, maybe even bigger than Mrs. Swerlin. Ella wasn't just black, but like our father, she was jet black. The way she sat, moved, talked, did everything, bespoke somebody who did and got exactly what she wanted. This was the woman my father had boasted of so often for having brought so many of their family out of Georgia to Boston. She owned some property, he would say, and she was "in society." She had come North with nothing, and she had worked and saved and had invested in property that she built up in value, and then she started sending money to Georgia for another sister, brother, cousin, niece or nephew to come north to Boston. All that I had heard was reflected in Ella's appearance and bearing. I had never been so impressed with anybody.

She was in her second marriage; her first husband had been a doctor.

Ella asked all kinds of questions about how I was doing; she had already heard from Wilfred and Hilda about my election as class president. She asked especially about my grades, and I ran and got my report cards. I was then one of the three highest in the class. Ella praised me. I asked her about her brother, Earl, and her sister, Mary. She had the exciting news that Earl was a singer with a band in Boston. He was singing under the name of Jimmy Carleton. Mary was also doing well.

Ella told me about other relatives from that branch of the family. A number of them I'd never heard of; she had helped them up from Georgia. They, in their turn, had helped up others. "We Littles have to stick together," Ella said. It thrilled me to hear her say that, and even more, the way she said it. I had become a mascot; our branch of the family was split to pieces; I had just about forgotten about being a Little in any family sense. She said that different members of the family were working in good jobs, and some even had small businesses going. Most of them were homeowners.

When Ella suggested that all of us Littles in Lansing accompany her on a visit to our mother, we all were grateful. We all felt that if anyone could do anything that could help our mother, that might help her get well and come back, it would be Ella. Anyway, all of us, for the first time together, went with Ella to Kalamazoo.

Our mother was smiling when they brought her out. She was extremely surprised when she saw Ella. They made a striking contrast, the thin near-white woman and the big black one hugging each other. I don't remember much about the rest of the visit, except that there was a lot of talking, and Ella had everything in hand, and we left with all of us feeling better than we ever had about the circumstances. I know that for the first time, I felt as though I had visited with someone who had some kind of physical illness that had just lingered on.

A few days later, after visiting the homes where each of us were staying, Ella left Lansing and returned to Boston. But before leaving, she told me to write to her regularly. And she had suggested that I might like to spend my summer holiday visiting her in Boston. I jumped at that chance.

## E. B. White, *The Trumpet of the Swan*

As the cob flew toward Billings on his powerful white wings, all sorts of troublesome thoughts whirled in his head. The cob had never gone looking for a trumpet before. He had no money to pay for a trumpet. He feared he might arrive after the shops had closed for the day. He realized that in the whole continent of North America he was undoubtedly the only Trumpeter Swan who was on his way to a city to get a trumpet.

"This is a queer adventure," he said to himself. "Yet it is a noble quest. I will do anything to help my son Louis—even if I run into real trouble."

Toward the end of the afternoon, the cob looked ahead and in the distance saw the churches and factories and shops and homes of Billings. He decided to act quickly and boldly. He circled the city once, looking for a music store. Suddenly he spied one. It had a very big, wide window, solid glass. The cob flew lower and circled so he could get a better look. He gazed into the store. He saw a drum painted gold. He saw a fancy guitar with an electric cord. He saw a small piano. He saw banjos, horns, violins, mandolins, cymbals, saxophones, marimbaphones, cellos, and many other instruments. Then he saw what he wanted: he saw a brass trumpet hanging by a red cord.

"Now is my time to act!" he said to himself. "Now is my moment for risking everything on one bold move, however shocking it may be to my sensibilities, however offensive it may be to the laws that govern the lives of men. Here I go! May good luck go with me!"

With that, the old cob set his wings for a dive. He aimed straight at the big window. He held his neck straight and stiff, waiting for the crash. He dove swiftly and hit the window going full speed. The glass broke. The noise was terrific. The whole store shook. Musical instruments fell to the floor. Glass flew everywhere. A salesgirl fainted. The cob felt a twinge of pain as a jagged piece of broken glass cut into his shoulder, but he grabbed the trumpet in his beak, turned sharply in the air, flew back through the hole in the window, and began climbing fast over the roofs of Billings. A few drops of blood fell to the ground below. His shoulder hurt. But he had succeeded in getting what he had come for. Held firmly in his bill, its red cord dangling, was a beautiful brass trumpet.

You can imagine the noise in the music store when the cob crashed through the window. At the moment the glass broke, one of the clerks was showing a bass drum to a customer, and the clerk was so startled at seeing a big white bird come flying through the window, he hit the drum a tremendous wallop.

. . .

"Make way!" shouted the owner. He ran for the door, stepped outside, and fired another shot—*bang!*—at the disappearing bird. His shot was too late. The cob was safe in the sky, beyond the range of gunfire. He was headed home, toward the southwest, high above the roofs and spires of Billings. In his beak was the trumpet. In his heart was the pain of having committed a crime.

"I have robbed a store," he said to himself. "I have become a thief. What a miserable fate for a bird of my excellent character and high ideals! Why did I do this? What led me to commit this awful crime? My past life has been blameless—a model of good behavior and correct conduct. I am by nature law-abiding. Why, oh, why did I do this?"

Then the answer came to him, as he flew steadily on through the evening sky. "I did it to help my son. I did it for love of my son Louis."

. . .

Back at the Red Rock Lakes, Louis's mother waited anxiously for her husband to return. When he showed up in the night sky, she saw that he had a trumpet with him. It was slung around his neck by its cord.

"Well," she said, as he glided to a stop in the water, "I see you made it."

"I did, my dear," said the cob. "I traveled fast and far, sacrificed my honor, and I have returned. Where is Louis? I want to give him his trumpet right away."

"He's over there sitting on a muskrat house, dreaming about that empty-headed young female he's so crazy about."

The cob swam over to his son and made a presentation speech.

"Louis," he said, "I have been on a journey to the haunts of men. I visited a great city teeming with life and commerce. Whilst there, I picked up a gift for you, which I now bestow upon you with my love and my blessing. Here, Louis, is a trumpet. It will be your voice—a substitute for the voice God failed to give you. Learn to blow it, Louis, and life will be smoother and richer and gayer for you! With the help of this horn, you will be able at last to say ko-hoh, like every other swan. The sound of music will be in our ears. You will be able to attract the attention of desirable young females. Master this trumpet, and you will be able to play love songs for them, filling them with ardor and surprise and longing. I hope it will bring you happiness, Louis, and a new and better life. I procured it at some personal sacrifice to myself and my pride, but we won't go into that now. The long and short of it is, I had no money; I took the trumpet without paying for it. This was deplorable. But the important thing is that you learn to play the instrument."

So saying, the cob removed the trumpet from around his neck and hung it on Louis, alongside the slate and the white chalk pencil.

"Wear it in health!" he said. "Blow it in happiness! Make the woods and the hills and the marshes echo with the sounds of your youthful desire!"

*It is blessed to receive as well as to give. As O. Henry shows, to do that gen-*
*erously makes it possible to deepen the bonds between people. The pig in*
The Builders, *who just couldn't keep the "I told you so" to himself, shows*
*the other side of the coin.*


## O. Henry, *The Gift of the Magi*

Della finished her cry and attended to her cheeks with the powder rag.
She stood by the window and looked out dully at a gray cat walking a
gray fence in a gray backyard. Tomorrow would be Christmas Day, and
she had only $1.87 with which to buy Jim a present. She had been saving
every penny she could for months, with this result. Twenty dollars a
week doesn't go far. Expenses had been greater than she had calculated.
They always are. Only $1.87 to buy a present for Jim. Her Jim. Many a
happy hour she had spent planning for something nice for him.
Something fine and rare and sterling—something just a little bit near to
being worthy of the honor of being owned by him.

. . .

Now, there were two possessions of the James Dillingham Youngs in
which they both took a mighty pride. One was Jim's gold watch that had
been his father's and his grandfather's. The other was Della's hair. Had
the Queen of Sheba lived in the flat across the airshaft, Della would have
let her hair hang out the window some day to dry just to depreciate Her
Majesty's jewels and gifts. Had King Solomon been the janitor, with all
his treasures piled up in the basement, Jim would have pulled out his
watch every time he passed, just to see him pluck at his beard from envy.

So now Della's beautiful hair fell about her rippling and shining like
a cascade of brown waters. It reached below her knee and made itself
almost a garment for her. And then she did it up again nervously and
quickly. Once she faltered for a minute and stood still while a tear or two
splashed on the worn red carpet.

On went her old brown jacket; on went her old brown hat. With a
whirl of skirts and with the brilliant sparkle still in her eyes, she fluttered
out the door and down the stairs to the street.

Where she stopped the sign read: "Mme. Sofronie. Hair Goods of All
Kinds." One flight up Della ran, and collected herself, panting. Madame,
large, too white, chilly, hardly looked the "Sofronie."

"Will you buy my hair?" asked Della.

"I buy hair," said Madame. "Take yer hat off and let's have a sight at
the looks of it."

Down rippled the brown cascade.

"Twenty dollars," said Madame, lifting the mass with a practiced hand.

"Give it to me quick," said Della.

Oh, and the next two hours tripped by on rosy wings. Forget the hashed metaphor. She was ransacking the stores for Jim's present.

She found it at last. It surely had been made for him and no one else. There was no other like it in any of the stores, and she had turned all of them inside out. It was a platinum fob chain simple and chaste in design, properly proclaiming its value by substance alone and not by meretricious ornamentation—as all good things should do. It was even worthy of The Watch. As soon as she saw it she knew that it must be Jim's. It was like him. Quietness and value—the description applied to both. Twenty-one dollars they took from her for it, and she hurried home with the 87 cents. With that chain on his watch Jim might be properly anxious about the time in any company. Grand as the watch was, he sometimes looked at it on the sly on account of the old leather strap that he used in place of a chain.

When Della reached home her intoxication gave way a little to prudence and reason. She got out her curling irons and lighted the gas and went to work repairing the ravages made by generosity added to love. Which is always a tremendous task, dear friends—a mammoth task.

Within forty minutes her head was covered with tiny, close-lying curls that made her look wonderfully like a truant schoolboy. She looked at her reflection in the mirror long, carefully, and critically.

"If Jim doesn't kill me," she said to herself, "before he takes a second look at me, he'll say I look like a Coney Island chorus girl. But what could I do—oh! what could I do with a dollar and eighty-seven cents?"

At 7 o'clock the coffee was made and the frying-pan was on the back of the stove hot and ready to cook the chops.

Jim was never late. Della doubled the fob chain in her hand and sat on the corner of the table near the door that he always entered. Then she heard his step on the stair away down on the first flight, and she turned white for just a moment. She had a habit of saying little silent prayers about the simplest everyday things, and now she whispered: "Please God, make him think I am still pretty."

The door opened and Jim stepped in and closed it. He looked thin and very serious. Poor fellow, he was only twenty-two—and to be burdened with a family! He needed a new overcoat and he was without gloves.

Jim stopped inside the door, as immovable as a setter at the scent of quail. His eyes were fixed upon Della, and there was an expression in them that she could not read, and it terrified her. It was not anger, nor surprise, nor disapproval, nor horror, nor any of the sentiments that she had been prepared for. He simply stared at her fixedly with that peculiar expression on his face.

. . .

Out of his trance Jim seemed quickly to wake. He enfolded his Della. For ten seconds let us regard with discreet scrutiny some inconsequential object in the other direction. Eight dollars a week or a million a year— what is the difference? A mathematician or a wit would give you the wrong answer. The magi brought valuable gifts, but that was not among them. This dark assertion will be illuminated later on.

Jim drew a package from his overcoat pocket and threw it upon the table.

"Don't make any mistake, Dell," he said, "about me. I don't think there's anything in the way of a haircut or a shave or a shampoo that could make me like my girl any less. But if you'll unwrap that package you may see why you had me going a while at first."

White fingers and nimble tore at the string and paper. And then an ecstatic scream of joy; and then, alas! a quick feminine change to hysterical tears and wails, necessitating the immediate employment of all the comforting powers of the lord of the flat.

For there lay The Combs—the set of combs, side and back, that Della had worshipped for long in a Broadway window. Beautiful combs, pure tortoise shell, with jewelled rims—just the shade to wear in the beautiful vanished hair. They were expensive combs, she knew, and her heart had simply craved and yearned over them without the least hope of possession. And now, they were hers, but the tresses that should have adorned the coveted adornments were gone.

But she hugged them to her bosom, and at length she was able to look up with dim eyes and a smile and say: "My hair grows so fast, Jim!"

And then Della leaped up like a little singed cat and cried, "Oh, oh!"

Jim had not yet seen his beautiful present. She held it out to him eagerly upon her open palm. The dull precious metal seemed to flash with a reflection of her bright and ardent spirit.

"Isn't it a dandy, Jim? I hunted all over town to find it. You'll have to look at the time a hundred times a day now. Give me your watch. I want to see how it looks on it."

Instead of obeying, Jim tumbled down on the couch and put his hands under the back of his head and smiled.

"Dell," said he, "let's put our Christmas presents away and keep 'em a while. They're too nice to use just at present. I sold the watch to get the money to buy your combs. And now suppose you put the chops on."

The magi, as you know, were wise men—wonderfully wise men—who brought gifts to the Babe in the manger. They invented the art of giving Christmas presents. Being wise, their gifts were no doubt wise ones, possibly bearing the privilege of exchange in case of duplication. And here I have lamely related to you the uneventful chronicle of two foolish children in a flat who most unwisely sacrificed for each other the greatest treasures of their house. But in a last word to the wise of these days let it be said that of all who give gifts these two were the wisest. Of all who give and receive gifts, such as they are wisest. Everywhere they are wisest. They are the magi.

### Sara Henderson Hay, *The Builders*

I told them a thousand times if I told them once:
Stop fooling around, I said, with straw and sticks;
They won't hold up. You're taking an awful chance.
Brick is the stuff to build with, solid bricks.
You want to be impractical, go ahead.
But just remember, I told them; wait and see,
You're making a big mistake. Awright, I said,
But when the wolf comes, don't come running to me.

The funny thing is, they didn't. There they sat,
One in his crummy yellow shack, and one
Under his roof of twigs, and the wolf ate
Them, hair and hide. Well, what is done is done.
But I'd been willing to help them, all along,
If only they'd once admitted they were wrong.

---

*In our most able moments, when like Esther in* The Endless Steppe *we are intensely aware of our own talents and skills, we need also to consider those less well-endowed. Then our talents are tools of service, not of conquest—used to animate, not to appropriate.*

### Esther Hautzig, *The Endless Steppe*

No one had seen it. The money was gone and with it our bread for the month.

I not only felt sick with despair, but also frightened. Mother didn't get angry with me often, but when she did, it was overwhelming. All of my past offenses dwindled to minor infractions compared to losing this money. I simply did not want to go back to the hut and stalled as long as I could. I walked around the village trying to figure out some way of replacing the money . . . or getting the bread. I had some quite desperate fantasies. Having already discovered that I was not much good as a thief, I wondered whether I would fare any better as a beggar. Finally, there was no escape: I had to go home.

It was very late and Mother was full of concern. Why was I so late? Had anything happened to me?

"I won't say. You can be as angry with me as your wish. I don't know what to say. And I don't know what happened. I don't. I don't." My voice began to quaver and my teeth to chatter. I didn't cry; I just shivered from head to foot. It was not calculated; it was unavoidable.

In a second both Mother and Grandmother were fussing over me: What in God's name was the trouble? Was I sick? Surely nothing could have happened that was terrible enough to make me act this way?

"But it did!" I cried out. "It did! The thirty rubles—they're gone—"

I had a rather spectacular fit of hysterics, weeping and gasping for breath.

The two women stood absolutely still for a minute or two, trying to absorb this latest misfortune.

The next thing I knew I was in Mother's arms and she was stroking my hair. "Oh, my darling, we have lost so much more in our lives than this thirty-ruble note. You must stop your crying and your shivering. Everything will be all right."

Grandmother had gone to the pot of very watery soup that was our supper for that night.

"A nice cup of soup, Esther . . . "

"No, no. I can't eat. Now or ever. There will be nothing to eat the rest of this month. . . ."

I was on the verge of starting my hysterics all over again.

And Mother started talking—to me, to Grandmother, and to herself I am sure. Standing in for Father, she was assuring us that everything was going to be all right: we would not starve, we had friends, didn't we? (Grandmother and I nodded, although we knew that for Mother to ask anyone for a crust of bread was unthinkable.) We would find something to sell.

She stopped talking.

Selling the food one got at the state store on the free market was illegal and punishable to an uncomfortable degree, rumor had it. When she picked up the piece of bread we had left, I knew what was going through her mind.

"I'll do it, Mamma."

"No, not you—"

We argued back and forth and, frightened to death about it as she was, and indeed as I was too, it was settled that I would try to sell the bread the next day.

"Before Tata left, he told us we were strong women and that we would get on well without him," Mother said. "And so we will." She put her hand on my head. "But you will be very very careful, Esther, won't you?"

The next day after school I went to the free market with our piece of bread. I carried it under my coat, as surreptitiously as the old women with the bread they wished to have blessed. I was becoming skilled in the ways of deception and no one caught me. I sold the piece of bread for twenty rubles, which reduced our loss to ten rubles.

Whether inspired by Mother's including me among the strong women who would get on well, or frightened by the prospect of starvation, that was the day that I decided that somehow or other I too must earn some rubles.

After supper, I waited for Grandmother to finish pushing back her cuticles—a process I thought would never end—and lie down on the mattress of straw, which even her tiny frail body had begun to make a bed of lumps. When I heard the pathetic little wheezes that accompanied her troubled sleep, I signaled to Mother that I wanted to talk to her. As I talked of my intention to become a breadwinner, I watched Mother's still beautiful but ravaged face for praise that surely was due me for being such an enterprising person. But Mother's face remained strangely opaque.

"What's the matter?" I asked, considerably deflated.

Then, as if she were pleading my case before some unearthly court, she murmured: "She is only twelve years old, she helps keep house like a little old woman, she studies like a Talmudic scholar, she carries bricks back and forth—" She caught her breath. "No. Enough is already too much. Esther, there is nothing more you can do that I will permit you to do. Just do well at school, that's all I ask. The way things are, you will need every drop of education you can get. For the rest—you leave the rubles to me."

"But, Mama—"

"Esther! Please not tonight. Tonight I don't have the strength for your 'buts.'"

"But I can knit and I can embroider, can't I? You and Miss Rachel taught me how, didn't you?"

Mother's lips twisted. "But of course. All the gentle arts—"

"Well, I will use them right here to make some money."

Mother was absolutely certain that rough as life was, every single woman in Rubtsovsk knew how to knit just as well as I did.

"But we can ask around, can't we? You ask your friends and I'll ask my friends. We'll spread the word."

For me, spreading the word meant that I had to admit to my friends that I needed work badly, that we really did not have enough food to see us through the winter. As my hunger grew, my pride shrank and so did my price—although I apparently still kept my head up as high as I could get it. I reduced it from "some" rubles to a little bit of milk or a cup of flour or some potatoes. Still there were no customers. Mother was right; everyone in Rubtsovsk did know how to knit and didn't need me.

I had given up all hope when a young woman came to our hut late one afternoon. She had some old white wool: would I knit a sweater for her little girl?

*Would* I? Presented at last with a real live customer, I was so flustered that I could barely talk.

"Don't *you* know how to knit?" I asked the lady, more incredulous than businesslike.

"Yes," she said.

"Then—?"

She held out her right arm and to my horror I saw that most of her hand was gone. I looked away quickly. Mother, who thought of everything, had not thought of this.

The woman showed me the wool—barely enough for a sweater for a midget—and said the sweater was to be a surprise for her little girl, who was not well.

"I cannot pay you much—"

A dreadful thought buzzed around me: Ought I to take anything at all from a poor crippled woman?

"—but I have a cow. Would one liter of milk and maybe a pail of potatoes be enough?"

Milk? And potatoes? The buzzing stopped. I was thrilled.

"Could you possibly have it ready for the New Year?"

Oh, yes, I assured the lady, although how this was to be done with everything else I had to do, I did not know.

"My little girl will be so happy," the lady said.

That makes two little girls, I thought.

Mother was amazed and, it turned out, delighted. She showed me how to start the sweater, but I had to rip it out a million times before I really got going. I worked on it whenever I had a spare minute and far into every night. The light in our hut was very poor. We had one we kept the wick down as low as possible. Moreover, the lamp had to rest on the one and only table, which was not close enough to be the stove to keep my fingers warm. In order for them to be nimble enough to knit, I had constantly to jump up to warm them at the stove. But at last the sweater was finished and neatly pressed with an iron borrowed from Anya, who had surely gone hungry to acquire one.

My customer greeted me warmly and said I must meet her little girl. Having been told only that her child was "not well," I was not prepared for the pinched and white-faced little creature who sat up in bed to stare at me in a most peculiar way, with her little eyes squinting and her head twisting this way and that.

After a few stilted words—the little girl spoke in a wee little voice— the mother ushered me out. "My little girl is going blind and there's nothing we can do about it. I am glad you did such a good job on the sweater. Whenever she wears it, it will make her happy."

She gave me the milk and potatoes and I walked home filled with pride.

That night, as we feasted on the milk and potatoes, I saw a bright future with customers lining up in front of our hut to offer me work.

"She is her father's daughter, always the optimist," Mother said, shaking her head.

"And a good thing it is," Grandmother retorted. "If she had not been such an optimist, would we be drinking this milk and eating these potatoes?"

---

*Edward, in* Ann of Avonlean, *is concerned that people be kind to each other, but that can be difficult when life is hard. Is it sound to let your worst experiences dominate how you deal with everybody else—or is it wiser to preserve the chance to do some good? Be sure to keep the end in view, as Papa reminds Rob in* A Day No Pigs Would Die. *Even though you may receive great appreciation for your generous actions, it's a good idea not to rest on your laurels but to be open to the challenge of new experience and of tasks not yet done. As Papa gently suggests, it's a mistake to think you have reached the end of a journey.*

## L. M. Montgomery, *Ann of Avonlea*

*Dear teacher,*

> *I think I will write you a composition about birds. birds is very useful animals. my cat catches birds. His name is William, but pa calls him tom. he is oll striped and he got one of his ears forz of last winter. only for that he would be a good-looking cat. My unkle had adopted a cat. it came to his house one day and wouldent go away and unkle says it has forgot more than most people ever knowed. he lets it sleep on his rocking chare and my aunt says he thinks more of it than he does of his children. that is not right. we ought to be kind to the cats and given them new milk but we ought not to be better to them than to our children. this is oll I can think of so no more at present.*

> *edward blake ClaY*

## Robert Newton Peck, *A Day No Pigs Would Die*

Somebody was yelling out Papa's name, but I couldn't see anything. And it was real strange, because my eyes were open. They sort of stinged. So I blinked, but the fog was still there.

There was a wool blanket around me. I could feel the wool rub against the raw place on my arm, but the hurt of it seemed to keep me awake. And keep me alive.

There were more voices now. I heard Papa answer, and the man who was carrying me asked him, "Is this your boy? There's so much blood and dirt and Satan on him, I can't tell for sure. Besides, he's near naked."

"Yes," said Papa. "That's our Robert."

And then I heard Mama's voice, soft and sweet like music; and I could feel her hands on my head and my hair. Aunt Carrie was there, too. She was Mama's oldest sister, who lived with us.

Strong hands were touching my legs now, and then my ribs. I tried to say something about not being in school. Somebody had some warm water and washed my face with it. The water had lilac in it, and smelled right restful.

"We're beholding to you, Benjamin Tanner," said Papa, "for fetching him home. Whatever he done, I'll make it right."

"Better look to his arm. It got tore up worse than proper. May be broke."

"Haven," I heard Mama say, "the boy's holding something in his hand. Can't make it out."

I felt them taking something from my right hand. I didn't want to render it up, but they took it.

"I never see the like of it," Mama said. "Like it's near to be alive."

I could hear Mr. Tanner's rough voice over the others. "I know what that is. It's a goiter."

"Goiter?"

"Where'd he get it?"

"It's an evil thing. But for now let's tend his arm. Mr. Tanner, we may got to cut away part of your blanket."

"Ain't mine. Belongs to my horse. So cut all you're a mind to."

I felt Papa pulling the blanket down off my right shoulder, until it got caught in the clotted blood. I heard his jackknife click open, and cut away part of the wool.

"I tied my bandana on his arm," said Mr. Tanner, "so he wouldn't bleed dry." When Papa loosened it up, Mr. Tanner said, "He'll bleed again with it loose, Haven."

"He will," said Papa, "and that'll be a good thing for his arm. Let it open up and holler out all the dirt. Only way to treat a wound is to bleed it, 'til it's clean as a cat's mouth."

"True."

"Lucy," Papa spoke soft to Mama, "better get a needle threaded. He'll want sewing."

He picked me up in his arms, carried me into the house and to the kitchen. He laid me flat on the long lammis table, face up. Mama put something soft under my head, and Aunt Carrie kept washing me off with the lilac water while Papa cut off my shirt and took off my boots.

"The poor lamb," said Mama.

Somebody put a hand on my forehead to see if I was cool. It was followed by a cold wet cloth, and it felt real good. Funny, but it was the only thing on my entire body that I could feel. Then I felt the first of Mama's stitches going into the meat of my arm. I wanted to yell out, but didn't have the will for it. Instead I just lay there on my back on that old kitchen table and let Mama sew me back together. It hurt. My eyes filled up with crying and the water ran in rivers to my ears, but I never let out a whimper.

When I had took all the sewing to be took (and by this time I must of been more thread than boy) Papa burdened me upstairs to my room. I could smell Mama, crisp and starched, plumping my pillow, and the cool muslin pillowcase touched both my ears as the back of my head sank into all those feathers.

"Tell Mr. Tanner," I said.

Mama rushed to where my head was, and Papa and Aunt Carrie were at bed foot.

"Tell Mr. Tanner," I said again, "that were he to look up on the ridge, he'll find a calf. I helped get it born. Afterward, old Apron was still choking so I had to rip the ball out of her throat. And I didn't mean to skip school."

"I'll be," said Papa.

"Where are your trousers, Rob?" said Aunt Carrie, who took quite a stock in appearances.

"Up on the ridge. When I tied 'em round a tree they got busted some. I'm sorry, Mama. You'll just have to cut me out another pair."

Mama put her face right down close to mine, and I could smell her goodness.

"I'm preferenced to mend busted pants than a busted boy."

"I . . . I can't feel nothing in my right hand."

"That's 'cause it's resting," said Mama. "It wants to get well, and so do you. So right about now your Pa and Carrie and I are going to tiptoe out of here and let you get some rest. You earned it."

They left. And I closed my eyes and went right off. Later I woke up when Mama brought me a dish of hot succotash and a warm glass of milking, fresh from the evening pail. The bubbles were still on it.

"That's real good," I said.

At bedtime, Papa came upstairs with his big shoes kicking one of the risers, and brought me one of the last of the winter apples from the cellar. He pulled up a chair close to my bed and looked at me for a long time while I ate the apple with my left hand.

"You mending?"

"Yes, Papa."

"I ought to lick you proper for leaving the schoolhouse."

"Yes, Papa. You ought."

"Someday you want to walk into the bank in Learning and write down your name, don't you?"

"Yes, sir."

# Empathy

One day Mr. Gumpy went out in his boat . . .
"Can I come along, Mr. Gumpy?" said the rabbit.
"Yes, but don't hop about."

Lots of animals want to go on Mr. Gumpy's Outing in the book by John Burningham. Serially, Mr. Gumpy tells the cat not to chase the rabbit, the dog not to tease the cat, the pig not to "muck" about, the sheep not to bleat. Mr. Gumpy is kind enough to include them all, but he is not empathetic. He offers a ride on his boat only if the animals promise not to be themselves, not to do what they do. Empathy means understanding and appreciating another person's most deeply felt self.

Emily and Little Bear in *Little Bear's Friend* (by Else Holmslund Minarik) are empathetic. In saying good-bye after a wonderful summer together, each wants to do and give something very special. They want to give the best, most important gift they can. They both feel exactly the same way. But each knows when Emily is tempted to give too much, and they are considerate and understanding in allowing her to change her mind:

Emily hugged her doll, and said, "Lucy wants to say good-by, too. Say good-by to Little Bear, Lucy."

Emily made Little Bear hold Lucy. Then she said to him, "Little Bear, you can have Lucy for keeps. I will give her to you."

"Oh—" began Little Bear. But before he could say anything, Emily took Lucy back again. "Oops," she said. "I forgot. Lucy has to come to school with me."

Emily opened her pocket book. She took out a fine new pen. "This is for you," she said. "I want you to have it."

Little Bear took the pen. "Thank you, Emily," he said. He ran into his room, and came back with a pretty toy boat.

In Sloppy Kisses (by Elizabeth Winthrop), Rosemary persuades Emmylou that kissing is for babies, even though Emmylou's family loves to kiss. Emmylou immediatley begins to reject her parent's kisses. "No more sloppy kisses," she tells them; in the morning at school time and evening at bedtime. Rosemary is very pleased and congratulates Emmylou, who lives without kissing for a while. But she misses family kissing a lot. Her parents do too. But they understand what she is feeling. They remain very warm and pat her good night on the shoulder. After a while Emmylou, in front of Rosemary at school, hugs her dad and gives him a big, sloppy kiss. Rosemary is quite upset: she insists kissing is only for babies.

"It is not," said Emmylou. "Kissing is for everybody." And she gave Rosemary a little kiss on the cheek and walked inside.

Emmylou was able to figure out that Rosemary was jealous so she gave her a kiss too. A kind of empathetic circle was created through the interplay of testing, patience, understanding, and self-control with love, friendship, and a little rivalry too.

---

*Empathy cannot be feigned. The grateful sparrow forgets it is a deeply authentic feeling between people and is not the same as pity. There are no rules to follow—and the rewards that can result from such a strong connection won't come if we try to imitate feeling involved. But there are times when the limits set by the differences in people's life experience run so deep that even the strongest personal connections will be frustrated. This was the case for the two loving and well-meaning children in* One More River.

## Anonymous, *The Grateful Sparrow,* translated by Donald Keene

In times now long ago, one bright sunny day in early spring an old woman of about sixty was sitting outside her house picking lice. In the courtyard a sparrow hopped about. Some children who were playing nearby started to throw stones at the bird, and one of them struck it, breaking its back. While it struggled about, helplessly flapping its wings, a crow came swooping down upon it. "Oh, what a pity! The crow will get it!" cried the old woman. She rushed over to the sparrow and picked it up. Then she blew on it with her warm breath and fed it. She put the bird into a little pail which she took indoors for the night. The next morning she fed it some rice and made it some medicine of copper dust.

Her children and grandchildren said sneeringly "What a dear old lady she is, to take care of a sparrow in her old age!"

Nevertheless, she tenderly looked after the bird for several months until at last it was hopping about again. Though a mere sparrow, it felt very happy and grateful that she had restored it to health. Whenever the old woman left the house, even on the briefest of errands, she would give instructions to her family. "Look after the sparrow and see that it gets something to eat." And her children and grandchildren laughed at her and teased her. "How touching! Why do you worry so much about a sparrow?" "Say what you please, it's a poor helpless creature," she would reply.

As a result of the good care she took of it, the bird finally was able to fly once more. "Now no crow will get it," said the old woman and took it outdoors to see how well it could fly. When she placed it on the palm of her hand and had it out at arm's length, away the sparrow flew with a flutter of its wings. After that the old woman, in the loneliness and tedium of her life, longed for the bird. She would say, "How sad that it has flown away after so many months and days of taking it in for the night and feeding it in the morning!" As usual, everyone laughed at her.

Some twenty days later the woman heard the loud chirping of a sparrow outside her house. "Why, that's a sparrow! Perhaps the same one has come back," she thought, going out to look. Indeed, it was the very same sparrow. "Oh, how touching! How touching that it has not forgotten me and has come back," she said. The sparrow, peering at the old woman's face, dropped something very small that it had in its beak, apparently intending to leave whatever it was for her, and then flew away. "What can the sparrow have dropped?" wondered the woman. She went over and discovered that it had let fall a single gourd seed. "It must have had some reason for bringing this," she said, picking it up. Her children mocked her, "How wonderful! She gets a present from a sparrow and acts as if it were some great treasure!" "Say what you will, I'll plant it and see what happens," she replied, and this she did.

When autumn came the plant bore a great many gourds. They were not of the usual kind, but much larger and more numerous. The old woman was exceedingly pleased. No matter how many she picked or gave away to the neighbors, more still remained than she could possibly use. Her children and grandchildren who had laughed at her ate the gourds every day.

At last, when she had distributed the gourds to everyone in the village, she decided that she would cure seven or eight of the largest and finest to use as containers. These she hung indoors and left to dry. When several months had elapsed, she inspected them, thinking that by this time they would be about ready. The gourds had indeed turned out very well but when she took one of them down, she was surprised to find how heavy it was. She cut open the gourd all the same, only to discover that it was stuffed with something. She poured it out to see what it might be— the gourd was full of white rice! Amazed at this prodigy, she emptied the gourd into a big container, but when she had finished it was full again, just as when she began. Astonished and overjoyed, she said, "This is most unusual. The sparrow must be back of this." She put the rice into containers and stored it away. When she examined the other gourds, she found that they were full of rice too. No matter how much she poured out or used, there was still more left than she knew what to do with, and she thus became a very wealthy person indeed. The other villagers were amazed and envious at her good fortune.

Now the children of the old woman who lived next door said to their mother, "Other people, though they're no different from you, manage to become rich, but you can't even do the simplest thing." As the result of such complaints, the old woman from next door went to visit the first old woman. "Now then, what's all this about? I've heard some rumors about a sparrow, but I really know nothing about it. Please tell me the whole story from the beginning, just as it happened."

"It all came about from planting a gourd seed that a sparrow dropped," replied the first old woman, and would not give any further details. But the second old woman kept pressing her. "I insist! Do tell me all about it!" And so, thinking that it would be wrong to be petty and keep the matter a secret, she said, "I took care of a sparrow that had a broken back, and nursed it back to health. It must have felt so grateful that it brought me a gourd seed which I planted, and this is what happened."

"Please give me just one of the seeds," said the second old woman, but she refused. "I will give you some of the rice that was inside the gourds, but I can't give you any seeds. Those I most certainly cannot give away."

Having been thus unsuccessful in getting a seed, the second old woman began to keep a sharp lookout in the hope that she too might find a sparrow with a broken back to take care of, but not a single sparrow of that description was to be seen.

**Lynne Reid Banks, *One More River***
'Shalom.'
    'Salaam.'

They looked at each other, awakened, happy, embarrassed. Then she put out her right hand and he took it and shook it and they half-laughed. Her hand was not soft like a little girl's nor hard like a woman's (all the grown girls and women he knew had hard, calloused hands) but something in between. It was very warm, and her grip was firm. Lesley, on her side, thought his hand felt somewhat too cool and limp, and she gripped harder than she usually did to encourage him to grip back, for she sensed his shyness and uncertainty. The strength in her hand challenged the man in him, and he suddenly pressed hers almost convulsively before letting go.

'How is your peace?' she asked in Hebrew, and he replied:

'My peace is good. And yours?'

'Also good.'

They spoke stiffly, but their eyes were shining. They were each strangely thrilled to see the other. Their meeting seemed to both uncanny, an event not to be dreamed of, not really part of normality.

'What are you doing here?' asked Lesley.

The boy shrugged and indicated the tray with hidden shame. 'What you see—selling. You want nuts?' He took a bag and offered it to her. 'Without money. I give you. Take.'

She took them and thanked him and ate one, and offered one to him. 'Are they yours?'

'My uncle's.'

'Won't he care?'

'He not know.'

They grinned. Then he asked her what she was doing in Tubas.

'I'm on a trip with my class.'

'You like our country?' he asked, with just a hint of irony.

She flushed and said, 'Yes, very much. I like the villages. Why did you leave your village?'

She at once noticed his withdrawn expression and knew she had touched him on the raw. He answered with his old roughness:

'That is my business.'

'I'm sorry.'

After a moment, feeling ashamed, he added, 'It was the war.'

'I understand.'

'I live now with my father and my uncle in this town.' He didn't consider his sister worth mentioning.

'It goes well with you?'

'Not bad.'

'And Eeyore?' she asked eagerly, without thinking.

'What?'

'Oh' . . . She giggled, and a smile twitched his tough mouth at the sight. 'Eeyore—that's what I used to call your donkey. Hee-haw—Eeyore—it's a donkey's name from a book.'

'He's okay.'

'Did you keep your promise?'

'Yes.'

'You don't beat him, ever?'

'Only when he is bad,' he said, to keep his pride, for he couldn't let her know how completely he had obeyed her.

'You shouldn't beat him at all! He doesn't mean to be bad.'

'He is lazy and no good,' he said sternly, but then he smiled.' But I like him—sometimes.'

'You have him with you here?'

'Yes, of course.'

'But this is your work now—the nuts?' He nodded. 'So why do you need him?'

'He carries things. He carries us. We would be nothings without a donkey,' he said. 'My father rode him here, all the way from our village, with all our stuff on his back too. He never gets tired.'

'I thought you said he was lazy and no good.'

'Oh, that is only sometimes.'

'I think you love him now.'

'Of course not. He's just an animal.'

They stood for a while saying nothing. Lesley waved lightly to Ofer, who was craning his neck to watch her.

'You can't go back to your village now?' Lesley asked suddenly.

'No.'

'Would you like—' she began, then hesitated. The war was over. Surely there would be proper peace soon, and yet . . . Would the kibbutz allow . . . ? What would her friends think of her? But she finished her sentence. 'Would you like to visit the kibbutz?'

'What?'

'My—village. Where I live. You can see your village from there.'

He stared at her. He was trying to come to grips with the idea of seeing his village like that, from the Jewish side of the river. To visiting that hated place which, had it not been for Lesley, he would long have dreamt of destroying. He wouldn't mind destroying it anyway, if he could just be sure she wouldn't be there at the time.

'No!'

'Why not? Why are you angry?' He turned his head away. His eyes had a curious burning in them. 'Mustapha . . . I understand how you feel about—us. About the war and everything, but—'

'No you don't. You can't understand.'

'But we're not enemies, are we? You and I?'

He looked round at her slowly. His eyes were lustrous like black olives, and just as bitter, but they softened as they looked at her.

'Perhaps no. But I am enemy to all your people, except only you.'

'Don't talk like that!'

'You want lies? That is the truth. You must know it.'

'But the war's over!'

'It is not over. It is not begun.'

She gazed at him with a deep sensation of horror swelling inside her. 'But Mustapha, it can't be like that! Don't you see that it can't go on and on? There's been so much fighting, so many people are dead. How can you want to go on? Let it stop, let it stop and let's have peace!'

'*You* can say that. You can talk of peace. You—won,' he said with great difficulty. 'But when you lose, it is different. Then you can't talk about stopping. You must talk about fighting and you must fight, until you lose your—' He groped desperately for the English word.

'Till you lose your life?' Lesley cried.

'No, no. Till you don't have to feel—' He curled his hand into a hard claw and made a savage gesture towards his chest as if some beast were tearing at him. And Lesley understood.

'Ashamed.'

'Yes, *yes!* Till you are not ashamed—any more.'

'Oh, Mustapha! Then there'll be no end to it—ever. Because someone must always lose.'

———⊶◈⊷———

*Joining in a strong, intuitive connection with another person is one of life's great wonders. It nourishes a feeling of wholeness in us and empowers us to take difficult steps and to make hard decisions. Grandpa gives this kind of help in* Flowers and Freckle Cream. *With his understanding, Elizabeth finds the strength to deal with her situation.*

### Elizabeth Ellis, *Flowers and Freckle Cream*

When I was a kid about 12 years old, I was already as tall as I am now, and I had a lot of freckles. I had reached the age when I had begun to really look at myself in the mirror, and I was underwhelmed. Apparently my mother was too, because sometimes she'd look at me and shake her head and say, "You can't make a silk purse out of a sow's ear."

I had a cousin whose name was Janette Elizabeth, and Janette Elizabeth looked exactly like her name sounds. She had a waist so small that men could put their hands around it . . . and they did. She had waist-length naturally curly blonde hair too, but to me her unforgivable sin was that she had a flawless peaches-and-cream complexion. I couldn't help comparing myself with her and thinking that my life would be a lot different if I had beautiful skin too—skin that was all one color.

And then, in the back pages of Janette Elizabeth's *True Confessions* magazine, I found the answer: an advertisement for freckle-remover cream. I knew that I could afford it if I saved my money, and I did. The ad assured me that the product would arrive in a "plain brown wrapper." Plain brown freckle color.

For three weeks I went to the mailbox every day precisely at the time the mail was delivered. I knew that if someone else in my family got the mail, I would never hear the end of it. There was no way that they would let me open the box in private. Finally, after three weeks of scheduling my entire day around the mail truck's arrival, my package came.

I went to my room with it, sat on the edge of my bed, and opened it. I was sure that I was looking at a miracle. But I had gotten so worked up about the magical package that I couldn't bring myself to put the cream on. What if it didn't work? What would I do then?

I fell asleep that night without even trying the stuff. And when I got up the next morning and looked at my freckles in the mirror, I said, "Elizabeth, this is silly. You have to do it now!" I smeared the cream all over my body. There wasn't as much of it as I had thought there would be, and I could see that I was going to need a part-time job to keep me in freckle remover.

Later that day I took my hoe and went with my brother and cousins to the head of the holler to hoe tobacco, as we did nearly every day in the summer. Of course, when you stay out hoeing tobacco all day, you're not working in the shade. And there was something important I hadn't realized about freckle remover: if you wear it in the sun, it seems to have a reverse effect. Instead of developing a peaches-and-cream complexion, you just get more and darker freckles.

By the end of the day I looked as though I had leopard blood in my veins, although I didn't realize it yet. When I came back to the house. my family, knowing nothing about the freckle-remover cream, began to say things like, "I've never seen you with that many freckles before." When I saw myself in the mirror, I dissolved into tears and hid in the bathroom.

My mother called me to the dinner table, but I ignored her. Then she came to the bathroom door and demanded that I come out and eat, I burst out the door and ran by her, crying I ran out to the well house and threw myself down, and I was still sobbing when my grandfather came out to see what was wrong with me. I told him about how I'd sent for the freckle remover, and he didn't laugh—though he did suggest that one might get equally good results from burying a dead black cat when the moon was full.

It was clear that Grandpa didn't understand, so I tried to explain why I didn't want to have freckles and why I felt so inadequate when I compared my appearance with Janette Elizabeth's. He looked at me in stunned surprise, shook his head, and said, "But child, there are all kinds of flowers, and they are all beautiful." I said, "I've never seen a flower with freckles!" and ran back to my room, slamming the door.

When my mother came and knocked, I told her to go away. She started to say the kinds of things that parents say at times like that, but my grandfather said, "Nancy, leave the child alone." She was a grown-up, but he was her father. So she left me alone.

I don't know where Grandpa found it. It isn't at all common in the mountains where we lived then. But I know he put it in my room because my mother told me later. I had cried myself to sleep that night, and when I opened my swollen, sticky eyes the next morning, the first thing I saw, lying on the pillow next to my head, was a tiger lily.

---

*Sometimes we will be lucky enough to find empathetic support with strangers, sometimes with people we know. Suddenly, we can make great discoveries about other people and about ourselves, just like the Lion, the Tin Woodman, and the Scarecrow do in* The Wizard of Oz, *because we've recognized ourselves and one another fully for the first time.*

## L. Frank Baum, *The Wizard of Oz*

'I am Oz, the Great and Terrible,' said the little man, in a trembling voice. 'But don't strike me—please don't—and I'll do anything you want me to.'

Our friends looked at him in surprise and dismay.

'I thought Oz was a great Head,' said Dorothy.

'And I thought Oz was a lovely Lady,' said the Scarecrow.

'And I thought Oz was a terrible Beast,' said the Tin Woodman.

'And I thought Oz was a Ball of Fire,' exclaimed the Lion.

'No, you are all wrong,' said the little man meekly. 'I have been making believe.'

'Making believe!' cried Dorothy. 'Are you not a great Wizard?'

'Hush, my dear,' he said. 'Don't speak so loud, or you will be overheard—and I should be ruined. I'm supposed to be a Great Wizard.'

'And aren't you?' she asked.

'Not a bit of it, my dear; I'm just a common man.'

'You're more than that,' said the Scarecrow, in a grieved tone. 'You're a humbug.'

'Exactly so!' declared the little man, rubbing his hands together as if it pleased him. 'I am a humbug.'

'But this is terrible,' said the Tin Woodman. 'How shall I ever get my heart?'

'Or I my courage?' asked the Lion.

'Or I my brains?' wailed the Scarecrow, wiping the tears from his eyes with his coat sleeve.

'My dear friends,' said Oz. 'I pray you not to speak of these little things. Think of me, and the terrible trouble I'm in at being found out.'

'Doesn't anyone else know you're a humbug?' asked Dorothy.

'No one knows it but you four—and myself,' replied Oz. 'I have fooled everyone so long that I thought I should never be found out. It was a great mistake my ever letting you into the Throne Room. Usually I will not see even my subjects, and so they believe I am something terrible.'

. . .

'Really,' said the Scarecrow, 'you ought to be ashamed of yourself for being such a humbug.'

'I am—I certainly am,' answered the little man sorrowfully. 'But it was the only thing I could do. Sit down, please, there are plenty of chairs. I will tell you my story.'

So they sat down and listened while he told the following tale:

'I was born in Omaha—'

'Why, that isn't very far from Kansas!' cried Dorothy.

'No, but it's farther from here,' he said, shaking his head at her sadly. 'When I grew up I became a ventriloquist, and at that I was very well trained by a great master. I can imitate any kind of bird or beast.' Here he mewed so like a kitten that Toto pricked up his ears and looked everywhere to see where she was. 'After a time,' continued Oz, 'I tired of that, and became a balloonist.'

. . .

'I think you are a very bad man,' said Dorothy.

'Oh, no, my dear; I'm really a very good man, but I'm a very bad Wizard, I must admit.'

'Can't you give me brains?' asked the Scarecrow.

'You don't need them. You are learning something every day. A baby has brains, but it doesn't know much. Experience is the only thing that brings knowledge, and the longer you are on earth the more experience you are sure to get.'

'That may all be true,' said the Scarecrow, 'but I shall be very unhappy unless you give me brains.'

The false Wizard looked at him carefully.

'Well,' he said with a sigh, 'I'm not much of a magician, as I said. But if you will come to me tomorrow morning, I will stuff your head with brains. I cannot tell you how to use them, however. You must find that out for yourself.'

'Oh, thank you—thank you!' cried the Scarecrow. 'I will find a way to use them, never fear!'

'But how about my courage?' asked the Lion anxiously.

'You have plenty of courage, I am sure,' answered Oz. 'All you need is confidence in yourself. There is no living thing that is not afraid when it faces danger. True courage is in facing danger when you are afraid, and that kind of courage you have in plenty.'

'Perhaps I have, but I'm scared just the same,' said the Lion. 'I shall really be very unhappy unless you give me the sort of courage that makes one forget he is afraid.'

'Very well, I will give you that sort of courage tomorrow,' replied Oz.

'How about my heart?' asked the Tin Woodman.

'Why, as for that,' answered Oz, 'I think you are wrong to want a heart. It makes most people unhappy. If you only knew it, you are in luck not to have a heart.'

'That must be a matter of opinion,' said the Tin Woodman. 'For my part, I will bear all the unhappiness without a murmur, if you will give me the heart.'

'Very well,' answered Oz meekly. 'Come to me tomorrow and you shall have a heart. I have played Wizard for so many years that I may as well continue the part a little longer.'

'And now,' said Dorothy, 'how am I to get back to Kansas?'

'We shall have to think about that,' replied the little man. 'Give me two or three days to consider the matter and I'll try to find a way to carry you over the desert. In the meantime you shall all be treated as my guests, and while you live in the Palace my people will wait upon you and obey your slightest wish. There is only one thing I ask in return for my help—such as it is. You must keep my secret and tell no one I am a humbug.'

They agreed to say nothing of what they had learned, and went back to their rooms in high spirits. Even Dorothy had hope that 'The Great and Terrible Humbug', as she called him, would find a way to send her back to Kansas, and if he did she was willing to forgive him everything.

---

*When people are mutually attuned and show strong empathy for one another, as Canisy finds, they can sense their friends' positive and negative feelings almost as if they were their own. It is as though each of us had a third ear designed to pick up the feelings—below the surface of what's visible to others—of those we care most about. At times our own wishes will color our perspective, as they do in* Rainbow Valley *for Faith, who badly wants Dan to fight for her. But Una, who has not been personally hurt, can see the terrible risks Dan is running.*

### Jean Follain, *Canisy,* translated by Louise Guiney

Whenever we lined up to march into class, the assistant at my grandfather's school always had us sing the kind of civic-minded song in which words like peace, justice and blood are intermingled. These songs in no way arrested the attention of my paternal grandmother as she slowly crossed the courtyard to the storehouses to get grain, or coal.

I often cried in the assistant's class and then he would send me into my grandfather's class where behind his schoolmaster's desk, up on his raised chair, my grandfather sat with his scarlet, black polka-dotted handkerchief sticking out of his pocket, ready to welcome me as if nothing had happened and let me climb the steps to his chair, sit right under his desk, and tuck myself in as best I could between his legs. In that shadowy realm I smelled chalk dust and heard slates squeaking and the map of the world snapping as it unfolded. Sometimes a gnat would pay me a visit. After a succession of long quarters of an hour my grandfather and I would abandon the room where now only the boy whose turn it was that day to sweep remained, and who hurried so as to finish before the deep red death of the sun.

Sometimes I stayed for supper and the night with my paternal grandparents. Often, after the soup, there would be a knock at the door and at the words, "come in," someone would cross the threshold. A woman with a favor to ask, making as little noise as possible with her wooden shoes as she stepped forward, or else a mailman leaving messages people had given him during his rounds. Day laborers, a little drunk, their eyes blank, come to sign up for the next day, or it might be a young seamstress, hair upswept in a chignon, face starred with burning, candid eyes, leaving again a little fearfully, sewing machine slung over her shoulder, to set out towards the stagnant darkness of the hamlets.

A world of care, peace and Christianity, lightly governed by the ancient fear.

For me it was a joy to sleep beside my grandfather the schoolmaster, in his bed. Together we climbed the stairs to the room where the bed curtains had black flowers on them, against a background the color of dried blood. My grandfather would don a pale cotton nightcap with a pompom, a grotesque headdress that cast a shadow profile on the wall evocative of gnomes, and royal jesters, perhaps, who in the dark of ages past were clothed in crimson and buttercup gold.

My grandmother stayed behind to tidy up downstairs.

Upstairs in bed my grandfather would embark on a story, spinning felony and fear, precious gems and crafty animals together into baroque harmonies, provoking my laughter and his own. We could hear my grandmother downstairs muttering, "can't he let him sleep" and sometimes, louder, "Father, will you quiet down?" but all we ever did to mollify her was to muffle his golden words and both of us our mirth, until at length the ashen sleep of villages emerged from the palace of the ages, and closed our eyes.

## L. M. Montgomery, *Rainbow Valley*

Next day school was a different matter. At noon recess Faith encountered Dan in the little spruce plantation behind the school and Dan shouted once more,

"Pig-girl! Pig-girl! Rooster-girl!"

Walter Blythe suddenly rose from a mossy cushion behind a little clump of firs where he had been reading. He was very pale, but his eyes blazed.

"You hold your tongue, Dan Reese!" he said.

"Oh, hello Miss Walter," retorted Dan, not at all abashed. He vaulted aerily to the top of the rail fence and chanted insultingly,

Cowardy, cowardy-custard!
Stole a pot of mustard
Cowardy, cowardy-custard!

"You are a coincidence!" said Walter scornfully, turning still whiter. He had only a very hazy idea of what a coincidence was, but Dan had none at all and thought it must be something peculiarly opprobrious.

"Yah! Cowardy!" he yelled again. "Your mother writes lies-lies-lies! And Faith Meredith is a pig-girl-a-pig-girl-a-pig-girl! And she's a rooster-girl-a rooster-girl-a-rooster-girl! Yah! Cowardy-cowardy-cust—"

Dan got no further. Walter had hurled himself across the intervening space and knocked Dan off the fence backward with one well-directed blow. Dan's sudden and glorious sprawl was greeted with a burst of laughter and a clapping of hands from Faith. Dan sprang up, purple with rage, and began to climb the fence. But just then the school-bell rang and Dan knew what happened to boys who were late during Mr. Hazard's regime.

"We'll fight this out," he howled. "Cowardy!"

"Any time you like," said Walter.

"Oh, no, no, Walter," protested Faith. "Don't fight him. I don't mind what he says—I wouldn't condescend to mind the likes of *him*."

"He insulted you and he insulted my mother," said Walter, with the same deadly calm. "Night after school, Dan."

"I've got to get right home from school to pick the taters after the harrows, Dad says," answered Dan sulkily. "But to-morrow night'll do."

"Alright, here to-morrow night," agreed Walter.

"And I'll smash your sissy-face for you," promised Dan.

Walter shuddered—not so much from fear of the threat as repulsion over the ugliness and vulgarity of it. But he held his head high and marched into school. Faith followed in a conflict of emotions. She hated to think of Walter fighting that little sneak, but oh, he had been splendid! And he was going to fight for her—for Faith Meredith—to punish her insulter! Oh course he would win—such eyes spelled victory.

Faith's confidence in her champion had dimmed a little by evening, however. Walter had seemed so very quiet and dull the rest of the day in school.

"If it were only Gem," she sighed to Una, as they sat on Hezekiah Pollock's tombstone in the graveyard. "He is such a fighter—he could finish Dan off in no time. But Walter doesn't know much about fighting."

"I'm so afraid he'll be hurt," sighed Una, who hated fighting and couldn't understand the subtle, secret exultation she divined in Faith.

"He oughtn'd to be," said Faith uncomfortably. "He's every bit as big as Dan."

"But Dan's so much older," said Una. "Why, he's nearly a year older."

"Dan hasn't done much fighting when you come to count up," said Faith. "I believe he's really a coward. He didn't think Walter would fight, he wouldn't have called names before him. Oh, if you could have seen Walter's face when he looked at him, Una! It made me shiver—with a knife shiver. He looked just like Sir Gallahad in that poem Father read us on Saturday."

"I hate the thought of them fighting and I wish it could be stopped," said Una.

"Oh, it's got to go on now," cried Faith. "It's a matter of honour. Don't you dare tell anyone, Una. If you do I'll never tell you secrets again!"

"I won't tell," agreed Una. "But I won't stay to-morrow to watch the fight. I'm coming right home."

---

*When we are in tune in this empathetic way we can be sensitive to the humiliation or pain a friend is feeling, even when nobody else seems to care. In* The Pioneers, *James Fenimore Cooper shows us dramatically how one person can lend strength to another who is up against great difficulty or strength is flagging.*

## James Fenimore Cooper, *The Pioneers*

The punishments of the common law were still known, at the time of our tale, to the people of New-York; and the whipping-post, and its companion the stocks, were not yet supplanted by the more merciful expedients of the public prisons. Immediately in front of the gaol, those relics of the elder times were situated, as a lesson of precautionary justice to the evil-doers of the settlement.

Natty followed the constables to this spot, bowing his head with submission to a power that he was unable to oppose, and surrounded by the crowd, that formed a circle about his person, exhibiting in their countenances strong curiosity. A constable raised the upper part of the stocks, and pointed with his finger to the holes where the old man was to place his feet. Without making the least objection to the punishment, the Leather-stocking quietly seated himself on the ground, and suffered his limbs to be laid in the openings, without even a murmur; though he cast one glance about him, in quest of that sympathy that human nature always seems to require under suffering. If he met no direct manifestations of pity, neither did he see any unfeeling exultation, or hear a single reproachful epithet. The character of the mob, if it could be called by such a name, was that of attentive subordination.

The constable was in the act of lowering the upper plank, when Benjamin, who had pressed close to the side of the prisoner, said, in his hoarse tones, as if seeking for some cause to create a quarrel—

"Where away, master constable, is the use of clapping a man in them here bilboes? it neither stops his grog nor hurts his back; what for is it that you do the thing?"

"'Tis the sentence of the court, Mr. Penguillum, and there's law for it, I s'pose."

"Ay, ay, I know that there's law for the thing; but where away do you find the use, I say? it does no harm, and it only keeps a man by the heels for the small matter of two glasses."

"Is it no harm, Benny Pump," said Natty, raising his eyes with a piteous look to the face of the steward—"is it no harm to show off a man in his seventy-first year, like a tamed bear, for the settlers to look on! Is it no harm to put an old soldier, that has sarved through the war of 'fifty-six, and seen the inimy in the 'seventy-six business, into a place like this, where the boys can point at him and say, I have known the time when he was a spictacle for the county! Is it no harm to bring down the pride of an honest man to be the equal of the beasts of the forest!"

Benjamin stared about him fiercely, and, could he have found a single face that expressed contumely, he would have been prompt to quarrel with its owner; but meeting every where with looks of sobriety, and occasionally of commiseration, he very deliberately seated himself by the side of the hunter, and placing his legs in the two vacant holes of the stocks, he said—

"Now lower away, master constable, lower away, I tell ye! If-so-be there's such a thing hereabouts as a man that wants to see a bear, let him look and be d—d, and he shall find two of them, and mayhap one of the same that can bite as well as growl."

"But I've no orders to put you in the stocks, Mr. Pump," cried the constable; "you must get up and let me do my duty."

"You've my orders, and what do you need better, to meddle with my own feet? so lower away, will ye, and let me see the man that chooses to open his mouth with a grin on it."

"There can't be any harm in locking up a creater that will enter the pound," said the constable, laughing, and closing the stocks on them both.

It was fortunate that this act was executed with decision, for the whole of the spectators, when they saw Benjamin assume the position he took, felt an inclination for merriment, which few thought it worth while to suppress. The steward struggled violently for his liberty again, with an evident intention of making battle on those who stood nearest to him; but the key was already turned, and all his efforts were vain.

"Hark ye, master constable," he cried, "just clear away your bilboes for the small matter of a log-glass, will ye, and let me show some of them there chaps who it is they are so merry about."

"No, no, you would go in, and you can't come out," returned the officer, "until the time has expired that the Judge directed for the keeping of the prisoner."

Benjamin, finding that his threats and his struggles were useless, had good sense enough to learn patience from the resigned manner of his companion, and soon settled himself down by the side of Natty, with a contemptuousness expressed in his hard features, that showed he had substituted disgust for rage. When the violence of the steward's feelings had in some measure subsided, he turned to his fellow sufferer, and, with a motive that might have vindicated a worse effusion, he attempted the charitable office of consolation.

"Taking it by and large, Master Bump-ho, 'tis but a small matter, after all," he said. "Now I've known very good sort of men, aboard of the Boadishey, laid by the heels, for nothing, mayhap, but forgetting that they'd drunk their allowance already, when a glass of grog has come in their way. This is nothing more than riding with two anchors ahead, waiting for a turn in the tide, or a shift of wind, d'ye see, with a soft bottom and plenty of room for the sweep of your hawse. Now I've seen many a man, for overshooting his reckoning, as I told ye, moored head and starn, where he couldn't so much as heave his broadside round, and mayhap a stopper clapt on his tongue too, in the shape of a pump-bolt lashed athwart-ship his jaws, all the same as an out-rigger alongside of a taffrel-rail."

The hunter appeared to appreciate the kind intentions of the other, though he could not understand his eloquence; and raising his humbled countenance, he attempted a smile, as he said—

"Anan!"

"'Tis nothing, I say, but a small matter of a squall, that will soon blow over," continued Benjamin. "To you that has such a length of keel it must be all the same as nothing; thof, seeing that I'm a little short in my lower timbers, they've triced my heels up in such a way as to give me a bit of a cant. But what cares I, Master Bump-ho, if the ship strains a little at her anchor; it's only for a dog-watch, and dam'me but she'll sail with you then on that cruise after them said beaver. I'm not much used to small arms, seeing that I was stationed at the ammunition-boxes, being sum'mat too low-rigged to see over the hammock-cloths; but I can carry the game, d'ye see, and mayhap make out to lend a hand with the traps; and if-so-be you're any way so handy with them as ye be with your boathook, 'twill be but a short cruise after all. I've squared the yards with Squire Dickens this morning, and I shall send him word that he needn't bear my name on the books again till such time as the cruise is over."

"You're used to dwell with men, Benny," said Leather-stocking, mournfully, "and the ways of the woods would be hard on you, if"

"Not a bit—not a bit," cried the steward; "I'm none of your fair-weather chaps, Master Bump-ho, as sails only in smooth water. When I find a friend I sticks by him, d'ye see."

<hr />

*We do have a wonderful ability to renew another person's faith or energy to go on. This can happen because, like Grandma in* Orange Cheeks, *people love each other so much or, as in* Mary Poppins, *because someone has an uncanny sense of how much good a little bit of encouragement can do.*

### Jay O'Callahan, *Orange Cheeks*

Willie was 6 years old, and he lived in the country. One day the phone rang, and Willie picked it up. He had a habit of breathing into the phone instead of talking.

"Hello, Willie," his grandmother's voice said to the breathing.

"How'd you know it was me?"

"I just knew, Willie. Willie, I want you to spend the night."

"Oh, Grandma! I'll get Mama!"

His mother took the phone, talked a while, and hung up.

"Willie," his mother said, "I never let you spend the night at your grandmother's because you get in trouble."

"I won't get in trouble," Willie burbled. He shone with excitement, so his mother said quietly, seriously, "I don't want to get a call tonight and have to drive 30 miles to pick you up."

"No troublllllle," he said.

"Your grandmother can be difficult late in the day," she went on. "She can be a bit of a grump."

"I'll be good. I promise."

"If there's any trouble, you won't go overnight again for a year. Go up and pack your bag."

Willie ran upstairs and put six T-shirts and a toothbrush in his bag.

They drove all the way into Cambridge. Willie loved Cambridge because all the houses were squeezed together. They drove around Harvard Yard and down Trowbridge Street and took a left on Leonard Avenue. The houses were all wooden triple-deckers, and his grandmother lived at Number 9. They parked, and Willie ran up the outside stairs, pushed the outside door open, and pressed the buzzer inside.

Zzzzzttt! The door wouldn't open until his grandmother pressed another buzzer from the inside. It made a click, then the door unlocked. It was magic. Willie pushed the door in and stood at the bottom of the stairs. The stairs were narrow and dark and filled with the wonderful smells of his grandmother's house. He could have spent the whole weekend right there, but his grandmother was standing at the head of the stairs, calling him.

"Come on up, Willie."

"Here I come, Grandmaaaaa."

He rushed up to the top, and his grandmother leaned down for a hug. He kissed her on those wrinkled, crinkled cheeks. He loved those cheeks but never said anything about them.

"You'll be in the guest room upstairs," his grandmother said. "There's a prize up there for you."

"Thank you, Grandmaaaaa," he said, hurrying up the stairs. His mother's voice caught up with him: "You remember what I said, Willie. "

"Don't worry. No troublllle."

Willie loved the guest room because his grandmother had done something wonderful. She had pasted six large silver stars to the ceiling. He loved those.

The prize lay on the table. Two pieces of orange paper, a small pair of scissors, glue, and a sharp pencil. Willie took the scissors and cut two circles from the paper and put glue on the back of the circles. He pasted the circles to his cheeks. Now he had orange cheeks.

Looking out the window, he saw his mother driving off. "Good-bye, Mamaaaaa," he said with a victorious grin.

He ran downstairs, and his grandmother said just the right thing: "Wonderful cheeks."

"Thank you, Grandmaaaaa," he said jouncing his shoulders.

"We'll have tea in the dining room, but first I'll hang out wash, and you'll go to Mr. Murchison's. You know him."

"The fruit man."

"Yes. He's right next door. He's expecting you. Get four pounds of bananas. Here's a dollar. Do a good job."

. . .

Willie took the bananas to the back yard, where his grandmother was hanging clothes on the line. "Good for you, Willie. You're a regular businessman. You go up and play till I finish, and we'll have tea."

Willie thought he was a businessman. To him a businessman was someone who made pencil marks on the walls. Secret ones. But they were real. Willie went up and down the back stairway, making small pencil marks. Then he decided to make a secret mark in the dining room.

He pushed a chair against the white wall in the dining room, stood on the chair, reached way up, and started to make a tiny dot. Willie heard something. Terrified, he called, "Grandma!" In his panic he made a scratch mark two feet long on the wall.

"Oh, no! I have to go home now," he cried. He tried to erase it, but that made it worse. He spat on his hands and tried to wipe the mark off. Now it was all over the wall. It was horrible. Now he was in trouble.

He jumped off the chair and ran to the window. His grandmother was hanging the last few socks. He had to do something, or he'd have to go home. Willie opened the drawer in the pantry and saw a hammer and two nails. He took them and went in the dining room. He took the dining room tablecloth off the table and stood on the chair. He nailed the tablecloth to the wall. Now you couldn't see the scratch mark, but you could see the dining-room tablecloth.

His grandmother made the tea and put everything on a tray.

"Come on, Willie. We'll have tea in the dining room."

His head seemed to be sinking into his shoulders. "Let's have tea here," he said.

"We always have tea in the dining mom," she said and went into the dining room alone.

"Willie, the dining-room tablecloth is not on the table," she said in a voice slightly changed. A voice that had new information. "The dining-room tablecloth is nailed to the wall."

After a silence Willie said, "Which wall?"

"You come in and see which wall."

Willie came slowly in. His head sank further into his shoulders. "Oh, that wall," Willie said. "I nailed it to that wall."

Suddenly, he began to shake. His whole body trembled, and he burst out crying. "Now I have to go home." He was crying so hard the tears ran down onto his paper orange cheeks. He began to rub the cheeks and the paper was tearing and shredding. That overwhelmed his grandmother. "Willie!" she said, rushing over, kneeling down, holding him. She was crying now, and her tears were falling onto his paper orange cheeks. She held him until she could get hold of herself, then breathed deeply, saying, "Willie, look at the two of us. This is absurd. Everything's all right."

"No, it isn't," Willie sobbed. "Now I have to go home. I can't come for a whole year."

"You don't have to go home," she said, standing. "It's perfectly all right."

"No, it isn't," Willie persisted. "Mama says late in the day you're a grump."

His grandmother's eyes seemed to open rather wide. "Hmm. She does, does she?" His grandmother pursed her lips in thought. "Well, I'll tell you this, Willie—your mother's no prize either."

They sat down at the table. "Now we'll have tea, and then we'll take care of the wall. How many sugars, Willie?"

"Five."

"One." she corrected.

The tea seemed to calm his whole body.

"Now, your mother won't know about this." she said with assurance. "It's our secret."

"She'll know," Willie pouted. "She always knows."

"She's my daughter. She won't know."

His grandmother took the hammer and pulled out the nails. She put the tablecloth on the table saying, "I'll sew the holes up another time, but your mother won't know. I'll put a bowl of fruit over one hole and flowers over the other." His grandmother put putty in the holes in the wall, and that afternoon she and Willie painted over the scratch mark.

In three hours the paint was dry, and the mark was gone. "Now your mother won't know about this," she said with assurance. "It's our secret."

"She'll know," Willie pouted. "She always knows."

"She's my daughter. She won't know."

"She's my mother. She'll know." Willie grumped.

Willie was scared to death as his mother came up the dark secret stairs the next morning. The three of them would have tea before leaving.

They sat at the dining table drinking tea. Willie was quiet as long as he could be. Finally, he looked at his mother and said, "Don't pick the bowl of fruit up."

"Why would I pick the bowl of fruit up?" she asked.

An extraordinary look of total innocence filled his face. "I don't knooooow."

Tea continued, and Willie kept staring at the wall.

"What are you staring at?" his mother asked.

"The wall," Willie replied. "It's a nice wall."

"Ah!" his mother said. "There was trouble, just like I said. What happened?"

Defeated, Willie said, "Tell the trouble, Grandma."

"Well, there was trouble," his grandmother said kindly. "The trouble was, we didn't have enough time. Is that what you mean, Willie?"

"That's what I mean," he said, bouncing.

A few minutes later his grandmother stooped over at the top of the stairs, and Willie kissed her on those wrinkled, crinkled cheeks. And then he and his mother went down the dark narrow stairway with the wonderful smells. His mother didn't know what had happened. It was a secret.

When he got home, Willie ran up to his room, unzipped his bag, and took out the orange paper. He cut two circles and put them in an envelope with a note saying, "Dear Grandma, Here's orange cheeks for you. Love, Willie."

## P. L. Travers, *Mary Poppins*

Suddenly they heard voices on the stairs.

"Children, children!" Mrs. Banks was calling as she opened the door. "Children—I am very cross. Mary Poppins has left us—"

"Yes," said Jane and Michael.

"You knew, then?" said Mrs. Banks, rather surprised. "Did she tell you she was going?"

They shook there heads, and Mrs. Banks went on:

"It's outrageous. One minute here and gone the next. Not even an apology. Simply said, 'I'm going!' and off she went. Anything more preposterous, more thoughtless, more discourteous—What is it, Michael?" She broke off crossly, for Michael had grasped her skirt in his hands and was shaking her. "What *is* it, child?"

"Did she say she'd come back?" he cried, nearly knocking his Mother over. "Tell me—did she?"

"I don't remember *what* she said, except that she was going. But I certainly shan't have her back if she does want to come. Leaving me high and dry with nobody to help me and without a word of notice."

"Oh, Mother!" said Jane reproachfully.

"You are a very cruel woman," said Michael, clenching his fist, as though at any minute he would have to strike her.

"Children! I'm ashamed of you—really I am! To want back anybody who has treated your Mother so badly. I'm utterly shocked."

Jane burst into tears.

"Mary Poppins is the only person I want in the world!" Michael wailed, and flung himself on to the floor.

"Really, children, really! I don't understand you. Do be good, I beg of you. There's nobody to look after you tonight. I have to go out to dinner and it's Ellen's Day Off. I shall have to send Mrs. Brill up." And she kissed them absentmindedly, and went away with an anxious little line on her forehead. . . .

"Well, if I ever did! Her going away and leaving you pore dear children in the church like that," said Mrs. Brill, a moment later, bustling in and setting to work on them.

"A heart of stone, that's what that girl had *and* no mistake, or my name's not Clara Brill. Always keeping herself to herself, too, and not even a lace handkerchief or a hatpin to remember her by. Get up, will you please, Master Michael!" Mrs. Brill went on, panting heavily.

"How we stood here so long, I *don't* know, with her airs and graces and all. What a lot of buttons, Miss Jane! Stand still, do now, and let me undress you, Master Michael. Plain she was, too, nothing much to look at. Indeed, all things considered, I don't know that we won't be better off, after all. Now, Miss Jane, where's your nightgown—why, what's this under your pillow—?"

Mrs. Brill had drawn out a small nobbly parcel.

"What is it? Give it to me—give it," said Jane, trembling with excitement, and she took it from Mrs. Brill's hands very quickly. Michael came and stood near her and watched her undo the string and tear away the brown paper. Mrs. Brill, without waiting to see what emerged from the package, went in to the Twins.

The last wrapping fell to the floor and the thing that was in the parcel lay in Jane's hand.

"It's her picture," she said in a whisper, looking closely at it.

And it was!

Inside a little curly frame was a painting of Mary Poppins, and underneath it was written, "Mary Poppins by Bert."

"That's the Match-Man—he did it," said Michael, and took it in his hand so that he could have a better look.

Jane found suddenly that there was a letter attached to the painting. She unfolded it carefully. It ran:

*Dear Jane,*

*Michael had the compass so the picture is for you. Au revoir.*

*Mary Poppins*

She read it out loud till she came to the words she couldn't understand.

"Mrs. Brill!" she called. "What does 'au revoir' mean?"

"Au revore, dearie?" shrieked Mrs. Brill from the next room. "Why, doesn't it mean—let me see, I'm not up in these foreign tongues—doesn't it mean 'God bless you'? No. No, I'm wrong. I think, Miss Jane dear, it means To Meet Again."

Jane and Michael looked at each other. Joy and understanding shone in their eyes. They knew what Mary Poppins meant.

Michael gave a long sigh of relief. "That's all right," he said shakily. "She always does what she will." He turned away.

"Michael, are you crying?" Jane asked.

He twisted his head and tried to smile at her.

"No, I'm not," he said. "It is only my eyes."

She pushed him gently towards the bed, and as he got in she slipped the portrait of Mary Poppins into his hand—hurriedly, in case she should regret it.

"You have it for tonight, darling," whispered Jane, and she tucked him in just as Mary Poppins used to do. . . .

# Honesty

—◆—

In *My Mama Says There Aren't Any Zombies, Ghosts, Vampires, Creatures, Demons, Fiends, Goblins or Things,* Judith Viorst portrays a little boy joshing his mother:

> My mama says that a creature
> isn't reaching out his hand
> to pinch me.

The little boy goes on to complain about his mother's refusal to acknowledge any of the weird fantasies that frighten him. Finally he realizes that "even mothers make mistakes." And, of course, sometimes they don't . . . make mistakes—or tell the truth?

This good-natured tale reminds us that little white lies can be a way for children to reassure themselves of the security their parents provide and to give concrete, if imaginary form to their fears. In all this fantasy, deep truths lie close by.

A similar untruthful approach to the truth is illustrated by Mr. Jones (in *Bea and Mr. Jones* by Amy Schwartz), who has exchanged places with his daughter Bea. He goes to kindergarten; she goes to his office to work. "So," the author tells us, "remember that big kid you saw getting in for half price at the movie matinee, and you just couldn't believe he was under 12? Well, you were probably right." Is this deception? Dishonesty? Mr. Jones in his pretense mirrors children playing grown-up. The little white lie which gets him a reduced rate at the movie house is a reminder of the limits of the game: Daddy is still Daddy.

But the serious side of honesty is crucial if we are to have reliable relationships and safety in society. Interestingly, the Ten Commandments do not actually prohibit lying—the relevant command is "not to bear false witness." Truth is seen as a social exchange, taking its meaning from the good or harm to be done between people.

The philosopher Spinoza believed that truth in friendship was a great blessing, and that friendship was a celebration of and a sanctuary for the search for truth in our lives.

> *Sir and Very Welcome Friend,*
>
> *Your letter of December 12th (enclosed in another letter of December 24th) didn't reach me until the 26th, while I was at Schiedham. I gathered from it that you have a great love for the truth, and that it alone is the aim of all your efforts. Since I too aim at nothing else, this made me decide not only to grant your request, as well as I can, by answering the questions you have sent me or will send me in the future, but also to do everything I can to further a closer acquaintance and a sincere friendship between us. Of all things beyond my power, I value nothing more than friendship with people who sincerely love the truth. For I believe that of the things beyond our power, there is nothing in the world we can love with tranquillity except such people. For the love such people feel for one another is founded on the love each one has for the truth, and it is as impossible to disturb it as it is not to embrace the truth once it has been perceived. Moreover, it is the greatest and the most satisfying source of happiness that we can find among things beyond our power, since nothing but the truth can unite different opinions and temperaments.*

For Spinoza the goal of truth was foremost—an ideal to be striven for, since in daily life certain truths might wax and wane with circumstance and knowledge. The standard of honesty has to reach beyond the facts we can know to our very desire to be clear and truthful with one another.

———•◦•———

*Alice Walker's father understood the temptation to lie, and the importance of resisting it. As a result, she learned to favor truthfulness, which, as she found, pays off in greater personal strength and deeper ties with other people. Dishonesty can be very destructive.* Pinocchio *is an age-old reminder of this. People who care so little about others that they lie without thinking for personal gain are diminished by their lying and are likely to feel empty and quite lonely.*

## Alice Walker, *Fathers*

I recall a scene when I was only three or so in which my father questioned me about a fruit jar I had accidentally broken. I felt he knew I had broken it, at the same time I couldn't be sure. Apparently breaking it was, in any event, the wrong thing to have done. I could say, Yes, I broke the jar, and risk a whipping for breaking something valuable, or No, I did not break it, and perhaps bluff my way through.

I've never forgotten my feeling that he really wanted me to tell the truth. And because he seemed to desire it—and the moments during which he waited for my reply seemed quite out of time, so much so I can still feel them, and, as I said, I was only three—I confessed. I broke the jar, I said. I think he hugged me. He probably didn't, but I still feel as if he did, so embraced did I feel by the happy relief I noted on his face and by the fact that he didn't punish me at all, but seemed, instead, pleased with me. I think it was at that moment that I resolved to take my chances with the truth, although as the years rolled on I was to break more serious things in his scheme of things than fruit jars.

### Carlo Collodi, *Pinocchio*

As soon as the three doctors had left the room, the Fairy went to Pinocchio and felt his forehead and discovered that he had a high fever. Quickly, she put some medicine in half a glass of water and offered it to the puppet, saying affectionately, "Here, drink this down, and soon you'll feel better."

Pinocchio looked at the glass, made a wry face, and then asked in a very unhappy voice, "Is it sweet or bitter?"

"It's bitter, but it'll help you."

"If it's bitter, I won't drink it!"

"Now, see here—! Drink it!"

"I don't like bitter things!"

"Drink it down! Then after you've drunk it, I'll give you a lump of sugar to eat to take away the bitter taste."

"Where's the lump of sugar?"

"Right here," said the Fairy as she took a lump from a golden sugar bowl.

"First, give me the lump of sugar, and then I'll drink that glass of bitter medicine."

"Do you promise—?"

"Yes."

The Fairy gave him the lump of sugar and Pinocchio quickly crunched it between his teeth and swallowed it in an instant. Then, as he licked his lips, he said, "Wouldn't it be nice if sugar was medicine! I'd take it every day!"

"All right now, keep your promise and drink this little bit of medicine. It'll make you all better again."

Very unwillingly, Pinocchio took the glass of medicine in his hand. Then he put the tip of his nose to it and sniffed it. He brought the glass almost up to his lips, but then he stopped again to sniff it. Finally, he said, "It's too bitter! too bitter! I can't drink it!"

"How can you say that when you haven't even tasted it?"

"I can tell! I can tell from the smell of it! First give me another lump of sugar, and then I'll drink it!"

With all the patience of a little mother, the Fairy put another lump of sugar into Pinocchio's mouth. Then she gave him the glass of medicine again.

"I can't drink it like this!" cried the puppet as he made an awful face.

"Why not?"

"Well—because that pillow on my feet is uncomfortable."

The Fairy took the pillow away.

"It's no use! I still can't drink it."

"Now what's the matter?"

"That bedroom door bothers me. It's half open."

The Fairy went and closed the bedroom door.

"Even so," shouted Pinocchio as he burst into tears, "I won't take that bitter medicine—I won't! I won't! I won't!"

"Pinocchio, you'll be sorry if you don't take it."

"I don't care!"

"You're a very sick boy."

"I don't care!"

"In a very short while that fever is going to kill you."

"I don't care!"

"Aren't you afraid to die?"

"No, I'm not afraid! It'd be better to die than to drink that awful medicine!"

At this point, the door flew open and into the room marched four huge jet-black rabbits who carried a little coffin on their shoulders.

"What do you want?" cried the terrified Pinocchio as he sat bolt upright in his bed.

"We have come to take you away," replied the biggest of the black rabbits.

"Take me away—? But I'm not *dead* yet!"

"No, not yet. But you have only a few minutes left to live. You wouldn't take the medicine that would have cured your fever."

"Oh Fairy! dear Fairy!" the puppet screamed, "Give me that glass of medicine! Quick, for heaven's sake! I don't want to die—No! I don't want to die!" He then seized the glass in both hands and emptied it in a single gulp.

"Well, I guess we'll just have to wait," said the biggest of the black rabbits. "This time we came for nothing." Then, taking up the little coffin again, they put it on their shoulders and marched out of the room muttering and grumbling to themselves.

Hardly a moment later, Pinocchio leaped out of bed completely cured. As you probably know, wooden puppets don't often get sick, but when they do, they get well again very quickly.

The Fairy, seeing him running and romping about the room as frisky and happy as a young rooster, said to him, "Then my medicine was really good for you?"

"Good? More than good! It brought me back to life!"

"Then, why in the world did I have to beg you to take it?"

"Why? It's simply because boys are all alike! It's just because we're more afraid of the medicine than we are of the sickness."

"Shame on you! Boys should realize that good medicine taken in time can keep them from being very sick and perhaps even from dying. . . ."

"Ah yes, but the next time you won't have to beg me! I'll just remember those four black rabbits with the coffin on their shoulders—then I'll take up that glass of medicine and down it'll go!"

"All right, now suppose you tell me how you happened to fall into the hands of those murderous thieves."

"Well, it happens that the puppetmaster, Fire Eater, gave me some gold pieces and told me to take them to my Daddy. Instead, on the road I met a Fox and a Cat, two very honest and respectable people, who said, 'Would you like to see your money turn into a thousand—even two thousand—gold pieces? Come along with us and we'll take you to the Field of Miracles,' and then I said, 'Let's go!' and then they said, 'Let's stop for a while at the Inn of The Red Lobster, and after midnight we'll go on our way,' and then when I woke up, I discovered that they'd already left, and then I started out again and it was so dark you wouldn't believe it, and then, on the road I met two robbers wearing coal sacks who said, 'Give us your money!' and then I said, 'I haven't got any money,' 'cause I had hidden the four gold pieces in my mouth, and then one of the robbers tried to put his hand in my mouth, and then with one bite I bit off his hand and spat it out, but—and you know, it's a funny thing—it wasn't a hand at all, it was a cat's paw, and then the robbers chased me and I ran, till finally they caught me and hanged me by the neck from The Great Oak in the woods, and then they said, 'Tomorrow we'll come back and you'll be dead with your mouth hanging wide open and then it'll be easy to take out the money you hid under your tongue."

"And the gold pieces," asked the Fairy, "now where are they?"

"I lost them!" said Pinocchio with a perfectly straight face. But this was a lie, because he really had the money in his pocket. As soon as he told this lie, his nose—which, as you know, was already a pretty long nose—suddenly grew two inches longer.

"And where did you lose them?"

"In the woods."

With this second lie, Pinocchio's nose grew even longer.

"If you lost your gold pieces in the woods," said the Fairy, "we'll look for them there, and I know we'll find them, because anything that is lost there is always found."

"Ah! now I remember," the puppet stammered in confusion, "I didn't really lose the gold pieces. By accident I swallowed them while I was taking your medicine."

With this third lie, his nose grew so long that poor Pinocchio couldn't turn in any direction. If he turned this way, his nose would hit against the bed or the window panes. If he turned that way, it would bang against the walls or the bedroom door. If he even so much as raised his head, he ran the risk of sticking his nose into the Fairy's eye.

The Fairy just looked at him and laughed.

"What are you laughing at?" demanded the puppet who, by now, was completely confused and worried about his nose which had so quickly grown to such an enormous size.

"I'm laughing at the lie you told me."

"How could you ever know that I told a lie?"

"My dear boy," she replied, "it's so very easy to tell when someone is lying, because there are only two kinds of lie. There are lies that have short legs, and there are lies that have long noses. It just so happens that your kind of lie is the kind with the long nose."

Pinocchio wanted to hide himself in shame, but when he tried to run out of the room, he couldn't do it because his nose had grown so long that he could no longer pass through the door.

---

*As Barry Lopez shows, differences between people can be an excuse for mean behavior. All too often, calculated dishonesty can also be a form of group or clique identity, making people fear to be left out—as is the case for the Emperor and his advisers in the famous tale* The Emperor's New

Clothes. *George Orwell shows too how dishonesty can be a way of equating one's own side as right and honest—regardless of the truth.*

### Barry Lopez, "Coyote and the Skunk Kill Game," from *Giving Birth to Thunder, Sleeping with His Daughter*

There was a place where a lot of prairie dogs and rabbits were living. Coyote knew about the place but he didn't know how to get the animals. There was a stream close by. He thought he might change the course of that stream and drown them all.

Skunk lived near the stream. Coyote was walking along there, trying to think how to get those animals, when he met Skunk. He told Skunk all about the rabbits and the prairie dogs. "Let's make a plan to catch them," said Coyote.

"All right," said Skunk.

Coyote said he was going to go upstream a ways and that Skunk should go get some slime grass. The water level would drop off in the stream said Coyote, and Skunk would find him lying in some driftwood. He should take the slime grass, which looked like maggots, and stuff it in Coyote's ears and mouth and all around underneath him, under his tail and in his nose. After he did this, Skunk was to go over and tell all the prairie dogs and rabbits that Coyote was dead.

It was a hot day and as he went along Coyote wished for a cloud. A cloud appeared over him. Then he wished it would sprinkle so he could run on cool ground. It began to sprinkle. Coyote wished it would rain hard so that the water would come up around his knees, and it did. He wished the water would become deep enough to reach his stomach, and the water came up that far. Then he wished the water would come up so that only his ears would stick out, and the water came up that far. Then Coyote wished he'd be carried downstream by the water, and he was. Then he wished he'd be caught in a pile of driftwood, and he was.

When the water went down Skunk went looking for Coyote. When he found him he put the grass in his ears and mouth and under his tail and in his nose. Then he went over and told the rabbits and the prairie dogs that the person they hated was dead.

Two rabbits came over to see if Skunk was telling the truth, Jack Rabbit and White Rabbit. Coyote had told Skunk to take a stick and hit him in the stomach when the animals came over, so they could see he was dead.

Skunk hit Coyote in the stomach and the two rabbits thought he was dead. They went back and told the others that Skunk was telling the truth. The others did not trust Skunk, so they sent over two other rabbits to see if Coyote was dead, Furry Rabbit and Gray Rabbit. They went over and again Skunk hit Coyote in the belly with the stick. The two rabbits went back and told the other animals that Coyote was dead. But some of them still didn't believe it, so they sent over two prairie dogs to see. Again, Skunk hit Coyote in the belly with the stick. Then the prairie dogs got up close to look at the maggots in Coyote's ears and nose and mouth and in his anus. They returned and told the others. Everyone now believed Coyote was dead.

When the animals arrived, Skunk told them they must dance because their enemy was dead. Some of the rabbits didn't like this and they hung back. But the prairie dogs, they wanted to dance, and started right in. They made a ring around Coyote. Then the rabbits finally came over and started dancing. Soon everyone was dancing. Skunk was singing along with them making a lot of noise when suddenly he said, "Look up there! Look at that pretty bird!" They all stopped dancing and looked up and Skunk turned around and sprayed everyone. The liquid got in their eyes and they couldn't see anything. Coyote had two sticks hidden under him. He jumped up and began to club rabbits and prairie dogs. Only a few got away.

Coyote built a fire and then told Skunk to carry the rabbits and prairie dogs over. Skunk took four big loads to the fire. Then he cleaned all the animals and singed off all their hair. He was doing all the work. Coyote told him to dig a pit and put the animals in with some saltbush. He buried them with just their tails sticking out and built another fire on top of the pit.

While the meat was cooking, Coyote and Skunk sat in the shade of some big rocks. Coyote was thinking. "Cousin," he said, "let's run a race. Whoever wins can eat all the rabbits and prairie dogs. We'll run over to that mountain and back."

"No, I can't run fast at all. Anyway, that's too far to go."

But Coyote kept asking and asking. Finally, Skunk gave in. "All right," he said, "but you must let me start first because I can't run very fast."

At first Coyote said no, but finally agreed. Skunk said to wait until he got over the first hill.

When Skunk reached the first hill he looked around for a badger hole. He found one and pulled a tumbleweed in behind him. Soon Coyote raced past like he was on fire. Skunk came out of the hole and went back to where the rabbits and prairie dogs were cooking. They were done just right, very tender and dripping with juices. He took them all out of the pit, cut off the tails of the prairie dogs and put them back in the ground so it looked like they were still cooking, and then he went up on a high rock and began eating.

Just as Skunk was finishing his meal, Coyote came back. He was sweating and so out of breath. He was holding on to his knee. He dug up some wet sand in the stream bed to wipe over himself to cool down. "I wonder where Skunk is?" he thought. "He has such short legs, he must be way back there."

Coyote went over to the prairie dog pit and saw the tails sticking up. "They must be done by now," he thought. He reached down and pulled at their tails. "They must be nice and tender. Their tails come right off." He took a stick and dug around in the ashes, but he couldn't find any prairie dogs. He kept digging but there wasn't anything there. He got angry and he began looking for tracks. "Skunk did this," he thought. "When I find him I'll kill him."

While Coyote was running around looking for the right set of tracks to follow, Skunk threw down a piece of bone. Coyote looked up and saw Skunk. "Please, give me some of that meat." But Skunk did not answer. He finished his meal and stretched out for a nap.

## Hans Christian Andersen, *The Emperor's New Clothes,* adapted by Colin Greer

One day, two swindlers came to a great town. They told everyone they were weavers and said they knew how to weave the most beautiful cloth. Not only were the colors and patterns gorgeous, but the clothes that were made of this cloth has the quality of becoming invisible to every person who was not fit for the office he held or was impossibly stupid.

"Those must be splendid clothes," said the Emperor. "By wearing them I should be able to discover who in my kingdom are fit for their posts. I will be able to distinguish the wise from the fools."

The Emperor paid the two swindlers cash in advance so they could being work at once.

Soon, the Emperor grew anxious to know how the work was proceeding. But he felt embarrassed to call on the weavers. Instead, he decided to send one of his faithful ministers. "He will be able to see how the cloth looks, for he is a clever man and fulfills his duties well."

So the old minister went to the swindlers and watched them working at their empty looms. "Good heavens," he said, is it possible that I am a fool? Am I not fit for my office? I see no cloth."

The swindlers asked the minister what he thought of the cloth they were pretending to weave. "Oh, it's quite beautiful," said the minister.

"Such beautiful colors. I will tell the Emperor how well the cloth is coming along."

The Emperor was pleased to hear the good news. But soon he grew anxious again. "I know, I'll send another minister to see how the work is proceeding."

The next minister visited the swindlers working at their empty looms. "I know I'm not a fool," he thought, but perhaps I'm not fit for my post. But I must not let it appear so." So he praised the cloth on his return to the Emperor.

Now the Emperor thought he would like to see the weavers at work at their looms. So he, accompanied by a number of courtiers, went to visit the two swindlers.

"What?" thought the Emperor, "I see nothing at all. Am I a fool? Am I not fit to be Emperor?"

"Oh," said the Emperor to the swindlers, "what beautiful work. I cannot wait to wear the clothes made from such cloth." The courtiers accompanying the Emperor applauded the Emperor's remarks, all calling the clothes magnificent! gorgeous! excellent!"

In a matter of weeks, the swindlers decided they were ready to bring the Emperor his new clothes. "See, these are the trousers. This is the coat. Here is the robe."

"Yes, I see," said the Emperor

"Will Your Majesty be pleased to take off your clothes?" said the swindlers. "Then we may put the new ones on you."

The Emperor took off his clothes, and the weavers pretended to give him one article of dress after another. The Emperor's courtiers called for the Emperor to walk through the town so all of his subjects could see the beautiful new clothes the Emperor was wearing.

"Yes," said the Emperor, "I am quite ready to show my new clothes to my people. Don't they fit well?"

Then the Emperor walked in procession from his palace through the streets of the town. "How beautiful the Emperor's clothes are! What a splendid gown!" the townspeople called from the streets and windows. Nobody would let it appear that he or she could see nothing, for then they would not be fit for their posts or they would be thought to be fools.

"But he has nothing on," said a little child.

"Oh, listen to the child," said his father. And one person whispered to another what the child has said. "He has nothing on! He has nothing on!"

At last, all the people cried, "The Emperor has nothing on!"

The Emperor blushed deep red, for he knew it was true. Only a little child had dared to speak the truth and let it appear that he was a fool.

## George Orwell, *Shooting an Elephant*

I had halted on the road. As soon as I saw the elephant I knew with perfect certainty that I ought not to shoot him. It is a serious matter to shoot a working elephant—it is comparable to destroying a huge and costly piece of machinery—and obviously one ought not to do it if it can possibly be avoided. And at that distance, peacefully eating, the elephant looked no more dangerous than a cow. I thought then and I think now that his attack of "must" was already passing off; in which case he would merely wander harmlessly about until the mahout came back and caught him. I decided that I would watch him for a little while to make sure that he did not turn savage again, and then go home.

But at that moment I glanced round at the crowd that had followed me. It was an immense crowd, two thousand at the least and growing every minute. It blocked the road for a long distance on either side. I looked at the sea of yellow faces above the garish clothes—faces all happy and excited over this bit of fun, all certain that the elephant was going to be shot. They were watching me as they would watch a conjurer about to perform a trick. They did not like me, but with the magical rifle in my hands I was momentarily worth watching. And suddenly I realized that I should have to shoot the elephant after all. The people expected it of me and I had got to do it; I could feel their two thousand wills pressing me forward, irresistibly. And it was at this moment, as I stood there with the rifle in my hands, that I first grasped the hollowness, the futility of the white man's dominion in the East. Here was I, the white man with his gun, standing in front of the unarmed native crowd—seemingly the leading actor of the piece; but in reality I was only an absurd puppet pushed to and fro by the will of those yellow faces behind. I perceived in this moment that when the white man turns tyrant it is his own freedom that he destroys. He becomes a sort of hollow, posing dummy, the conventionalized figure of a sahib. For it is the condition of his rule that he shall spend his life in trying to impress the "natives," and so in every crisis he has got to do what the "natives" expect of him. He wears a mask, and his face grows to fit it. I had got to shoot the elephant. I had committed myself to doing it when I sent for the rifle. A sahib has got to act like a sahib; he has got to appear resolute, to know his own mind and do definite things. To come all that way, rifle in had, with two thousand people marching at my heels, and then to trail feebly away, having done nothing—no, that was impossible. The crowd would laugh at me. And my whole life, every white man's life in the East, was one long struggle not to be laughed at.

But I did not want to shoot the elephant. I watched him beating his bunch of grass against his knees, with that preoccupied grandmotherly air that elephants have. It seemed to me that it would be murder to shoot him. At that age I was not squeamish about killing animals, but I had never shot an elephant and never wanted to. (Somehow it always seems worse to kill a *large* animal.) Besides, there was the beast's owner to be considered. Alive, the elephant was worth at least a hundred pounds; dead, he would only be worth the value of his tusks, five pounds, possibly. But I had got to act quickly. I turned to some experienced-looking Burmans who had been there when we arrived, and asked them how the elephant had been behaving. They all said the same thing: he took no notice of you if you left him alone, but he might charge if you went too close to him.

It was perfectly clear to me what I ought to do. I ought to walk up to within, say, twenty-five yards of the elephant and test his behavior. If he charged, I could shoot; if he took no notice of me, it would be safe to leave him until the mahout came back. But also I knew that I was going to do no such thing. I was a poor shot with a rifle and the ground was soft mud into which one would sink at every step. If the elephant charged and I missed him, I should have about as much chance as a toad under a steam-roller. But even then I was not thinking particularly of my own skin, only of the watchful yellow faces behind. For at that moment, with the crowd watching me, I was not afraid in the ordinary sense, as I would have been if I had been alone. A white man mustn't be frightened in front of "natives"; and so, in general, he isn't frightened.

. . .

I often wondered whether any of the others grasped that I had done it solely to avoid looking a fool.

———————

*Slavery was a situation in which a lie, an untruth about people, dominated—humanity was denied to people who could be owned and sold like cars or houses, and slaveowners could believe that very big lie.*

## The Constitution of the United States
### Article I, Section 2
Section 2. The House of Representatives shall be composed of members chosen every second year by the people of the several states, and the electors in each state shall have the qualifications requisite for electors of the most numerous branch of the state legislature.

No person shall be a Representative who shall not have attained to the age of twenty five years, and been seven years a citizen of the United States, and who shall not, when elected, be an inhabitant of that state in which he shall be chosen.

Representatives and direct taxes shall be apportioned among the several states which may be included within this union, according to their respective numbers, which shall be determined by adding to the whole number of free persons, including those bound to service for a term of years, and excluding Indians not taxed, three fifths of all other Persons.

## The Slaves Speak

I was here in slavery days. I was here. When I came here, colored people didn't have their ages. The boss man had it.

anon: Library of Congress

Half the time a slave didn't know that he was sold 'til the master'd call him to the Big House and tell him he had a new master.

Mingo White: Library of Congress

When us black folks get set free us'n change our names, so effen the white folks get together and change their minds and don't let us be free anymore, then they have a hard time finding us.

Alice Wilkins: Library of Congress

## The Emancipation Proclamation

[On January 1, 1863, President Lincoln declared free all slaves residing in territory in rebellion against the federal government:]

And by virtue of the power and for the purpose aforesaid, I do order and declare that all persons held as slaves within said designated States and parts of States are, and henceforward shall be, free; and that the Executive Government of the United States, including the military and naval authorities thereof, will recognize and maintain the freedom of said persons.

And I hereby enjoin upon the people so declared to be free to abstain from all violence, unless in necessary self-defence; and I recommend to them that, in all case when allowed, they labor faithfully for reasonable wages.

And I further declare and make known that such persons of suitable condition will be received into the armed service of the United States to garrison forts, positions, stations, and other places, and to man vessels of all sorts in said service.

And upon this act, sincerely believed to be an act of justice, warranted by the Constitution upon military necessity, I invoke the considerate judgment of mankind and the gracious favor of Almighty God.

## The Constitution of the United States, Amendment XIII

Section 1. Neither slavery nor involuntary servitude, except as a punishment for crime whereof the party shall have been duly convicted, shall exist within the United States, or any place subject to their jurisdiction.

Section 2. Congress shall have power to enforce this article by appropriate legislation.

---

*When telling the truth challenges the fundamental disregard for it that underlies routine practices of powerful figures or entrenched mores, the truth teller might find herself under great pressure, as in* Northanger Abbey, *or might be punished—perhaps quite severely, as happened to Nancy, who was finally killed by Bill Sikes in* Oliver Twist.

### Jane Austen, *Northanger Abbey*

"It would be so easy to tell Miss Tilney that you had just been reminded of a prior engagement, and must only beg to put off the walk till Tuesday."

"No, it would not be easy. I could not do it. There has been no prior engagement." But Isabella became only more and more urgent, calling on her in the most affectionate manner, addressing her by the most endearing names. She was sure her dearest, sweetest Catherine would not seriously refuse such a trifling request to a friend who loved her dearly. She knew her beloved Catherine to have so feeling a heart, so sweet a temper, to be so easily persuaded by those she loved. But all in vain; Catherine felt herself to be in the right, and though pained by such tender, such flattering supplication, could not allow it to influence her. Isabella then tried another method. She reproached her with having more affection for Miss Tilney, though she had known her for so little a while, than for her best and oldest friends, with being grown cold and indifferent, in short, towards herself. "I cannot help being jealous, Catherine, when I see myself slighted for strangers, I, who love you so excessively! When once my affections are placed, it is not in the power of anything to change them. But I believe my feelings are stronger than anybody's; I am sure they are too strong for my own peace; and to see myself supplanted in your friendship by strangers does cut me to the quick, I own. These Tilneys seem to swallow up everything else."

Catherine thought this reproach equally strange and unkind. Was it the part of a friend thus to expose her feelings to the notice of others? Isabella appeared to her ungenerous and selfish, regardless of everything but her own gratification. These painful ideas crossed her mind, though she said nothing. Isabella, in the meanwhile, had applied her handkerchief to her eyes; and Morland, miserable at such a sight, could not help saying, "Nay, Catherine. I think you cannot stand out any longer now. The sacrifice is not much; and to oblige such a friend—I shall think you quite unkind, if you still refuse."

This was the first time of her brother's openly siding against her, and anxious to avoid his displeasure, she proposed a compromise. If they would only put off their scheme till Tuesday, which they might easily do, as it depended only on themselves, she could go with them, and everybody might then be satisfied. But "No, no, no!" was the immediate answer; "that could not be, for Thorpe did not know that he might not go into town on Tuesday." Catherine was sorry, but could do no more; and a short silence ensued, which was broken by Isabella, who in a voice of cold resentment said, "Very well, then there is an end of the party. If Catherine does not go, I cannot. I cannot be the only woman. I would not, upon any account in the world, do so improper a thing."

"Catherine, you must go," said James.

. . .

"I did not think you had been so obstinate, Catherine," said James, "you were not used to be so hard to persuade; you once were the kindest, best-tempered of my sisters."

"I hope I am not less so now," she replied, very feelingly; "but indeed I cannot go. If I am wrong, I am doing what I believe to be right."

## Charles Dickens, *Oliver Twist*

"This is far enough," said a voice, which was evidently that of the gentleman. "I will not suffer the young lady to go any farther. Many people would have distrusted you too much to have come even so far, but you see I am willing to humour you."

"To humour me!" cried the voice of the girl whom he had followed. "You're considerate indeed, sir. To humour me! Well, well, it's no matter."

"Why, for what," said the gentleman in a kinder tone, "for what purpose can you have brought us to this strange place? Why not have let me speak to you, above there, where it is light, and there is something stirring, instead of bringing us to this dark and dismal hole?"

"I told you before," replied Nancy, "that I was afraid to speak to you there. I don't know why it is," said the girl shuddering, "but I have such a fear and dread upon me tonight that I can hardly stand."

"A fear of what?" asked the gentleman, who seemed to pity her.

"I scarcely know of what," replied the girl. "I wish I did. Horrible thoughts of death, and shrouds with blood upon them, and a fear that has made me burn as if I was on fire, have been upon me all day. I was reading a book to-night, to wile the time away, and the same things came into the print."

"Imagination," said the gentleman, soothing her.

"No imagination," replied the girl in a hoarse voice. "I'll swear I saw 'coffin' written in every page of the book in large black letters,—aye, and they carried one close to me in the streets to-night."

"There is nothing unusual in that," said the gentleman. "They have passed me often."

"*Real ones*," rejoined the girl. "This was not."

There was something so uncommon in her manner, that the flesh of the concealed listener crept as he heard the girl utter these words, and the blood chilled within him. He had never experienced a greater relief than in hearing the sweet voice of the young lady as she begged her to be calm, and not allow herself to become the prey of such fearful fancies.

"Speak to her kindly," said the young lady to her companion. "Poor creature! She seems to need it."

"Your haughty religious people would have held their heads up to see me as I am to-night, and preached of flames and vengeance," cried the girl. "Oh, dear lady, why ar'n't those who claim to be God's own folks as gentle and as kind to us poor wretches as you, who, having youth and beauty and all that they have lost, might be a little proud instead of so much humbler?"

"Ah!" said the gentleman. "A Turk turns his face, after washing it well, to the East, when he says his prayers; these good people, after giving their faces such a rub against the World as to take the smiles off, turn with no less regularity, to the darkest side of Heaven. Between the Mussulman and the Pharisee, commend me to the first!"

These words appeared to he addressed to the young lady, and were perhaps uttered with the view of affording Nancy time to recover herself. The gentleman shortly afterwards, addressed himself to her.

"You were not here last Sunday night," he said.

"I couldn't come," replied Nancy: "I was kept by force."

"By whom?"

"Him that I told the young lady of before."

"You were not suspected of holding any communication with any-body on the subject which has brought us here to-night, I hope?" asked the old gentleman.

"No," replied the girl, shaking her head. "It's not very easy for me to leave him unless he knows why; I couldn't have seen the lady when I did, but that I gave him a drink of laudanum before I came away."

"Did he awake before you returned?" inquired the gentleman.

"No; and neither he nor any of them suspect me."

"Good," said the gentleman "Now listen to me."

"I am ready," replied the girl, as he paused for a moment.

"This young lady," the gentleman began, "has communicated to me, and to some other friends who can be safely trusted, what you told her nearly a fortnight since. I confess to you that I had doubts, at first, whether you were to be implicitly relied upon, but now I firmly believe you are."

"I am," said the girl earnestly.

"I repeat that I firmly believe it. To prove to you that I am disposed to trust you, I tell you without reserve, that we propose to extort the secret, whatever it may be, from the fears of this man Monks. But if—if—" said the gentleman, "he cannot be secured, or, if secured, cannot be acted upon as we wish, you must deliver up the Jew."

"Fagin!" cried the girl, recoiling.

"That man must be delivered up by you." said the gentleman.

"I will not do it! I will never do it!" replied the girl "Devil that he is, and worse than devil as he has been to me, I will never do that."

"You will not?" said the gentleman, who seemed fully prepared for this answer.

"Never!" returned the girl.

"Tell me why."

"For one reason," rejoined the girl firmly, "for one reason, that the lady knows and will stand by me in, I know she will, for I have her promise; and for this other reason, besides, that, bad life as he has led, I have led a bad life too; there are many of us who have kept the same courses together, and I'll not turn upon them, who might—any of them—have turned upon me, but didn't, bad as they are."

"Then," said the gentleman, quickly, as if this had been the point he had been aiming to attain; "put Monks into my hands, and leave him to me to deal with."

"What if he turns against the others?"

"I promise you that in that case, if the truth is forced from him, there the matter will rest; there must be circumstances in Oliver's little history which it would be painful to drag before the public eye, and if the truth is once elicited, they shall go scot free."

"And if it is not?" suggested the girl.

"Then," pursued the gentleman, "this Fagin shall not be brought to justice without your consent. In such a case I could show you reasons, I think, which would induce you to yield it."

"Have I the lady's promise for that?" asked the girl.

"You have," replied Rose. "My true and faithful pledge."

"Monks would never learn how you knew what you do?" said the girl, after a short pause.

"Never," replied the gentleman. "The intelligence should be so brought to bear upon him, that he could never even guess."

"I have been a liar, and among liars from a little child," said the girl after another interval of silence, "but I will take your words."

After receiving all assurance from both, that she might safely do so, she proceeded in a voice so low that it was often difficult for the listener to discover even the purport of what she said, to describe, by name and situation, the public-house whence she had been followed that night. From the manner in which she occasionally paused, it appeared as if the gentleman were making some hasty notes of the information she communicated. When she had thoroughly explained the localities of the place, the best position from which to watch it without exciting observation, and the night and hour on which Monks was most in the habit of frequenting it, she seemed to consider for a few moments, for the purpose of recalling his features and appearance more forcibly to her recollection.

"He is tall," said the girl, "and a strongly made man, but not stout; he has a lurking walk; and as he walks, constantly looks over his shoulder, first on one side, and then on the other. Don't forget that, for his eyes are sunk in his head so much deeper than any other man's, that you might almost tell him by that alone. His face is dark, like his hair and eyes; and, although he can't be more than six or eight and twenty, withered and haggard. His lips are often discoloured and disfigured with the marks of teeth; for he has desperate fits, and sometimes even bites his hands and covers them with wounds—why did you start?" said the girl, stopping suddenly.

The gentleman replied, in a hurried manner, that he was not conscious of having done so, and begged her to proceed.

"Part of this," said the girl, "I've drawn out from other people at the house I tell you of, for I have only seen him twice, and both times he was covered up in a large cloak. I think that's all I can give you to know him by. Stay though," she added. "Upon his throat: so high that you can see a part of it below his neckerchief when he turns his face: there is—"

"A broad red mark, like a burn or scald?" cried the gentleman.

"How's this?" said the girl "You know him!"

The young lady uttered a cry of surprise, and for a few moments they were so still that the listener could distinctly hear them breathe.

"I think I do," said the gentleman, breaking silence. "I should by your description. We shall see. Many people are singularly like each other. It may not be the same."

As he expressed himself to this effect, with assumed carelessness, he took a step or two nearer the concealed spy, as the latter could tell from the distinctness with which he heard him mutter, "It must be he!"

"Now," he said, returning: so it seemed by the sound: to the spot where he had stood before, "you have given us most valuable assistance, young woman, and I wish you to be the better for it. What can I do to serve you?"

"Nothing," replied Nancy

"You will not persist in saying that," rejoined the gentleman, with a voice and emphasis of kindness that might have touched a much harder and more obdurate heart. "Think now. Tell me."

"Nothing, sir," rejoined the girl, weeping. "You can do nothing to help me. I am past all hope, indeed."

"You put yourself beyond its pale," said the gentleman. "The past has been a dreary waste with you, of youthful energies mis-spent, and such priceless treasures lavished, as the Creator bestows but once and never grants again, but, for the future, you may hope. I do not say that it is in our power to offer you peace of heart and mind, for that must come as you seek it; but a quiet asylum, either in England, or, if you fear to remain here, in some foreign country, it is not only within the compass of our ability but our most anxious wish to secure you. Before the dawn of morning, before this river wakes to the first glimpse of daylight, you shall be placed as entirely beyond the reach of your former associates, and leave as utter an absence of all trace behind you, as if you were to disappear from the earth this moment. Come! I would not have you go back to exchange one word with any old companion, or take one look at any old haunt, or breathe the very air which is pestilence and death to you. Quit them all, while there is time and opportunity!"

"She will be persuaded now," cried the young lady. "She hesitates, I am sure."

"I fear not, my dear," said the gentleman.

"No, sir, I do not," replied the girl, after a short struggle, "I am chained to my old life. I loathe and hate it now, but I cannot leave it. I must have gone too far to turn back,—and yet I don't know, for if you had spoken to me so, some time ago, I should have laughed it off. But," she said, looking hastily round, "this fear comes over me again. I must go home."

"Home!" repeated the young lady, with great stress upon the word.

"Home, lady," rejoined the girl. "To such a home as I have raised for myself with the work of my whole life. Let us part. I shall be watched or seen. Go! Go! If I have done you any service, all I ask is, that you leave me, and let me go my way alone."

"It is useless," said the gentleman, with a sigh. "We compromise her safety, perhaps, by staying here. We may have detained her longer than she expected already."

# Adaptability

A few years ago, the press reported on a young family lost in a blizzard while they were camping. It was days before they were rescued. As might be expected, the parents described how they had managed to forage and protect themselves—but they also told about how surprised they had been to find the strength in themselves to keep going, to believe in survival even though things looked pretty grim. That strength, the mother said, "will be with us from now on in all we do. We never imagined we were that kind of person."

A personal treasury of possibilities can be opened up to us from what we learn about ourselves when we successfully adapt in the face of danger. Sometimes the perils we face are not physical but emotional, as when we fear that we are not being sufficiently respected, when we think we've disappointed or hurt somebody important to us, when we ourselves have been disappointed or hurt by vows not made or promises not kept. All too often who we are gets wrapped up in how we want to be seen and what we want to own. When we lose ourselves in any of these ways, our best hope is to relocate the person we are deep inside, distinct and apart from the external trappings of position and reward. The Chinese sage Laotzu asked the key questions well:

> What means more to you
> You or how important you are?
> What would you miss more
> You or the things you own?
> If you're stingy, it will cost you in the long run.
> If you hoard, you will lose in the long run.
> But if you're humble enough to be generous
> You can be generous to yourself.
> You'll know how to start over
> When the path you are on is blocked,
> You'll know you can start again.

Changing to deal with hardship is one thing, making simple or large changes to have a grand time is another—and it is not to be underestimated. City kids in the country or at the seaside have to learn new ways, and tired parents eager for their children to have a good time will, now and then, have to find one last ounce of energy so that can happen. When it does, people can look just a little bit different, some new dimensions—some simple but pleasing elements of who they are—will come to life, as they do for Mama in Sidney Taylor's *All-of-a-Kind Family*:

> Suddenly Henry looked up and said, "Ma, are we going to Playland today?"
>
> "Oh, are we ma? Are we?" the others echoed eagerly.
>
> Mama hesitated before answering. The section where the colorful booths and sideshows were located was a good distance away. She was already tired, and it would be quite a job to lead five young ones through the crowds along the boardwalk. But the children's faces were so pleading. They seldom had such treats. She was always so busy at home and there was very little extra money. She couldn't say no. After all they just wanted to see the sights, and that wouldn't cost any money. "All right," she said, finally, and the children squealed with delight.
>
> "But," Mama continued, "we will have to hurry. We must get back to the cars early in order to avoid the crowds. So just go into the water once, wash the sand off your bodies and bathing suits, and we'll get dressed as quickly as we can."
>
> "It is amazing," thought Mama, "how quickly the girls can do things when they have something to look forward to." In no time at all they were proceeding towards what seemed to the children to be fairyland.

And so whether it's fairyland or the tough realities of personal change and physical survival, resources for new possibilities are to be found in us and between us.

————•>•<•————

*One of the most challenging demands on us is how to deal with the inevitable blows we experience, especially blows to our self-esteem. Getting up when we've been laid low emotionally is often a touchy project. We can experience this kind of emotional toll when we feel humiliated—when some piece of ourselves has been injured and also when another person or animal we love and depend on gets hurt or dies.*

**Ishmael Reed,** *Sky Diving*
"It's a good way to live and
A good way to die"
From a Frankenheimer video about
Sky diving
The hero telling why he liked to

      The following noon he leaped
      But his parachute wasn't with him
      He spread out on the field like
      Scrambled eggs

Life is not always
Hi-lifting inside
Archibald Motley's
"Chicken Shack"
You in your derby
Your honey in her beret
Styling before a small vintage
Car

Like too many of us
I am a man who never had much
Use for a real father
And so when I'm heading
For a crash
No one will catch me but
Me

The year is only five days old
Already a comet has glittered out
Its glow sandbagged by
The jealous sun

      Happens to the best of us
      Our brilliance falling off
      Like hair from Berkeley's roving
      Dogs

Even on Rose Bowl day
An otherwise joyous occasion

A float veered into the crowd
Somebody got bruised over the incident
Like a love affair on second ave.

It's a good lesson to us all
In these downhill days of a
Hard-hearted decade
Jetting through the world
Our tails on fire

> You can't always count
> On things opening up for you
> Know when to let go
> Learn how to fall

## James Herriot, *All Things Bright and Beautiful*

"Good God, Cliff, what have you been doing to yourself?" His face was a patchwork of cuts and scratches and his nose, almost without skin, jutted from between two black eyes.

He grinned through the wounds, his eyes dancing with merriment. "Came off me bike t'other day. Hit a stone and went right over the handlebars, arse over tip." He burst out laughing at the very thought.

"But damn it, man, haven't you been to a doctor? You're not fit to be out in that state."

"Doctor? Nay, there's no need to bother them fellers. It's nowt much." He fingered a gash on his jaw. "Ah lapped me chin up for a day in a bit o' bandage, but it's right enough now."

I shook my head as I followed him into the stable. He hung up the oil lamp then went over to the horse.

"Can't reckon t'awd feller up," he said. "You think there wasn't much ailing him but there's a summat."

There were no signs of violent pain but the animal kept transferring his weight from one hind foot to the other as if he did have a little abdominal discomfort. His temperature was normal and he didn't show symptoms of anything else.

I looked at him, doubtfully. "Maybe he has a bit of colic. There's nothing else to see, anyway. I'll give him an injection to settle him down."

"Right you are, maister, that's good." Cliff watched me get my syringe out then he looked around him into the shadows at the far end of the stable.

"Funny seeing only one 'oss standing here. I remember when there was a great long row of 'em and the barfins and bridles hangin' there on the stalls and the rest of the harness behind then all shinin' on t'wall." He transferred his plug of tobacco to the other side of his mouth and smiled. "By Gaw, I were in here at six o' clock every morning feedin' them and gettin' them ready for work and ah'll tell you it was a sight to see us all goin' off ploughing at the start o' the day. Maybe six pairs of 'osses setting off with their harness jinglin' and the ploughmen sittin' sideways on their backs. Like a regular procession it was."

I smiled. "It was an early start, Cliff."

"Aye, by Gaw, and a late finish. We'd bring the 'osses home at night and give 'em a light feed and take their harness off, then we'd go and have our own teas and we'd be back 'ere again afterwards, curry-combing and dandy-brushin' all the sweat and dirt off 'em. Then we'd give them a right good stiff feed of chop and oats and hay to set 'em up for the next day."

"There wouldn't be much left of the evening then, was there?"

"Nay, there wasn't. It was about like work and bed, I reckon, but it never bothered us."

I stepped forward to give Badger the injection, then paused. The old horse had undergone a slight spasm, a barely perceptible stiffening of the muscles, and as I looked at him he cocked his tail for a second then lowered it.

"There's something else here," I said. "Will you bring him out of his stall, Cliff, and let me see him walk across the yard."

And watching him clop over the cobbles I saw it again; the stiffness, the raising of the tail. Something clicked in my mind. I walked over and rapped him under the chin and as the membrana nictitans flicked across his eye then slid slowly back I knew.

I paused for a moment. My casual little visit had suddenly become charged with doom.

"Cliff," I said. "I'm afraid he's got tetanus."

"Lockjaw, you mean?"

"That's right. I'm sorry, but there's no doubt about it. Has he had any wounds lately—especially in his feet?"

"Well he were dead lame about a fortnight ago and blacksmith let some matter out of his hoof. Made a right big 'ole."

There it was. "It's a pity he didn't get an anti-tetanus shot at the time," I said. I put my hand into the animal's mouth and tried to prise it open but the jaws were clamped tightly together. "I don't suppose he's been able to eat today."

. . .

"We'll have to put him down, won't we?"

"I'm afraid so."

"There's just one thing. Mallock will be taking him away but old Cliff says he doesn't want Mallock to shoot 'im. Wants you to do it. Will you come?"

I got out the humane killer and drove back to the farm, wondering at the fact that the old man should find the idea of my bullet less repugnant than the knacker man's. Mr. Gilling was waiting in the box and by his side Cliff, shoulders hunched, hands deep in his pockets. He turned to me with a strange smile.

"I was just saying to t'boss how grand t'awd lad used to look when I got 'im up for a show. By Gaw you should have seen him with 'is coat polished and the feathers on his legs scrubbed as white as snow and a big blue ribbon round his tail."

"I can imagine it, Cliff," I said. "Nobody could have looked after him better."

He took his hands from his pockets, crouched by the prostate animal and for a few minutes stroked the white-flecked neck and pulled at the ears while the old sunken eye looked at him impassively.

He began to speak softly to the old horse but his voice was steady, almost conversational, as though he was chatting to a friend.

"Many's the thousand miles I've walked after you, awd lad, and many's the talk we've had together. But I didn't have to say much to tha, did I? I reckon you knew every move I made, everything I said. Just one little word and you always did what ah wanted you to do."

He rose to his feet. "I'll get on with me work now, boss," he said firmly, and strode out of the box.

<hr/>

*Our sense of security derives from what we know, what we think we can be sure of. Staying open to new ideas, as the Professor in* The Lion, the Witch and the Wardrobe *advises, can be tough.*

## C. S. Lewis, *The Lion, the Witch and the Wardrobe*

"But it's all nonsense," said Edmund, very taken aback.

"Of course it's all nonsense," said Peter, "that's just the point. Lucy was perfectly all right when we left home, but since we've been down here she seems to be either going queer in the head or else turning into a most frightful liar. But whichever it is, what good do you think you'll do by jeering and nagging at her one day and encouraging her the next."

"I thought I thought—," said Edmund; but he couldn't think of anything to say.

"You didn't think anything at all," said Peter, "it's just spite. You've always liked being beastly to anyone smaller than yourself; we've seen that at school before now."

"Do stop it," said Susan; "it won't make things any better having a row between you two. Let's go and find Lucy."

It was not surprising that when they found Lucy, a good deal later, everyone could see that she had been crying. Nothing they could say to her made any difference. She stuck to her story and said:

"I don't care what you think, and I don't care what you say. You can tell the Professor or you can write to Mother or you can do anything you like. I know I've met a Faun in there and I wish I'd stayed there and you are all beasts, beasts!" It was an unpleasant evening. Lucy was miserable and Edmund was beginning to feel that his plan wasn't working as well as he had expected. The two older ones were really beginning to think that Lucy was out of her mind. They stood in the passage talking about it in whispers long after she had gone to bed. The result was that next morning they decided that they really would go and tell the whole thing to the Professor.

"He'll write to Father if he thinks there is really something wrong with Lucy," said Peter; "it's getting beyond us." So they went and knocked at the study door, and the Professor said "Come in," and got up and found chairs for them and said he was quite at their disposal. Then he sat listening to them with the tips of his fingers pressed together and never interrupting, till they had finished the whole story. After that he said nothing for quite a long time. Then he cleared his throat and said the last thing either of them expected.

"How do you know?" he asked, "that your sister's story is not true?"

"Oh, but—" began Susan, and then stopped.

Anyone could see from the old man's face that he was perfectly serious. Then Susan pulled herself together and said, "But Edmund said they had only been pretending."

"That is a point," said the Professor, "which certainly deserves consideration; very careful consideration. For instance if you will excuse me for asking the question does your experience lead you to regard your brother or your sister as the more reliable? I mean, which is the more truthful?"

"That's just the funny thing about it, Sir," said Peter.

"Up till now, I'd have said Lucy every time."

"And what do you think, my dear?" said the Professor, turning to Susan.

"Well," said Susan, "in general, I'd say the same as Peter, but this couldn't be true all this about the wood and the Faun."

"That is more than I know," said the, Professor, "and a charge of lying against someone whom you have always found truthful is a very serious thing; a very serious thing indeed."

"We were afraid it might not even be lying," said Susan.

"We thought there might be something wrong with Lucy."

"Madness, you mean?" said the Professor quite coolly.

"Oh, you can make your minds easy about that. One has only to look at her and talk to her to see that she is not mad."

"But then," said Susan and stopped. She had never dreamed that a grown-up would talk like the Professor and didn't know what to think.

"Logic!" said the Professor half to himself.

"Why don't they teach logic at these schools? There are only three possibilities. Either your sister is telling lies, or she is mad, or she is telling the truth. You know she doesn't tell lies and it is obvious that she is not mad. For the moment then and unless any further evidence turns up, we must assume that she is telling the truth."

Susan looked at him very hard and was quite sure from the expression on his face that he was not making fun of them.

"But how could it be true, Sir?" said Peter.

"Why do you say that?" asked the Professor.

"Well, for one thing," said Peter, "if it was real why doesn't everyone end this country every time they go to the wardrobe? I mean, there was nothing there when we looked; even Lucy didn't pretend there was."

"What has that to do with it?" said the Professor.

"Well, Sir, if things are real, they're there all the time."

"Are they?' said the Professor; and Peter did not know quite what to say. "But there was no time," said Susan, "Lucy had no time to have gone anywhere, even if there was such a place. She came running after us the very moment we were out of the room. It was less than a minute, and she pretended to have been away for hours."

That is the very thing that makes her story so likely to be true," said the Professor. "If there really is a door in this house that leads to some other world (and I should warn you that this is a very strange house, and even I know very little about it)—if, I say, she had got into another world, I should not be at all surprised to find that other world had a separate time of its own; so that however long you stayed there it would never take up any of our time. On the other hand, I don't think many girls of her age would invent that idea for themselves. If she had been pretending, she would have hidden for a reasonable time before coming out and telling her story."

"But do you really mean, Sir," said Peter, "that there could be other worlds all over the place, just round the corner like that?"

"Nothing is more probable," said the Professor, taking off his spectacles and beginning to wonder what they do teach them at these schools.

"But what are we to do?" said Susan. She felt that the conversation was beginning to get off the point.

"My dear young lady," said the Professor, suddenly looking up with a very sharp expression at them, while he muttered to himself, "I have both of them," "there is one plan which no one has yet suggested and which is well worth trying."

"What's that?" said Susan.

"We might all try minding our own business," said he. And that was the end of that conversation.

---

*Of course, as Yehuda Amichai tells us, physical trials and personal dangers require adaptability and resourcefulness. Catherine in* Catherine, Called Birdy, *shows us how the youngest among us can summon up strong personal resources to withstand unusual risk and threat.*

**Yehuda Amichai,** *Now That the Water Presses Hard,* **translated by Benjamin and Barbara Harshaw**
Now that the water presses hard
On the walls of the dam,
Now that the returning white storks
In the middle of the firmament
Turn into flocks of jet planes,
We will feel again how strong are the ribs,
How bold the warm air in the lungs,
How urgent the daring of love in the open plain,
When great dangers arch overhead,
And how much love is needed
To fill all the empty vessels
And the watches that stopped telling time,
And how much breath,

A blizzard of breath,
To sing a little Song of Spring.

## Katherine Cushman, *Catherine, Called Birdy*
24TH DAY OF SEPTEMBER

The stars and my family align to make my life black and miserable.
My mother seeks to make me a fine lady—dumb, docile, and accomplished—so I must take lady-lessons and keep my mouth closed. My
brother Edward thinks even girls should not be ignorant, so he taught
me to read holy books and to write, even though I would rather sit in an
apple tree and wonder. Now my father, the toad, conspires to sell me like
a cheese to some lack-wit seeking a wife.

What makes this clodpole suitor anxious to have me? I am no
beauty, being sun-browned and gray-eyed, with poor eyesight and a
stubborn disposition. My family holds but two small manors. We have
plenty of cheese and apples but no silver or jewels or boundless acres to
attract a suitor.

Corpus bones! He comes to dine with us in two days' time. I plan to
cross my eyes and drool in my meat.

. . .

I rubbed my nose until it shone red, blacked out my front teeth with
soot, and dressed my hair with the mouse bones I found under the
rushes in the hall. All through dinner, while he talked of his warehouses
stuffed with greasy wool and the pleasures of the annual Yarmouth herring fair, I smiled my gaptooth smile at him and wiggled my ears.

My father's crack still rings my head but Master Lack-wit left without a betrothal.

. . .

Then she told a story about this man who was so stupid that he forgot how to get dressed in the morning. Where was his shirt? Did it go on
his legs or his arms? And how did it fasten? Such trouble it was every
morning. Finally he decided to hire the boy next door to come in each
day and tell him, "Your shoes are there and your cloak is here and your
hat goes on your head." The first day the boy comes in. "First," he says to
the stupid man, "wash yourself." "That's all very well," says the stupid
man, "but where is myself? Where in the world am I? Am I here? Am I
here? Or am I here?" And he looked under the bed and behind the chair
and in the street, but it was all in vain for he never did find himself.

As she spoke, the children stopped their snuffling and chanted with
her, "Am I here? Or am I here?" And then shyly they began to shove each

other and giggle, wiping their runny noses on their sleeves and skirts.

"Listen to me, my children," said the old woman then, "do not be like the stupid man. Know where you yourself are. How? By knowing who you are and where you come from. Just as a river by night shines with the reflected light of the moon, so too do you shine with the light of your family, your people, and your God. So you are never far from home never alone, wherever you go."

---

*Finding personal strength as Betsy does in* Understood Betsy, *means encountering one of the big surprises in life: that we are so much more than we are likely to let ourselves know most of the time. The Tin Woodman and the Scarecrow make this discovery, too.*

### Dorothy Canfield Fisher, *Understood Betsy*

Uncle Henry looked down at her soberly, his hard, weather-beaten old face unmoved. "Here, you drive, will you, for a piece?" he said briefly, putting the reins into her hands, hooking his spectacles over his ears, and drawing out a stubby pencil and a bit of paper. "I've got some figgering to do. You pull on the left-hand rein to make 'em go to the left and t'other way for t'other way, though 'tain't likely we'll meet any teams."

Elizabeth Ann had been so near one of her wild screams of terror that now, in spite of her instant absorbed interest in the reins, she gave a queer little yelp. She was all ready with the explanation, her conversations with Aunt Frances having made her very fluent in explanations of her own emotions. She would tell Uncle Henry about how scared she had been, and how she had just been about to scream and couldn't keep back that one little . . . But Uncle Henry seemed not to have heard her little howl, or, if he had, didn't think it worth conversation, for he . . . oh, the horses were *certainly* going to one side! She hastily decided which was her right hand (she had never been forced to know it so quickly before) and pulled on that rein. The horses turned their hanging heads a little, and, miraculously, there they were in the middle of the road again.

Elizabeth Ann drew a long breath of relief and pride, and looked to Uncle Henry for praise. But he was busily setting down figures as though he were getting his 'rithmetic lesson for the next day and had not noticed . . . Oh, there they were going to the left again! This time, in her flurry, she made a mistake about which hand was which and pulled wildly on the left line! The horses docilely walked off the road into a shallow ditch, the wagon tilted . . . help! Why didn't Uncle Henry help! Uncle Henry continued intently figuring on the back of his envelope.

Elizabeth Ann, the perspiration starting out on her forehead, pulled on the other line. The horses turned back up the little slope, the wheel grated sickeningly against the wagon-box—she was *sure* they would tip over! But there! somehow there they were in the road, safe and sound, with Uncle Henry adding up a column of figures. If he only knew, thought the little girl, if he only *knew* the danger he had been in, and how he had been saved! . . . But she must think of some way to remember, for sure, which her right hand was, and avoid that hideous mistake again.

And then suddenly something inside Elizabeth Ann's head stirred and moved. It came to her, like a clap, that she needn't know which was right or left. If she just pulled the way she wanted them to go—the horses would never know whether it was the right or the left rein!

It is possible that what stirred inside her head at that moment was her brain, waking up. She was nine years old, and she was in the third-A grade at school, but that was the first time she had ever had a whole thought of her very own. At home, Aunt Frances had always known exactly what she was doing, and had helped her over the hard places before she even knew they were there; and at school her teachers had been carefully trained to think faster than the scholars. Somebody had always been explaining things to Elizabeth Ann so carefully that she had never found out a single thing for herself before. This was a very small discovery, but it was her own. Elizabeth Ann was as excited about it as a mother bird over the first egg that hatches.

She forgot how afraid she was of Uncle Henry, and poured out to him her discovery. "It's not right or left that matters!" she ended triumphantly; "it's which way you want to go!" Uncle Henry looked at her attentively as she talked, eyeing her sidewise over the top of one spectacle glass. When she finished—"Well, now, that's so," he admitted, and returned to his 'rithmetic.

### L. Frank Baum, *The Wizard of Oz*

'This funny tin man,' she answered, 'killed the Wildcat and saved my life. So hereafter you must all serve him, and obey his slightest wish.'

'We will!' cried all the mice, in a shrill chorus. And then they scampered in all directions, for Toto had awakened from his sleep, and seeing all these mice around him he gave a bark of delight and jumped right into the middle of the group. Toto had always loved to chase mice when he lived in Kansas, and he saw no harm in it.

But the Tin Woodman caught the dog in his arms and held him tight, while he called to the mice: 'Come back! Come back! Toto shall not hurt you.'

At this the Queen of the Mice stuck her head out from underneath a clump of grass and asked, in a timid voice, 'Are you sure he will not bite us?'

'I will not let him,' said the Woodman; 'so do not be afraid.'

One by one the mice came creeping back, and Toto did not bark again, although he tried to get out of the Woodman's arms, and would have bitten him had he not known very well he was made of tin. Finally one of the biggest mice spoke.

'Is there anything we can do,' it asked, 'to repay you for saving the life of our Queen?'

'Nothing that I know of,' answered the Woodman; but the Scarecrow, who had been trying to think, but could not because his head was stuffed with straw, said, quickly, 'Oh, yes; you can save our friend, the Cowardly Lion, who is asleep in the poppy bed.'

'A Lion!' cried the little Queen. 'Why, he would eat us all up.'

'Oh, no,' declared the Scarecrow; 'this Lion is a coward.'

'Really?' asked the Mouse.

'He says so himself,' answered the Scarecrow, 'and he would never hurt anyone who is our friend. If you will help us to save him I promise that he shall treat you all with kindness.'

'Very well,' said the Queen, 'we trust you. But what shall we do?'

'Are there many of these mice which call you Queen and are willing to obey you?'

'Oh, yes; there are thousands,' she replied.

'Then send for them all to come here as soon as possible, and let each one bring a long piece of string.'

The Queen turned to the mice that attended her and told them to go at once and get all her people. As soon as they heard her orders they ran away in every direction as fast as possible.

'Now,' said the Scarecrow to the Tin Woodman, 'you must go to those trees by the riverside and make a truck that will carry the Lion.'

So the Woodman went at once to the trees and began to work; and he soon made a truck out of the limbs of trees, from which he chopped away all the leaves and branches. He fastened it together with wooden pegs and made the four wheels out of short pieces of a big tree-trunk. So fast and so well did he work that by the time the mice began to arrive the truck was all ready for them.

They came from all directions, and there were thousands of them:

big mice and little mice and middle-sized mice; and each one brought a piece of string in his mouth. It was about this time that Dorothy woke from her long sleep and opened her eyes. She was greatly astonished to find herself lying upon the grass with thousands of mice standing around and looking at her timidly. But the Scarecrow told her about everything, and turning to the dignified little Mouse, he said:

'Permit me to introduce to you her Majesty, the Queen.'

Dorothy nodded gravely and the Queen made a curtsy, after which she became quite friendly with the little girl.

The Scarecrow and the Woodman now began to fasten the mice to the truck, using the strings they had brought. One end of a string was tied around the neck of each mouse and the other end to the truck. Of course the truck was a thousand times bigger than any of the mice who were to draw it; but when all the mice had been harnessed they were able to pull it quite easily. Even the Scarecrow and the Tin Woodman could sit on it, and were drawn swiftly by their queer little horses to the place where the Lion lay asleep.

After a great deal of work, for the Lion was heavy, they managed to get him up on the truck. Then the Queen hurriedly gave her people the order to start, for she feared if the mice stayed among the poppies too long they also would fall asleep.

At first the little creatures, many though they were, could hardly stir the heavily loaded truck; but the Woodman and the Scarecrow both pushed from behind, and they got along better. Soon they rolled the Lion out of the poppy bed to the green fields, where he could breathe the sweet, fresh air again, instead of the poisonous scent of the flowers.

Dorothy came to meet them and thanked the little mice warmly for saving her companion from death. She had grown so fond of the big Lion she was glad he had been rescued.

Then the mice were unharnessed from the truck and scampered away through the grass to their homes. The Queen of the Mice was the last to leave.

'If ever you need us again,' she said. 'Come out into the field and call, and we shall hear you and come to your assistance. Good-bye!'

'Good-bye!' they all answered, and away the Queen ran, while Dorothy held Toto tightly lest he should run after her and frighten her.

After this they sat down beside the Lion until he should awaken; and the Scarecrow brought Dorothy some fruit from a tree near by, which she ate for her dinner.

*What we expect of other people changes over time, and what other people are willing and able to do changes as well. Relationships change too, as Aesop often reminds us. The Scotty, in* The Scotty Who Knew Too Much, *is a reminder that people are not always the particular personalities we have come to know. They can surprise us for good and for ill.*

## Aesop, *The Lion and the Boar*, retold by Ann McGovern

One hot summer's day a Lion and a Boar came to a small well at the same moment. They were both very thirsty and began at once to argue as to who should be the first to drink. Neither would give in to the other. They were about to come to blows when the Lion looked up and saw some vultures in the sky above them.

"Look!" said the Lion. "Those vultures see us fighting and they are hungry. They are waiting to feed upon the loser."

"Then let us settle our quarrel," said the Boar. "It is better for us to make friends than to become the food of vultures."

"I agree," the Lion said. "In the face of common danger, small differences are best forgotten."

## James Thurber, *The Scotty Who Knew Too Much*

Several summers ago there was a Scotty who went to the country for a visit. He decided that all the farm dogs were cowards, because they were afraid of a certain animal that had a white stripe down its back. "You are a pussy-cat and I can lick you," the Scotty said to the farm dog who lived in the house where the Scotty was visiting. "I can lick the little animal with the white stripe, too. Show him to me." "Don't you want to ask any questions about him?" said the farm dog. "Naw," said the Scotty. "*You* ask the questions."

So the farm dog took the Scotty into the woods and showed him the white-striped animal and the Scotty closed in on him, growling and slashing. It was all over in a moment and the Scotty lay on his back. When he came to, the farm dog said, "What happened?" "He threw vitriol," said the Scotty, "but he never laid a glove on me."

A few days later the farm dog told the Scotty there was another animal all the farm dogs were afraid of. "Lead me to him," said the Scotty. "I can lick anything that doesn't wear horseshoes." "Don't you want to ask any questions about him?" said the farm dog. "Naw," said the Scotty. "Just show me where he hangs out." So the farm dog led him to a place in the woods and pointed out the little animal when he came along. "A clown," said the Scotty, "a pushover," and he closed in, leading with his left and exhibiting some mighty fancy footwork. In less than a second the Scotty was flat on his back, and when he woke up the farm dog was pulling quills out of him. "What happened?" said the farm dog. "He pulled a knife on me," said the Scotty, "but at least I have learned how you fight out here in the country, and now I am going to beat *you* up." So he closed in on the farm dog, holding his nose with one front paw to ward off the vitriol and covering his eyes with the other front paw to keep out the knives. The Scotty couldn't see his opponent and he couldn't smell his opponent and he was so badly beaten that he had to be taken back to the city and put in a nursing home.

*Moral: It is better to ask some of the questions than to know all the answers.*

---

*If we are open to the prospect of change, we become better able to withstand disappointment. As it does for Izzy in* Izzy, Willy-Nilly, *facing unpleasant reality can help us rise to meet uncertain and frightening events.*

### Cynthia Voigt, *Izzy, Willy-Nilly*

Leigh sprayed and trimmed, then worked over my head with a blow drier, then trimmed a little more. She must have been half an hour solid on that haircut. When she finally gave me a hand mirror, she sounded pretty pleased with herself.

I didn't mind the hand mirror, I looked into it. My face looked pale and my eyes dark blue, and my mother was right about my eyelashes. Somehow, the short hair, feathered around my head and blown back from my face, looked especially good on my eyes. I looked—I thought, a little older. My hair even looked more blonde. "Thank you," I said over my shoulder. "It's really nice."

I guess that's five words already. I meant it, of course, because it was a good haircut. I looked pretty. I thought if I was going to have to be crippled I'd rather not look pretty. I thought, any other time she would have teased me about boyfriends loving it. I thought I wouldn't be able to stand the way all the women, who had been pretending not to notice me, now had some comment to make about how nice I looked—the other hairdressers and the women with curlers all over their heads.

"That wasn't so bad," my mother, said once we were settled in the car again. "Was it?"

"It's a really good haircut," I answered her. Because it was bad, and these were only strangers. It would be worse, I knew, if they had been people I already knew, from before.

Adelia had me working on crutches that week, getting ready. She recommended the old-fashioned kind, tall wooden crutches that fitted into my armpits, because eventually I'd have canes and things and the tall crutches would keep me walking straighter. I propped myself up on them, trying to remember how the people I'd seen with broken legs or ankles had used them. My blouse pulled up out of the waist of my skirt because of them.

"It'll be much more comfortable once that cast comes off," Adelia told me.

I nodded, concentrating on how wide to space the crutches, how to step them forward. After a couple of days, I could really sort of move around. Not fast, or anything, but I could go where I wanted, turn or go forward, and keep my balance easily. I started going down the whole length of the room, moving between the other PT patients and their nurses.

That was my mistake, because while I was looking at the floor and concentrating on balance, I walked myself right up to a full length mirror.

I couldn't stop myself from looking. There was this blonde girl with feathery hair, on crutches, with her shirt pulled up and hanging out over her plaid skirt. Her right leg hung down about two inches from the hem, and then stopped.

It was grotesque.

It wasn't so bad, actually. It wasn't anything as bad as Jeannette Wheatley's face, in terms of looking at it and wanting to never have to see it again. The skin looked sort of normal colored. There wasn't a big mass of lumpy flesh at the end of my leg. Just a stump.

The stump hung down about two inches below my skirt. It looked grotesque.

Adelia stood behind me, and I looked at the two of us in the mirror. She was much bigger than I was, taller and broader. Her ankles were thick and her calves muscular. I looked at myself again, trying to make myself see it and accept it. That was my grotesque stumpy leg there. I'd never seen it like this, the way it would look to other people. I had to accept it, I guessed, but I couldn't accept it, and I didn't want to have to.

Adelia spoke from behind me. I kept my eyes on the stump, making myself look at it. "There isn't anything you can do about it, Izzy."

I didn't need her to tell me that.

"Except maybe wear trousers. You'd pin them up in the back."

I'd never thought of that. My mother had removed all my pants from my drawers, so I thought there was some reason not to wear them. But maybe there wasn't, maybe my mother just thought pinned-up pants looked too crippled, or something.

. . .

"Definitely pants," I told her, turning away from the mirror.

As my mother drove me home, my legs covered with a car blanket and the wheelchair folded in the rear of the station wagon, I asked her. "Why did you take away all my pants?"

She didn't answer.

"I need some pants to wear. These skirts are too short—and—and—I wish you hadn't gotten rid or my pants."

"But I didn't."

"Oh. Do we have any safety pins? To pin them up with."

"You wouldn't rather have a hem?"

"No. That would look worse."

"But we can't get pants over the cast, Izzy." My mother sounded like she was apologizing.

"Oh."

"After Friday, though. Unless—how much does it matter to you? We could certainly sacrifice a pair of jeans. We could easily slit the leg to make room for the cast."

All along the road the dried leaves were being blown by the wind. Leaves rushed toward us, brown and yellow and red, skittering along the roadway, just being blown along.

"Yes please," I said to my mother, suddenly exhausted.

"I'm sorry.

"Oh Love, it's OK. That wasn't even much of a show of temper. It wasn't anything like the performances you put on last year."

"I'll have to try harder," I joked back.

"You're doing just fine," my mother said, serious again. "You're doing just right. I'm so proud of the way you've adjusted."

You adjust the hem of the skirt, making it longer of shorter, so in that sense I guess I adjusted. You adjust the temperature in a room, or in attitude, which means changing it, and in that sense too I had been adjusted. But these were all, as we said in Latin, passive verbs: I was the subject but I didn't do anything. Everything was done to me, had been done to me. I thought about that, and then, when we got home again, I took out the bag Rosamunde's mother had given me in the hospital, to think about a design for a blank canvas, to stop thinking about adjustment.

My mother was going out for lunch and then doing errands and the grocery shopping, so I had the house to myself until Francie came home.

I spread out the square of canvas and looked at it: It was brown mesh, with white tape sewn all around the edges, about a yard long and a foot and a half wide. I tried to see a picture on it but I couldn't. So I took the pad of graph paper and a pencil and started sketching.

It was something to do, I thought, making a lot of little pictures all over the paper, trying to find a shape I liked. It didn't matter if I couldn't do it, because there was nobody but me in the house. It didn't even matter, I thought, looking at a sketch with a tree that looked like one of those rocket lollipops and a straight line for the grass and pillows for clouds, if I couldn't draw—which I couldn't. When I got a general design I liked, I took a fresh sheet of graph paper and tried it larger. The tree was in the middle, at stage center. Behind it, I put clouds in layers, trying to make the edges wavy so the sky wouldn't look striped.

The hardest thing, I discovered, with that sketch by my side as I tried to x in the squares, the way Rosamunde had said I should, was to get a sense of the tree. I couldn't figure out how to get the leaves in, the layers and layers, each individual leaf there by making only a part of the whole golden tree.

Just before Francie was due, I packed all the papers away into the bag and returned them to my room. When Francie came in, I was sitting in the den, reading a beginning needlepoint book. I was looking at different stitches, wondering how I might use them to get the effect I wanted.

I was having a good time. I was entirely happy right then. I remember recognizing the feeling and looking up, surprised. As soon as I had recognized it, however, I lost it. Like a little kid grabbing at a soap bubble, I thought: When you touch it, it bursts.

Francie slouched into the room and dumped her knapsack on the floor. "There's nothing to eat."

"Have some fruit. Have a jam sandwich. Have some milk. Do you have any colored pens I could use?" I asked her.

"What for?"

"Just something. Do you?"

"Yeah, I have some upstairs."

"May I borrow them?"

She shook her head.

"Why not? What's the matter with letting me just borrow your pens? I won't break them or anything."

"I don't have to," Francie said. "You can't make me."

I knew that. I tried to think of some bribe I could offer her.

Francie dropped her vest down on top of her knapsack and put her hands on her hips, glaring at me.

"Boy, what's wrong with you today?" I asked.

"Wendy's having a birthday party."

"So what?"

"She said, she wasn't going to invite me."

"Yes, she will, Francie; she always does. Don't be silly. Why did she say that, anyway?"

"Because I didn't vote for her to be the princess in our Christmas play."

I almost burst out laughing. It was just like Francie. "And you told her about it, right? Why did you tell her?"

"Because she was saying it wasn't fair and somebody must have counted the votes wrong. Because I don't think they did count the votes wrong."

"Who did you vote for?"

"Me."

"Oh." I knew I shouldn't laugh, and I didn't. "Did you win?"

Francie shook her head emphatically. "It's going to be a slumber party. But I told her."

"Told her what?"

"Her mother will make her ask me. So that's all right."

Francie left the room and I sat there in my wheelchair wishing my mother would come home right then, so I could tell her about that conversation. She would get a kick out of that conversation.

"Anyway," I called after Francie, wheeling down the hallway to follow her into the kitchen, "can I please, please, borrow your colored pens. Just for an hour?"

"I told you, no. Ask Mommy to get you some. She gets you anything you want, anyway, now."

If I hadn't been in a wheelchair, I would have stomped out of the room. As it was, I had to back around a couple of times to reverse my direction. If they hadn't taken the door off the hinges, I could have swung it behind me so hard it would rock back and forth, *clump, clump, clump.*

I went back to my own room and took out some homework. If my parents had been home, Francie would never have said that. I scratched out the answer to a problem, waiting for the tightness in my throat to ease up. No wonder Francie didn't have any real friends.

There was a knock on the door. "Who is it?"

"It's me, Francie."

"Go away," I said.

She opened the door and came in. "What are you doing?'

"I said go away. That means, don't come in. I meant what I said."

"Yeah, but you can't do anything about it," Francie told me.

I thought I would burst into tears of shame and frustration. I thought I was angry enough to get out of the wheelchair and hustle my sister out of the room by the scruff of her neck. I was angry enough to move normally. Inside my head, the little Izzy blew up like a red balloon. I thought I would throw the math book at Francie's head.

I did none of those things. I sat there, half turned toward her, getting control, holding control. I don't know what I looked like, but Francie got up from the bed and started backing toward the door. I paid no attention to her. It had nothing to do with Francie. It had only to do with me, with my relationship to me.

"I'm telling," Francie said. "I'm going to tell Mommy on you. You're being mean and you're jealous and I'm telling."

She didn't close the door but that didn't matter, because she wouldn't be coming back. I didn't have to worry about Francie. She was my parents' problem: handling her, teaching her how to behave like a human being.

I felt sorry for her, and I would have liked to help. I even knew what was wrong with her. Here was this older sister she envied and admired, who could do anything, as far as Francie knew, and I had turned into a cripple. For years, she had been sort of comparing herself to me, with me as the example, and however she felt about it, she still thought I was the perfect example. Then a terrible thing had happened to me. Francie had to figure out—she was smart enough, that was half her trouble—that terrible things could happen to anybody, whether you were the good sister or the bad sister, or anybody.

I knew Francie was frightened, but I couldn't do anything about that. I had myself to take care of, first. Because I was frightened too.

I was sorry to be the cause of Francie's fears, but she was also blaming me for them. As long as she did that, I knew, thinking about it, as long as she couldn't stand to feel sorry for me—which she couldn't stand, because she felt so sorry for me—I couldn't say anything to her, couldn't tell her in any way, or show in any way, that this wasn't as bad as she thought.

Unless, I thought grimly, it was just as bad as she was thinking it was. And I wasn't so sure it wasn't.

---

*When the time for leaving home arrives, we might not be ready to greet it. At times a person is reluctant but ready to set out alone. And at other times, as we see in the animals' discussion in* Jaguarandi, *staying home, hunkering down, and learning new ways to live is the right course to take.*

## Virginia Hamilton, *Jaguarandi*

The powerful jaguar with golden, spotted coat speaks up: "Day in, year out, hunters keep up their war. They want to sell my hide. But they will never destroy *me!*"

Some animals cringe in fear. Others bear their teeth.

"Each time I catch their scent," says Jaguar, "I turn about and race away. Oh, no," he gloats. "I'll never flee nor change my ways. I'll stay in these parts, hiding when I have to."

"That's the way to do it," Kit Fox says. "That's it! Rundy. I've made up my mind. I will stay here and take my chances."

"Unwise! Unwise!" Chattered Coati. "Run, Run with us!"

"No, you stay, too, Coati and Rundy! Stay with us," cry others.

The night is nearly over. The animals have spoken together. Each thinks and wonders how much time it has to be safe here.

---

*At times whole families have to uproot to escape unbearable hardship. There are also occasions when remembering where you come from, as James Mitsui does, will give you the know-how and fortitude to stay or to face the unknown, as necessary. That's the advice Catherine in* Catherine, Called Birdy, *gets too.*

## Katherine Cushman, *Catherine, Called Birdy*

Then she told a story about this man who was so stupid that he forgot how to get dressed in the morning. Where was his shirt? Did it go on his legs or his arms? And how did it fasten? Such trouble it was every morning. Finally he decided to hire the boy next door to come in each day and tell him, "Your shoes are there and your cloak is here and your hat goes on your head." The first day the boy comes in. "First," he says to the stupid man, "wash yourself." "That's all very well," says the stupid man, "but where is myself? Where in the world am I? Am I here? Am I here? Or am I here?" And he looked under the bed and behind the chair and in the street, but it was all in vain for he never did find himself.

As she spoke, the children stopped their snuffling and chanted with her, "Am I here? Or am I here?" And then shyly they began to shove each other and giggle, wiping their runny noses on their sleeves and skirts.

"Listen to me, my children," said the old woman then, "do not be like the stupid man. Know where you yourself are. How? By knowing who you are and where you come from. Just as a river by night shines with the reflected light of the moon, so too do you shine with the light of your family, your people, and your God. So you are never far from home, never alone, wherever you go."

It was a wonder. She was like a minstrel, or a magician spinning stories from her wrinkled mouth. And then she pulled from the sleeves of her gown bread and onions and herring and boiled cabbage and they ate. One tiny girl with soft eyes brought me an onion and some bread. Mayhap I wasn't hidden as well as I thought. It smelled like our food and I was hungry from hearing of the adventures of Moses, so I ate it. I did not die nor turn into a Jew. I think some stories are true and some stories are just stories.

**James Masao Mitsui, *Katori Maru*, October 1920**
Two weeks across a strange sea,
big waves, the ship
spilling its toilets.
People sick of the ocean
run from bulkhead to bulkhead,
trying to keep their balance
on the slick iron deck. . . .

Waves, floating waves,
rise above the railing,
drift out of sight.
Vancouver Island
is a memory of home, hills
soft & green as crushed velvet.

In Tacoma, Minoru buys
Western clothes: a pink taffeta dress
full of pleats, wide-brimmed hat,
white gloves, a leather handbag
and awkward high heels.

No more flowered silk,
obi sash and getas.
He brings out a used coat from the closet,
thick maroon wool, brown fur collar.
It is too full in the shoulders

the size & color
fit her sister.
But for now she accepts it.
The rain feels heavy
on the gray sidewalk to America

# Values That Relate to People One Doesn't Know and Nature (Idealism, Compassion, Responsibility, Balance, and Fairness)

# Introduction

The engineer, architect, author, and visionary Buckminster Fuller developed the notion of earth as one great spaceship and said of it:

> We are not going to be able to operate our spaceship earth successfully nor much longer unless we see it as a whole spaceship and our fate as common. It has to be everybody or nobody.
> —*Operating Manual for Spaceship Earth*

The challenge to live harmoniously in a complex world means that we have to learn to care for others we do not know and are not likely to know on a personal level. These people may live in the same city we live in and share our culture. They may live in places we know nothing of or be quite different culturally. However, we all share a common humanity, and learning to internalize that deeper sense of connectedness is an increasingly demanding call. Our own democracy, international peace, and the well-being of the Earth itself depend on it. As the poet Susan Griffith says:

> We know ourselves to be made from this earth. We know this earth is made from our bodies. For we see ourselves. And we are nature. We are nature seeing nature. We are nature with a concept of nature. Nature weeping. Nature speaking of nature to nature.
> —*The Earth: What She Says to Me*

The specific character values that develop as one grows into a larger world are *idealism, compassion, responsibility, balance,* and *fairness.*

IDEALISM
The ability to imagine a more perfect world or, on a more intimate level, to see beyond present troubles and imagine future happiness, is what keeps hope alive during times of trouble. It is the central force that sees

goodness in the world and makes it possible to maintain the most romantic and hopeful dreams of childhood. An idealist of any age can see beyond present troubles and envision future happiness.

## COMPASSION

A sense of shared identity with humanity and nature leads to reverence for life and humility in facing the complexity and beauty of the world. It is from this central feeling that people reach out to help others and also feel comfortable enough to ask for assistance. Young people need to experience our compassionate caring for their lives and feel free enough to show similar concern for the lives of others.

## RESPONSIBILITY

An acceptance of the role of responsibility for personal decisions in the molding of events, lies at the heart of learning to live with others. Young people have to learn about many levels of responsibility, beginning with responsibility for the person they are and moving out to responsibility due to loved ones, to society, to the environment, and to larger ideals of justice and fairness. The ability to act on the basis of conviction and not allow oneself to be victimized requires a developed sense of responsibility.

## BALANCE

An understanding of one's personal role in the complex interrelation-ships between all beings and the interrelatedness of action and thought is called upon throughout life. We face compelling and diverse desires in ourselves, and among those we love and work with. The Earth too offers opportunities and costs to be judged and assessed. In childhood it is very difficult to understand how one's place in the whole might affect every-day life. However, the abilities to function cooperatively, to analyze a complex situation, and to understand the systemic effects of one's actions are crucial, not merely for oneself but for the future of all of us. Appreciating this complexity and searching for ways to act in respect for it are what many spiritual traditions call wisdom.

## FAIRNESS

A sense that what is good for you should also be good for everyone else, that each person on Earth has worth and value, is the source of feelings about justice and equality. It is the generative center of reciprocity, the idea that harmony can be achieved through human effort. It makes tol-erance for difference possible and desirable. Along with compassion, fairness is the character value that gives rise to hope for a just world.

# Idealism

And he dreamed and behold a ladder set up on the earth and the top of it reached to heaven.

"I am clay, I am one of countless shards of clay. But my soul reaches to heaven and behold the angels of God ascending and descending on it. Even the ascent and descent of the angels depends on my deeds."
—Genesis, translated by Martin Buber

Jacob's dream image has long been a powerful one. The idea that we can soar despite our human frailties is reassuring and inspiring. Idealism is the force in us that keeps that idea alive: believing that we are in partnership with a grand vision of life.

To be sure people interpret that vision in quite diverse ways. Grand visions can also have salutary or destructive impact. But idealism carries the desire to recognize and aim for the best in individual and social life. Toni Morrison, in a commencement speech, called on graduating students this way: "As you enter positions of trust and power, dream a little before you think." Morrison imposes a social ethic on personal ambition. She seems to have Jacob's dream in mind—the deeds of those in positions of authority are central to our capacity as a society to keep "heaven" in view.

In Eric Carle's story *Papa, Please Get the Moon for Me*, Monica so loves the moon that she asks her father to get it for her. He places a ladder on a high mountain to reach up and ask the moon to come down to play with his daughter. The moon agrees:

And indeed, the moon got smaller and smaller
When the moon was just the right size,
Papa took it.
Down and down he climbed.
"Here," said Papa to Monica,
I have the moon for you."

Monica dances joyously with the moon. But of course the moon continues to get smaller until it disappears. Monica is back endlessly looking at the sky—until happily once again she sees a sliver of the moon; then:

> It got bigger
> And bigger
> And bigger
> Until it was the moon again.

All of us who have our eyes on the heavens will sometimes be fortunate to live with all we hope for, and sometimes we will count ourselves lucky if we can keep it in view, as it waxes and wanes in the course of our daily lives.

——◦◦◦——

*The pursuit of a great vision evokes a force that calls us all to wonder and to search, as in the poems by Walt Whitman and Emily Dickinson. When Wendy is shot by an arrow, Peter Pan and the children have to find a way to shelter their vision of the mother they're searching for.*

### Walt Whitman, *I hear it was charged against me*

I hear it was charged against me that I sought to destroy institutions,
But really I am neither for nor against institutions
(What indeed have I in common with them? or what with the destruc-
　　tion of them?)
Only I will establish in the Mannahatta and in every city of these States
　　inland and seaboard,
And in the fields and woods, and above every keel little or large that
　　dents the water,
Without edifices or rules or trustees or any argument,
The institution of the dear love of comrades.

### Emily Dickinson, *Tell All the Truth*

Tell all the truth but tell it skant.
Success in circuit lies
Too bright for our infirm delight,
The truth's super surprise

As lightning to the children eased
With explanation kind.
The truth must dazzle gradually
Or everyman be blind.


**James M. Barrie,** *Peter Pan*
They opened their mouths, but the cheers would not come. He overlooked it in his haste to tell the glorious tidings.

"Great news, boys," he cried, "I have brought at last a mother for you
all."

Still no sound, except a little thud from Tootles as he dropped on his
knees.

"Have you not seen her?" asked Peter, becoming troubled. "She flew
this way."

"Ah me!" one voice said, and another said, "Oh, mournful day."

Tootles rose. "Peter," he said quietly, "I will show her to you," and
when the others would still have hidden her he said, "Back, twins, let
Peter see."

So they all stood back, and let him see, and after he had looked for a
little time he did not know what to do next

"She is dead," he said uncomfortably. "Perhaps she is frightened at
being dead."

He thought of hopping off in a comic sort of way till he was out of
sight of her, and then never going near the spot any more. They would all
have been glad to follow if he had done this.

But there was the arrow. He took it from her heart and faced his
band.

"Whose arrow?" he demanded sternly.

"Mine, Peter," said Tootles on his knees.

"Oh, dastard hand," Peter said, and he raised the arrow to use it as a
dagger.

Tootles did not flinch. He bared his breast. "Strike, Peter," he said
firmly, "strike true."

Twice did Peter raise the arrow, and twice did his hand fall. "I cannot
strike," he said with awe, "there is something stays my hand."

All looked at him in wonder, save Nibs, who fortunately looked at
Wendy.

"It is she," he cried, "the Wendy lady, see, her arm!"

Wonderful to relate, Wendy had raised her arm. Nibs bent over her
and listened reverently. "I think she said 'Poor Tootles,'" he whispered.

"She lives," Peter said briefly.

Slightly cried instantly, "The Wendy lady lives."

Then Peter knelt beside her and found his button. You remember she had put it on a chain that she wore round her neck

"See," he said, "the arrow struck against this. It is the kiss I gave her. It has saved her life."

"I remember kisses," Slightly interposed quickly, "let me see it. Ay, that's a kiss."

Peter did not hear him. He was begging Wendy to get better quickly, so that he could show her the mermaids. Of course she could not answer yet, being still in a frightful faint; but from overhead came a wailing note.

"Listen to Tink," said Curly, "she is crying because the Wendy lives."

Then they had to tell Peter of Tink's crime, and almost never had they seen him look so stern.

"Listen, Tinker Bell," he cried, "I am your friend no more. Begone from me for ever."

She flew on to his shoulder and pleaded, but he brushed her off. Not until Wendy again raised her arm did he relent sufficiently to say, "Well, not for ever, but for a whole week."

Do you think Tinker Bell was grateful to Wendy for raising her arm? Oh dear no, never wanted to pinch her so much. Fairies indeed are strange, and Peter, who understood them best, often cuffed them.

But what to do with Wendy in her present delicate state of health?

"Let us carry her down into the house," Curly suggested.

"Ay," said Slightly, "that is what one does with ladies."

"No, no," Peter said, "you must not touch her. It would not be sufficiently respectful."

"That," said Slightly, "is what I was thinking."

"But if she lies there," Tootles said, "she will die."

"Ay, she will die," Slightly admitted, "but there is no way out."

"Yes, there is," cried Peter. "Let us build a little house round her."

They were all delighted. "Quick," he ordered them, "bring me each of you the best of what we have. Gut our house. Be sharp."

In a moment they were as busy as tailors the night before a wedding. They skurried this way and that, down for bedding, up for firewood, and while they were at it who should appear but John and Michael. As they dragged along the ground they fell asleep standing, stopped, woke up, moved another step and slept again.

"John, John," Michael would cry, "wake up! Where is Nana, John, and mother?"

And then John would rub his eyes and mutter, "It is true, we did fly."

You may be sure they were very relieved to find Peter.

"Hullo, Peter," they said.

"Hullo," replied Peter amicably, though he had quite forgotten them. He was very busy at the moment measuring Wendy with his feet to see how large a house she would need. Of course he meant to leave room for chairs and a table. John and Michael watched him.

"Is Wendy asleep?" they asked.

"Yes."

"John," Michael proposed, "let us wake her and get her to make supper for us," and as he said it some of the other boys rushed on carrying branches for the building of the house. "Look at them!" he cried.

"Curly," said Peter in his most captainy voice, "see that these boys help in the building of the house."

"Ay, ay, sir."

"Build a house?" exclaimed John.

"For the Wendy," said Curly.

"For Wendy?" John said, aghast. "Why, she is only a girl !"

"That," explained Curly, "it why we are her servants."

"You? Wendy's servants!"

"Yes," said Peter, "and you also. Away with them"

The astounded brothers were dragged away to hack and hew and carry. "Chairs and a fender first," Peter ordered. "Then we shall build the house round them."

"Ay," said Slightly, "that it how a house is built; it all comes back to me."

Peter thought of everything. "Slightly," he cried, "fetch a doctor."

"Ay, ay," said Slightly at once, and disappeared, scratching his head. But he knew Peter must be obeyed, and he returned in a moment, wearing John's hat and looking solemn.

"Please, sir," said Peter, going to him, "are you a doctor?"

The difference between him and the other boys at such a time was that they knew it was make-believe, while to him make-believe and true were exactly the same thing. This sometimes troubled them, as when they had to make-believe that they had had their dinners.

If they broke down in their make-believe he rapped them on the knuckles.

"Yes, my little man," anxiously replied Slightly, who had chapped knuckles.

"Please, sir," Peter explained, "a lady lies very ill."

She was lying at their feet, but Slighty had the sense not to see her.

"Tut, tut, tut," he said, "where does she lie?"

"In yonder glade."

"I will put a glass thing in her mouth," said Slightly, and he made-believe to do it, while Peter waited. It was an anxious moment when the glass thing was withdrawn.

"How is she?' inquired Peter.

"Tut, tut, tut," said Slighty, " this has cured her."

"I am glad!" Peter cried.

—◦◦◦—

*To make tough choices requires a rich inner sense of conviction, the song of oneself singing—the almost-perfect pitch of what is most important to us.*

### Julius Lester, *John Henry*

. . . folks swore the rainbow whispered it. I don't know. But whether it was a whisper or a thought, everyone had the same knowing at the same moment: "dying ain't important. Everybody does that. What matters is how well you do your living."

### Hans Christian Andersen, *The Candle*, retold by Colin Greer

Once there was a tallow candle, the commonest sort. Now this candle lived with a very poor family, but from its place in the kitchen window, it could look across the street and see into the house of a very rich family. "Oh, they have wax candles glittering in the house, how bright it is over there. I wish I could light up the house for my family like that, but alas I am just plain tallow."

Soon the children of the poor family came in to have supper. It was their father's birthday. The candle was brought to the table and lighted. The smallest of the children reached up and put her arms around the necks of her brother and sister, then her father and mother. Do you know," she asked, "Mama says we'll have warm potatoes tonight, this very night."

Her face beamed with happiness, and the candle beamed back at her. "Oh, how happy the light of the candle makes me feel," she cried. Warm gladness filled the candle as it wondered, "Little children manage to be happy here too, and my light helps." The candle wept tallow tears of joy as the family bathed happily in its light—and more than that a candle cannot do.

The table was spread, and the potatoes were eaten. There was a bright red apple for everyone. Everybody sang happy birthday, and Father blew out the tallow candle—which smiled, knowing it had the power to bring happiness, and would again.

---

*There is often a hopefulness in idealism which embraces us all. Anne Frank infuses joy and grand optimism into the very air we breathe; it's like hearing the birds singing before they are hatched, as Jean Little describes it in* Listen for the Singing.

## Jean Little, *Listen for the Singing*

The girl who had won last year's grade twelve oratorical contest recited "In Flanders Fields." Anna, along with every other Canadian child, had had to memorize it long ago. Still she found herself listening with interest.

"In Flanders fields, the poppies blow
Between the crosses, row on row
    That mark our place; and in the sky
    The larks, still bravely singing, fly
Scarce heard amid the guns below.

"We are the Dead. Short days ago
We lived, felt dawn, saw sunset glow,
    Loved, and were loved, and now we lie
    In Flanders fields.

"Take up our quarrel with the foe.
To you from failing hands we throw
    The torch; be yours to hold it high.
    If ye break faith with us who die
We shall not sleep, though poppies grow
    In Flanders fields."

Anna did not like the last verse as well as the first two. Suddenly she realized that there must be no skylarks in Canada, for she had never heard one here. Or even heard them mentioned. But there were skylarks in Germany, and she remembered how they sang. The day Papa had made her aware of them was, in that instant, as fresh in her memory as though it had happened last week. They had been out in the country, going for a walk, and she had just started to get tired when Papa said, "Listen. That's a lark singing."

The twins had stood, craning their necks back, searching the sky for the bird. Anna, who had never seen a bird in flight, did not bother to look up.

"Where is he, Papa?" Frieda demanded. "I can't see him."

"Larks fly so high they are only specks against the sun," Papa said, "but they keep singing as they mount up. Listen."

And Anna, too, had heard the shrill joyous song falling down to them out of the blue.

Now she said the line about the larks over to herself:

> . . . and in the sky
> The larks, still bravely singing, fly
> Scarce heard amid the guns below.

A Canadian doctor named John McCrae had written the poem, she knew. Wasn't he supposed to have written it in the middle of a battle, in between caring for wounded soldiers? How could he have noticed larks at a time like that? she wondered, coming on the thought unexpectedly. Most people would have heard only the guns.

Then everyone at the assembly stood while the names of graduates of Davenport Collegiate who had died in that war were read aloud. The students stood for two minutes of profound silence.

Then a boy from the band played "The Last Post" on his bugle. He played from behind them, so that the notes floated out over them, beautiful, infinitely sad. Although her father had fought in the wrong army, and not one of the names read out had special meaning for her, Anna felt her heart wrench at the thought of all those young men being killed. After all, they had been boys here, standing in this very hall. They must have wanted to go on living as much as she did.

Then, when they took their seats, the hush still holding, Mr. Appleby came out on the stage and began to talk to them.

"How many of you noticed that the poet, in the middle of a bloody and terrible battle, still could hear the singing of larks? Faintly but still bravely singing. In a sense, that is what I want to talk to you about. How important it is to stay aware of something other than the sounds of gunfire. Wartime is a time of despair and fear and loneliness and loss. Not many of us have had to face those things yet, but before this war is done most of you will have been touched by tragedy. Some of you may well be called on to fight in the armed services. You will all hear of hatred, violence, and slaughter. Some of you may already have experienced special tension, those of you with relatives in the British Isles or in Europe."

He does know, Anna thought. That was why he said all that about us on the first day of school. He used our family to stand for all the rest, Paula and Carl . . . She cut short her thoughts, not wanting to miss what he was saying.

"You will have to grow up more quickly than any group of students I have ever had before. We are facing a hard time and you are not children to be spared its pain, sheltered from its sorrow."

He paused for a moment. Though hundreds of young people sat facing him, there was not a sound.

He's talking to us as though we matter, Anna thought.

"But you have something special to give to the rest of us in this time of trial. You have faith. Once at a revival meeting, I heard a preacher say, 'Faith is when you hear the bird singing before the egg is hatched.' I thought it so perfect a definition, I have never forgotten it.

"Teachers have that kind of faith in their pupils or they would not be able to teach. They see promise, sometimes when no one else can see it, and over and over, because of their faith, they work hard enough to make the promise come true. Many people have faith in something.

"But I think that *you* must have faith in the whole world. It is going to appear hard and cruel in the months to come, and many of us will lose hope. You, with your young eyes which see more clearly, must look deeper. Keep believing that, somewhere, there is goodness, beauty, joy, love. When you find them, share them with us.

"To me, the world is like that unhatched egg. Older people, embittered by suffering, will tell you that it is rotten, that it is not worth saving. But you must warm the world the way the mother bird warms her egg. Warm it back into life and love. It is terribly important that young people like you listen for the singing.

"Because when this world breaks open, the new world will be yours. And your faith in it and in yourselves will shape the future, will decide whether there will still be a song.

"I am putting this badly. But remember the poet hearing the larks. And the preacher's words, 'Faith is when you hear the bird singing before the egg is hatched.' It is up to you to keep the faith . . . and listen for the singing."

He usually finished off with a joke, but this time he just stopped and looked out over the sea of faces. Anna, looking up at him, wanted to say out loud, "I will. I'll try." The whole student body seemed to be pledging the same thing. Mr. Appleby smiled, said "Thank you" quietly, and dismissed them.

Anna walked out with the others. She felt as though she had made a huge discovery, as though, at last, she understood why she was alive right now, today.

That night, she told Papa about the speech.

"He is a fine man," he said. "Tell me again."

## Frances Goodrich and Albert Hackett, *The Diary of Anne Frank*

ANNE: (*Looking up through skylight.*) Look, Peter, the sky. What a lovely day. Aren't the clouds beautiful? You know what I do when it seems as if I couldn't stand being cooped up for one more minute? I think myself out. I think myself on a walk in the park where I used to go with Pim. Where the daffodils and the crocus and the violets grow down the slopes. You know the most wonderful thing about thinking yourself out? You can have it any way you like. You can have roses and violets and chrysanthemums all blooming at the same time. . . . It's funny . . . I used to take it all for granted . . . and now I've gone crazy about everything to do with nature. Haven't you?

PETER: (*Barely lifting his face.*) I've just gone crazy. I think if something doesn't happen soon . . . if we don't get out of here . . . I can't stand much more of it! (*Warn change. Curtain light on. Warn £54.*)

ANNE: (*Softly.*) I wish you had a religion, Peter.

PETER: (*Bitterly, as he rolls over.*) No, thanks. Not me.

ANNE: Oh, I don't mean you have to be Orthodox . . . or believe in heaven and hell and purgatory and things. . . . I just mean some religion . . . it doesn't matter what. Just to believe in something! When I think of all that's out there . . . the trees . . . and flowers . . . and seagulls . . . when I think of the dearness of you, Peter . . . and the goodness of the people we know . . . Mr. Kraler, Miep, Dirk, the vegetable man, all risking their lives for us every day . . . When I think of these good things, I'm not afraid any more . . . I find myself, and God, and I . . .

PETER: (*Impatiently, as he gets to his feet.*) That's fine! But when I begin to think, I get mad! Look at us, hiding out for two years. Not able to move! Caught here like . . . waiting for them to come and get us . . . and all for what?

ANNE:          (*Rises and goes to him.*) We're not the only people that've
               had to suffer. There've always been people that've had to . . .
               sometimes one race . . . sometimes another . . . and yet . . .
PETER:         (*Sitting on upstage end of bed.*) That doesn't make me feel
               any better!
ANNE:          I know it's terrible, trying to have any faith . . . when people
               are doing such horrible . . . (*Gently lifting his face.*) but you
               know what I sometimes think? I think the world may be
               going through a phase, the way I was with Mother. It'll pass,
               maybe not for hundreds of years, but some day . . . I still
               believe, in spite of everything, that people are really good at
               heart.

<hr>

*To recognize the idealist, we frequently have to set aside our standard view
of things. Someone who offers us hope might also challenge our conventional
ways of doing things. A person of great hope will often see more in others
than we can see and recognize opportunities we don't recognize.*

## Ralph Ellison, *Invisible Man*

Let me be honest with you—a feat which, by the way, I find of the utmost
difficulty. When one is invisible he finds such problems as good and evil,
honesty and dishonesty, of such shifting shapes that he confuses one with
the other, depending upon who happens to be looking through him at
the time. Well, now I've been trying to look through myself, and there's a
risk in it. I was never more hated than when I tried to be honest. Or
when, even as just now I've tried to articulate exactly what I felt to be the
truth. No one was satisfied—not even I. On the other hand, I've never
been more loved and appreciated than when I tried to 'justify' and affirm
someone's mistaken beliefs; or when I've tried to give my friends the
incorrect, absurd answers they wished to hear. In my presence they could
talk and agree with themselves, the world was nailed down, and they
loved it. They received a feeling of security. But here was the rub: Too
often, in order to justify *them*, I had to take myself by the throat and
choke myself until my eyes bulged and my tongue hung out and wagged
like the door of an empty house in a high wind. Oh, yes, it made them
happy and it made me sick. So I became ill of affirmation, of saying 'yes'
against the nay-saying of my stomach—not to mention my brain.

There is, by the way, an area in which a man's feelings are more rational than his mind, and it is precisely in that area that his will is pulled in several directions at the same time. You might sneer at this, but I know now. I was pulled this way and that for longer than I can remember. And my problem was that I always tried to go in everyone's way but my own. I have also been called one thing and then another while no one really wished to hear what I called myself. So after years of trying to adopt the opinions of others I finally realized I am an *invisible* man. Thus I have come a long way and returned and boomeranged a long way from the point in society towards which I originally aspired.

So I took to the cellar; I hibernated. I got away from it all. But that wasn't enough. I couldn't be still even in hibernation. Because, damn it, there's the mind, the *mind*. It wouldn't let me rest. Gin, jazz, and dreams were not enough. Books were not enough. My belated appreciation of the crude joke that had kept me running, was not enough. And my mind revolved again and again back to my grandfather. And, despite the farce that ended my attempt to say 'yes' to the Brotherhood, I'm still plagued by his deathbed advice . . . Perhaps he hid his meaning deeper than I thought, perhaps his anger threw me off—I can't decide. Could he have meant—hell, he *must* have meant the principle, that we were to affirm the principle on which the country was built and not the men, or at least not the men who did the violence. Did he mean say 'yes' because he knew that the principle was greater than the men, greater than the numbers and the vicious power and all the methods used to corrupt its name? Did he mean to affirm the principle, which they themselves had dreamed into being out of the chaos and darkness of the feudal past, and which they had violated and compromised to the point of absurdity even in their own corrupt minds? Or did he mean that we had to take the responsibility for all of it, for the men as well as the principle, because we were the heirs who must use the principle because no other fitted our needs? Not for the power or for vindication, but because we, with the given circumstance of our origin, could only thus find transcendence. Was it that we of all, we, most of all, had to affirm the principle, the plan in whose name we had been brutalized and sacrificed—not because we would always be weak nor because we were afraid or opportunistic, but because we were older than they, in the sense of what it took to live in the world with others and because they had exhausted in us, some—not much, but some—of the human greed and smallness, yes, and the fear and superstition that had kept them running. (Oh, yes, they're running too, running all over themselves.) Or was it, did he mean that we should affirm the principle because we, through no fault of our own, were linked to all the others in the loud, clamoring semi-visible world, that world seen only as a fertile field for exploitation by Jack and his kind, and with condescension by Norton and his, who were tired of being the mere pawns in the futile game of 'making history'? Had he seen that for these too we had to say 'yes' to the principle, lest they turn upon us to destroy both it and us?

'Agree 'em to death and destruction,' grandfather had advised. Hell, weren't they their own death and their own destruction except as the principle lived in them and in us? And here's the cream of the joke: Weren't we *part of them* as well as apart from them and subject to die when they died? I can't figure it out; it escapes me. But what do I really want, I've asked myself. Certainly not the freedom of a Rinehart or the power of a Jack, nor simply the freedom not to run. No, but the next step I couldn't make, so I've remained in the hole.

I'm not blaming anyone for this state of affairs, mind you; nor merely crying *mea culpa*. The fact is that you carry part of your sickness within you, at least I do as an invisible man. I carried my sickness and though for a long time I tried to place it in the outside world, the attempt to write it down shows me that at least half of it lay within me. It came upon me slowly, like that strange disease that affects those black men whom you see turning slowly from black to albino, their pigment disappearing as under the radiation of some cruel, invisible ray. You go along for years knowing something is wrong, then suddenly you discover that you're as transparent as air. At first you tell yourself that it's all a dirty joke, or that it's due to the 'political situation'. But deep down you come to suspect that you're yourself to blame, and you stand naked and shivering before the millions of eyes who look through you unseeingly. *That* is the real soul-sickness, the spear in the side, the drag by the neck though the mob-angry town, the Grand Inquisition, the embrace of the Maiden, the rip in the belly with the guts spilling out, the trip to the chamber with the deadly gas that ends in the oven so hygienically clean—only it's worse because you continue stupidly to live. But live you must and you can either make passive love to your sickness or burn it out and go on to the next conflicting phase.

Yes, but what *is* the next phase? How often have I tried to find it! Over and over again I've gone up above to seek it out. For, like almost everyone else in our country, I started out with my share of optimism. I believed in hard work and progress and action, but now, after first being 'for' society and then 'against' it, I assign myself no rank or any limit, and such an attitude is very much against the trend of the times. But my world has become one of infinite possibilities. What a phrase—still it's a good phrase and a good view of life, and a man shouldn't accept any other; that much I've learned underground. Until some gang succeeds in putting the world in a strait jacket, its definition is possibility. Step out-side the narrow borders of what men call reality and you step into chaos—ask Rinehart, he's a master of it—or imagination. That too I've learned in the cellar, and not by deadening my sense of perception; I'm invisible, not blind.

No indeed, the world is just as concrete, ornery, vile and sublimely wonderful as before, only now I better understand my relation to it and it to me. I've come a long way from those days when, full of illusion, I lived a public life and attempted to function under the assumption that the world was solid and all the relationships therein. Now I know men are different and that all life is divided and that only in division is there true health. Hence again I have stayed in my hole, because up above there's an increasing passion to make men conform to a pattern. Just as in my nightmare, Jack and the boys are waiting with their knives, looking for the slightest excuse to . . . well, to 'ball the jack', and I do not refer to the old dance step, although what they're doing is making the old eagle rock dangerously.

Whence all this passion towards conformity anyway?—diversity is the word. Let man keep his many parts and you'll have no tyrant states. Why, if they follow this conformity business they'll end up by forcing me, an invisible man, to become white, which is not a colour but the lack of one. Must I strive towards colourlessness? But seriously, and without snobbery think of what the world would lose if that should happen. America is woven of many strands; I would recognize them and let it so remain. It's 'winner take nothing' that is the great truth of our country or of any country. Life is to be lived, not controlled; and humanity is won by continuing to play in face of certain defeat. Our fate is to become one, and yet many—This is not prophecy, but description.

### Gospel of Mark, 5

Seeing the crowds, he went up on the mountain, and when he sat down his disciples came to him. And he opened his mouth and taught them, saying:

"Blessed are the poor in spirit, for theirs is the kingdom of heaven.

"Blessed are those who mourn, for they shall be comforted.

"Blessed are the meek, for they shall inherit the earth.

"Blessed are those who hunger and thirst for righteousness, for they shall be satisfied.

"Blessed are the merciful, for they shall obtain mercy.

"Blessed are the pure in heart, for they shall see God.

"Blessed are the peacemakers, for they shall be called sons of God.

"Blessed are those who are persecuted for righteousness' sake, for theirs is the kingdom of heaven.

"Blessed are you when men revile you and persecute you and utter all hands of evil against you falsely on my account. Rejoice and be glad, for your reward is great in heaven, for so men persecuted the prophets who were before you.

"You are the salt of the earth; but if salt has lost its taste, how shall its saltness be restored? It is no longer good for anything except to be thrown out and trodden under foot by men.

"You are the light of the world. A city set on a hill cannot be hid. Nor do men light a lamp and put it under a bushel, but on a stand, and it gives light to all in the house. Let your light so shine before men, that they may see your good works and give glory to your Father who is in heaven.

"Think not that I have come to abolish the law and the prophets; I have come not to abolish them but to fulfill them. For truly, I say to you, till heaven and earth pass away, not an iota, not a dot, will pass from the law until all is accomplished. Whoever then relaxes one of the least of these commandments and teaches men so, shall be called least in the kingdom of heaven; but he who does them and teaches them shall be called great in the kingdom of heaven. For I tell you, unless your right-eousness exceeds that of the scribes and Pharisees, you will never enter the kingdom of heaven.

"You have heard that it was said, 'You shall love your neighbor and hate your enemy.' But I say to you, Love your enemies and pray for those who persecute you, so that you may be sons of your Father who is in heaven; for he makes his sun rise on the evil and on the good, and sends rain on the just and on the unjust. For if you love those who love you, what reward have you? Do not even the tax collectors do the same? And if you salute only your brethren, what more are you doing than others? Do not even the Gentiles do the same? You, therefore, must be perfect, as your heavenly Father is perfect."

———◦•◦———

*Knowing what we believe in, as was clear to Albert Einstein, is the key component of idealism. For some people, like Anouilh's* Antigone *and Al Young, the integrity of their own selves is the most precious gem of all.*

## Albert Einstein, *My Philosophy*

To ponder interminably over the reason for one's own existence or the meaning of life in general seems to me, from an objective point of view, to be sheer folly. And yet everyone holds certain ideals by which he guides his aspiration and his judgment. The ideals which have always shone before me and filled me with the joy of living are goodness, beauty, and truth. To make a goal of comfort or happiness has never appealed to me; a system of ethics built on this basis would be sufficient only for a herd of cattle.

Without the sense of collaborating with like-minded beings in the pursuit of the ever unattainable in art and scientific research, my life would have been empty. Ever since childhood I have scorned the commonplace limits so often set upon human ambition. Possessions, outward success, publicity, luxury, to me these have always been contemptible. I believe that a simple and unassuming manner of life is best for everyone, best both for the body and the mind.

My passionate interest in social justice and social responsibility has always stood in curious contrast to a marked lack of desire for direct association with men and women. I am a horse for single harness, not cut out for tandem or team work. I have never belonged wholeheartedly to country or state, to my circle of friends, or even to my own family. These ties have always been accompanied by a vague aloofness, and the wish to withdraw into myself increases with the years.

Such isolation is sometimes bitter, but I do not regret being cut off from the understanding and sympathy of other men. I lose something by it, to be sure, but I am compensated for it in being rendered independent of the customs, opinions, and prejudices of others, and am not tempted to rest my peace of mind upon such shifting foundations.

My political ideal is democracy. Everyone should be respected as an individual, but no one idolized. It is an irony of fate that I should have been showered with so much uncalled for and unmerited admiration and esteem. Perhaps this adulation springs from the unfulfilled wish of the multitude to comprehend the few ideas which I, with my weak powers, have advanced.

The most beautiful thing we can experience is the mysterious. It is the source of all true art and science. He to whom this emotion is a stranger, who can no longer pause to wonder and stand rapt in awe, is as good as dead: his eyes are closed. This insight into the mystery of life, coupled though it be with fear, has also given rise to religion. To know that what is impenetrable to us really exists, manifesting itself as the highest wisdom and the most radiant beauty which our dull faculties can comprehend only in their most primitive forms, this knowledge, this feeling, is at the center of true religiousness. In this sense, and in this sense only, I belong in the ranks of devoutly religious men.

I cannot imagine a God who rewards and punishes the objects of his creation, whose purposes are modeled after our own, a God, in short, who is but a reflection of human frailty. Neither can I believe that the individual survives the death of his body, although feeble souls harbor such thoughts through fear or ridiculous egotism. It is enough for me to contemplate the mystery of conscious life perpetuating itself through all eternity, to reflect upon the marvelous structure of the universe which we can dimly perceive, and to try humbly to comprehend even an infinitesimal part of the intelligence manifested in nature.

## Jean Anouilh, *Antigone,* translated by Lewis Galantiere

CREON: All this is really beside the point. You have your whole life ahead of you—and life is a treasure.

ANTIGONE: Yes.

CREON: And you were about to throw it away. Don't think me fatuous if I say that I understand you; and that at your age I should have done the same thing. A moment ago, when we were quarreling, you said I was drinking in your words. I was. But it wasn't you I was listening to; it was a lad named Creon who lived here in Thebes many years ago. He was thin and pale, as you are. His mind, too, was filled with thoughts of self-sacrifice. Go and find Haemon. And get married quickly, Antigone. Be happy. Life flows like water, and you young people let it run away through your fingers. Shut your hands; hold on to it, Antigone. Life is not what you think it is. Life is a child playing around your feet, a tool you hold firmly in your grip, a bench you sit down upon in the evening, in your garden. People will tell you that that's not life, that life is something else. They will tell you that because they need your strength and your fire, and they will want to make use of you. Don't listen to them. Believe me, the only poor consolation that we have in our old age is to discover that what I have just said to you is true. Life is nothing more than the happiness that you get out of it.

ANTIGONE: (*Murmurs, lost in thought.*) Happiness . . .

CREON: (*Suddenly a little self-conscious.*) Not much of a word, is it?

ANTIGONE: (*Quietly.*) What kind of happiness do you foresee for me? Paint me the picture of your happy Antigone. What are the unimportant little sins that I shall have to commit before I am allowed to sink my teeth into life and tear happiness from it? Tell me: to whom shall I have to lie? Upon whom

|   |   |
|---|---|
| | shall I have to fawn? To whom must I sell myself? Whom do you want me to leave dying, while I turn away my eyes? |
| CREON: | Antigone, be quiet. |
| ANTIGONE: | Why do you tell me to be quiet when all I want to know is what I have to do to be happy? This minute; since it is this very minute that I must make my choice. You tell me that life is so wonderful. I want to know what I have to do in order to be able to say that myself. |
| CREON: | Do you love Haemon? |
| ANTIGONE: | Yes, I love Haemon. The Haemon I love is hard and young, faithful and difficult to satisfy, just as I am. But if what I love in Haemon is to be worn away like a stone step by the tread of the thing you call life, the thing you call happiness, if Haemon reaches the point where he stops growing pale with fear when I grow pale, stops thinking that I must have been killed in an accident when I am five minutes late, stops feeling that he is alone on earth when I laugh and he doesn't know why—if he too has to learn to say yes to everything—why, no, then, no! I do not love Haemon! |
| CREON: | You don't know what you are talking about! |
| ANTIGONE: | I do know what I am talking about! Now it is you who have stopped understanding. I am too far away from you now, talking to you from a kingdom you can't get into, with your quick tongue and your hollow heart. (*Laughs.*) I laugh, Creon, because I see you suddenly as you must have been at fifteen: the same look of impotence in your face and the same inner conviction that there was nothing you couldn't do. What has life added to you, except those lines in your face, and that fat on your stomach? |
| CREON: | Be quiet, I tell you! |
| ANTIGONE: | Why do you want me to be quiet? Because you know that I am right? Do you think I can't see in your face that what I am saying is true? You can't admit it, of course; you have to go on growling and defending the bone you call happiness. |
| CREON: | It is your happiness, too, you little fool! |
| ANTIGONE: | I spit on your happiness! I spit on your idea of life—that life that must go on, come what may. You are all like dogs that lick everything they smell. You with your promise of a humdrum happiness—provided a person doesn't ask too much of life. |

**Al Young, *For Poets***
Stay beautiful
but don't stay down underground too long
Don't turn into a mole
or a worm
or a root
or a stone

Come out into the sunlight
Breathe in trees
Knock out mountains
Commune with snakes
& be the very hero of birds

Don't forget to poke your head up
& blink
Think
Walk all around
Swim upstream

Don't forget to fly

*By imagining more in their own lives, sometimes by taking hope from the most ordinary of circumstances, as do James Agee's characters in* Let Us Now Praise Famous Men *and Grace in* Lincoln's Famous Beard, *idealists give us all more space to live in and to grow.*

## James Agee, *Let Us Now Praise Famous Men*

. . . a house of simple people which stands empty and silent in the vast southern country morning sunlight, and everything which on this morning in eternal space it by chance contains, all thus left open and defenseless to a reverent and cold-laboring spy, shines quietly forth such grandeur, such sorrowful holiness of its exactitudes in existence, as no human consciousness shall ever rightly perceive, far less impart to another: that there can be more beauty and more deep wonder in the standings and spacings of mute furnishings on a bare floor between the squaring bournes of walls, than in any music ever made: that this square home as it stands in unshadowed earth between the winding years of heaven, is, not to me but of itself, one among the serene and final, uncapturable beauties of existence: that this beauty is made between hurt but unvanquishable nature and the plainest cruelties and needs of human existence in this uncured time, and is inextricable among these, and as impossible without them as a saint born in paradise:

## 2

There is plenty of time. We may stand here in front of it, and watch it, so long as it may please us to; watch its wood: move and be quiet among its rooms and meditate what the floor supports, and what is on the walls, and what is on shelves and tables, and hangs from nails, and is in boxes and in drawers: the properties, the relics of a human family; a human shelter: all in the special silence and perfection which is upon a dwelling undefended of its dwellers, undisturbed; and which is contracted between sunlight and a human shell; and in the silence and delicateness of the shame and reverence of our searching.

## 3

It is put together out of the cheapest available pine lumber, and the least of this is used which will stretch a skin of one thickness alone against the earth and air; and this is all done according to one of the three or four simplest, stingiest, and thus most classical plans contrivable, which are all traditional to that country: and the work is done by half-skilled half-paid men, under no need to do well, and who therefore take such vengeance upon the world as they may in a cynical and part wilful apathy; and—this is what comes of it. Most naive, most massive symmetry and simpleness. Enough lines, enough off-true, that this symmetry is strongly yet most subtly sprained against its centres, into something more powerful than either full symmetry, or deliberate breaking and balancing of 'monotonies' can hope to be. A look of being earnestly hand-made, again, as a child's drawing, a thing created out of need, love, patience and strained skill in the innocence of a race. Nowhere one ounce or inch, spent into ornament, not one trace of relief or of disguise: a matchless monotony, and in it a matchless variety, and this again throughout restrained, held rigid: and of all this, nothing which is not intrinsic between the materials of structure, the earth, and the open heaven. The major lines of structure, each horizontal of each board, and edge of shingle, the strictness yet subtle dishevelment of the shingles, the nailheads, which are driven according to geometric need yet are not in perfect order, the grain, differing in each foot of each board and in each board from any other, the many knots in this cheap lumber: all these fluencies and irregularities; all these shadows of pattern upon each piece of wood; all these in rectilinear ribbons caught into one squared; angled and curled music, compounding a chord of four chambers upon a soul and centre of clean air: and upon all these masses and edges and chances and flowerings of grain, the chances and colorings of all weathers, and the slow complexions and marchings of pure light.

## Lucille and Bren Breneman, *Lincoln's Famous Beard*

It was an October evening in 1860 in the town of Westfield, New York. Grace Bedell, an 11-year-old girl, was in her room, looking at a picture that her father had just given her.. It was not a drawing or a painting, yet she could see every hair on Lincoln's head and all the details of his clothing.

Her lamp threw shadows about his face and covered the hollow cheeks. Whiskers! she thought.

"How becoming it would be," she said to herself. "Somebody should tell him. All the ladies like whiskers. They would tell their husbands to vote for him, and he would become president. I must tell him!"

She reached for a pen, and began to write the following letter.

*Mr. Abraham Lincoln*

*Dear Sir,*

*I am a little girl, 11 years old, but I want you to be president of the United States very much. So I hope you won't think me very bold to write to such a great man as you are.*

*Have you a little girl about as large as I am? If so, give her my love and tell her to write me if you cannot answer this letter. I have four brothers, and some of them will vote for you. If you will let your whiskers grow, I will try to get the others to vote for you. You would look a good deal better, for your face is so thin. All the ladies like whiskers, and they would ask their husbands to vote for you. Then you would become president.*

*Grace Bedell*

At that time about 50 letters a day arrived at the Lincoln campaign headquarters. Lincoln saw only those from friends and very important people. His two secretaries, John Nicolay and John Hay, considered all other mail unimportant and usually did not give it to Lincoln.

Grace's letter was picked up by John Hay, and he was intrigued by her original idea. But John Nicolay was not impressed and suggested that Grace's letter be tossed into the wastebasket. The two secretaries began to argue, and neither of them would give in.

Just then Mr. Lincoln walked into the room. Now, Abe Lincoln liked little girls. No little girl's letter should be tossed into the wastebasket. He took the letter and began to read it. Soon a pleased expression came to his face.

A few days later Grace received this letter from Springfield, Illinois:

*My dear little Miss:*

*Your very agreeable letter of October 15th has been received. I regret the necessity of saying that I have no daughters. But I have three sons, one 17, one 9, and one 7 years of age. They, with their mother, constitute my entire family.*

*As to the whiskers, having never worn any, do you not think people would call it a piece of silly affectation if I were to begin now?*

> *Your very sincere well-wisher,*
> *A. Lincoln*

You can imagine the thrill and excitement the young girl felt when she read this letter.

On February 16 the following year a special train carried the newly elected President Lincoln from Illinois to the White House. The people of Westfield learned that the train would stop briefly at a station near their town. The Bedell family also heard the news, and on that day they took Grace and went to the station. As they approached, they saw a huge banner, which read HAIL TO THE CHIEF, and the Stars and Stripes flying from the roof of the station.

As Grace looked around at the many strange faces, there was a sudden silence. A thousand people were straining to hear. "Here comes the train!" someone shouted.

Grace raised her eyes as high as she could and saw the top of the black railway engine pass slowly beyond the heads of the people in front of her. Then she saw the top of a flat railway car, and another, and a third with the Stars and Stripes waving from the back of it.

Then she saw a tall black hat a little higher than a lot of other hats— that was all that she could see. Some of the people were shouting "Speech! Speech!" Grace held her breath. All the people around her were quiet.

"Ladies and gentlemen," she heard, "I have no speech to make, nor do I have the time to make one. I appear before you so that I may see you and you may see me."

Grace was ice-cold. That was Lincoln—that was his voice. He was up there on the platform. She tried hard to see him, but all she could see was the tall black hat.

Lincoln was speaking again. "I have but one question, standing here beside the flag: Will you give me the support a man needs to be president of our country?"

The people threw their hats into the air, waved their arms, and shouted, "We will, Abe, we will!" And then they were quiet again because Lincoln had something else to say.

"I have a little correspondent in this place. She wrote me what I should do to improve my appearance. I want to thank her. If she is present, I would like to speak to her. Her name is Grace Bedell."

Grace's father took her hand and started leading her toward the platform. People made a path for them as they went. Her father lifted her up to the platform, up high where she saw a pair of huge feet.

Somewhere above her she heard a slow chuckle. "She wrote me that I would look better if I wore whiskers."

Then Grace felt strong hands under her arms. She was lifted high in the air, kissed on both cheeks, and gently set down again. She forgot all about the people. Grace looked up and laughed happily, for up there on the rugged face, she saw the whiskers.

"You see, Grace, I let them grow just for you."

All Grace could do was stand there and look at this great, tall, wonderful man. She would have been willing to stay there forever. But Lincoln took her hand, and she heard him say, "I hope to see you again sometime, my little friend." Then she knew the moment had to end. Lincoln helped her down the railway steps, and she obediently went back to her proud father.

She heard the train whistle and the noise of the engine as it started on its way again. People waved and cheered after the train until it was far down the tracks, but in her mind Grace heard only three words—three words repeated over and over: "My little friend."

# Compassion

---

In his poem *The Dream Keeper*, Langston Hughes reaches out and says:

> Bring me all of your dreams,
> You dreamers,
> Bring me all of your
> Heart melodies
> That I may wrap them
> In a blue cloud-cloth
> Away from the too-rough fingers
> Of the world.

This poem is an embrace, one that expresses compassion for the best within all of us. Compassion is a sense of identification with all that is. It leads to reverence for life and humility facing the very fact of existence. It is from this core that people reach out to help others and feel safe enough to accept assistance. Without compassion we can turn away from other people's pain with impunity and not worry about things that do not directly affect us. We can also become hard within and forget that a compassionate embrace of the world includes ourselves as well and is therefore a central source of love and self-respect.

Young people need to experience our compassionate caring for their lives and feel free enough to show similar concern for the lives of others. The selections in this part of the book illuminate the meaning of compassion and illustrate what happens when it is lacking.

The poet Emily Dickinson embodies the character value compassion in this simple poem:

> It's all I have to bring to-day
> This, and my heart beside,

This, and my heart, and all the fields,
        And all the meadows wide.
Be sure you count, should I forget,
        Some one the sum could tell,
This, and my heart, and all the bees
        Which in the clover dwell.

———⟫•⟪———

*Here is a miscellany of short quotations, poems, and dialogues that, taken together, give a deeper view of how compassion manifests itself in life and thought:*

### Russell Hoban, *A Bargain for Frances*

"Well," said Thelma, "from now on, I will have to be careful when I play with you." "Being careful is not as much fun as being friends," said Frances. "Do you want to be careful or do you want to be friends?"

### *Psalm 133*, translated by Stephen Mitchell

How wonderful it is to live
        in harmony with all people:
like stepping out of the bath,
        your whole body fresh and vibrant;
like the morning dew, glistening
        on the tiniest blade of grass.
It is God's infinite blessing,
        a taste of eternal life.

### Yehuda Amichai, "The Courage of Plants . . . ," from *A Life of Poetry*

. . . I lay on my back and thought
About the courage of plants to climb.

### Anon.

It's better to light one candle than to curse the darkness.

My feet are tired, but my soul is rested.
                        Civil Rights marcher

**Bashō**
Learn about a pine tree from a pine tree,
and about a bamboo plant from a bamboo plant.

**Laotzu, "A Sound Man's Heart . . . ," from *The Way of Life*, adapted by Witter Bynner**
A sound man's heart is not closed upon himself
But open to other people's hearts.

<hr />

*Compassion involves recognizing the humanity in others. It often consists of reaching out to people rather than waiting for them to come to you. After reading these three selections, you might talk about how you reach out to others or are afraid to do so. Expanding the circle of one's acquaintances is a way of becoming larger oneself and contributing to the cohesion of our common social life.*

**Mary Kay Boyd, *Among the Tribes . . .***
Among the tribes of northern Natal in South Africa, the most common greeting, equivalent to "hello" in English, is the expression: Sawu Bona, which means, "I see you." If you are a member of the tribe, you might reply by saying Sikhona, "I am here." The order of the exchange is important: until you see me, I do not exist. It's as if, when you see me, you bring me into existence.

The word ubuntu stems from the folk saying Umuntu ngumentu magabantu, which, from Zulu, literally translates as: "A person is a person because of other people." Your identity is based upon the fact that you are seen—that the people around you respect and acknowledge you as a person, according to the spirit of ubuntu.

**Traditional Japanese, *Book of Songs*, translated by Arthur Waley**
Tall stands that pear tree;
Its leaves are fresh and fair.
But alone I walk, in utter solitude.
True indeed, there are other men;
But they are not like children of one's own father.
Heigh, you that walk upon the road,

Why do you not join me?
A man that has no brothers and sisters.
Why do you not help him?

## Leon Garfield, *Smith*

They made poor progress. In two hours something less than three quarters of a mile. No more. Every once in a while, the boy would turn his back to the weather and face the blind man, drawing him on and, at the same time, seeming to retreat under the impassive stare of the snow-stained face. For there was no doubt the blind man sensed the scrutiny of unseen eyes (or did he feel warm breath softening the bitter wind?) and, as was his old habit, emptied his face of all telltale expression . . . Then the boy would grunt and turn about, to plod on in the scourging snow.

Sometimes, when they passed among the heavily bandaged trees, the wind would dislodge snow from the lower branches so's it thumped down, knocking the breath out of the two travelers and forcing them to halt for recovery. Then the blind man would once more ask his guide who he was and why he'd saved him and was leading him through this huge and bitter night. Perhaps he knew? Hard to say.

"Very well, then, speak . . . anything . . . anything at all. Or are you dumb? A fine pair, we two! One with no tongue to tell what he sees, and the other with no eyes to see what's worth the telling. A humorous pair! Well, then, if you won't speak, sing!"

But Smith uttered never a word. Why? He was deeply frightened of the magistrate's mania for justice. He dreaded the blind man would give him up at the first opportunity. "So let 'im think it's a perishing angel what's leading 'im!" thought Smith cunningly: and held his tongue.

At about seven o'clock the snow began to abate, though the wind did not, and a great clearness and brilliancy settled upon the landscape, across which the boy and the blind man seemed to be the only moving things.

The magistrate, having worn out his conversation, turned to singing and chanting (maybe in the hope his silent guide would join in and betray himself?).

"The Lord is my shepherd, I shall not want." ("You said it!" thought Smith, plodding on.)

"He maketh me to lie down in green pastures . . . " ("You should see 'em," mouthed Smith with fierce irony.)

"Oh you should see 'em!" He blinked about him where the hills were white and the valleys were white: likewise the slopes between. The sky alone offered relief, being of a velvety blackness, pricked out with some fifteen or twenty frosty stars.

"Thou preparest a table before me in the presence of mine enemies . . ." went on the blind man: and Smith scowled through his windy tears, for he'd not eaten that day . . .

The thought struck him that Mr. Mansfield knew who he was all the time and was subtly mocking him, till the chance should offer of giving him up. Certainly, everything the blind man said seemed now to be cruelly humorous: and he said a great deal! Songs and poems and lumps of the Scriptures came puffing out his mouth with much issuage of smoking breath. For this was Mr. Mansfield's stock-in-trade, his vision of the world, seen through other men's eyes who'd digested their vision into words: and it made him a supper for to last him all of his life.

His own memories of what the world looked like he no longer trusted. He was a sensible man and knew full well the changes that must have been wrought since last he'd looked. His beloved daughter could no longer have been the fearful child caught in the fire he'd remembered for so long. Even the Town itself he knew to be much changed, for everywhere he heard sounds of building and of tumbling and of men losing their way. Even Nature herself he suspected of ageing, and the wind and the cold seemed crueller than he recalled.

Maybe, they were even breeding a new style of boy, now? He smiled, or tried to, but his cheeks were partly frozen. The child, Smith, for instance . . . He frowned as he recalled the powerful evidence against him. No. Whatever else might alter, justice remained fixed—like God Himself. Justice: the last refuge of a blind man.

Suddenly, he felt the grip on his wrist disappear! Frightened, he stopped, turned his face this way and that in the lonely wind. Had he been left? Oh God! Why?

Smith, beaten breathless by the weather, with a lock of his black hair (his hat was in "Bob Bellamy's") frozen solid so's it banged against his forehead like a doorknocker, was suddenly attacked by commonsense. The old mole-in-the-hole was not changed. Stern and cold was his face, colder even than the snow that spotted it. Smith was not leading him, but he was leading Smith: back into the horrible house of bondage! A thousand windy voices shouted in his ears, bidding him leave the old Justice and be gone! The world was a freezing, lonely place. No one would give Smith quarter in it. Not his sisters, not his treacherous friend, and, least of all, the stern-faced magistrate. Not even the howling weather!

Further and further off backed Smith, amazed by his own madness in coming thus far. He stared at the stark, menacing form of the blind man with his stony heart. "Take, take, take! And never give nought in return! I'm done with you!"

And then, as Smith watched, the blind man raised his hands. He turned about: tried to take a step: stumbled: recovered himself, and cried out:

"Am I alone? Am I alone?"

His face, though much limited in expression by his shrouded eyes, was suddenly and deeply wretched. A desolate face, bespeaking a starved soul. For that soul of his had been nourished on thin fare these past twelve years: it had grown weak without his knowing it so that, when the wind blew, it bowed as if to break. And the wind blew as hard for the blind man as it did for the boy.

"You old blind Justice, you!" mumbled Smith, lurching back to Mr. Mansfield. "Give us your hand, then!"

The magistrate stretched out his hands, and Nature made strange amends for a certain disability of his. Snow, dislodged from his spectacles and fallen against his eyes, had begun to melt. Water trickled down his cheeks as if it was doing what he could not: weeping.

Bewildered, Smith gazed on Mr. Mansfield's melting face. He took both the oustretched hands.

" 'ere, 'ere, then! Both me hands! You ain't alone, Mister Mansfield, nor never was! I, I was only resting."

"Smith—Smith—Smith!" cried the blind man, grasping in return the hands he'd never forgot. "Your voice at last! How I longed to hear it!"

"You knew it was me, then?"

"Yes, yes!"

"Then, why didn't you say?"

"You didn't want me to know, did you?"

"No. I was thinking you'd 'and me over to the law."

"And even so you came back?"

"I'm only a 'uman bein'."

"Only!"

Smith freed one of Mr. Mansfield's hands and turned once more into the weather.

"We'd best be moving, or we'll freeze in situation!"

They stumbled on a while longer, but no more in silence. A curious warmth seemed to've sprung up between them and rendered the wind less savage. Mr. Mansfield told Smith that his daughter had stayed behind to attend his trial and, maybe, to keep Mr. Billing to his promise of the adjournment. It seemed she, the "Saint of Vine Street," had kept her faith in Smith.

"Not you, Mister Mansfield?" asked Smith, wistfully.

"No, alas, not me. I'm no saint, Smith. Like you, I'm only a human being."

"Queer, then, being an old mole-in-the-hole and 'elpless, you should come out in sich weather for . . . for what, Mister Mansfield? For the 'ealthy cold air?"

Mr. Mansfield grinned awkwardly.

"That's it, Smith! For my health!"

Smith grinned back, then remembered his companion's disability and said:

"I'm a-smiling, Mister Mansfield!"

"Pleased to hear it, Smith."

"You, too, Mister Mansfield. And a very cheering thing to see. You got a friendly smile, you know."

"I didn't know, Smith. But now you've mentioned it, I'll take a special pride in it!"

And Mr. Mansfield continued to smile into the icy wind in the firm hope that Smith would sometimes turn and get the benefit. Which Smith did, and always remembered to return the compliment aloud. Then he'd turn back again and chatter about what he could see and what he'd seen . . . describing his life and the doings of his sisters . . . and even his escape from Newgate Jail. But he never mentioned Lord Tom nor any of the darkness that hemmed him in. Likewise, with Mr. Mansfield. Though he confided in Smith much of his warmer past, he, too, said nothing of what must have lain deepest in both their thoughts: viz. the murder of Mr. Field.

Presently, they reached the top of a gentle slope.

"Cottage, Mister Mansfield. Quarter mile off. Light in the window. Nice, snug little place. Looks warm. What say we knock on the door?"

"Don't mind if we do."

So Smith tucked his head as far as it would go into his collar, and began the descent toward the cottage which lay in a snow-filled hollow.

---

*Compassion implies solidarity, which consists of standing with others who are in pain or are less fortunate than you are. It means accepting their struggles as part of your struggles and implies making conscious sacrifices in their service. It is important to reflect on how much of your life is given over to serving yourself and how much to serving others. These two selections illuminate the meaning of solidarity and provide examples of such compassionate action.*

**Francisco X. Alarcón, *Promised Land***

*To the students of the Yo Puedo program, 1989, and their families*

let us carry our roots
with us all the time
let us roll them up and
use them as our pillow

let us be the dream
of our elders,
the promise of their ribs,
the answer to their prayers

let us fill up all gaps,
tear down all barriers,
let us find godliness
in every face, every tree

may our ears hear
what nobody wants to hear,
may our eyes see
what everyone wants to hide

may our mouths speak up
the truth of our hearts,
may our arms be branches
that give shade to the needy

let us be a drizzle,
the salt of the earth,
the horizon that unites
the beginning and the end

let us accept ourselves
the way we are,
let us take presents in
and give them back manifold

let us see ourselves
twenty years from now

who is now the doctor,
the nurse who can heal

who is now the teacher
who can really teach
and learn from students,
the social worker who cares

the lawyer who defends
the poor, the innocent,
the organizer who makes
dreams come true

who is now the mother
that takes a child to school,
the lover that can forgive
and love again

let us keep forever
the child within each of us,
may our shoulders grow wings
so we can be butterflies

let us be the key that opens
new doors to our people,
let tomorrow be today,
yesterday has never left

let us all right now
take the first step:
let us finally arrive
at our Promised Land!

### Si Kahn, *Hunger,* a story song

"Hunger" concerns a strike and lockout in a coal camp. When the children begin crying because there is no food left anywhere to eat, Aunt Molly Jackson, accompanied by her own young child, robs the company store at gunpoint and distributes the stolen food throughout the coal camp. When the deputy sheriff comes to arrest her, she persuades him that what she's done is just and he lets her go. From retelling this story, using my own voice by Aunt Molly Jackson's words, I would go directly into the unaccompanied song "People Like You." I start with my song "What You Do With What You've Got."

> *It's not just what you're born with*
> *It's what you choose to bear*
> *It's not how large your share is*
> *But how much you can share*
> *It's not the fights you dream of*
> *But those you really fought*
> *It's not just what you're given*
> *But what you do with what you've got*

> *For what's the use of two strong legs*
> *If you only run away*
> *What good is the finest voice*
> *If you've nothing good to say*
> *What good are strength and muscle*
> *If you only push and shove*
> *What's the use of two good ears*
> *If you can't hear those you love*

> *It's not just what you're born with*
> *It's what you choose to bear*
> *It's not how large your share is*
> *But how much you can share*
> *It's not the fights you dream of*
> *But those you really fought*
> *It's not just what you're given*
> *But what you do with what you've got*

So there was a young family
that had one child
that lived just below me
and I heard that little child a-crying
for two days

And I went down
and I asked the mother, I said
Daisy, what is the matter with that baby?

She said, Aunt Molly
she's a-crying for something to eat
I don't have a crust of bread
for that child

So I said. Is it possible
that I will do more for your children.
you people
than you will do yourselves?
I said. In the name of common sense
have you got a fifty pound feed sack
or a sugar sack
or something to give me?

Yes. she said.
I took that sugar sack
and I went back to the house.
Me being a midwife
I had a permit
to carry me a gun

I had a good .38 special
that I'd used for my protection
through them hills
for fifteen years then
And I put it under my arm
and put my coat on over it
and I started to the commissary

But when I got down to the foot of the hill
there was another family of children of seven a-crying
all small children
And I said
Well, what is the matter with your children, Ann?
That was Bob Stringer's wife
a good, hard-working man
and kept his family plenty
when he was allowed to work
So she says
they're hungry and I don't have a thing
and she was a-crying

I said. Come on. Henry
to my little son, Henry Jackson, I said
come on and go with me
I went into the commissary
and I went in laughing
and I said to the commissary clerk
I said. Well, it don't make any difference
how hard times gets
Mister Martin
I said, I can always have a little money
or a little scrip
or something to get by on
Give me a 24-pound sack of flour

He handed me over
the 24-pound sack of flour
and I whispered to my little son, I said
Henry, take this 24-pound sack of flour
and walk out and wait for me
at the tipple
That was where they weighed the coal
and dumped it into cars

The boy took that sack of flour
and he walked out
Then I begin to call
for the things that was needed the worst
for them little starving children
And I filled my sugar sack full
and I said: How much is this?

Five dollars
and ninety cents

Well, I said, Now, Martin
I'll see you in 90 days
as quick as I can get around
and collect enough money
to pay you
I have to feed some children
they're starving
they can't wait

for me to go around
and try to collect
by nickels and dimes
enough to get them something to eat
They have to eat now
And I'll pay you
don't worry

He says, Aunt Molly Jackson
don't you offer to walk out
without them groceries

I reached under my arm
and I pulled my pistol
and I walked out backwards
and I said
Martin, if you try to take this grub
away from me, I said
God knows if they electrocute me for it tomorrow
I says, I'll shoot you six times in a minute

I walked out
I got home
And these seven little children
was so hungry
that when their mother was making up the dough
to cook the bread
they was a-grabbing the raw dough
off of their mother's hands
and cramming it into their mouth
and swallowing it

I left part of the food
with that big family of children
I went on up to Bill Allen's house
and give Daisy Allen his wife the rest
for her little child

My house was the next house
and by the time I got into the door
the deputy sheriff was there to arrest me

And he said to me, he says,
Well, Aunt Molly, what in the world, he says
have you turned out, he says, to be a robber?

I said Oh. no. Frank, I said
I am no robber
but I said it was the last chance
I have heard these little hungry children cry
for something to eat
'til I'm desperate
I'm almost out of my mind
And, I said, I will get out
as I said
and collect that money
just as quick as I can
and pay them
I said, You know
I'm as honest
as the days is long

And the tears come in his eyes
And he said
Well, Aunt Molly, he says
They sent me up here, he says
to arrest you
The coal operator
well, Goodman, sent me here
to arrest you
(he was the coal operator)
for that
But, he says
if you've got the heart
to do that much, he says
for other people's children
that's not got one drop
of your blood in their bodies, he says
I will pay that bill myself, he says
and, he says, if they fire me
for not arresting you, he said
I will be damned glad of it
That's just the way he said it

He walked out
and he didn't arrest me

---

*Compassion for others can lead to a commitment to healing. Medicine is a healing profession, but so are teaching and psychology. However, within any vocation or work, a healing component can be crafted. These two selections suggest that you reflect on how the way work is done in your family can contribute to the healing of others.*

### Lorraine Hansberry, *A Raisin in the Sun*

BENEATHA:    Me? . . . Me? . . . Me I'm nothing. . . . me. When I was very small . . . we used to take our sleds out in the wintertime and the only hills we had were the ice covered stone steps of some houses down the street. And we used to fill them in with snow and make them smooth and slide down them all day . . . and it was very dangerous you know . . . far too steep . . . and sure enough one day a kid named Rufus came down too fast and hit the sidewalk . . . and we saw his face just split open right there in front of us . . . and I remember standing there looking at his bloody open face thinking that was the end of Rufus. But the ambulance came and they took him to the hospital and they fixed the broken bones and they sewed it all up . . . and the next time I saw Rufus he just had a little line down the middle of his face . . . I never got over that.

ASAGAI:    What?

BENEATHA:    That was what one person could do for another, fix him up—sew up the problem, make him right again. That was the most marvelous thing in the world . . . I wanted to do that, I always thought it was the one concrete thing in the world that a human being could do. This was truly being God . . .

ASAGAI:    You wanted to be God?

BENEATHA:    [No] I wanted to cure. It used to be so important to me. I wanted to cure. It used to matter. I used to care. I mean about people and how their bodies hurt . . .

*Ojibway Prayer*
Grandfather,
Look at our brokenness.

We know that in all creation
Only the human family
Has strayed from the Sacred Way.
We know that we are the ones.
Who are divided
And we are the ones
Who must come back together
To walk the Sacred Way.
Grandfather,
Sacred One,
Teach us love, compassion
          and honor
That we may heal the earth
And heal each other.

———⟶•⟵———

*Sometimes people act cruelly and hurt others. Occasionally one can make things up and, through an expression of compassion and love, bring things together again. Other times, as in this selection, it is too late, and the best one can do is always remember that one's actions can have serious consequences in other people's lives.*

## Eleanor Estes, *The Hundred Dresses*

"Dear teacher: My Wanda will not come to your school any more. Jake also. Now we move away to big city. No more holler Polack. No more ask why funny name. Plenty of funny names in the big city. Yours truly, Jan Petronski."

A deep silence met the reading of this letter. Miss Mason took her glasses off, blew on them and wiped them on her soft white handkerchief. Then she put them on again and looked at the class. When she spoke her voice was very low.

"I am sure none of my boys and girls in Room 13 would purposely and deliberately hurt anyone's feelings because his name happened to be a long unfamiliar one. I prefer to think that what was said was said in thoughtlessness. I know that all of you feel the way I do, that this is a very unfortunate thing to have happen. Unfortunate and sad, both. And I want you all to think about it."

The first period was a study period. Maddie tried to prepare her lessons, but she could not put her mind on her work. She had a very sick feeling in the bottom of her stomach. True, she had not enjoyed listening to Peggy ask Wanda how many dresses she had in her closet, but she had said nothing. She had stood by silently, and that was just as bad as what Peggy had done. Worse. She was a coward. At least Peggy hadn't considered they were being mean, but she, Maddie, had thought they were doing wrong. She had thought, supposing she was the one being made fun of. She could put herself in Wanda's shoes. But she had done just as much as Peggy to make life miserable for Wanda by simply standing by and saying nothing. She had helped to make someone so unhappy that she had had to move away from town.

Goodness! Wasn't there anything she could do? If only she could tell Wanda she hadn't meant to hurt her feelings. She turned around and stole a glance at Peggy, but Peggy did not look up. She seemed to be studying hard.

Well, whether Peggy felt badly or not, she, Maddie, had to do something. She had to find Wanda Petronski. Maybe she had not yet moved away. Maybe Peggy would climb the Heights with her and they would tell Wanda she had won the contest. And that they thought she was smart and the hundred dresses were beautiful.

When school was dismissed in the afternoon, Peggy said with pretended casualness, "Hey, let's go and see if that kid has left town or not."

So Peggy had had the same idea as Maddie had had! Maddie glowed. Peggy was really all right, just as she always thought. Peg was really all right. She was o.k.

———————

*Lack of compassion can lead to horrible behavior. Compassion checks the worst in us; without it people become a menace to themselves and others. Here is one comment on and two examples of the effects of having no feeling for others or for nature.*

### The Wisdom of the Jewish Sages, translated by Rami Shapiro
Yochanan said to his disciples:

Go out and see
which is the wrong path for a person to follow.

Rabbi Eliezer said: Blind the eye to Reality.
Rabbi Joshua: Be a bad friend.
Rabbi Jose: Be a bad neighbor.
Rabbi Shimon: Borrow without repaying.
Rabbi Elazar: Inure the heart to compassion.

Yochanan said:

I prefer the words of Elazar ben Arach,
for his words include all other words.

II:13

### Anna Sewell, *Black Beauty*

Whether the man was partly blind, or only very careless, I can't say; but he drove me with that stone in my foot for a good half mile before he saw anything. By that time I was going so lame with the pain that at last he saw it and called out, "Well, here's a go! Why, they have sent us out with a lame horse! What a shame!"

He then chucked the reins and flipped about with the whip, saying, "Now, then, it's no use playing the old soldier with me; there's the journey to go, and it's no use turning lame and lazy."

Just at this time a farmer came riding up on a brown cob. He lifted his hat and pulled up.

"I beg your pardon, sir," he said, "but I think there is something the matter with your horse. He goes very much as if he had a stone in his shoe. If you will allow me, I will look at his feet; these loose scattered stones are confounded dangerous things for the horses."

"He's a hired horse," said my driver. "I don't know what's the matter with him, but it's a great shame to send out a lame beast like this."

The farmer dismounted, and slipping his rein over his arm at once took up my near foot.

"Bless me, there's a stone! lame! I should think so!"

At first he tried to dislodge it with his hand, but as it was now very tightly wedged, he drew a stone-pick out of his pocket, and very carefully, and with some trouble, got it out. Then holding it up, he said, "There, that's the stone your horse had picked up. It is a wonder he did not fall down and break his knees into the bargain!"

"Well, to be sure!" said my driver. "That is a queer thing! I never knew that horses picked up stones before."

"Didn't you?" said the farmer, rather contemptuously. "But they do, though, and the best of them will do it, and can't help it sometimes on such roads as these. And if you don't want to lame your horse, you must look sharp and get them out quickly. This foot is very much bruised," he said, setting it gently down and patting me. "If I might advise, sir, you had better drive him gently for a while. The foot is a good deal hurt, and the lameness will not go off directly."

Then mounting his cob and raising his hat to the lady, he trotted off.

When he was gone my driver began to flop the reins about and whip the harness, by which I understood that I was to go on, which of course I did, glad that the stone was gone, but still in a good deal of pain.

This was the sort of experience we job horses often came in for.

### Raymond R. Patterson, *Birmingham 1963*

Sunday morning and her mother's hands
Weaving the two thick braids of her springing hair,
Pulling her sharply by one bell-rope when she would
Not sit still, setting her ringing,
While the radio church choir prophesied the hour
With theme and commercials, while the whole house tingled;
And she could not stand still in that awkward air;
Her dark face shining, her mother now moving the tiny buttons,
Blue against blue, the dress which took all night making,
That refused to stay fastened;
There was some pull which hurried her out of Sunday School
Toward the lesson and the parable's good news,
The quiet escape from the warring country of her feelings,
The confused landscape of grave issues and people.

But now we see
Now we see through the glass of her mother's wide screaming
Eyes into the room where the homemade bomb
Blew the room down where her daughter had gone:
Under the leaves of hymnals, the plaster and stone,
The blue dress, all undone—
The day undone to the bone—
Her still, dull face, her quiet hair;
Alone amid the rubble, amid the people
Who perish, being innocent.

*When compassion is lacking, it is easy to divide the world into those with you and those against you, the former being good and the latter being bad. Here's a delightful game of Us and Them made up by Robert Cormier. See if you can contribute to the list.*

### Robert Cormier, *I Have Words to Spend*

The world is made up of two kinds of people—them and us. Oh, I'm not talking about friends versus enemies or the Western nations against the rest of the world or the North against the South. Nothing like that. I mean those of us who share common things, who are loyal to each other, and those who aren't. And with people who are with Us, we have special rules and very special ways of looking at Them and Us.

For instance:

We are always Cautious but they are Chicken.

When we lose a football game by a 7 to 6 score, we achieve a Moral Victory. But when they lose a football game to us by a 7 to 6 score, we say that it's the score that counts.

When we don't dress, we go Casual. But when they don't dress, they're Slobs.

Our house has character—theirs is rundown. Or our house has that lived-in look—their house looks worn out.

A friend of ours is colorful, but that same friend of theirs is nutty.

Our friend has an even disposition and never loses his cool—their friend is dull, dull, dull.

Our friend is the life of the party—but their friend always makes a fool of himself after a few drinks.

See how it works?

Our garden could have used more luck this year—their garden was an utter failure.

Or: We have a green thumb—but they happen to have good soil.

We are slender—but they are skinny.

We have been putting on a little weight lately, but they are getting fat.

We are contemplative—they are lazy.

We are daredevils—they are reckless.

The Them or Us syndrome extends to the arts, as well.

As in:

Our friend got a character part in a new movie—their friend got a small role.

Our friend has written a book with a plot as light as a soufflé—their friend has written a book with a flimsy plot.

Our friend is very emotional—their friend is temperamental.

Our friend is always "on"—their friend is a show-off.

Our friend is multi-talented—their friend can sing a little, dance a little, play a little.

The world of diplomacy has also been invaded by this kind of thing and, in fact, it has reached the stage where the magazine *Horizon* devotes an article to what it calls "Newspeak." Samples:

They have terrorists—we have freedom fighters

They are moralistic—we are moral.

They are reactionary— we are traditional.

They are racist—we want to preserve our identity.

They have emotions—we have feelings.

But most of all, it is used in our daily lives, and it goes unnoticed.

Our friend is fastidious—their friend is fussy.

Our friend hasn't been feeling well for some time—their friend is a hypochondriac.

Our children are inquisitive—their children are nosy.

Our friend is very well informed—their friend is a know-it-all.

Our friend can go on at length on any topic—their friend never stops talking.

Our friend is aging gracefully—their friend is getting old.

Ah, but you get the idea. Because you, my friend, are so perceptive . . .

———◆◆———

*The following two selections are instances of compassion extended to animals. Feeling for animals is akin to feeling the smallness of one's own place in the whole of creation and provides a sense of reverence. Life without the presence of animals is diminished, and the longing for connection with all forms of life is a central component of compassion. For city people, pets often make this connection.*

## John Berger, *Pig Earth*

Joseph paced it out and found she had rolled a hundred metres. How she finally stopped herself was another mystery. He shrugged his shoulders. Yet she had stopped just in time. A few metres below, the slope increased to nearly forty five degrees, and then nothing could have saved her. She would have hit the boulders at the bottom, a mass of unsellable broken meat and bone.

"Rousa's come back!" he shouted.

Martine came running, and stopped short to see the cow unexpectedly on the ground.

"Has she broken a leg?"

Joseph shook his head.

Together they pushed and pulled to get the cow on to her feet. She would not budge.

"We can't move her, the two of us by our selves."

"In the morning I'll go down to get help," he said.

"I'm not leaving her alone all night," Martine insisted.

"A cow is an animal," he said.

"I'm staying with her. She could roll down there on to the rocks."

He walked away with his despondent walk.

"Twenty seven years, and this is the first time I've had an accident with a cow." She said this quietly as she felt the cow's horns and ears. "A stupid accident. A stupid cow accident!"

With her complacent eyes Rousa followed the woman's movement. Her horns were unhealthily cold.

Joseph came back with some blankets draped over his shoulders. Something had mollified him.

"I will stay with her," he said.

"I won't sleep anyway," said Martine.

They spread the blankets over Rousa, and then over themselves.

"She knows what's happening," said Martine.

Cows rarely make any sound when in pain. At the most they blow heavily through their immense nostrils.

From under the blankets the two of them looked down at the far lights in the valley. The sky was clear, the Milky Way like a vast misty white goose pecking at the lip of a jug.

"If only she'd move," whispered Martine, "I could milk her."

She lay by the cow's head, the halter rope coiled round her wrist. He lay between the cow's four legs.

"The lights stay on all night in the villages," he said. "One, two, three, four, five, six, seven, but none of them is my village."

From out of his pocket he took a mouth-organ. He had had this mouth-organ for fifty years, since he was a conscript in the army. At that time, when he was young, he used to pretend to play an invisible trumpet, using only his lips and hands. If asked, he would entertain the whole barrack room by playing this trumpet which did not exist. One evening a friendly sergeant said: "You play well enough to have something to play on. Here, I've got two. Take this."

And so he acquired a mouth-organ.

As he played now, he tapped his foot on the mountainside and looked at the tiny clusters of lights below—no larger than grains of sugar, fallen from a spoon.

He played a polka, a quadrille, a waltz, "The Nightingale of the Sweet Wood," a rigadoon. Neither she nor he could have said afterwards for how long he played. The night turned colder. As his foot beat time on the mountainside, his hands in the moonlight smoothed and ruffled each tune as if it were a bird miraculously perched on the instrument. All music is about survival, addressed to survivors. Once Rousa stirred, but she could not move her numb hindquarters.

When he stopped playing, Martine spoke very gently as if talking about a child being born. "I remember you used to play your mouth organ when you first came to us."

"Twelve years ago."

"The Patron asked you"—she was laughing now—"if you could play The Charming Rosalie!"

"Twelve years and two months."

"You remember the month!"

"Yes, it was April. There was snow. I knocked on the door and asked if I could sleep in the barn. You said Yes. The next day it thawed, and the day after I helped plant the potatoes. If it hadn't thawed that day, I wouldn't be here now."

"We had only daughters," she said, by way of explanation.

The two of them listened to Rousa's difficult breathing.

"The Patron is as cunning as a fox, isn't he? He used to leave money on the table. Did you know that? He used to leave it there at night to see if I was honest. One day I said to him, 'You needn't worry! I eat my own money but I'm not going to eat yours or the Patronne's!'"

The thought of this riposte of ten years ago made him burst into song:

"Bon Soir! Bon Soir.
You gave me the moon!"

When he could remember no more words, he continued on the mouth-organ. He serenaded her. He addressed her across Rousa's head, which rested on the ground. Every so often, out of tact, he looked away from her and across to the peak opposite. He played to the mountain and the woman. To the dead and the unborn.

Then, laughing, he broke into words again:

"Bon Soir! Bon Soir.
You give me the moon."

On the last note his voice creaked like a pine tree in a storm. On the slope there was not a breath of wind. Then he pulled his beret over his ear and laid his head down to sleep.

Five minutes later Martine said: "If we can set her on to her feet in the stable tomorrow she has a chance. She wants to get up, I can feel it, Joseph."

He was already asleep with his knees drawn up. His open hand, palm uppermost, had fallen across the cow's udder. Beside it was an empty wine bottle which he must have brought with him under the blankets.

Next morning eight neighbours came to pull Rousa, with ropes attached to each of her legs, across the grass and into the stable. They talked of using a pulley and rope to hoist her to her legs, but the stable ceiling was too low. After they had gone, Martine continued to puzzle on how she could save the cow.

She pushed planks under her in the hope of levering her up. She asked Joseph to stand on the far end of a plank. He jumped up and down with all his weight until he had to stop to pull up his trousers. But nothing moved the cow. The complacency of her look was turning into indifference. Her white patches were muddied with shit and with the soil she had been pulled across.

Between carrying out Martine's instructions, Joseph kept shaking his head.

Now she had the idea that they should nail blocks of wood to the floor by her hind feet, so that if she tried to get up by herself, she would have something to push against. Joseph cut the blocks of wood and nailed them to the floor.

The day the butcher's lorry came, Rousa was dragged through the door and up the ramp into the lorry. She made no sound. All she did was to roll her eyes, rolling them upwards, until only the blue grey of the underneath of her eyeballs was visible.

In the lorry she tried for the last time to shift the dead weight of the body, muscles, tissue, organs, passages and vessels which had turned her mad for a bull, and had made her a cow with a yield of twenty- five litres of milk. But she couldn't. The cold from the mountainside was creeping up her back.

Martine stepped into the lorry and stuffed an armful of straw between Rousa's flank and the sharp metal housing round the back wheel. The road down was full of pot-holes, and she did not want the

animal, who could not move, to suffer by her skin being chafed against
the metal.

"She's a cow," one of the men said, when the back doors of the lorry
were shut.

"A poor beast," said another.

Joseph stared after the lorry and remained standing in the middle of
the rutted road long after it was out of sight.

"Hey, Joseph," a neighbour shouted.

He turned round, waved and made three dance steps.

"Come and have a drink!"

He disappeared into the stable where he looked at the horse who was
older than him.

**Garrison Keillor, *In Memory of Our Cat, Ralph***

When we got home, it was almost dark.
Our neighbor waited on the walk.
"I'm sorry, I have bad news," he said.
"Your cat, the gray-black one, is dead.
I found him by the garbage an hour ago."
"Thank you," I said, "for letting us know."

We dug a hole in the flower bed
With lilac bushes overhead,
Where this cat loved to lie in spring
And roll in dirt and eat the green
Delicious first spring buds,
And laid him down and covered him up,
Wrapped in a piece of tablecloth,
Our good old cat laid in the earth.

We quickly turned and went inside
The empty house and sat and cried
Softly in the dark some tears
For that familiar voice, that fur,
That soft weight missing from our laps,
That we had loved too well perhaps
And mourned from weakness of the heart:
A childish weakness, to regard
An animal whose life is brief
With such affection and such grief.

If such is weakness, so it be.
This modest elegy
Is only meant to note the death
Of one cat so we won't forget
His face, his name, his gift
Of cat affection while he lived,
The sweet shy nature
Of this graceful creature,
The simple pleasure of himself,
The memory of our cat, Ralph.

# Responsibility

Many families tell stories of grandmothers or grandfathers who never threw anything out, and who worried endlessly about staining the new furniture or new clothes. Those are usually stories about poor families whose survival depended on people taking responsibility not to spoil what was new and to mend what was old so it could be used again.

Stories about responsibility for survival often tell about giving. In *Dracula*, for example, it's crucial for someone to take responsibility for what is needed in order for a sick person to survive:

> Van Helsing and I were shown up to Lucy's room. If I was shocked when I saw her yesterday, I was horrified when I saw her to-day. She was ghastly, chalkly pale; the red seemed to have gone even from her lips and gums, the bones of her face stood out prominently; her breathing was painful to see or hear. . . .
>
> "My God!" he said; "this is dreadful. There is no time to be lost. She will die from sheer want of blood to keep the heart's action as it should be. There must be a transfusion of blood at once. Is it you or me?"
>
> "I am younger and stronger, professor. It must be me."
>
> "Then get ready at once. I will bring up my bag. I am prepared."
>
> —*Dracula*, by Bram Stoker

There is no point in simply being a sympathetic shadow when circumstances call for a dedicated companion and comrade. In this sense, responsibility is not simply a state of mind, as Gandhi pointed out, but a readiness to step forward as needed, a capacity to make sound preparations for certain and uncertain prospects.

> What is faith worth if it is not translated into action.
> —Mohandas Gandhi

This means paying attention, because it is inattention to the hurt, which can be caused by thoughtless habit and ill-considered convention, that produces so much ill will and conflict between people. Taking responsibility for changing begins with paying attention to the active if invisible role that is played in keeping harmful traditions alive.

Dag Hammarskjöld, the peace-loving and visionary Secretary General of the United Nations, warned: "No one should preserve a corner of his heart or mind for weeds; once they start growing, there's no stopping them." The weeds that suffocate our capacity for responsible action grow in any soil. We must all keep in mind that whenever we are in situations for which we can reasonably be expected to bear some responsibility, we have to be responsible.

*Responsibility is, as this fable tells, about understanding how much of what needs to be done or what we would like to see done can be in our own hands.*

### Anonymous, *Fable,*

There was once a wise old man who could answer any question, no matter how difficult. One day, two young people decided they were going to fool the old man. They planned to catch a bird and take it to the old man saying, "Is what we have in our hands alive or dead?" If he says "dead," we'll turn it loose, and it will fly away; if he says "alive," we'll crush it.

They caught a bird and went with it to the old man. They said, "Is what we have in our hands alive or dead?" The wise old man considered them and smiled. Then he said, "It's in your hands."

*Responsibility can begin by paying due respect to those we love and care about, as* The Growing *suggests. But it can also involve our imaginative intelligence drawing inspiration from "just above my head," as James Baldwin describes it. And so we can be open enough to keep challenges within the bounds of our own ability to take action, as Ken learns in* My Friend Flicka.

### Mongane Wally Serote, *The Growing*

No!
This is not dying when the trees

Leave their twigs
To grow blindly long into windows like fingers into eyes.
And leave us unable
To wink or to blink or to actually close the eye,
The mind—
Twigs thrusting into windows and leaves falling on the sills,
Are like thoughts uncontrolled and stuffing the heart.
Yes,
This is teaching about the growing of things:
If you crowd me I'll retreat from you,
If you still crowd me I'll think a bit,
Not about crowding you but about your right to crowd me;
If you still crowd me, I will not, but I will be thinking
About crowding you.
If my thoughts and hands reach out
To prune the twigs and sweep the leaves,
There was a growth of thought here,
Then words, then action.
So if I say prune instead of cut,
I'm teaching about the growing of things.


### Mary O'Hara, *My Friend Flicka*

When she turned her head to the south and pricked her ears and stood tense and listening, Ken knew she heard the other colts galloping on the upland.

"You'll go back there someday, Flicka," he whispered. "You'll be three and I'll be twelve. You'll be so strong and you won't know I'm on your back, and we'll fly like the wind. We'll stand on the very top where we can look over the whole world, and smell the snow from the Neversummer range. Maybe we'll see antelope—"

As her leg got better, Flicka took to following Ken around. She came hopping at his whistle or call and turned and kept beside him as he walked. He would have his hand under her chin, or around under her neck and up the other side of her face, hugging her, or just resting on her neck lightly, with a strand of her mane between his fingers.

This was what he had always dreamed of. That he should have a horse of his own that would come at his call and follow him of its own accord.

Now and then, walking down to give her her oats, he stopped and thought about it in a daze of bliss. Just what his father had said . . . she looked for him as if he was her whole life. She didn't seem to think of anything but him. Before breakfast, when he came through the cow-barn corrals, carrying the can of oats, she was waiting at the gate for him, nickering. She nosed for the can of oats. He held it away and hurried down the path, telling her that the proper place for her to have her oats was in her nursery. Flicka hopped along by his side. She knew as well as he where they were going, and then they reached the Hill, ran ahead and was standing over the box when he poured the oats in.

After breakfast, when Ken went down again, his mother was with him, and Pauly, the cat, at her heels. And again Flicka knew what to expect, and was waiting at the corral gate. She turned and hopped in front of them, leading the way to the nursery, and when she got there, stood in the accustomed place, holding up her hind leg for Ken to take the bandage off.

All her timidity had gone. Nothing frightened her now. With her acceptance of Ken there seemed to have come to her a conviction that all men were friendly and safe and their queer doings harmless.

Every day, when the bandage was removed, the wound sponged and washed with disinfectant, and the new poultice and bandage put on, Ken made a fire on the other side of the fence in the Practice Field, and burned the old dressings.

All the time Flicka listened to Ken talking to his mother, turning from one to the other, as if she could understand them.

"Dad says she *can* understand," said Ken. "Anyway, she can talk. I understand about six of the things she says."

His mother boasted, "Pauly can talk too. She can say seven things."

"What?" challenged Ken.

"She can say, *Oh, good morning, good morning, good morning. I have been waiting the longest time for you!* That's when she's been waiting in the kitchen for me to come down and make breakfast. And she can say, *Oh, please, can't I have it?* And, *All right for you!* And, *Well, what do you want now?* And, *Isn't this a lovely day? Let's do something!* And, *Oh, leave me alone!* That's when she's a nervous woman. And, *I'm just a poor little helpless cat trying to get along in the world.*"

"That's seven," said Ken.

"She can really say more than that, because she says something every time I speak to her, just a word, maybe."

"What word?" demanded Ken enviously.

"It depends. *What?* or *Yes,* or *Thanks,* or *Oh, the dickens!* "To prove it, Nell looked at Pauly who was lying on the bank, crouched like a Sphinx, her yellow eyes half open, and spoke her name sharply.

Pauly's reply was as quick as the bounce of a ball. A little sharp, questioning, cry. *Well, what do you want?* This, Ken had to admit, was more than he could get out of Flicka.

The filly's physical condition was improving. She ran all over the Calf Pasture on three legs. She was up on the hillside near the three pines in the early morning, broadside to the sun, getting what Nell said was her radium treatment; and the first thing when Ken woke in the morning, he looked out his window and saw her there, standing in profile, motionless as a statue, her head hanging low and relaxed, as all horses stand for their sunbaths.

The poultices drained and cleansed the deep wound above the hock, and the soreness was relieved, so that Flicka had no difficulty in getting up from either side alone. Soon she began to use the leg in walking; and then Nell said it was time to discontinue the poultices.

The achievement which Ken had been getting just a hint of, like the scent of something delicious but far away tickling the nostrils of a hound, was more than a hint now. It was a reality. A victory that filled his lungs and shone from his eyes and gave strength to his hands. Flicka was his. Flicka had recovered. Flicka loved him. There was only one more thing . . .

"Dad," he said at supper that night, Flicka's my friend now. She likes me."

"I'm glad of that, son," said McLaughlin. "It's a fine thing to have a horse for a friend."

### James Baldwin, *Just above My Head*

And when the dream was slaughtered, and all that love and labor seemed to have come to nothing, we scattered: it was not a time to compare notes. We had no notes to compare. We knew where we had been, what we had tried to do, who had cracked, gone mad, died, or been murdered around us. We scattered, each into his or her own silence. It was in the astounded eyes of the children that we realized, had to face, how immensely we had been feared, despised, and betrayed. Each had, with speed, to put himself together again as best he could, and begin again. Everything was gone, but the children: children allow no time for tears. Many of us who were on that road then, may now be lost forever, that is true, but not everything is lost: responsibility cannot be lost, it can only be abdicated. If one refuses abdication, one begins again. The dream was repudiated: so be it.

My father said to me, a long time ago, "Son, whatever really gets started never gets stopped. The trouble is," he added thoughtfully, after a moment, "so little ever gets started."

I was far more the pragmatic American then than I am now. Now, watching my children grow, old enough to have some sense of where I've been, having suffered enough to be no longer terrified of suffering, and knowing something of joy, too, I know that we must attempt to be responsible for what we know. Only this action moves us, without fear, into what we do not know, and what we do not know is limitless.

But we had no trouble at all on the road the next day, and it was a very beautiful, bright day. The leaves on the trees were turning, like the changing colors in the sky, and, as the miles increased behind us, our apprehensions dropped, and we were very comfortable with each other. We were comfortable with each other, among other reasons, because, whatever was coming now, we were in it together, and we could not turn back: this sense of having crossed a river brings one a certain peace.

---

*"Deeds not words!" we've been told by sages and poets through the millennia. Whether or not we act responsibly determines how we are seen—since what we do will, to a great extent, determine whether we are worthy of self-respect and the respect of other people. As these selections show, responsibility often requires timely action, not simply good intentions.*

**Yehuda Amichai, *To all my wars . . .***
. . . To all my wars it's I who have to go

**Ogden Nash, *Isabel***
Isabel once was asleep in bed
When a horrible dream crawled into her head.
It was worse than a dinosaur, worse than a shark,
Worse than an octopus oozing in the dark.
"Boo!" said the dream, with a dreadful grin,
"I'm going to scare you out of your skin!"

Isabel, Isabel, didn't worry,
Isabel didn't scream or scurry.
Isabel had a cleverer scheme;
She just woke up and fooled that dream.

**Gwendolyn Brooks, *Strong Men, Riding Horses***
Strong Men, riding horses. In the West
On a range five hundred miles. A Thousand. Reaching

From dawn to sunset. Rested blue to orange.
From hope to crying. Except that Strong Men are
Desert-eyed. Except that Strong Men are
Pasted to stars already. Have their cars
Beneath them. Rentless, too. Too broad of chest
To shrink when the Rough Man hails. Too flailing
To redirect the Challenger, when the challenge
Nicks; slams; buttonholes, Too saddled.

I am not like that, I pay rent, am addled
By illegible landlords, run, if robbers call.

What mannerisms I present, employ,
Are camouflage, and what my mouths remark
To word-wall off that broadness of the dark
Is pitiful.
I am not brave at all.


### Abraham Joshua Heschel, *Not Coming Too Late*

Heschel feared, like many of us, that people of conscience would neither speak nor act in relation to Vietnam until it was too late, and in his speech at the first Clergy and Laity Concerned mobilization in Washington, in January 1967, he indicated how this fear of coming too late replicated his boyhood fears when studying Torah at age seven with a rebbe in Poland. Together they confronted the Akeda, the story of the sacrifice of Isaac. Heschel reconstructs the scene:

> Isaac was on the way to Mount Moriah with his father; then he lay on the altar, bound, waiting to be sacrificed. My heart began to beat even faster; it actually sobbed with pity for Isaac. Behold, Abraham now lifted the knife. And now my heart froze within me with fright. Suddenly the voice of the angel was heard: "Abraham, lay not thine hand upon the lad, for now I know that thou fearest God." And here I broke into tears and wept aloud.
>
> "Why are you crying?" asked the Rabbi. "You know Isaac was not killed."
>
> And I said to him, still weeping, "But Rabbi, supposing the angel had come a second too late?"
>
> The Rabbi comforted me, and calmed me by telling me that an angel cannot come late.

And then Heschel, lifting his eyes from his manuscript and looking directly into our eyes, concluded:

An angel cannot come late, my friends, but we, made of flesh and blood, we may come late.

I have never forgotten that it is possible to come too late.

**E. F. Schumacher,** *I Cannot Predict*
I cannot predict the wind but I can have my sail ready

———※◆※———

*The call to take responsibility for who we are as individuals is usually an opportunity to find new strength to endure routine necessity as well as to be ready for more apparently grand tests of character.*

**Edgar Lee Masters,** *Spoon River Anthology*
I went to the dances at Chandlerville,
And played snap-out at Winchester
One time we changed partners,
Driving home in the moonlight in middle June,
And then I found Davis.
We were married and lived together for seventy years,
Enjoying, working, raising the twelve children,
Eight of whom we lost
Ere I had reached the age of sixty.
I spun, I wove, I kept the house, I nursed the sick,
I made the garden, and for holiday
Rambled over the fields where sang the larks,
And by Spoon River gathering many a shell,
And many a flower and medicinal weed—
Shouting to the wooded hills, singing to the green valleys.
At ninety-six I had lived enough, that is all,
And passed to a sweet repose.
What is this I hear of sorrow and weariness,
Anger, discontent and drooping hopes?
Degenerate sons and daughters,
Life is too strong for you—
It takes life to love life.

**Gary Soto, "The School Plays," from *Local News***
In the school play at the end of his sixth-grade year, all Robert Suarez had to remember to say was, "Nothing's wrong, I can see," to a pioneer woman who was really Belinda Lopez. Belinda was one of the toughest girls since the beginning of the world. She was known to slap boys and grind their faces into the grass until they bit into chunks of wormy earth. More than once Robert had witnessed Belinda staring down the janitor's pit bull, a dog that licked his frothing chops but didn't dare mess with her.

The class rehearsed the play for three weeks, at first without costumes. Early one morning Mrs. Bunnin wobbled into the classroom carrying a large cardboard box. She wiped her brow and said, "Thanks for the help, Robert."

Robert was at his desk etching a ballpoint tattoo, D-U-D-E, on the mountaintops of his knuckles. He looked up and stared at his teacher. "Oh, did you need some help?" he asked.

She rolled her eyes at him and told him to stop writing on his skin. "You'll look like a criminal," she scolded.

Robert stuffed his hands into his pockets as he rose from his seat. "What's in the box?" he asked.

She popped open the Scotch-taped top and brought out skirts, hats, snowshoes, scarves, and vests. She tossed Robert a red beard, which he held up to his face thinking it made him look handsome.

"I like it," Robert said. He sneezed and ran one hand across his moist nose.

His classmates looked at Robert in awe. "That's *bad*," Alfredo said. "What do I get?"

Mrs. Bunnin threw him a wrinkled shirt. Alfredo raised it to his chest and said, "My dad could wear this. Can I give it to him after the play is done?"

Mrs. Bunnin turned away in silence.

Most of the actors didn't have speaking parts. They were given cut-out crepe-paper snowflakes to pin to their shirts or crepe-paper leaves to wear.

During the blizzard scene in which Robert delivered his line, Belinda asked, "Is there something wrong with your eyes?" Robert looked at the "audience," which for rehearsal was all the things that filled the classroom: empty chairs, a dented world globe that had been dropped by almost everyone, one limp flag, one wastebasket, and a picture of George Washington, whose eyes seemed to follow you around the room when you got up to sharpen your pencil. Robert answered, "Nothing's wrong. I can see."

Mrs. Bunnin, biting on the end of her pencil, said, "Louder, both of you."

Belinda stepped forward, her nostrils flaring so that the shadows on her nose quivered, and said louder, "Sucka, is there something wrong with your eyeballs?"

"Nothing's wrong. I can see."

"Louder! Make sure the audience can hear you," Mrs. Bunnin directed. She tapped her pencil hard against the desk. "Robert, I'm not going to tell you again to quit fooling with the beard."

"It's itchy."

"We can't do anything about that. Actors need props. You're an actor. Now try again."

Robert and Belinda stood center stage as they waited for Mrs. Bunnin to call "Action!" When she did Belinda approached Robert slowly. "Sucka face, is there anything wrong with your mug?" Belinda asked. Her eyes were flecked with anger. For a moment Robert saw his head grinding into the playground grass.

"Nothing's wrong. I can see."

Robert giggled behind his red beard. Belinda popped her gum and smirked. She stood with her hands on her hips.

"What? What did you say?" Mrs. Bunnin asked, pulling off her glasses. "Are you chewing gum, Belinda?"

"No, Mrs. Bunnin," Belinda lied. "I just forgot my lines."

The play, The Last Stand, was about the Donner party, with the action taking place just before the starving members of the expedition started eating each other. Everyone who scored twelve or more out of fifteen on the spelling tests got to say at least one line. Everyone else had to stand around and be trees or snowflakes.

Mrs. Bunnin wanted the play to be a success. She couldn't risk having kids with bad memories on stage. The nonspeaking trees and snowflakes hummed to create the effects of snow flurries and blistering wind. They produced hail by clacking their teeth.

Robert's mother was proud of him because he was living up to the legend of Robert DeNiro, for whom he was named. During dinner he said, "Nothing's wrong. I can see," when his brother asked him to pass the dish towel, their communal napkin. His sister said, "It's your turn to do dishes," and he said, "Nothing's wrong. I can see." His dog, Queenie, begged him for more than water and a Milkbone. He touched his dog's own hairy beard and said, "Nothing's wrong. I can see."

One warm spring night Robert lay in the backyard counting shooting stars. He was up to three when David, a friend who was really more his brother's friend, hopped the fence and asked, "What's the matter with you?"

"Nothing's wrong. I can see," Robert answered. He sat up, feeling good because the line came naturally, without much thought. He leaned back on his elbow and asked David what he wanted to be when he grew up.

"I don't know yet," David said, plucking at the grass. "Maybe a fighter pilot. What do you want to be?"

"I want to guard the president. I could wrestle the assassins and be on television. But I'd pin those dudes, and people would say, 'That's him, our hero.'" David plucked at a blade of grass and frowned.

Robert thought of telling David that he really wanted to be someone with a super-great memory who could recall facts that most people thought were unimportant. He didn't know if there was such a job, but he thought it would be great to sit at home by the telephone waiting for scientists to call him and ask hard questions.

The three weeks of rehearsal passed quickly. The day before the play, Robert felt happy as he walked home from school with no homework. As he turned onto his street, he found a dollar floating over the currents of wind.

"A buck," he screamed to himself. He snapped it up and looked for others. But he didn't find any more. It was his lucky day, though. At recess he had hit a fluke home run on a bunt, a fluke because the catcher had kicked the ball, another player had thrown it into center field, and the pitcher wasn't looking when Robert slowed down at third, then burst home with dust flying behind him.

That night was his sister's turn to do the dishes. They had eaten enchiladas with "the works," so she slaved away in suds up to her elbows. Robert bathed in Mr. Bubble, the suds peaked high like the Donner Pass. He thought about how full he was and how those poor people had had nothing to eat but snow. I can live on nothing, he thought, and whistled like wind through a mountain pass, flattening the Mr. Bubble suds with his palm.

The next day after lunch he was ready for the play, red beard in hand, his one line trembling on his lips. Classes were herded into the auditorium. As the actors dressed and argued about stepping on each other's feet, Robert stood near a cardboard barrel full of toys, whispering over and over to himself: "Nothing's wrong. I can see." He was hot, itchy, and confused. When he tied on the beard, he sneezed. He said louder: "Nothing's wrong. I can see," but the words seemed to get caught in the beard. "Nothing, no, no. I can see great," he said louder, then under his breath because the words seemed wrong. "Nothing's wrong, can't you see?" "Nothing's wrong. I can see you." Worried, he approached Belinda and asked if she remembered his line. Balling her hand into a fist, Belinda warned, "Sucka, I'm gonna bury your ugly face in the ground if you mess up."

"I won't," Robert said as he walked away. He bit a fingernail and looked into the barrel of toys. A clown's mask stared back at him. He prayed that his line would come back to him. He would hate to disappoint his teacher and didn't like the thought of his face being rubbed into spiky grass.

The curtain parted slightly and the principal stepped out, smiling, onto the stage. She said some words about pioneer history and then, stern-faced, warned the people in the audience not to scrape their chairs on the freshly waxed floor. The principal then introduced Mrs. Bunnin, who told the audience about how they had rehearsed for weeks.

Meanwhile the class stood quietly in place behind the curtain. They were ready. Belinda had swallowed her gum because she knew this was for real. The snowflakes clumped together and began howling.

Robert retied his beard. Belinda, smoothing her skirt, looked at him and said, "If you know what's good for you, you better do it right." Robert felt nervous when the curtain parted, and his classmates—the snow, wind, and hail—broke into song.

Alfonso stepped forward with his narrative about a blot on American history that would live on forever. He looked at the audience, lost for a minute. But he continued, saying that if the Donner party could come back, hungry from not eating for over a hundred years, they would be sorry for what they had done.

The play began with some boys in snowshoes shuffling around the stage, muttering that the blizzard would cut them off from civilization. They looked up, held out their hands, and said in unison, "Snow." One stepped center stage and said, "I wish I had never left the prairie." Another said, "California is just over there." He pointed, and some of the first-graders looked in the direction of the piano.

"What are we going to do?" one kid asked, pretending to brush snow off his vest.

"I'm getting pretty hungry," another said, rubbing her stomach.

The audience seemed to be following the play. A ribbon of sweat ran down Robert's face. When it was time for his scene he staggered to center stage and dropped to the floor, just as Mrs. Bunnin had directed, just as he had seen Robert DeNiro do in that movie about a boxer. Belinda, bending over him with an "Oh, my," yanked him up so hard that something clicked in his elbow. She boomed: "Is there anything wrong with your eyes?"

Robert rubbed his elbow, then his eyes, and said, "I can see nothing wrong. Wrong is nothing, I can see."

"How are we going to get through?" Belinda boomed, wringing her hands together in front of her schoolmates in the audience, some of whom had their mouths taped shut because they were known talkers. "My husband needs a doctor." The drama advanced through snow, wind, and hail that sounded like chattering teeth.

Belinda turned to Robert and muttered, "You messup. You're gonna hate life."

But Robert thought he'd done OK. At least, he reasoned to himself, I got the words right. Just not in the right order.

After finishing his scene he joined the snowflakes and trees, chattering his teeth the loudest. He bayed like a hound to suggest the howling wind and snapped his fingers furiously in a snow flurry. He trembled from the cold.

The play ended with Alfonso saying again that if they were to come back to life, the members of the Donner party would be sorry for having eaten each other. "It's just not right," he argued. "You gotta suck it up in bad times."

Robert remembered how one day his sister had locked him in the closet and he didn't eat or drink for five hours. When he got out, he hit his sister, but not so hard it left a bruise. Then he ate three sandwiches and felt a whole lot better. Robert figured that Alfonso was right.

The cast paraded up the aisle through the audience. Belinda pinched Robert hard, but only once because she was thinking that it could have been worse. As he passed a smiling and relieved Mrs. Bunnin, she patted Robert's shoulder and said, "Almost perfect."

Robert was happy. He'd made it through without passing out from fear. Now the first- and second-graders were looking at him and clapping. He was sure everyone wondered who the actor was behind that smooth voice and red, red beard.

---

*Society is more or less democratic depending on how many of its members recognize and fulfill their responsibility to make it work, even when that's simply a matter of saying enough is enough.*

**Carl Ewald,** *A Fairy Tale about God and Kings,* **translated by Jack Zipes**

Once upon a time the people became so sick and tired of their kings that they decided to send some deputies to God to ask for his help against their monarchs.

The deputies arrived at the gates of heaven and were allowed to enter heaven in turn. But when the speaker of the group presented their case, God shook his head in surprise and said, "I don't understand one word you've said. I never gave you kings."

The entire group began to yell in confusion that the earth was full of kings, all of whom declared that they ruled with God's blessings.

"I don't know a thing about this!" God responded. I created you all equal. I made you in my image. Good-bye!"

So ended the audience with God. But the deputies sat down in front of the gates of heaven and shed bitter tears. When God learned about this, he took pity on them and let them enter heaven again. Then he summoned an archangel and said, "Get the book in which I listed all of the plagues that were to fall upon human beings if they sinned, and check to see whether I wrote something about kings there."

The book was very thick, so the angel needed an entire day to complete his task. In the evening, when he was finished, he reported to the Lord that he had found nothing. So the deputies were led before God, who stated, "I don't know a thing about kings. Good-bye!"

The poor deputies became so desperate that God took pity on them once again. And again he summoned the angel and said to him, "Get the books in which I've recorded everything human beings must suffer for their foolish prayers so that they might learn that my teachings are wiser than theirs. Check to see whether I wrote anything about kings there."

And the angel did as he was commanded. However, since he had to read twelve thick books, it took him twelve days to finish the work. And he found nothing. So God granted the deputies an audience for the last time and said, "You'll have to return home without fulfilling your mission. There's nothing I can do for you. Kings are your own invention, and if you're sick and tired of them, then you must find your own way to get rid of them."

## *Gospel of Luke, 15*

Now the tax collectors and sinners were all drawing near to him. And the Pharisees and the scribes murmured, saying, "This mans receives sinners and eats with them."

So he told them this parable: "What man of you, having a hundred sheep, if he has lost one them, does not leave the ninety-nine in the wilderness, and go after the one which is lost until he finds it? And when he has found it, he lays it on his shoulders, rejoicing. And when he comes home, he calls together his friends and his neighbors, saying to them, 'Rejoice with me, for I have found my sheep which was lost.' Just so, I tell you, there will be more joy in heaven over one sinner who repents than over ninety-nine righteous persons who need no repentance.

"Or what woman, having ten silver coins, if she loses one coin, does not light a lamp and sweep the house and seek diligently until she finds it? And when she has found it, she calls together her friends and neighbors, saying, 'Rejoice with me, for I have found the coin which I had lost.' Just so, I tell you, there is joy before the angels of God over one sinner who repents."

And he said, "There was a man who had two sons, and the younger of them said to his father, 'Father, give me the share of property that falls to me.'" And he divided his living between them. Not many days later, the younger son gathered all he had and took his journey into a far country, and there he squandered his property in loose living. And when he had spent everything, a great famine arose in that country, and he began to be in want. So he went and joined himself to one of the citizens of that country, who sent him into his fields to feed swine.

"And he would gladly have fed on the pods that the swine ate; and no one gave him anything. But when he came to himself he said, 'How many of my father's hired servants have bread enough and to spare, but I perish here with hunger! I will arise and go to my father, and I will say to him, "Father, I have sinned against heaven and before you; I am no longer worthy to be called your son; treat me as one of your hired servants."' And he arose and came to his father. But while he was yet at a distance, his father saw him and had compassion and ran and embraced him and kissed him. And the son said to him, 'Father, I have sinned against heaven and before you; I am no longer worthy to be called your son.' But the father said to his servants, 'Bring quickly the best robe and put it on him; and put a ring on his hand, and shoes on his feet; and bring the fatted calf and kill it, and let us eat and make merry, for this my son was dead and is alive again; he was lost and is found.' And they began to make merry.

"Now his elder son was in the field; and as he came and drew near to the house, he heard music and dancing. And he called one of the servants and asked what this meant. And he said to him, 'Your brother has come and your father has killed the fatted calf, because he has received him safe and sound.' But he was angry and refused to go in. His father came out and entreated him, but he answered his father, 'Lo, these many years I have served you, and I never disobeyed your command; yet you never gave me a kid, that I might make merry with my friends. But when this son of yours came who has devoured your living with harlots, you killed for him the fatted calf!' And he said to him, 'Son, you are always with me, and all that is mine is yours. It was fitting to make merry and be glad, for this your brother was dead and is alive; he was lost, and is found.'"

*Whether in small groups, nations, or international bodies, individuals must participate fully if unfair or punitive systems are to be avoided or reversed. Little tyrants can be resisted through an individual's strength to say no. As in* How the Children Stopped the War, *it is the vision of young people that shines the beacon for responsible action brightly.*

## Jan Wahl, *How the Children Stopped the Wars*

"Grown-up people are continually fighting about something," interrupted the stranger. He heaved a sigh full of meaning, and kept dwindling.

"Well then—why doesn't somebody stop it?" asked Uillame, bending down beside the miniature figure.

"*Why don't you?*" screamed the stranger in the tiniest, squeakiest voice imaginable, so that Uillame was scarcely able to hear it above the din.

Then suddenly the stranger was gone. Nothing was left of him except the peculiar smelling cloak and a few curly stray hairs from his beard.

For a long while Uillame sat pondering what the stranger had told him. "*Why don't you?*" stuck in his ear like a burr; it grew inside his head. The vision of the battle scene had vanished from between the stars. He turned to his flock. They lay in a circle together, asleep. Then he heard a flapping.

The brown cloak was flying off, before he could grab it.

THE STOPPING

Uillame waited for the twin red stars to show themselves. Or for the stranger's brown cloak to appear. None of these came in the sky, though the morning light exploded and shadows were streaked with wildness. What seemed to be flares glided and fell like sparks pulled into the fire. At last the children were near to the thing itself!

They left the rocks and the cave and reached a long dry empty tree-less plain and got very hungry, but after a while they did not think about their hunger or their thirst any more, because they had already been hungry and thirsty many times.

As if a tide were rolling across the plain, the children advanced. Their sheep bells seemed to draw down all the buzzards out of the sky; the birds wheeled by with greedy interest. They came to the ruins of a smoking city. Some of the buildings were still in flames. Among the ruins some very skinny, hollow-eyed children wandered, carefully searching in the rubble, drifting through the gray and yellow streets. These zombie children did not speak; however, they looked up and made little motions toward their mouths with their fingers.

"They are hungry too," whispered Uillame to Flora. The zombie children looked more like ancient men and women with all their bones showing. They did not run away, because there was nowhere to go. These were the children of the people on the other side. Their fathers were at the war and their mothers were wearily sweeping up the rubble, and looking at Uillame and his followers with grave faces.

"Come with us," motioned Uillame. The zombie children stood bewildered. The marching children took them one by one by the hand and they led them, slowly, away from the city. When the zombie children realized what direction they were heading in, they trembled and dragged their feet and shook their heads.

But Uillame's confidence was catching, so they couldn't help following. Uillame rode up and down the line to keep everybody together.

On the plain there were two more villages, burned nearly to the ground. In each, more of these children were seized by the hand. Then the procession approached what had once been a muddy swamp, now dried by the scorched air, and crossed over its cracked crust. Beyond it sat a great rock, and Uillame climbed up to its jagged top and raised his arms and shouted, "Don't hang back! Don't hang back! Soon we'll be face to face with it! It's just a little farther!" All the children were clinging to each other. Ahead of them they spied the flashing smoke and the bursting of rockets. The trembling of the earth grew worse and worse. Uillame leaped off the rock and got back on Paraquin. "Go now," he yelled into his ear.

The long line of children walked near, nearer, to the smoking battle-ground. Still no exact plan had come to Uillame, no matter how hard he thought.

"Bim!" and "Bam!" and "Bim" sang out a chorus of children bravely.

"BOOM!" answered the war.

The pony Paraquin jogged along at a sturdy pace. Loyal friend! Recklessly and fearlessly the children followed Uillame and moved on— advancing.

It was now full daylight but *there*, the two red, red stars were shining. Like two immense iron pots in flame, of great weight, about to spill over. They hung at either side of the battleground, which was wider than the plain.

. . .

During the lull, Uillame cleared his parched throat. He raised himself up and stood on Paraquin's back, with two children steadying his feet, two others steadying Paraquin. He felt this might be the time to speak. "Sirs!" he said. "We have arrived from very far away, to see for ourselves what it is you are doing here. Back at your homes, land is growing dry, the orchards have gone, your houses are falling to ruin or are burnt. We want to see the victory you are achieving here. Don't you remember us? Don't you remember who we are?" That was about all he could think of to say, after countless nights of lying awake, wondering what his magnificent plan would be. That was *all* he could say to stop them; simply to show them they were there.

Could the fathers fight again, now, with their children watching?

The soldiers on both sides were infinitely tired, and they had begun to feel that the wars might last forever, that they would never get finished. Some soldiers blew their noses; they started wiping some of their grime off, also. Their eyes were tired and their minds were tired. Now what would happen?

Suddenly one of them shouted, "That's my son! I think! He's bigger now. Well, I think that's him. Boy, might your name be Hullbo?"

It was Hullbo, and he ran into his father's arms. He had not seen his father in four years.

One by one, the fathers, the uncles, the older brothers, the cousins were recognized. The furious combat was forgotten.

Which side had been fighting which was forgotten and each man tried to find the child who was related to him. A breeze arose and the banners drifted in it. It took time to match up the living children with their living kinsfolk. When each soldier located the child he was looking for, he would toss his helmet and weapons down with a clatter.

The men stepped up, joyfully, to hug the children they had long missed. Uillame found his own father, who looked old and gray; but that didn't matter.

"Hello, Father," Uillame said.

"Hello, Son," said his father, his eyes glistening with tears.

They embraced.

Till evening, the fathers and the children talked. All the fathers asked questions about home and the children tried to answer them and everybody was speaking at the same time.

That night they slept together, huddled like grown bears and bear cubs, the fathers, the sons, and the daughters, among the ruins of that broken battleground.

By morning the fathers were ashamed to remain at this place any longer. They couldn't fight, with their children looking on. Some of the children gathered Red flowers from beyond the battleground, which they strewed over the corpses. They all, fathers, uncles, brothers, cousins, daughters, sons, walked across the wide plain to the sea. Those who belonged on the other side of the sea mounted the ships which had brought the men to war. The others stayed on shore and watched them go. Winds came from the south, filling the sails, pushing them homeward. And, where the war scars were worst, sand blew, filling full the holes in the ground. The cannons sat there rusting. The buzzards and vultures gave up and flew off, disappointed. The two red stars faded.

Listen!

Out over the sea, can't you hear the children and their fathers singing?

---

*Reminiscences like Nelson Mandela's remind us of the role of leadership and the possibility of responsibility being shared jointly by all members of a community.*

## Nelson Mandela, *Long Walk to Freedom*

Because of the universal respect the regent enjoyed—from both black and white—and the seemingly untempered power that he wielded, I saw chieftaincy as being the very center around which life revolved. The power and influence of chieftaincy pervaded every aspect of our lives in Mqhekezweni and was the pre-eminent means through which one could achieve influence and status.

My later notions of leadership were profoundly influenced by observing the regent and his court. I watched and learned from the tribal meetings that were regularly held at the Great Place. These were not scheduled, but were called as needed, and were held to discuss national matters such as drought, the culling of cattle, policies ordered by the magistrate, or new laws decreed by the government. All Thembus were free to come—and a great many did, on horseback or by foot.

On these occasions, the regent was surrounded by his *amaphakathi*, a group of councilors of high rank who functioned as the regent's parliament and judiciary. They were wise men who retained the knowledge of tribal history and custom in their heads and whose opinion carried great weight.

Letters advising these chiefs and headmen of a meeting were dispatched from the regent, and soon the Great Place became alive with important visitors and travelers from all over Thembuland. The guests would gather in the courtyard in front of the regent's house, and he would open the meeting by thanking everyone for coming and explaining why he had summoned them. From that point on, he would not utter another word until the meeting was nearing its end.

Everyone who wanted to speak did so. It was democracy in its purest form. There may have been a hierarchy of importance among the speakers, but everyone was heard, chief and subject, warrior and medicine man, shopkeeper and farmer, landowner and laborer. People spoke without interruption and the meetings lasted for many hours. The foundation of self-government was that all men were free to voice their opinions and equal in their value as citizens. (Women, I am afraid, were deemed second-class citizens.)

A great banquet was served during the day; and I often gave myself a bellyache by eating too much while listening to speaker after speaker. I noticed how some speakers rambled and never seemed to get to the point. I grasped how others came to the matter at hand directly, and who made a set of arguments succinctly and cogently. I observed how some speakers used emotion and dramatic language, and tried to move the audience with such techniques, while other speakers were sober and even, and shunned emotion.

At first, I was astonished by the vehemance—and candor—with which people criticized the regent. He was not above criticism—in fact, he was often the principal target of it. But no matter how flagrant the charge, the regent simply listened, not defending himself, showing no emotion at all.

The meetings would continue until some kind of consensus was reached. They ended in unanimity or not at all. Unanimity, however, might be an agreement to disagree, to wait for a more propitious time to propose a solution. Democracy meant all men were to be heard, and a decision was taken together as a people. Majority rule was a foreign notion. A minority was not to be crushed by a majority.

Only at the end of the meeting, as the sun was setting, would the regent speak. His purpose was to sum up what had been said and form some consensus among the diverse opinions. But no conclusion was forced on people who disagreed. If no agreement could be reached, another meeting would be held. At the very end of the council, a praise-singer or poet would deliver a panegyric to the ancient kings, and a mixture of compliments to and satire on the present chiefs, and the audience, led by the regent, who would roar with laughter.

As a leader, I have always followed the principles I first saw demonstrated by the regent at the Great Place. I have always endeavored to listen to what each and every person in a discussion had to say before venturing my own opinion. Oftentimes, my own opinion will simply represent a consensus of what I heard in the discussion. I always remember the regent's axiom: a leader, he said, is like a shepherd. He stays behind the flock, letting the most nimble go out ahead, whereupon the others follow, not realizing that all along they are being directed from behind.

# Balance

At a council meeting in 1877, as a reaffirmation of his love for his people's land and his willingness to defend it, the Lakota leader Tatanka Yotanka, or Sitting Bull, proclaimed:

Behold, my brothers, the spring has come;
the earth has received the embraces of the sun
and we shall soon see the results of that love!

Every seed is awakened and so has all animal life.
It is through this mysterious power that we too
have our being and we therefore yield to our
neighbors, even our animal neighbors, the same
right as ourselves, to inhabit this land.

This statement expresses a sense of balance and reverence for the whole of creation. It manifests a respect for the place of each living thing within that whole. This complex understanding of people and nature implies perspective, the ability to see things from many points of view and learn and communicate across culture. It also implies a distance from ego—that is, an ability to judge things without self-interest being the central motivating factor.

Balance does not require a denial of self so much as positioning one's self in social and planetary dimensions. It is out of this sense of balance that a regard for other people's lives, for the survival of all living creatures and the spirit of cooperative and peaceful living develops.

In personal life balance means being able to integrate thought and action and maintain internal consistency and decency. Throughout life we face compelling and often contradictory desires in ourselves and among those we love and work with. We have to learn how to shape our impulses and balance our desires so that they do not impinge on or exploit others. We also have to learn the crafts and arts of self-healing and social healing so that when things get out of balance we have resources to call upon for the restoration of balance.

Children find it difficult to recognize how their place in the whole might affect everyday life. It thus takes time to develop a view of the whole that leads to balanced living.

The selections in this part of the book concern the development, maintenance, collapse, and restoration of balance. They can provide opportunities for you and your children to reflect on how to balance different perspectives on some of the biggest questions—the meaning of life, our place on the planet, in history, in our communities and homes, and in our own selves—as Heather McHugh does in *A Night in a World*:

> I wouldn't have known if I didn't stay home
> where the big dipper rises from, time
> and again: one mountain ash.
>
> And I wouldn't have thought without traveling out
> how huge that dipper was,
> how small that tree.

———— ≫•◦•≪ ————

*This poem by William Stafford is a reminder that within the balance of the whole we all have a center, a home, a starting place. The poem provides an occasion to talk about the meaning of home.*

**William Stafford, *Allegiances***
It is time for all the heroes to go home
if they have any, time for all of us common ones
to locate ourselves by the real things
we live by.

Far to the north, or indeed in any direction,
strange mountains and creatures have always lurked,
elves, goblins, trolls, and spiders:—we
encounter them in dread and wonder,

But once we have tasted far streams, touched the gold,
found some limit beyond the waterfall,

a season changes, and we come back, changed
but safe, quiet, grateful.

Suppose an insane wind holds all the hills
while strange beliefs whine at the traveler's ears,
we ordinary beings can cling to the earth and love
where we are, sturdy for common things.

———⊶•⊷———

*Some creatures think their home is everywhere in the world. Coyote, the
Native American trickster figure, tries to be every creature and explore every
place, whether he is welcome or not. He disrupts balance, is full of mischief,
and for all his troublemaking is endearing. This short coyote tale provides
the opportunity to share moments of mischief: annoying but funny stories of
testing out power and crossing boundaries.*

### Peter Blue Cloud/Aroniawenrate, "Coyote, Coyote, Please Tell Me," from *Elderberry Flute Song*

"Coyote, do you understand the theory of relativity?"

"Yes, yes, I do. It's much easier that way. When I'm hungry I just stop
at anyone's place and get a meal. Yes, it's really good to know that all creatures are related."

———⊶•⊷———

*Balance and difference are thoroughly compatible. In this lovely story of a
father, his children, and their dog, we see the harmony that can emerge
through difference. The story leads us to wonder about times when difference
becomes a force that builds love instead of causing hatred and dissension.*

### George Dennison, *Shawno*

"Wake up, dad!" she called. "It's forty-forty!"

She was seven. I had told her the night before how when she was four
years old and could not count or tell time she had invented that urgent
hour, forty-forty, and had awakened me one morning proclaiming it.

When she saw that I was awake, she said eagerly, "Look out the window, daddy! Look!"

I did, and saw a world of astonishing whiteness. Clinging, heavy snow had come down copiously in the night and had stopped before dawn. There was no wind at all. Our white garden was bounded by a white rail fence, every post of which was capped by a mound of white. The pines and firs at the wood's edge were almost entirely white, and the heavy snow had weighted down their upward-sweeping branches, giving the trees a sharp triangular outline and a wonderfully festive look.

The whiteness was everywhere. Even the sky was white, and the just-risen sun was not visible as a disk at all but as a lovely haze of orange between whitenesses I knew to be hills.

An hour later Ida, Shawno, and I were walking through the silent, utterly motionless woods. We took the old county road, which for decades now had been a mere trail, rocky and overgrown. It went directly up the wooded high ridge of Folsom Hill and then emerged into broad, shaggy fields that every year became smaller as the trees moved in. We gathered blueberries there in the summer, and in the fall apples and grapes, but for almost two years now we had been going to the old farm for more sociable reasons.

After breakfast Ida had wanted to hear stories of her earlier child-hood, and now as we walked through the woods she asked for them again, taking my bare hand with her small gloved one, and saying, "Daddy, tell me about when I was a kid."

"You mean like the time you disappeared in the snow?"

This was a story I had told her before, and that she delighted in hearing.

"Yes!" she said.

"Well . . . that was it, you disappeared. You were two years old. You were sitting on my lap on the toboggan and we went down the hill beside the house. We were going really fast, and the toboggan turned over and you flew into a snowbank and disappeared."

She laughed and said, "You couldn't even see me?"

"Nope. The snow was light and fluffy and very deep."

"Not even my head?"

"Not even the tassel on your hat."

"How did you find me?"

"I just reached down and there you were, and I pulled you out."

She laughed triumphantly and said, "Tell me some more."

While we talked in this fashion the dog trotted to and fro among the snow-heavy close-set trees, knocking white cascades from bushes and small pines. Often he would range out of sight, leaping over deadfalls and crouching under gray birches that had been pressed almost flat by the snows of previous years, and then he would come back to us, sniffing at the six-inch layer of wet snow, and chuffing and snorting to clear his nose. Occasionally, snorting still more vigorously, he would thrust his snout deep into the snow, and then step back and busily pull away snow and matted leaves with his paws.

Watching all this, I understood once again that the world of his experience was unimaginably different from the world of mine. What were the actual sensations of his sense of smell? How could I possibly know them? And how were those olfactory shapes and meanings structured in his memory? Snout, eyes, tongue, ears, belly all were close to the ground, his entire life was close to it, and mine was not. I knew that in recent weeks complex odors had sprung up in the woods, stirring him and drawing him excitedly this way and that. And I could see that last night's snowfall had suppressed the odors and was thwarting him, and that was all, really, that I could know.

After three-quarters of a mile the trail grew steep. We couldn't walk side by side; I let Ida go in front, and our conversation now consisted of the smiles we exchanged when she looked back at me over her shoulder. I watched her graceful, well-proportioned little body in its blue one-piece snowsuit, and felt a wonderful happiness and peace.

Milky sky appeared between the snowy tops of the trees. A few moments later there was nothing behind the trees but the unmarked white of a broad field-at which moment there occurred one of those surprises of country life that are dazzling in much the way that works of art are dazzling, but that occur on a scale no artwork can imitate. I called to Ida, and she too cried aloud. The dog turned to us and came closer, lifting his head eagerly.

The sight that so astonished us was this: several hundred starlings, perhaps as many as five hundred, plump and black, were scattered throughout the branches of one of the maples at the wood's edge. The branches themselves were spectacular enough, thickened by snow and traced elegantly underneath by thin black lines of wet bark, but the surprising numbers of the birds and their glossy blackness against the white of the field were breathtaking.

I threw a stick at them. I couldn't resist. The entire tree seemed to shimmer and crumble, then it burst, and black sparks fluttered upward almost in the shape of a plume of smoke. The plume thinned and tilted, then massed together again with a wheeling motion, from which a fluttering ribbon emerged, and the entire flock streamed away in good order down the field to another tree.

Shawno, who had remained baffled and excluded, resumed his foraging. He stopped and raised his head alertly, then leaped forward in a bounding, enthusiastic gallop, and in a moment was out of sight. When Ida and I came to that very place, she too brightened, and with no more ceremony than had been shown me by the dog, let go of my hand and ran.

And if I had been a child, I would have followed, since it was here, at this very point, that due to the lay of the land, that is, the acoustics of the field, the playful gaiety of two voices could be heard quite clearly, a girl's voice shouting, "I *did*, Leo! I *did!*"—and the voice of her brother, who was eight, replying, "Ha, ha, ha!" and then both shouting, "Shawno! Shawno!" I stood there and watched Ida's diminutive figure as she ran by herself across the snowy field toward the house that had not yet come in sight.

I looked back for a moment down the long slope of the field, toward the woods, the way we had come. I had intended to look for the birds, but our three sets of footprints caught my eye, and I couldn't help but smile at the tale they told. They were like diagrams of our three different ways of being in the world. Mine seemed logical, or responsible, or pre-occupied: they kept on going straight ahead. Ida's footprints, in contrast to mine, went out to the sides here and there; they performed a few curlicues and turns, and were even supplanted at one place by a star-shaped bodyprint where she had thrown herself laughing onto the snow.

But the footprints of the dog! . . . this was a trail that was wonderful to see! One might take it as erratic wandering, or as continual inspiration, or as continual attraction, which may come to the same thing. It consisted of meandering huge loops, doublings, zigzags, festoons. . . . The whole was traveling as a system in the direction I had chosen, yet it remained a system and was entirely his own.

---

*This selection illustrates the marvelous balance that can be achieved when human beings work or play together with a common goal. It is set among the Mbuti people, who live in the Ituri Forest in northeastern Zaire. The selection leads to the questions: How can competitive play be turned into cooperative play? And what kinds of cooperative activities can families engage in throughout life?*

## Colin Turnbull, *The Human Cycle*
Two pastimes illustrate the kind of education that takes place in the *bopi*. The youngest children begin to explore hanging vines. They pull

themselves upward, developing their young muscles while getting to know the vines. They climb and they swing and soon they learn skipping and hoop-jumping, which, like climbing and swinging, can be done in a variety of ways and can be done alone or with others. This ultimately leads to the most difficult of all these vine pastimes, which the children will be able to indulge in only when they are youths when it is mainly a male activity. An enormous vine is strung from high up between two trees with a clear space between them. Swinging from an axis perhaps thirty feet above ground, but with the loop a bare two feet from the earth, one youth sits in the swing and swings himself higher and higher. Then the others join in. As their companion starts his backward arc one runs after him, grabs one side of the vine swing, and, when it soars upward, leaps with it, and does a somersault over the head of his companion, who jumps to the ground, allowing the other to take his place. It requires perfect coordination, as well as considerable strength and agility. There are variations that at first may look like competitiveness, but that in fact demand just the opposite. The "jumper" may swing himself right over the head of the youth sitting in the swing and land on the ground in front of him as the swing descends. If the "sitter" does not sense what is happening and also jumps, expecting the other to take his place, there is a moan from the spectators; both have failed, the perfection of the ballet has been spoiled. Alternatively, the "sitter" may decide to remain sitting and the "jumper" has to make the extra effort demanded to complete the swing over his head and land safely. There can be no question of the one trying to outdo the other, for the fun is in developing daring maneuvers spontaneously and executing them together.

Similarly, climbing leads gently and steadily from individual development to social development. The children are all adept at tree-climbing by the age of four or five, limited only by their physical size and the size of the trunk and the limbs of the tree. At first they climb alone, exploring every branch, testing every way of getting from one branch to another, one tree to another. The idea is never just to get to the top, it is to know more about the tree. The younger are constantly stopping, riveted with fascination at a tiny detail of the bark they had not seen or felt or smelled before, or to examine the movement of ants up and down the tree, or to taste some sap oozing from its side. Put your own ear to a tree one day, as they told me to do, and see if, like an Mbuti child, you can hear it sing with happiness or cry with sorrow.

A little later, the Mbuti children develop tree-climbing into a pastime that like the vine swing, has serious educational import at a social rather than a personal level. A group of anything up to about ten children in the *bopi* climb a young sapling. When they reach the top, the sapling bends down until they are all within a few feet of the ground. At that point they all jump together with precision. If one lingers, either because of fear, or more likely out of bravado, it is not something it will do again. The child is flung upward as the sapling springs back, and it may well fall and be injured. Even if it survives with nothing worse than a minor bruise, it receives no credit for "bravery," because again it has spoiled the joint effort to "dance" (which is *their* term: *bina*) life's ballet of perfect cooperation and coordination. These are precisely the qualities demanded in adult life for the hunt. And in the same way that the sapling will not bend to the ground unless the majority of older children in the *bopi* climb it together, so the hunt will be unsuccessful if the majority of hunters in the *apa* do not participate.

---

*People often disregard balance and act solely from self-interest or greed. Sometimes they reach for things that they can't achieve and find themselves defeated and out of balance. Other times they are pulled in opposite directions, goodness and wealth vying for primacy. This happens in childhood too, as questions such as these confront young people: Should I share my money or spend it all on myself? Should I like people for what they own instead of who they are? Stories acknowledge that, short of sainthood, there is no pure person and the struggle to restore balance is part of the development of character.*

*The following two selections illustrate the consequences of being out of balance and celebrate the complexity that is moral life.*

### Aesop, *The Frog and the Ox*, retold by William Caxton

A frog was in a meadow when she espied and saw an OX which pastured. She would make herself as great and as mighty as the OX, and by her great pride she began to swell against the OX, and demanded of her children if she was not as great as the OX, and as mighty. And her children answered and said, "Nay Mother, for to look and behold on the OX it seemeth of you to be nothing." And then the frog began more to swell. And when the OX saw her pride, he trod and threshed her with his foot, and broke her belly.

Moral: Swell not thyself to the end that thou break not.

**Lawrence Ferlinghetti, *Pictures of the Gone World***
The world is a beautiful place

                              to be born

if you don't mind happiness

                         not always being

                                   so very much fun

             if you don't mind a touch of hell

                              now and then

        just when everything is fine

                           because even in heaven

            they don't sing

            all the time

---

*The restoration of balance is a major problem for human beings. We have made much of the world out of joint through war, social irresponsibility, and careless disregard for the resources that are available to us. The struggle to reestablish balance is both an inner one and a social and economic one worldwide. Ge Vue, a Hmong who was one of Herbert Kohl's college students, wrote the following paper on how he came to understand his father's quest to restore balance. The essay itself is a testament to the power of stories to bind adults and children and teach in depth and with love.*

## Ge Vue, *A Childhood Story to Treasure*

Growing up in a refuge camp along the border of Thailand and Laos, I remembered sneaking out onto the porch at night to sit on rice sacks with other children from the village and listened to folktales that men young and old were telling. Some of them were great orators and told elaborate tales about ghosts, love, wars, and broken promises. Other story tellers tend to be more cunning and told series of funny tales about a goofy but extremely intelligent court jester who constantly made a fool out of the emperor by playing tricks on him. Yet, others would recall tales about the innocent sufferings of orphans. In a rigid clan system where one's worth was measured by the size of one's clan and the parent (more specifically the father) was one's intrinsic link to the community, an orphan child with no parent was disconnected from the community and dangled at the bottom of the social status. However, because of the orphan boy's kind heart, Shoua, the all powerful being who overlooked all living creatures on earth, rewarded him with a beautiful wife and riches. Although the orphan boy tales always have a happy ending, such tales would grab me and drown me in my own sopping nonetheless. I was about four or five years old then, but I already could locate myself in the stories because many of my village friends whom I played with every day lost their father in the war. Although my family was "safe" in the refugee camp, every day my dad still attended meetings with the Nationalists who were determined to regain the home country back. As a child with a wild imagination, it frightened me to see my dad leave every day; for I feared he may not return.

I don't remember the exact circumstances surrounding this story I am about to tell. May be my brothers and I got into a fight so Dad set us all down to tell us this tale so we would understand the power of kinship. May be Dad noticed my weeping eyes one morning as I watched him leave and told me this tale to comfort me. May be he thought that as a quintessent five year old, I was old enough to internalize something consequential or as the feeble child who was deprived of his mother's milk, I must learn to be astute. Whatever the reasons, this is the tale Dad impart with me when I was a little child.

There once was a huge elephant. He was the biggest, "baddest," most feared creature in the jungle. Where ever he went, animals, trees, and rocks would move out of his path. Because the elephant was so powerful, he became very arrogant and all the creatures of the jungle despised him. Every day, the elephant would marched tall and proud through the jungle recklessly knocking trees down and ripping branches from here and there to eat. One day as the arrogant elephant was about to tear a branch off with his powerful trunk, he heard a mother bird cried out from behind the leaves.

"Mr. kind elephant! Please don't eat the branches from this tree. My little baby birds have just hatched and they are too young to fly to safely. If you eat this branch, my nest will be knocked down and my fragile babies will surely die. There are many trees in the jungle and around you that are just as good or better than this one. Please spare my babies and don't eat this tree. If you must, at least wait a few days until they are strong enough to fly away."

The mother bird pleaded and pleaded with the elephant, however, being such a pompous elephant, her persistent pleading only infuriated him more. He was the king of this jungle, yet this frail, tiny bird was trying to tell him what he should and should not do. Furious, the elephant torn the whole tree down and stumped on the mother bird's nest killing all her babies. Horrified but helpless, all the mother bird could do was weep and weep.

When the father bird came home and saw the mother bird weeping, he knew what had happened and tried to console her, "Please stop crying. Your tears cannot bring them back nor will it solve anything. I have a friend who might be able to help us. Why don't we go find him instead."

So the mother gathered herself together and they both flew out to find their friend, a large bird with broad, powerful wings and could see far and soar high—a falcon. When they told the falcon their story, the falcon was appalled but she was not surprised because she had heard of this elephant and the atrocity that he has committed before. The falcon was very eager to help them and told them that she has another friend who would willingly help them too once they told him their story. With that the falcon brought them to another bird.

This bird was very colorful and had a very sharp, sturdy beak which can peck holes in the toughest tree in the forest—a woodpecker. After the mother and father bird told the woodpecker about the elephant and what had happened, the woodpecker also acknowledged that he knew that contemptuous elephant and would be more than willing to aid them.

The woodpecker also had a friend who shared their grievance and he was confident his friend would help them too. Thus the woodpecker led the mother and father bird to the edge of a pond to meet his friend—a big, fat, and ugly frog. After hearing their tale, the frog agreed to help them and also introduced them to yet another friend, a fly this time.

So between the five of them, they devised a plan. The falcon with her keen eyes and powerful wings soared high and far to search for the elephant. Once she located the elephant, she flew quickly back and tell the group. The woodpecker then sneaked up on the elephant and with his sharp and fierce beak, pecked furiously at both the elephant's eyes, blinding him. Next, the fly flew over and laid hundreds of tiny eggs on the elephant's bleeding eyes infecting both immediately. Blind, terrified, and in pain, the elephant rampaged aimlessly throughout the jungle. Alter the elephant was worn out from his reckless running, the frog hopped to a steep cliff and began croaking loudly. Up on hearing the croaking sound, the elephant was misled to believe that there was water nearby. Remembering how thirsty he was, the elephant rushed toward the croaking noise. Instead of finding water to quench his thirst however, the elephant plunged to his death instead.

At different stages in my life I find myself reflecting back on this tale.

And each time, the story takes on new meaning. The true power of stories does not lie solely in its context. Stories are powerful because they are personal. When someone imparts with you parts of his life experience, when he shares with you something from his heart, it touches your heart. Words especially when spoken eloquently as story tellers often can do, paint images in your mind that are difficult to forget, and therefore you will always remember a tale once it touches you.

———※◦※———

*The philosopher Bertrand Russell's summing of his personal philosophy,* What I Have Lived For, *provides an eloquent example of a life devoted to the restoration and maintenance of balance. It makes us think about the question he addresses, only in the present tense: What am I living for?*

### Bertrand Russell, *What I Have Lived For*

Three passions, simple but overwhelmingly strong, have governed my life: the longing for love, the search for knowledge, and unbearable pity for the suffering of mankind. These passions, like great winds, have blown me hither and thither, in a wayward course, over a deep ocean of anguish, reaching to the very verge of despair.

I have sought love, first, because it brings ecstasy – ecstasy so great that I would often have sacrificed all the rest of life for a few hours of this joy. I have sought it, next, because it relieves loneliness – that terrible loneliness in which one shivering consciousness looks over the rim of the world into the cold unfathomable lifeless abyss. I have sought it, finally, because in the union of love I have seen, in a mystic miniature, the prefiguring vision of the heaven that saints and poets have imagined. This is what I sought, and though it might seem too good for human life, this is what—at last—I have found.

With equal passion I have sought knowledge. I have wished to understand the hearts of men. I have wished to know why the stars shine. And I have tried to apprehend the Pythagorean power by which number holds sway above the flux. A little of this, but not much, I have achieved.

Love and knowledge, so far as they were possible, led upward toward the heavens. But always pity brought me back to earth. Echoes of cries of pain reverberate in my heart. Children in famine, victims tortured by oppressors, helpless old people a hated burden to their sons, and the whole world of loneliness, poverty, and pain make a mockery of what human life should be. I long to alleviate the evil, but I cannot, and I too suffer.

This has been my life. I have found it worth living, and would gladly live it again if the chance were offered me.

***

*The next three examples, in different ways, also describe healing and the restoration of balance. They show how closely related balance is to other virtues, such as compassion, empathy, honesty, integrity, and fairness. They also illustrate how much healing occurs in ordinary places, away from the fields of medicine and therapy, and can lead to interesting discussions on how in one way or another we all can be healers.*

## Loren Eiseley, *The Immense Journey*

I have said that I saw a judgment upon life, and that it was not passed by men. Those who stare at birds in cages or who test minds by their closeness to our own may not care for it. It comes from far away out of my past, in a place of pouring waters and green leaves. I shall never see an episode like it again if I live to be a hundred, nor do I think that one man in a million has ever seen it, because man is an intruder into such silences. The light must be right, and the observer must remain unseen. No man sets up such an experiment. What he sees, he sees by chance.

You may put it that I had come over a mountain, that I had slogged through fern and pine needles for half a long day, and that on the edge of a little glade with one long, crooked branch extending across it, I had sat down to rest with my back against a stump. Through accident I was concealed from the glade, although I could see into it perfectly.

The sun was warm there, and the murmurs of forest life blurred softly away into my sleep. When I awoke, dimly aware of some commotion and outcry in the clearing, the light was slanting down through the pines in such a way that the glade was lit like some vast cathedral. I could see the dust motes of wood pollen in the long shaft of light, and there on the extended branch sat an enormous raven with a red and squirming nestling in his beak.

The sound that awoke me was the outraged cries of the nestling's parents, who flew helplessly in circles about the clearing. The sleek black monster was indifferent to them. He gulped, whetted his beak on the dead branch a moment and sat still. Up to that point the little tragedy had followed the usual pattern. But suddenly, out of all that area of woodland, a soft sound of complaint began to rise. Into the glade fluttered small birds of half a dozen varieties drawn by the anguished outcries of the tiny parents.

No one dared to attack the raven. But they cried there in some instinctive common misery, the bereaved and the unbereaved. The glade filled with their soft rustling and their cries. They fluttered as though to point their wings at the murderer. There was a dim intangible ethic he had violated, that they knew. He was a bird of death.

And he, the murderer, the black bird at the heart of life, sat on there, glistening in the common light, formidable, unmoving, unperturbed, untouchable.

The sighing died. It was then I saw the judgment. It was the judgment of life against death. I will never see it again so forcefully presented. I will never hear it again in notes so tragically prolonged. For in the midst of protest, they forgot the violence. There, in that clearing, the crystal note of a song sparrow lifted hesitantly in the hush. And finally, after painful fluttering, another took the song, and then another, the song passing from one bird to another, doubtfully at first, as though some evil thing were being slowly forgotten. Till suddenly they took heart and sang from many throats joyously together as birds are known to sing. They sang because life is sweet and sunlight beautiful. They sang under the brooding shadow of the raven. In simple truth they had forgotten the raven, for they were the singers of life, and not of death.

### Sterling North, *Rascal*

I told my father that Rascal and I would be away all afternoon and evening on a long canoe ride. I think he knew what I was planning. He looked at us quite sympathetically. . . . I led Rascal to where my canoe was waiting near the edge of the flooded creek. In a moment it was launched upon the racing stream. All unknowing, my raccoon stood at the prow, occasionally coming back to me for another pecan. . . . It was an evening of full moon, much like the one when I had found my little friend and carried him home in my cap. Rascal was a big, lusty fellow now, thirteen times the weight of the helpless creature to whom I had fed warm milk through a wheat straw. He was very capable in many ways— able to catch all the food he needed along a creek or in a marshy bay. He could climb, swim, and almost talk. As I thought over his accomplishments I was both proud and sad. . . . It came at last, the sound I had been waiting for, almost exactly like the crooning tremolo we had heard when the romantic female raccoon had tried to reach him through the chicken wire. Rascal became increasingly excited. Soon he answered with a slightly deeper crooning of his own. The female was now approaching along the edge of the stream, trilling a plaintive call, infinitely tender and questing. Rascal raced to the prow of the canoe, straining to see through the moonlight and shadow, sniffing the air, and asking questions. "Do as you please, my little raccoon. It's your life," I told him. He hesitated for a full minute, turned once to look back at me, then took the plunge and swam to the near shore. He had chosen to join that entrancing female somewhere in the shadows. I caught only one glimpse of them in a moonlit glade before they disappeared to begin their new life together.

### Gianni Rodari, *The War of the Bells,* translated by Jack Zipes

Once upon a time there was a war, a great and terrible war that caused many soldiers on both sides to die. We were from here and our enemies were from there, and we fired on them day and night. But the war was so long that at a certain point we ran out of bronze for the cannons and steel for the bayonets and other weapons.

Our commander, the four-star general "Bing-Bang" Bombardi, ordered all the bells of the churches to be taken down from the steeples and to be smelted so that he could build an enormous cannon, just one, but large enough to win the war with one single blow.

In order to erect this cannon we needed one hundred thousand cranes. To transport it to the front we needed ninety-seven trains. General Bombardi rubbed his hands with glee and said, "When my cannon is fired, the enemy will flee to the moon."

Finally the grand moment arrived. The enormous cannon was pointed at the enemy, and we filled our ears with cotton because the thunderous roar could break our ear drums.

General Bing-Bang Bombardi ordered, "Fire!"

A gunner pushed a button. And all at once, from one end of the front to the other, a gigantic chiming could be heard:

"Ding! Dong! Dell!"

We took the cotton out of our ears so that we could hear better. "Ding! Dong! Dell!" the cannon sounded. And a hundred thousand echoes could be heard repeatedly throughout the valley and mountains.

"Ding! Dong! Dell!"

"Fire!" screamed the general the second time. "Fire, darn it!"

The gunner pushed the button another time, and again a joyful concert of bells spread from trench to trench. It seemed that all the bells of our country were sounding. General Bombardi began pulling his hair in rage and continued to pull his hair until there was only one left on his head.

Then there was a moment of silence. And soon, from the other side of the front, came a cheerful deafening answer like a signal: "Ding! Dong! Dell!"

Why this noise? Well, you have to know that the commander of the enemy forces, General Storming-Steve Sterman, had also come up with the idea of building an enormous cannon with all the bells of his country.

"Ding! Dong!" sounded our cannon now.

"Dell!" responded the cannon of our enemy, And the soldiers from the two armies leapt from the trenches, ran toward one another, danced and cried out, "The bells, the bells. It's a holiday! Peace has broken out!"

General Bing-Bang Bombardi and General Storming-Steve Sterman jumped into their cars and drove far away. They used up all their gas, but the sound of the bells is following them even today.

---

*This selection from Ron Jones shows how, when things are in balance, people can often do the impossible. The story shows how the spirit and a sense of wholeness can lead what are usually considered handicaps to become strengths.*

### Ron Jones, *The Acorn People*

The breakup of the schedule and the giving of the necklaces drew the camp together and gave us all a feeling of confidence and a penchant for adventure. One particular adventure, I shall never forget. It was the mountain. Our interest and knowledge of the hill came from the ever-present loudspeaker. One evening the normal recorded taps and Boy Scout pledge were followed by an announcement that special merit badges would be awarded to all those completing the climb to Lookout Mountain.

Benny B. picked up this errant message, "If the Boy Scouts can climb that mountain, can we?" Dominic and I exchanged glances of doubt and surprise. Our thoughts were picked up. Spider sided with Benny. Thomas was quiet. Arid didn't think it was too neat an idea. Martin just stood there, and then, with all our attention fixed on him, he started stamping his feet in an exaggerated march step. Hefting his knee high and then softly pulling his foot to the floor. Then with his whole body in movement, he pumped his arms and in mime fashion demonstrated that he was going to climb that mountain. He was marching off to Pretoria. There was nothing to do but follow.

In the morning we made plans to find and climb Lookout Mountain. Maps in the camp office gave the trail markings and location of the mountain. It was a six-mile hike round trip. We had no idea of the terrain. For supplies we took a bag of apples, some carrots, raisins, canteens of water and three kitchen knives. The knives were for protection. Like a military convoy we broke from camp at the first sign of morning. As we passed down the rows of cabins a few sleepy campers heard our clanking progress and asked where we were going. Benny was our voice, "To Lookout Mountain."

Dominic led the way pushing Spider. Next came Benny B. wheeling himself, followed by Martin pushing Arid. I took up the rear of the column pushing Thomas Stewart. We looked and sounded like a wagon train. Like the pioneers before us, our faces were pushed into silence by the unknown that lay ahead. There was little talk and a strange absence of humor. A sense of fear overwhelmed any thought of adventure. Each curve in the trail presented an obstacle. Our greatest hardship was trailside bushes and branches. They slashed against the wheels and, if we were not careful, entwined themselves like tentacles around the spokes and footrests. Forging through this undergrowth reminded me of Humphrey Bogart's voyage of the *African Queen*. The trail kept getting narrower. It went from a walkway to a path to a skinny trail. As the trail narrowed, our effort to push the chairs increased tremendously. In methodic lunges we crossed fields and cut into a dark wood. For the first time in my experience of pushing a wheelchair, I felt Thomas shift and lift his weight in an effort to ease the strain of movement. It was a slight adjustment but it meant he was pulling his body as hard as I was pushing. I strained ahead to see that Arid and Spider were equally at work, lifting their weight and pushing branches aside, using whatever energy they had to help our progress. The trail started upward. We had to turn around and pull the chairs from behind. Benny was forced to pull his wheels and then brake with each stroke. Our movement was reduced to pull, stop. Pull, stop. Pull.

Perspiring and heaving for breath, I was haunted by the thought of going back. I just didn't want to turn around. It would be better to inch our way forever than to stop. Pull. Stop. Within this exertion my thoughts wandered. I felt the sensation of escape experienced in long-distance running. It's as if the mind detaches from the body. In flight it finds refreshment in abstract wonder. I pondered the condition in which people work at intricate tasks and behavior without knowing where they are headed. Surely that is the situation I am in. Where am I going? And why am I at the base of this mountain fighting to see the top? Is it the climb that's important? Or the summit? Can it be both? Or something else? Perhaps it's how we go down from the hill that counts. Or is it in simply enduring that we find the strength and purpose we seek?

Reaching exhaustion, Benny had to stop. He didn't say a word. Just stopped pushing. His chair slowly slid to a halt against Martin. Like a train being derailed we twisted to a halt. Chairs and bodies stacked upon each other. Without giving anyone the chance to think about our predicament Spider started talking. In a shrill and quick voice he began playing the role of expedition padre. Dramatically taking his canteen he sprinkled water on the hillside and proclaimed, "I hereby name this place Benny's Landing." Everyone looked up. Spider was still talking, "and claim this place and all its riches for the Acorn Society." He crossed himself and blessed the soil. Finding a willing audience Spider continued, "Mr. Thomas, I appoint you expedition recorder. Martin, you're expeditionary leader. You counselors, you're, let's see, you're soldiers. Benny, you're our scout." The drama gave us a chance to relax and realize our accomplishment. To look around for the first time in our journey. Feel the warmth of the day and the aroma of damp grass. We were in the rib of a small hill. The sun angled through the trees as if in search of someone. It splintered against the mass of rising moisture and cascaded to the ground. The air was heavy, full of light and flying things. We seemed surrounded by a soft but definable noise. A humming of insects on the move. Leaves turning to the sun. Seeds in flight. Morning dew evaporating and billowing upward. The ground drying and pulling tight.

Everyone seemed entranced by our discovery. Here we were, sitting in the middle of a forest with wheelchairs that had until now known only city streets and "convenience ramps." Spider again broke the concentration. "Well," he said, "what are you waiting for, Aaron? You're the exploration cook; break out the food." Spider was still talking as we took up the food, passed it around, and started eating. "We have more places to explore than this place, you know." With this moment of rest and Spider's encouragement our journey became enjoyable. We knew there were more places to meet, and with some patience we would find them. And so we started off again. Benny, pleased to have a place named after him, was thrilled that each time we halted there would be a similar honor. Sure enough, we "discovered" and marked our progress with Benny's Rock, Benny's Fall, Benny's Number 2 (in reference to a toilet break), and Benny's Vista.

By the end of the morning we had climbed steadily into the foothills toward Lookout Mountain. Spider was talking all the way. Naming birds, plants, and historic sights of interest. Thomas was keeping a mental diary, repeating points of importance to Benny and the rest of us. Arid was directing our culinary use of supplies and dreaming up delicious ice cream sodas and banana splits. Martin seemed to spread out. He swung erratically from side to side in his effort to pull Aaron. His head moved constantly as if it were an antenna tracking some wondrous delight. Spider finally ran out of things to name or count. Without hesitation he created and performed what he called the Acorn Marching Song. If you've ever heard the slave song "Mary Mac," you will have some notion of the noise we made crossing the wilderness.

After our succession of ceremonious starts and stops, we reached the final grade to the summit. We had covered over two-and-a-half miles. The final half mile looked straight up. More forbidding than the incline, however, was the deterioration of the trail. It simply stopped. The final grade was a hillside of slate rock and loose gravel. There would be no way to pull or push the chairs up this. The wheels simply spun around for lack of traction. Spider called this place "Desperation," but no one laughed. Dominic suggested, "How about us trying to carry everyone?" Thomas nixed the idea, "Not me, I'm not going up there on someone's back." Aaron had a similar plan, "I'll watch." Spider and Benny were talking wildly about a movie they saw in which climbers used ropes and things. During our deliberation Martin had moved several feet up the hill without our noticing. He called down to us, "Hey, you guys, it's easy." Martin was sitting down, facing downhill. By moving his legs under him in a squat position and then pushing back, he edged up the hill in this sitting posture. He looked like he was rowing a boat. Only instead of rowing across water he was literally rowing up the hill on his bottom. Using legs and arms in an accordion fashion, he made steady progress. Benny was delighted, "Martin, you're amazing." Spider added to the compliment, "Make sure that man gets the mountain cross." Thomas and Aaron were still doubtful. Leaving their wheelchairs was not an easy thing to do.

After a long debate and several demonstrations by Martin, we decided to make the ascent. Dominic sat against the hill and I placed Spider in his lap. Using belt buckles and safety straps from the wheelchairs I tied the two together. Dominic tried a few rows up the hill. It worked. Spider strapped to Dominic's stomach gave both of them the opportunity to look down the hill as they inched upward. It also freed Dominic's legs and arms for the hingelike movement and balance necessary to squeeze up the hill and not slip back. Benny was next in line. He wanted to try it by himself. In a trial effort he worked his way up the hill and right out of his pants. At his insistence we tied a pillow from one of the chairs to his butt. He was ready. With his strength he just might be able to drag his body the distance. Martin and Aaron were next. Martin's confidence helped Aaron. In a sitting position Martin shaped his body and legs into a lap. I gently placed Aaron against Martin and bound them together. Thomas and I were at the end of the ladder. I sat on the ground in front of Thomas and pulled him first out of the chair and onto me. We twisted and rotated until both of us were comfortable. Then tied ourselves together.

Like a caterpillar we edged our way up the slate. The loose rock gave and slipped into pockets that could be used as footholds. Our trail looked like a smooth slide bordered by tractor-like gouges. I thought to myself how a hiker someday would discover our tracks and the Santa Cruz Mountains would have evidence of its very own Bigfoot. Martin's invention was marvelous. Who would have thought of going up hill backward, sitting on our bottoms? We moved in a syncopated rhythm. First the legs pushing against the hill, followed quickly by a push with both hands. We would stop to rest and then continue. (Observing the valley floor below us, we saw the tree line slipping beneath our vision, aware that we could now see valleys moving away from our vantage point like huge green waves.) At two o'clock, according to Spider, we reached the top of Lookout Mountain. He gently gave the mountain one of his necklaces. Not the act of a conqueror, but a friend. We had done it.

As with all accomplishments our attention shifted from the joy of lying across the peak of this mountain to another vision. The sky above us. Even Martin seemed to study the traces of clouds and the blueness of the space. It was strange, there was no jubilation. What had been the ulti-mate victory was now matter of fact. The sky beckoned. It gave us peace. There were seven of us lying faces up, just watching. A lonely piston-engine plane droned by. I love that distant whining sound. I don't think any of us had ever seen the sky in quite this way. The wheelchair and city life we all knew just didn't give us the chance. It was wonderful. This must be the exhilaration that drives explorers. The surprise of always finding another vista, a new thought, an unexpected strength. The com-radeship of doing something together. Doing something no one else would dare. And in the end finding something as simple and everpresent as the sky.

The return trip to camp seemed half the time. We passed things we knew and places that were familiar. We knew where we were going. It was a quiet return. Our pace increased as we approached camp. Perhaps it was the idea of a waiting dinner or the chance to tell everyone about our climb. We wouldn't tell about the sky. It was our secret.

We arrived late to the dining hall. In dusty halos we tramped and rolled in. I guess all explorers expect a tickertape parade of some kind. Surely the world knew of our exploits. But the dining room was unexplainably quiet.

Thoughts tumbled into the void. Did we do something wrong? Would Mr. Bradshaw drum us out of camp? Had something happened to one of the kids? What's going on? Where is the laughter, the questioning, the noise? It's as if we had left a party of friends and returned to find another set of people engaged in a ritual we knew nothing about. We blended into the silence rather than interrupt it. Became a part of the stillness. Ate quickly without much emotion, anxious to get outside and learn what was wrong. It was like the first day of camp. I felt afraid.

It didn't take long to find out what had happened. The camp director, Mr. Bradshaw, had been "alarmed at the randomness of camp activities" and "concerned that parents visiting the camp on the following day would not find camp as it should be." To prepare the camp for Parent Visitation Day he announced strict adherence to the camp schedule. He had finished his remarks with ". . . We don't want to demonstrate *unruly behavior* at camp in front of our parents, now do we?"

We all knew what unruly behavior meant. Dominic had started teaching boys and girls the skills of cooking. He made up delicious meals. In fact he was famous for his chopped hamburger, apple, cheese, and onion delight. It was a mixture of these ingredients rolled into a ball and covered with aluminum foil for cooking in an open fire. It was delicious but rather unruly. Especially since most of the food was swiped from the camp kitchen. Dominic began holding a late afternoon "eating club" attended regularly by forty or fifty kids. Aaron became assistant chef and apprentice. Most of these kids had never held a knife, let alone sliced a carrot. Dominic was a master at closing his eyes and trusting that determination could beat any palsy or lack of sight. He was right. Dominic's success with kids prompted other forms of unruly behavior.

Several women counselors had gotten interested in archery. They went to town and bought a set of inexpensive bows and arrows. It wasn't the safest place to be when they held their practice, but it was a thrill to watch children struggle to use their chairs and bodies as the means to hold the bow and draw an arrow. It was pure joy to watch arrows take flight following long moments of intensive effort and patience.

Another type of unruly conduct came from Lenny X. Lenny was a black African. He was mean looking. His face scarred and twisted. You wouldn't dare meet him if it were not for his songs. Wherever he went he would be humming or whistling. You couldn't help but join in. Pretty soon you'd be humming the same song, catch Lenny's eye and smile. One day Lenny X. sat down in a shady place and just started singing. It was just after lunch when he started. He sat in that one place and sang until the late afternoon. By the time he finished every child and counselor had learned Lenny's songs. It was such a relief from the Boy Scout anthems and bugle calls that pounced from the camp loudspeaker. Lenny taught songs that, once started, could go on forever. Evenings at camp were blessed by these sounds. One cabin would start and others would softly join in until everyone was singing. These were the most tranquil hours I have ever experienced. Lenny considered songs a greeting. He explained to the children that in America you greet someone with "how are you?", whereas in Europe the greeting is "good day," and in China it's "have you eaten?" "The greetings of Senegal and Gambia," Lenny explained, "are like their songs. They ask 'do you have peace?'" His songs were like this greeting. They were expressions of peace.

The most unruly act of camp was perpetuated by the camp nurse, Mrs. Nelson. She was an older matronly looking woman who had probably served as a nurse in World War II. She always wore the same dark blue dress with matching socks rolled under at the ankles. The aging process had not been kind to Mrs. Nelson. Although she walked with a quick gait that bespoke a once-spry woman, she was now quite heavy. Her face was always overmade-up with bright red lipstick and swooping eyebrows. Well, it was just this sight that caught some of the girls' attention. They started asking to see how she did it. I guess this might have been the first time in a long while that anyone noticed this labored beauty. She responded by giving impromptu lessons in makeup for the girls. For most, this must have been their first taste of rouge. All of a sudden half the girls had bright red lipstick. The next day they smelled like a field of lilacs and all showed up wearing face cream. Of course they thought they were beautiful. Mr. Bradshaw saw them as unruly.

The prospect of ending Dominic's eating club, the straight arrow archery team, Lenny's songfest, or Mrs. Nelson's beauty salon was out of the question. The children were learning, growing, and most important of all, they were happy. (I gauged my own change in these days by realizing what a benefit it was to be in this Boy Scout camp.) I walked around thanking stairs, bunk beds, and hills, because they made all of us behave a little more normally. The camp was not a place for handicapped children and the kids knew it. Camp Wiggin was a summer camp for children who could shoot arrows, cook goulash, take hikes, and sing songs. It wasn't a place for ramps, sanitized medical facilities, swimming pool rails, or activity schedules. It was a place for children and their expectations and fantasies for life.

*These last two selections have to do with attunement, with learning how to listen and look for patterns and rhythms in the world—that is, how to perceive balance. The second selection also suggests that the search for balance is a creative one that calls upon the resources of the imagination and that every one of us is a creator with something important to add to the beauty in the world.*

## Karen Kennerly, *The Story of the Hungry Elephant*

Once there lived an elephant, and he said to himself, "I am very hungry." He went along a path in the forest, and came to a bamboo-palm standing in a swamp. Roughly he tore down the palm; he saw a tender bud in one of its leaves. But as he took the bud from the leaf, it fell into the water. He hunted and hunted, yet could not find it because he had riled up the water and it blinded his eyes. Then a frog spoke and said, "Listen!" The Elephant did not hear, thrashing the water hard with his trunk. The frog spoke again: "Listen!" The Elephant heard this time, and stood perfectly still, curious. Thereupon the water became clear so that he found the palm-bud and ate it.

## Barbara Cooney, *Miss Rumphius*

All that summer Miss Rumphius, her pockets full of seeds, wandered over fields and headlands, sowing lupines. She scattered seeds along the highways and down the country lanes. She flung handfuls of them around the schoolhouse and back of the church. She tossed them into hollows and along stone walls.

Her back didn't hurt her any more at all.

Now some people called her That Crazy Old Lady.

The next spring there were lupines everywhere. Fields and hillsides were covered with blue and purple and rose-colored flowers. They bloomed along the highways and down the lanes. Bright patches lay around the schoolhouse and back of the church. Down in the hollows and along the stone walls grew the beautiful flowers.

Miss Rumphius had done the third, the most difficult thing of all! Sometimes my friends stand with me outside her gate, curious to see the old, old lady who planted the fields of lupines. When she invites us in, they come slowly. They think she is the oldest woman in the world. Often she tells us stories of faraway places.

"When I grow up," I tell her, "I too will go to faraway places and come home to live by the sea."

"That is all very well, little Alice," says my aunt, "but there is a third thing you must do."

"What is that?" I ask.

"You must do something to make the world more beautiful."

"All right," I say.

But I do not know yet what that can be.

# Fairness

The poet Robert Browning, in *Bishop Blougram's Apology*, wrote:

The common problem, yours, mine, everyone's
Is—not to fancy what were fair in life
Provided it could be—but, finding first
What may be, then find how to make it fair
Up to our means.

As Browning implies, fairness, the conviction that what is good for you should be considered in relation to what is good for everyone else, presents a constant challenge. Whether it is a matter of sharing a pie, giving Christmas or Chanukah presents, or figuring out how to have everyone get a fair share of attention within the family; or a question of providing equal educational and job opportunities in society at large, being fair is an overriding challenge. In our society prejudice, racism, and discrimination on the basis of gender loom as challenges to the value of fairness. Many young and older people also feel that they are victims of unfair treatment because of their age.

The selections in this part of the book are meant to encourage thought and discussion about issues of fairness and justice. Some of the issues are immediate: How do I get my fair share and what do I owe you? Others are more universal: How do I understand issues of justice and work to nurture justice among my friends and in the world? We assume that the great majority of people, and in particular young people, want to believe in fairness and justice, and that growth as a whole person is dependent upon a sense of reciprocity.

Fairness is the character value that gives rise to hope and supports the impulse to act in the service of others. As Mohandas Gandhi phrased it, "I do not believe . . . that an individual may gain spiritually while those who surround him suffer. I believe in *advaita*, I believe in the essential unity of man and for that matter, of all that lives. Therefore, I believe that if one man gains spiritually, the whole world gains with him and if one man falls the whole world falls to that extent."

———————

*The United Nations Declaration of the Rights of the Child articulates principles that are meant to apply to all children. They are not well enough known in the United States, yet they provide a wonderful basis for discussion of rights within the family and within the world.*

### The Ten Principles (Abbreviated) from the United Nations' Declaration of the Rights of the Child, 1959

1.  All children, without regard to race, color, sex, language, religion, political or other opinion, national or social origin, property, birth or other status, are entitled to the rights set out in the Declaration of the Rights of the Child, adopted by the United Nations, 1959.
2.  The child shall enjoy special protection and be given opportunities and facilities to develop physically, mentally, morally, spiritually, and socially.
3.  The child shall be entitled to a name and nationality.
4.  The child shall have the right to adequate nutrition, housing, recreational, and medical services.
5.  The child who is physically, mentally, or socially handicapped shall be given special treatment, education and care.
6.  Wherever possible, the child should grow up with its parents. Society and public authorities have the duty to extend special care to children without a family and means of support.
7.  The child is entitled to free and compulsory education. The child shall have the opportunity for play and recreation.
8.  The child shall always be among the first to receive protection and relief.
9.  The child shall be protected against all forms of neglect, cruelty, and exploitation. Child labor shall not be allowed.
10. The child shall be protected from practices which foster discrimination in any form. The child shall be brought up in a spirit of understanding, tolerance, friendship among peoples, peace and universal brotherhood.

———————

*Sometimes something is required of you that you feel just isn't fair, even though other people may not think it's that big a deal. It may be a need to share a bedroom, wake up too early to go to school or work, or always have to wear hand-me-down clothes. Gary Soto's* The Jacket *is about the effects of having to live with what you can't stand. After you read the story, it might be interesting to make and share lists of things people in your family find unfair.*

## Gary Soto, *The Jacket*

My clothes have failed me. I remember the green coat that I wore in fifth and sixth grade when you either danced like a champ or pressed yourself against a greasy wall, bitter as a penny toward the happy couples.

When I needed a new jacket and my mother asked what kind I wanted, I described something like bikers wear: black leather and silver studs, with enough belts to hold down a small town. We were in the kitchen, steam on the windows from her cooking. She listened so long while stirring dinner that I thought she understood for sure the kind I wanted. The next day when I got home from school, I discovered draped on my bedpost a jacket the color of day-old guacamole. I threw my books on the bed and approached the jacket slowly, as if it were a stranger whose hand I had to shake. I touched the vinyl sleeve. the collar, and peeked at the mustard-colored lining.

From the kitchen mother yelled that my jacket was in the closet. I closed the door to her voice and pulled at the rack of clothes in the closet, hoping the jacket on the bedpost wasn't for me but my mean brother. No luck. I gave up. From my bed, I stared at the jacket. I wanted to cry because it was so ugly and so big that I knew I'd have to wear it a long time. I was a small kid, thin as a young tree, and it would be years before I'd have a new one. I stared at the jacket, like an enemy, thinking bad things before I took off my old jacket, whose sleeves climbed halfway to my elbow.

I put the big jacket on. I zipped it up and down several times and rolled the cuffs up so they didn't cover my hands. I put my hands in the pockets and flapped the jacket like a bird's wings. I stood in front of the mirror, full face, then profile, and then looked over my shoulder as if someone had called me. I sat on the bed, stood against the bed, and combed my hair to see what I would look like doing something natural. I looked ugly. I threw it on my brother's bed and looked at it for a long time before I slipped it on and went out to the backyard, smiling a "thank you" to my mom as I passed her in the kitchen. With my hands in my

pockets I kicked a ball against the fence, and then climbed it to sit looking into the alley. I hurled orange peels at the mouth of an open garbage
can, and when the peels were gone I watched the white puffs of my
breath thin to nothing.

I jumped down, hands in my pockets, and in the backyard, on my
knees, I teased my dog, Brownie, by swooping my arms while making
bird calls. He jumped at me and missed. He jumped again and again,
until a tooth sunk deep, ripping an L-shaped tear on my left sleeve. I
pushed Brownie away to study the tear as I would a cut on my arm.
There was no blood, only a few loose pieces of fuzz. Damn dog, I
thought, and pushed him away hard when he tried to bite again. I got up
from my knees and went to my bedroom to sit with my jacket on my lap,
with the lights out.

That was the first afternoon with my new jacket. The next day I wore
it to sixth grade and got a D on a math quiz. During the morning recess
Frankie T., the playground terrorist, pushed me to the ground and told
me to stay there until recess was over. My best friend, Steve Negrete, ate
an apple while looking at me, and the girls turned away to whisper on
the monkey bars. The teachers were no help: they looked my way and
talked about how foolish I looked in my new jacket. I saw their heads
bob with laughter, their hands half covering their mouths.

Even though it was cold, I took off the jacket during lunch and
played kickball in a thin shirt, my arms feeling like braille from goose
bumps. But when I returned to class I slipped the jacket on and shivered
until I was warm. I sat on my hands, heating them up, while my teeth
chattered like a cup of crooked dice. Finally warm, I slid out of the jacket
but put it back on a few minutes later when the fire bell rang. We
paraded out into the yard where we, the sixth graders, walked past all the
other grades to stand against the back fence. Everybody saw me.
Although they didn't say out loud, "Man, that's ugly," I heard the buzz-
buzz of gossip and even laughter that I knew was meant for me.

And so I went, in my guacamole-colored jacket. So embarrassed, so
hurt, I couldn't even do my homework. I received C's on quizzes and forgot the state capitals and the rivers of South America, our friendly neighbor. Even the girls who had been friendly blew away like loose flowers to
follow the boys in neat jackets.

I wore that thing for three years until the sleeves grew short and my
forearms stuck out like the necks of turtles. All during that time no love
came to me, no little dark girl in a Sunday dress she wore on Monday. At
lunchtime I stayed with the ugly boys who leaned against the chainlink
fence and looked around with propellers of grass spinning in our

mouths. We saw girls walk by alone, saw couples, hand in hand, their heads like bookends pressing air together. We saw them and spun our propellers so fast our faces were blurs.

I blame that jacket for those bad years. I blame my mother for her bad taste and her cheap ways. It was a sad time for the heart. With a friend I spent my sixth-grade year in a tree in the alley, waiting for something good to happen to me in that jacket, which had become the ugly brother who tagged along wherever I went. And it was about that time that I began to grow. My chest puffed up with muscle and, strangely, a few more ribs. Even my hands, those fleshy hammers, showed bravely though the cuffs, the fingers already hardening for the coming fights. But that L-shape rip on the left sleeve got bigger; bits of stuffing coughed out of its wound after a hard day of play. I finally Scotch-taped it closed, but in rain or cold weather the tape peeled off like a scab and more stuffing fell out until that sleeve shriveled into a palsied arm. That winter the elbows began to crack and whole chunks of green began to fall off. I showed the cracks to my mother, who always seemed to be at the stove with steamed-up glasses, and she said that there were children in Mexico who would love that jacket. I told her that this was America and yelled that Debbie, my sister, didn't have a jacket like mine. I ran outside, ready to cry, and climbed the tree by the alley to think bad thoughts and watch my breath puff white and disappear.

But whole pieces still casually flew off my jacket when I played hard, read quietly, or took vicious spelling tests at school. When it became so spotted that my brother began to call me "camouflage," I flung it over the fence into the alley. Later, however, I swiped the jacket off the ground and went inside to drape it across my lap and mope.

I was called to dinner: steam silvered my mother's glasses as she said grace; my brother and sister with their heads bowed made ugly faces at their glasses of powdered milk. I gagged too, but eagerly ate big rips of buttered tortilla that held scooped-up beans. Finished, I went outside with my jacket across my arm. It was a cold sky. The faces of clouds were piled up, hurting. I climbed the fence, jumping down with a grunt. I started up the alley and soon slipped into my jacket, that green ugly brother who breathed over my shoulder that day and ever since.

———⊷◦⊶———

*Sometimes it makes sense to bend and not exact, at the price of bad feelings, precisely your fair share. Peace in the family can demand that some people accept less than everything they want or feel entitled to. Witter Bynner's short poem raises the issue of making concessions and restoring peace. Leonard Jenkin's fable, on the other hand, shows what happens when you try to get everything and take advantage of everyone.*

### Laotzu, *The Way of Life*, adapted by Witter Bynner

If terms to end a quarrel leave bad feeling,
What good are they?
So a sensible man takes the poor end of the bargain
Without quibbling.
It is sensible to make terms,
Foolish to be a stickler:
Though heaven prefer no man,
A sensible man prefers heaven.

### Leonard Jenkin, *Birds, Beasts, and Bat*

Not too long ago one of the higher-ups among the hawks spotted a succulent fish in a stream far below him, and began his dive for it. He had been flying high, for by the time he got there, a bear had the fish hooked on one paw and was about to take a bite. "Get your dumb paws off that fish," screeched the hawk, "it's mine." "You must be kidding," said the bear, and with one swipe of his free paw he broke the hawk's right wing. The hawk limped off through the brush, cursing and screaming. He gathered his friends, and the bear gathered his friends, and before anybody realized what was happening, a full scale war between the birds and the beasts had begun. Every creature in the world took sides, except for one.

"I figure it this way," said the Bat to himself: "I'll see which side looks like it'll come out on top, and join that one." He knew that with his leathery wings he could easily pass for a bird, and with his ears and claws he could pass for a beast.

Bat made himself a tricky reversible soldier's uniform, with bird insignia on one side and beast insignia on the other. When the beasts looked as if they would wipe out the bird forces, Bat turned his uniform beast-side and joined them screaming, "God is on our side" and "Liberate the air!" He killed all the tiny birds he could find. When the birds had the upper hand, Bat went home, reversed his uniform, and flew back into the fray crying, "God is on our side" and "Liberate the land!" He killed all the mice and other little animals he could find.

The war went on for many months. At last the beasts and birds, tired of fighting, decided to make peace. Both sides wrote and signed many complicated treaties and documents, and set up commissions and organizations to make sure there would never be another war. Despite all the promises, there were other wars anyway; but whether they were at peace or war, from that time on neither side would have Bat.

"You fought for the Beasts," screamed the Eagle, "so you must be one. Go live with your friends."

"You were on the side of the birds," roared the lion, "so of course, you are a bird. Go live with them."

After all this, Bat became so confused and unhappy that he himself no longer knew if he was bird, beast, or anything at all. From that time until today, rejected by all sides, he has sneaked around at night, and lived in dank caves and old barns. He can fly like a bird, but he never sits in trees. Nobody knows exactly what kind of creature he is, and nobody cares.

---

*Prejudice consists of prejudging a group of people as negative or inferior. It knows no boundaries, is color-blind and cruel. The three selections here illustrate prejudice against Jews, poor whites, and Mexican Americans. They also show the humanity of the victims and, in Claire Bishop's tale, the decency of people who choose to oppose prejudice. It is important to acknowledge the reality of prejudice in our society and work actively within the family to discuss and oppose it.*

## Claire Huchet Bishop, *Twenty and Ten*

He laughed nastily. "Thought we were gone, eh? Didn't know we've been watching you for hours?"

We shuddered. Henry had been right.

"We've been looking around too," went on the Nazi. "We were told there are caves around this countryside. Don't you know about them, children? Let us go inside, we can talk better. Inside! Inside! *Schnell! Schnell!*"

Heavyhearted, we dragged our wooden shoes up to the house. The old soldier came in, carrying a large cardboard box. "Open it," ordered the young Nazi. While this was being done he said, "You did not have much to eat at noon. Rutabagas! I saw the peels in the garbage can. Poor children! Wouldn't you like a little extra? Look!"

He pointed to the box, out of which the old soldier proceeded to take out chocolate bars and colored candy. Our eyes popped, and we began to shift on our benches. But when the old soldier brought out oranges, real oranges, we couldn't help it: we shrieked. It was unbelievable. We had not seen oranges for years. Louis did not remember them at all—he was much too small—so he became very excited and clapped his hands, calling, "Pretty ball! Pretty ball for Louis!"

We were aghast. Up to this time Louis had been so good. He just had paid no attention at all to the Nazis. Of course he did not have the slightest idea of what was going on, but he had fallen in with the rest of us, naturally acting as we did. And now this!

The young Nazi was delighted. "Good! Good!" he said. "Come down here, little boy."

Denise snatched Louis and held him tight in her arms.

"All right," said the Nazi. "Then you both come."

So Denise had to get up. Carrying Louis, whose hand was stretched toward the oranges, she went up to the Nazi.

"Yes, little boy," he said, "you can have that pretty ball if you just tell me what I want to know. Now be a good little boy and tell me: don't you have some Jewish friends?"

"I forbid you to annoy my little brother!" yelled Denise.

"Oh yeah?" mocked the Nazi. "How funny! How very funny! You forbid me! And you talk, don't you? Better and better. Now we are getting somewhere."

Deliberately he took Louis away from Denise and sat him on his lap. "Go and sit down," he ordered Denise, who went back to her seat, crying. Then he spoke to Louis. "Listen carefully, little boy. You tell me the truth, and you can have the pretty ball, and the chocolate, and the candy. And all the others in the room can have it too. Tell me the truth. Don't you have some Jewish friends, boys and girls? Just say yes or no."

"Yes," said Louis.

In the hushed silence that followed, Henry got up slowly and said, "He does not understand. He is just trying to get the orange." Then I knew that Henry was playing the last card. Would it work?

"Did you hear?" the Nazi asked Louis, and he laughed. "It is not true of course. You know very well what I am talking about, don't you?"

Louis nodded triumphantly. I felt I was getting sick to my stomach.

"Of course!" rejoiced the Nazi. "You are a big boy! You know about Jewish boys and girls. Now tell me: where are they?"

"There!" said Louis at once, and he pointed to George, and me, and himself.

For a fraction of a second I was thunderstruck. Then I understood. Bless his heart! Louis remembered The Flight into Egypt and that George and I had held him. And, of course, we were the Jews.

"Pretty ball! Pretty ball!" Louis was demanding his due, but the Nazi seemed utterly dazed. He narrowed his eyes and peered from George to me, muttering, "Incredible! The nerve! Better even than I thought! Right here all the time!" Suddenly he shouted at George, "Get up! You!"

George got up. My heart was in my mouth. Had he understood?

"What's your name?" yelled the Nazi.

"Joseph," said George. Just like that. It was magnificent. I could have kissed him.

"And yours?" snarled the Nazi to me.

"Mary," I said.

"Fantastic!" sputtered the Nazi, wiping his forehead. And suddenly, as if waking up, he pushed Louis quickly off his knees with disgust and bellowed, "And what is your name?"

"Jesus!" shouted Louis proudly.

The whole room burst out laughing as the stunned Nazi opened his mouth wide. His eyes popped out and his arms fell to his sides. Then he caught sight of Louis walking toward the oranges.

"Everything back in the box," he barked to the other soldier. But we did not care. Nothing could stop us from laughing. We roared. We shook all over. We shrieked. We cat-called. We hissed. The boys started to turn cartwheels in the aisles, and we girls threw ourselves on the floor and rolled all over.

Suddenly there was the sharp crack of a gun. We scrambled to our feet in a hurry, and there, in the doorway, stood a Nazi officer holding the gun he had fired into the air. And, next to him, was Sister Gabriel, very pale, anxiously taking the whole room in at a glance. In her eyes we read the burning question: "Where are our ten Jewish children?" And we could only look at her.

The officer said sharply, "Sister, are these your charges?"

"Yes," answered Sister Gabriel.

"Very badly brought up," snapped the Nazi officer. He turned to the young soldier. "Anything to report?"

"No, sir," said the young Nazi, red as a beet. Together with the other, he had been standing at stiff attention since the officer had come in.

"Where are the Jewish children?" asked the officer.

"No Jewish children have been found, sir, except those three," said the young Nazi, snarling and pointing to George, Louis, and me. "Those

three Jews whose names are Jesus, Mary, Joseph, so they say, the impudent brats, and—"

"Oh, but, sir," interrupted Sister Gabriel hurriedly with a gay little
light in her eyes, "let me explain. It's a game the children play, The Flight
into Egypt. You know, when Jesus' family had to flee because Herod's soldiers were hunting—" She stopped short. She was very red.

The officer did not seem to hear her. He barked to the young Nazi,
"You have made a fool of yourself! A fool! Away with you! Report at
once to the Normandy front. That will teach you."

The soldier clicked his heels and went out.

"You," said the officer to the other, "you come with me."

The officer clicked his heels, saluted Sister Gabriel, and recited like
an automaton, "I am sorry for the inconvenience. You shall not be disturbed again. My advice, though, is that you give your charges a little
taste of German discipline. They need it." He glared at us ferociously and
then went out.

We crowded around the door. In the yard was a motorcycle with a
side seat in which the officer sat down, while the old soldier drove him.
There was also a truck with three SS troopers. Our tormentor, the young
Nazi soldier, put his bicycle in the truck, next to that of the old soldier,
and climbed in. There were some sharp commands, and down they went
at top speed.

At last Sister Gabriel turned to us. "Where are they?"

And we all were still so afraid that we told her the whole story in
whispers.

She kept laughing softly and saying, "Good! Good! Very good!" Then
she said, "The Nazis arrested me as I went into Dieulefit. They had come
back unexpectedly, and they questioned me. Of course I would not
answer, so they threw me in jail. This morning they told me that they
had sent two men up here, and that the Jewish children had been found.
But still I would not talk. I figured out that perhaps they were lying,
though I could not see how they could help catching the children. They
said, "You don't believe us? We'll take you back to the school now, and
you will watch the Jewish children being taken away in that truck." That
was the truck you saw," added Sister Gabriel.

We all shuddered. Then Denise asked, "Do you think, Sister, that it is
safe now, if one of us goes to the cave and tells the others that the coast is
clear?"

"By all means," said Sister Gabriel. "Show me the way, Denise. I'll go
with you."

Off they went.

## John Steinbeck, *The Grapes of Wrath*

The kids are hungry. We got no place to live. Like ants scurrying for work, for food, and most of all for land.

We ain't foreign. Seven generations back Americans, and beyond that Irish, Scotch, English, German. One of our folks in the Revolution, an' they was lots of our folks in the Civil War—both sides. Americans.

They were hungry, and they were fierce. And they had hoped to find a home, and they found only hatred. Okies—the owners hated them because the owners knew they were soft and the Okies strong, that they were fed and the Okies hungry; and perhaps the owners had heard from their grandfathers how easy it is to steal land from a soft man if you are fierce and hungry and armed. The owners hated them. And in the towns, the storekeepers hated them because they had no money to spend. There is no shorter path to a storekeeper's contempt, and all his admirations are exactly opposite. The town men, little bankers, hated Okies because there was nothing to gain from them. They had nothing. And the laboring people hated Okies because a hungry man must work, and if he must work, if he has to work, the wage payer automatically gives him less for his work; and then no one can get more.

And the dispossessed, the migrants, flowed into California, two hundred and fifty thousand, and three hundred thousand. Behind them new tractors were going on the land and the tenants were being forced off. And new waves were on the way, new waves of the dispossessed and the homeless, hardened, intent, and dangerous. And while the Californians wanted many things, accumulation, social success, amusement, luxury, and a curious banking security, the new barbarians wanted only two things, land and food; and to them the two were one. And whereas the wants of the Californians were nebulous and undefined, the wants of the Okies were beside the roads, lying there to be seen and coveted: the good fields with water to be dug for the good green fields, earth to crumble experimentally in the hand, grass to smell, oaten stalks to chew until the sharp sweetness was in the throat. A man might look at a fallow field and know, and see in his mind that his own bending back and his own straining arms would bring the cabbages into the light, and the golden eating corn, the turnips and carrots.

And a homeless hungry man, driving the roads with his wife beside him and his thin children in the back seat, could look at the fallow fields which might produce food but not profit, and that man could know how a fallow field is a sin and the unused land a crime against the thin children. And such a man drove along the roads and knew temptation at every field, and knew the lust to take these fields and make them grow strength for his children and a little comfort for his wife. The temptation was before him always. The fields goaded him, and the company ditches with good water flowing were a goad to him.

And in the south he saw the golden oranges hanging on the trees, the little golden oranges on the dark green trees; and guards with shotguns patrolling the lines so a man might not pick an orange for a thin child, oranges to be dumped if the price was low.

He drove his old car into a town. He scoured the farms for work. Where can we sleep tonight?

Well, there's Hooverville on the edge of the river. There's a whole raft of Okies there.

He drove his old car to Hooverville. He never asked again, for there was a Hooverville on the edge of every town.

The rag town lay close to water; and the houses were tents, and weed-thatched enclosures, paper houses, a great junk pile. The man drove his family in and became a citizen of Hooverville, always they were called Hooverville. The man put up his own tent as near to water as he could get; or if he had no tent, he went to the city dump and brought back cartons and built a house of corrugated paper. And when the rains came the house melted and washed away. He settled in Hooverville and he scoured the countryside for work, and the little money he had went for gasoline to look for work. In the evening the men gathered and talked together. Squatting on their hams they talked of the land they had seen.

There's thirty thousan' acres, out west of here. Layin' there. Jesus, what I could do with that, with five acres of that! Why, hell, I'd have ever'thing to eat.

Notice one thing? They ain't no vegetables nor chickens nor pigs at the farms. They raise one thing, cotton, say, or peaches, or lettuce. 'Nother place'll be all chickens. They buy the stuff they could raise in the dooryard.

Jesus, what I could do with a couple pigs!

Well, it ain't yourn, an' it ain't gonna be yourn.

What we gonna do? The kids can't grow up this way.

In the camps the word would come whispering, There's work at Shafter. And the cars would be loaded in the night, the highways crowded, a gold rush for work. At Shafter the people would pile up, five times too many to do the work. A gold rush for work. They stole away in the night, frantic for work. And along the roads lay the temptations, the fields that could bear rood.

That's owned. That ain't our'n.

Well, maybe we could get a little piece of her. Maybe—a little piece. Right down there—a patch. Jimson weed now. Christ, I could git enough potatoes off'n that little patch to feed my whole family!

It ain't our'n. It got to have Jimson weeds.

Now and then a man tried; crept on the land and cleared a piece, trying like a thief to steal a little richness from the earth. Secret gardens hidden in the weeds. A package of carrot seeds and a few turnips. Planted potato skins, crept out in the evening secretly to hoe in the stolen earth.

Leave the weeds around the edge, then nobody can see what we're a-doin'. Leave some weeds, big tall ones, in the middle.

Secret gardening in the evenings, and water carried in a rusty can.

And then one day a deputy sheriff: Well, what you think you're doin'? I ain't doin' no harm.

I had my eye on you. This ain't your land. You're trespassing.

The land ain't plowed, an' I ain't hurtin' it none.

You goddamned squatters. Pretty soon you'd think you owned it. You'd be sore as hell. Think you owned it. Get off now.

And the little green carrot tops were kicked off and the turnip greens trampled. And then the Jimson weed moved back in. But the cop was right. A crop raised—why, that makes ownership. Land hoed and the carrots eaten—a man might fight for land he's taken food from. Get him off quick! He'll think he owns it. He might even die fighting for the little plot among the Jimson weeds.

Did you see his face when we kicked them turnips out? Why, he'd kill a fella soon's he'd look at him. We got to keep these here people down or they'll take the country. They'll take the country.

Outlanders foreigners.

Sure, they talk the same language, but they ain't the same. Look how they live. Think any of us folks'd live like that? Hell, no!

In the evenings, squatting and talking. And an excited man: Whyn't twenty of us take a piece of lan'?

### Luis J. Rodríguez, *"Race" Politics*

My brother and I
—shopping for *la jefita*—
decided to get the "good food"
over on the other side
        of the tracks.

We dared each other.
Laughed a little.

Thought about it.
Said, what's the big deal.
Thought about that.
Decided we were men,
not boys.
Decided we should go wherever
we damn wanted to.

Oh, my brother—now he was bad.
Tough dude. Afraid of nothing.
I was afraid of him.

So there we go,
climbing over the iron and wood ties,
over discarded sofas
          and bent-up market carts,
over a weed-and-dirt road,
into a place called South Gate
—all white. All-American.

We entered the forbidden
narrow line of hate,
imposed,
transposed,
supposed,
a line of power/powerlessness
full of meaning.
meaning nothing—
those lines that crisscross
the abdomen of this land,
that strangle you
in your days, in your nights.
When you dream.

There we were, two Mexicans,
six and nine—from Watts, no less.
Oh, this was plenty reason
to hate us.

Plenty reason to run up behind us.
Five teenagers on bikes.

Plenty reason to knock
the groceries out from our arms—
　　　a splattering heap of soup
　　　cans, bread and candy.

Plenty reason to hold me down
on the hot asphalt, melted gum
　　　and chips of broken
　　　beer bottle on my lips and cheek.

Plenty reason to get my brother
by the throat, taking turns
　　　punching him in the face,
　　　cutting his lower lip,
　　　punching, him vomiting.
Punching until swollen and dark blue
he slid from their grasp
like a rotten banana from its peeling.

When they had enough, they threw us back,
dirty and lacerated,
back to Watts, its towers shiny
across the orange-red sky.

My brother then forced me
to promise not to tell anybody
how he cried.
He forced me to swear to God,
to Jesus Christ, to our long-dead
Indian Grandmother—
keepers of our meddling souls.

---

The Nobel Peace Prize winner Elie Wiesel said: "Racism is stupid, just as it is
ugly. Its aim is to destroy, to pervert, to distort innocence in human beings
and their quest for human equality." The prevalence of racism in our society
is a national disgrace, and it is up to all of us to work to eliminate it. This
selection, from Claire de Duras's Ourika, recounts the true story of a
Senegalese girl who, in the eighteenth century, was rescued from slavery and

*raised in a French aristocratic family. The part of the narrative excerpted here describes how Ourika discovers the way racism will transform her life.*

## Claire de Duras, *Ourika,* translated by John Fowles

I was brought here from Senegal when I was two years old by the Chevalier de B., who was then governor there. One day he saw me being taken aboard a slaver that was soon to leave port. My mother had died and in spite of my cries I was being carried to the ship. He took pity and bought me and then, when he returned to France, gave me to his aunt, Mme la Maréchale de B. She was one of the most attractive women of her time, combining a fine mind with a very genuine warmth of heart.

Rescued from slavery, placed under the protection of Mme de B.—it was as if my life had been twice saved. I have shown ingratitude to Providence by being so unhappy since. But does understanding bring happiness? I suspect the reverse is true. The privileges of knowledge have to be bought at the cost of the consolations of ignorance. The myth doesn't say whether Galatea was given happiness as well as life.

I didn't learn of the circumstances of my earliest childhood till long afterward. My first memories are of Mme de B.'s drawing room. I spent my life there, loved by her, fondled, spoiled by all her friends, loaded with presents, praised, held up as the most clever and endearing of children.

The chief characteristic of her circle was enthusiasm, but it was an enthusiasm governed by good taste and hostile to all excess. One praised all that might be praised: and one excused all that might be blamed. Often, by a charming mental sleight of hand, a person's defects were transformed into virtues. Popularity brings boldness of judgment and with Mme de B. one was as highly valued as one could be—perhaps overvalued, since without realizing it she lent something of her own character to her friends. Watching her, listening to her, people began to feel they resembled her.

Dressed in oriental costume, seated at her feet, I used to listen—long before I could understand it—to the conversation of the most distinguished men of the day. I had none of the usual boisterousness of children. I was thoughtful before I could think, and I was content to be at her side. For me "to love" meant to be there, to hear her talk, to obey her—above all, to watch her. I wanted no more of life. I couldn't marvel at my living in the lap of luxury, at my being surrounded by grace and intelligence, because I knew no other way of life. But without realizing it, I acquired a sharp contempt for everything that didn't belong in that world. *My* world. To possess good taste is like having perfect pitch in music. Even as a small child, bad taste offended me. I could sense it before I could define it, and habit made good taste an essential requirement of my life. Such a demand would have been dangerous, even if I'd had a future. But I had no future, though I was totally unaware of that then.

I reached the age of twelve without its once occurring to me that there might be other ways of being happy besides mine. I didn't regret being black. I was told I was an angel. There was nothing to warn me that the color of my skin might be a disadvantage. I saw very few other children. I had only one friend of my own age and my dark skin never meant he did not like me.

My benefactress had two grandsons, children of a daughter who had died young. The younger brother, Charles, was about the same age as myself. Brought up beside me, he was my champion, adviser, and defender in all my small misdemeanors. He went away to school when he was seven and the tears I shed when he was leaving were my first sorrow. I used to think of him a great deal, but I no longer saw him except at rare intervals. He studied. And I for my part learned, to please Mme de B., all that is considered essential for a girl's perfect education.

She wanted me to be accomplished at everything. I had a good voice and was trained by the best singing masters. I liked painting, and a famous painter, a friend of Mme de B.'s, took it upon himself to direct my efforts. I learned English and Italian and Mme de B. herself made sure I was well read. She guided my intellect and formed my judgment. When I talked with her and discovered the treasures of her mind, I felt my own exalted. It was admiration for her that opened my own intelligence to me. Alas, I didn't know then that these innocent studies would ripen into such bitter fruit. I thought only of pleasing her. All my future was a smile of approval on her lips.

However, my extensive reading, especially of poetry, began to exercise my young imagination. I had no goal in life, no plan, so I allowed my thoughts to wander where they would. With the naive self-confidence of my age, I told myself that Mme de B. would certainly find a way to make me happy. Her fondness for me, the kind of life I was leading, everything prolonged my mistaken view of existence and made my blindness natural.

Let me give you an example of the attention and favor I was accorded. Today perhaps, you'll find it hard to believe that I was considered once to have a fashionably beautiful figure. Mme de B. often praised what she called my natural grace and she had had me taught to dance to perfection. To show this talent of mine to the world she gave a ball—ostensibly for her grandsons, but really to display me, much to my advantage, in a quadrille symbolizing the four corners of the globe. I was to represent Africa. Travelers were asked for advice, books of costumes were ransacked, and learned tomes on African music consulted. At last a *comba*—the national dance of my country—was chosen. My partner covered his face in a mask of black crepe, a disguise I did not need. I say that sadly now. But at the time, it meant nothing to me.

I threw myself into the pleasures of the ball and danced the *comba* with all the success one might expect from so novel a spectacle. The audience were for the most part friends of Mme de B. and they thought the warmer their applause, the more she would be pleased. But the dance was in any case something fresh and different. It consisted of stately steps broken by various poses, describing love, grief, triumph, and despair. I was totally ignorant of such violent emotions, but some instinct taught me how to mimic their effects. In short, I triumphed. I was applauded, surrounded, overwhelmed with congratulations. It was unalloyed pleasure. Still nothing troubled my sense of security.

But a few days after the ball, a chance-heard conversation dropped the scales from my eyes and ended my childhood.

There was, in Mme de B.'s drawing room, a large lacquer screen. It was meant to hide a door, but it also reached as far as one of the windows—and there, between the window and the screen, was a table where I used sometimes to draw. One day I was taking great care over a miniature I had almost finished. Absorbed in what I was doing, I'd sat motionless for some time, and no doubt Mme de B. thought I had left the room. One of her friends was announced.

She was a certain marquise, a bleakly practical lady with an incisive mind, and frank to the point of dryness. She was like this even with her friends. She would do anything for them but she made them pay dearly for her concern on their behalf. Inquisitorial and persistent, her demands were matched only by her sense of duty. She was the least agreeable of Mme de B.'s circle and though she was kind to me in her fashion, I was afraid of her. When she interrogated you, even though it was with great severity, she meant well and to show her interest in you. But unfortunately I'd grown so accustomed to kinder methods that I was alarmed by her bluntness.

"Now that we're alone," said the marquise to Mme de B., "I must speak to you about Ourika. She's become a charming girl and her mind is mature. Soon she'll be able to converse as well as you. She's talented, unusual, has ease of manner. But what next? To come to the point—what do you intend doing with her?"

I heard Mme de B. sigh. "It's very much on my mind. And, I confess, sadly on my mind. I love her as if she were my own daughter. I'd do anything to make her happy. And yet—the more seriously I think about it, the further away a solution seems. I see the poor girl alone, always alone in the world."

I could never describe to you the effect those few words had on me. Lightning does not strike more swiftly. I comprehended all. I was black. Dependent, despised, without fortune, without resource, without a single other being of my kind to help me through life. All I had been until then was a toy, an amusement for my mistress; and soon I was to be cast out of a world that could never admit me. I was seized by a frightful trembling, everything grew dark, and for a moment the pounding of my heart prevented me from hearing more. At last I recovered enough to listen to the continuation of their conversation. The marquise was speaking.

"What concerns me is that you are making her future misery certain. What could please her now, having spent all her life close by your side?"

"But she will continue there!"

"Very well—so long as she remains a child. But she's fifteen already. To whom do you propose marrying her? With her intelligence, with the education you've given her? What kind of man would marry a negress? Even supposing you could bribe some fellow to father mulatto children, he could only be of low birth. She could never be happy with such a man. She can only want the kind of husband who would never look at her."

"I can't dispute all that," said Mme de B. "But mercifully she still knows nothing. And she has an affection for me that may save her from having to face reality for many years yet. To have made her happy I'd have had to try to turn her into a common servant. I sincerely believe that could never have been done. And who knows? Since she's too remarkable to be anything less than she is, perhaps one day she will rise above her fate."

"Wishful thinking!" snapped the marquise. "Reason may help people overcome bad luck. But it's powerless against evils that arise from deliberately upsetting the natural order of things. Ourika has flouted her natural destiny. She has entered society without its permission. It will have its revenge."

"But she's most obviously innocent of such a crime!" exclaimed Mme de B. "You're very hard on the poor child."

"I have her interests at heart more than you. I want her happiness, and you are destroying it."

Mme de B. answered with some heat, and I was about to become the cause of a quarrel between the two friends. But another visitor was announced. I slipped behind the screen and escaped from the room. I ran to my own. There a flood of tears temporarily relieved my swollen heart.

This loss of the till-then-unshaken sense of my own worth effected a profound change in my life. There are illusions like daylight. When they go, all becomes night. In the turmoil of new ideas that besieged me, I lost sight of everything that had engaged my mind in the past. It was a yawning gulf of horrors. I saw myself hounded by contempt, misplaced in society, destined to be the bride of some venal "fellow" who might condescend to get half-breed children on me. Such thoughts rose up one after the other like phantoms and fastened on me like furies. Above all, it was the isolation. Had I not heard it from Mme de B.'s own mouth— "alone, always alone in the world"? Again and again I repeated that phrase: alone, always alone. Only a day before, being alone had meant nothing. I knew nothing of loneliness, I had never felt it. I needed what I loved and it had never crossed my mind that what I loved did not need me in return. But now my eyes were opened, and my misfortune had already introduced mistrust into my heart.

When I went back to the drawing room, everyone was struck by my altered appearance. Questions were asked, I said I didn't feel well. I was taken at my word. Mme de B. sent for Doctor Barthez, who examined me carefully and took my pulse, and then announced curtly that I was fit as a fiddle. Her fears calmed, Mme de B. tried to take me out of myself by means of all sorts of amusements. I'm ashamed to tell you how ungrateful I was to her; my soul had crept back inside itself. The best kindnesses are those that touch deepest. But I was too full of resentment to be generous. Endless permutations of the same thoughts obsessed every hour of my day. They reproduced themselves in a thousand different shapes, and my imagination endowed them with the darkest colors. Often I passed whole nights weeping. All my pity was for myself.

My face revolted me, I no longer dared to look in a mirror. My black hands seemed like monkey's paws. I exaggerated my ugliness to myself, and this skin color of mine seemed to me like the brand of shame. it exiled me from everyone else of my natural kind. It condemned me to be alone, always alone in the world. And never loved! For the price of a dowry, a fellow might consent to have mulatto children! My whole being rose in rage against that idea. I thought for a moment of asking Mme de B. to send me back to my homeland. But I would still have been alone. Who there could listen to me now, or understand me?

I no longer belonged anywhere. I was cut off from the entire human race.

———→•◦•←———

*This selection from* Farewell to Manzanar *shows how a young Japanese American woman learns to become strong in the face of prejudice and racism. In addition to showing how strength emerges in the most difficult of circumstances, it suggests that we all have resources we can draw upon to grow and live fully.*

### Jeanne Wakatsuki Houston and James D. Houston, *Farewell to Manzanar*

As for me, the shapeless dread of that great dark cloud in my imagination gradually receded, soothed away by a sky the same blue it had always been, lawns the same green, traffic signals that still changed with dependable regularity, and familiar radio programs to fill up the late afternoons and evenings: *Jack Armstrong, Captain Midnight, The Whistler, I Love a Mystery.* That dread was gone. But those premonitions proved correct, in a way I hadn't been at all prepared for, on the first day back in public school, when the shape of what I truly had to deal with appeared to me for the first time.

When the sixth-grade teacher ushered me in, the other kids inspected me, but not unlike I myself would study a new arrival. She was a warm, benevolent woman who tried to make this first day as easy as possible. She gave me the morning to get the feel of the room. That afternoon, during a reading lesson, she finally asked me if I'd care to try a page out loud. I had not yet opened my mouth, except to smile. When I stood up, every one turned to watch. Any kid entering a new class wants, first of all, to be liked. This was uppermost in my mind. I smiled wider, then began to read. I made no mistakes. When I finished, a pretty blond girl in front of me said, quite innocently, "Gee, I didn't know you could speak English."

She was genuinely amazed. I was stunned. How could this have even been in doubt?

It isn't difficult, now, to explain her reaction. But at age eleven, I couldn't believe anyone could think such a thing, say such a thing about me, or regard me in that way. I smiled and sat down, suddenly aware of what being of Japanese ancestry was going to be like. I wouldn't be faced with physical attack, or with overt shows of hatred. Rather, I would be seen as someone foreign, or as someone other than American, or perhaps not be seen at all.

During the years in camp, I had never really understood why we were there, nor had I questioned it much. I knew no one in my family had committed a crime. If I needed explanations at all, I conjured up vague notions about a *war* between America and Japan. But now I'd reached an age where certain childhood mysteries begin to make sense. This girl's guileless remark came as an illumination, an instant knowledge that brought with it the first buds of true shame.

From that day on, part of me learned to be invisible. In a way, nothing would have been nicer than for no one to see me. Although I couldn't have defined it at the time, I felt that if attention were drawn to me, people would see what this girl had first responded to. They wouldn't see me, they would see the slant-eyed face, the Oriental. This is what accounts, in part, for the entire evacuation. You cannot deport 110,000 people unless you have stopped seeing individuals. Of course, for such a thing to happen, there has to be a kind of acquiescence on the part of the victims, some submerged belief that this treatment is deserved, or at least allowable. It's an attitude easy for nonwhites to acquire in America. I had inherited it. Manzanar had confirmed it. And my feeling. at eleven, went something like this: you are going to be invisible anyway, so why not completely disappear.

But another part of me did not want to disappear. With the same sort of reaction that sent Woody into the army, I instinctively decided I would have to prove that I wasn't different, that it should not be odd to hear me speaking English. From that day forward I lived with this double impulse: the urge to disappear and the desperate desire to be acceptable.

I soon learned there were certain areas I was automatically allowed to perform in: scholarship, athletics, and school-time activities like the yearbook, the newspaper, and student government. I tried all of these and made good grades, became news editor, held an office in the Girls Athletic League.

I also learned that outside school another set of rules prevailed. Choosing friends, for instance, often depended upon whether or not I could be invited to their homes, whether their parents would allow this. And what is so infuriating, looking back, is how I accepted the situation. If refused by someone's parents, I would never say, "Go to hell!" or "I'll find other friends," or "Who wants to come to your house anyway?" I would see it as my fault, the result of my failings. I was imposing a burden on *them*.

I would absorb such rejections and keep on looking, because for some reason the scholarship society and the athletic league and the year-book staff didn't satisfy me, were never quite enough. They were too lim-ited, or too easy, or too obvious. I wanted to declare myself in some dif-ferent way, and, old enough to be marked by the internment but still too young for the full impact of it to cow me, I wanted *in*.

At one point I thought I would like to join the Girl Scouts. A friend of mine belonged, that blond girl who had commented on my reading. Her name was Radine. Her folks had come west from Amarillo, Texas, and had made a little money in the aircraft plants but not enough yet to get out of Cabrillo Homes. We found ourselves walking partway home together every day. Her fascination with my ability to speak English had led to many other topics. But she had never mentioned the Girl Scouts to me. One day I did.

"Can I belong?" I asked, then adding as an afterthought, as if to ease what I knew her answer would have to be, "You know, I'm Japanese."

"Gee," she said, her friendly face suddenly a mask. "I don't know. But we can sure find out. Mama's the assistant troop leader.

And then, the next day, "Gee, Jeannie, no. I'm *really* sorry."

Rage may have been simmering deep within me, but my conscious reaction was, "Oh well, that's okay, Radine. I understand. I guess I'll see you tomorrow."

"Sure, I'll meet you at the stoplight."

I didn't hold this against her, any more than I associated her personally with the first remark she made. It was her mother who had drawn the line, and I was used to that. If anything, Radine and I were closer now. She felt obliged to protect me. She would catch someone staring at me as we walked home from school and she would growl, "What are *you* look-ing at? *She's* an American citizen. She's got as much right as anybody to walk around on the street!"

Her outbursts always amazed me. I would much rather have ignored those looks than challenged them. At the same time I wondered why my citizenship had to be so loudly affirmed, and I couldn't imagine why affirming it would really make any difference. (If so, why hadn't it kept me out of Manzanar?) But I was grateful when Radine stuck up for me. Soon we were together all the time. I was teaching her how to twirl baton, and this started a partnership that lasted for the next three years.

I hadn't forgotten what I'd learned in camp. My chubby teacher had taught me well. Radine and I would practice in the grassy plots between the buildings, much as I used to in the firebreaks near Block 28: behind the back, between the legs, over the shoulder, high into the air above the two-story rooftops watching it, timing its fall for the sudden catch. We practiced the splits, and bending backward, the high-stepping strut, and I saw myself as a sequined princess, leading orchestras across a football field, the idol of cheering fans.

There happened to be a Boy Scout drum and bugle corps located in the housing project next to ours. They performed in local parades, and they were looking for some baton twirlers to march in front of the band. That fall Radine and I tried out, and we suited them just fine. They made me the lead majorette, in the center between Radine and Gloria, another girl from the seventh grade. Those two wore blue satin outfits to accent their bright blond hair. My outfit was white, with gold braid across the chest. We all wore white, calf-high boots and boat-shaped hats. We worked out trio routines and practiced every weekend with the boys, marching up and down the streets of the project. We performed with them at our junior high assemblies, as well as in the big band reviews each spring, with our batons glinting out in front of the bass drums and snares and shiny bugles, their banners, merit badges, khaki uniforms, and their squared-off military footwork.

This was exactly what I wanted. It also gave me the first sign of how certain intangible barriers might be crossed.

The Girl Scouts was much like a sorority, of the kind I would be excluded from in high school and later on in college. And it was run by mothers. The Boy Scouts was like a fraternity and run by fathers. Radine and I were both maturing early. The boys in the band loved having us out there in front of them all the time, bending back and stepping high, in our snug satin outfits and short skirts. Their dads, mostly navy men, loved it too. At that age I was too young to consciously use my sexuality or to understand how an Oriental female can fascinate Caucasian men, and of course far too young to see that even this is usually just another form of invisibility. It simply happened that the attention I first gained as a majorette went hand in hand with a warm reception from the Boy Scouts and their fathers, and from that point on I knew intuitively that one resource I had to overcome the war-distorted limitations of my race would be my femininity.

---

*These three selections speak of hope and the will to struggle to make a fair world. They suggest that we all examine and celebrate the sources of hope within ourselves.*

**Muriel Rukeyser, *Poem***
I lived in the first century of world wars
Most mornings I would be more or less insane,
The newspapers would arrive with their careless stories,
The news would pour out of various devices
Interrupted by attempts to sell products to the unseen.
I would call my friends on other devices;
They would be more or less mad for similar reasons.
Slowly I would get to pen and paper,
Make my poems for others unseen and unborn.
In the day I would be reminded of those men and women
Brave, setting up signals across vast distances,
Considering a nameless way of living, of almost unimagined values.
As the lights darkened, as the lights of night brightened,
We would try to imagine them, try to find each other.
To construct peace, to make love, to reconcile
Waking with sleeping, ourselves with each other,
Ourselves with ourselves. We would try by any means
To reach the limits of ourselves, to reach beyond ourselves,
To let go the means, to wake.

I lived in the first century of these wars.


***Psalm 15,* translated by Stephen Mitchell**
Lord, who can be trusted with power,
    and who may act in your place?
Those with a passion for justice,
    who speak the truth from their hearts;
who have let go of selfish interests
    and grown beyond their own lives;
who see the wretched as their family
    and the poor as their flesh and blood.
They alone are impartial
    and worthy of the people's trust.
Their compassion lights up the whole earth,
    and their kindness endures forever.


**Martin Luther King Jr., *I Have a Dream***
I am happy to join with you today in what will go down in history as the
greatest demonstration for freedom in the history of our nation.

Fivescore years ago, a great American, in whose symbolic shadow we stand today, signed the Emancipation Proclamation. This momentous decree came as a great beacon light of hope to millions of Negro slaves who had been seared in the flames of withering injustice. It came as a joyous daybreak to end the long night of their captivity.

But one hundred years later, the Negro still is not free; one hundred years later, the life of the Negro is still sadly crippled by the manacles of segregation and the chains of discrimination; one hundred years later, the Negro lives on a lonely island of poverty in the midst of a vast ocean of material prosperity; one hundred years later, the Negro is still languished in the corners of American society and finds himself in exile in his own land.

So we've come here today to dramatize a shameful condition. In a sense we've come to our nation's capital to cash a check. When the architects of our republic wrote the magnificent words of the Constitution and the Declaration of Independence, they were signing a promissory note to which every American was to fall heir. This note was the promise that all men, yes, black men as well as white men, would be guaranteed the unalienable rights of life, liberty, and the pursuit of happiness.

It is obvious today that America has defaulted on this promissory note in so far as her citizens of color are concerned. Instead of honoring this sacred obligation, America has given the Negro people a bad check; a check which has come back marked "insufficient funds." We refuse to believe that there are insufficient funds in the great vaults of opportunity of this nation. And so we've come to cash this check, a check that will give us upon demand the riches of freedom and the security of justice.

We have also come to this hallowed spot to remind America of the fierce urgency of now. This is no time to engage in the luxury of cooling off or to take the tranquilizing drug of gradualism. Now is the time to make real the promises of democracy; now is the time to rise from the dark and desolate valley of segregation to the sunlit path of racial justice; now is the time to lift our nation from the quicksands of racial injustice to the solid rock of brotherhood; now is the time to make justice a reality for all God's children. It would be fatal for the nation to overlook the urgency of the moment. This sweltering summer of the Negro's legitimate discontent will not pass until there is an invigorating autumn of freedom and equality.

Nineteen sixty-three is not an end, but a beginning. And those who hope that the Negro needed to blow off steam and will now be content, will have a rude awakening if the nation returns to business as usual.

There will be neither rest nor tranquillity in America until the Negro is granted his citizenship rights. The whirlwinds of revolt will continue to shake the foundations of our nation until the bright day of justice emerges.

But there is something that I must say to my people who stand on the warm threshold which leads into the palace of justice. In the process of gaining our rightful place we must not be guilty of wrongful deeds.

Let us not seek to satisfy our thirst for freedom by drinking from the cup of bitterness and hatred. We must forever conduct our struggle on the high plane of dignity and discipline. We must not allow our creative protest to degenerate into physical violence. Again and again we must rise to the majestic heights of meeting physical force with soul force.

The marvelous new militancy which has engulfed the Negro community must not lead us to a distrust of all white people, for many of our white brothers, as evidenced by their presence here today, have come to realize that their destiny is tied up with our destiny and they have come to realize that their freedom is inextricably bound to our freedom. This offense we share mounted to storm the battlements of injustice must be carried forth by a biracial army. We cannot walk alone.

And as we walk, we must make the pledge that we shall always march ahead. We cannot turn back. There are those who are asking the devotees of civil rights, "When will you be satisfied?" We can never be satisfied as long as the Negro is the victim of the unspeakable horrors of police brutality.

We can never be satisfied as long as our bodies, heavy with fatigue of travel, cannot gain lodging in the motels of the highways and the hotels of the cities. We cannot be satisfied as long as the Negro's basic mobility is from a smaller ghetto to a larger one.

We can never be satisfied as long as our children are stripped of their selfhood and robbed of their dignity by signs stating "for whites only." We cannot be satisfied as long as a Negro in Mississippi cannot vote and a Negro in New York believes he has nothing for which to vote. No, we are not satisfied, and we will not be satisfied until justice rolls down like waters and righteousness like a mighty stream.

I am not unmindful that some of you come here out of excessive trials and tribulation. Some of you have come fresh from narrow jail cells. Some of you have come from areas where your quest for freedom left you battered by the storms of persecution and staggered by the winds of police brutality. You have been the veterans of creative suffering. Continue to work with the faith that unearned suffering is redemptive.

Go back to Mississippi; go back to Alabama; go back to South Carolina; go back to Georgia; go back to Louisiana; go back to the slums and ghettos of the northern cities, knowing that somehow this situation can, and will be changed. Let us not wallow in the valley of despair.

So I say to you, my friends, that even though we must face the difficulties of today and tomorrow, I still have a dream. It is a dream deeply rooted in the American dream that one day this nation will rise up and live out the true meaning of its creed, we hold these truths to be self-evident, that all men are created equal.

I have a dream that one day on the red hills of Georgia, sons of former slaves and sons of former slave-owners will be able to sit down together at the table of brotherhood.

I have a dream that one day, even the state of Mississippi, a state sweltering with the heat of injustice, sweltering with the heat of oppression, will be transformed into an oasis of freedom and justice.

I have a dream my four little children will one day live in a nation where they will not be judged by the color of their skin but by the content of their character. I have a dream today!

I have a dream that one day, down in Alabama, with its vicious racists, with its governor having his lips dripping with the words of interposition and nullification, that one day, right there in Alabama, little black boys and black girls will be able to join hands with little white boys and white girls as sisters and brothers. I have a dream today!

I have a dream that one day every valley shall be exalted, every hill and mountain shall be made low, the rough places shall be made plain, and the crooked places shall be made straight and the glory of the Lord will be revealed and all flesh shall see it together.

This is our hope. This is the faith that I go back to the South with.

With this faith we will be able to hew out of the mountain of despair a stone of hope. With this faith we will be able to transform the jangling discords of our nation into a beautiful symphony of brotherhood.

With this faith we will be able to work together, to pray together, to struggle together, to go to jail together, to stand up for freedom together, knowing that we will be free one day. This will be the day when all of God's children will be able to sing with new meaning—"my country 'tis of thee; sweet land of liberty; of thee I sing; land where my fathers died, land of the pilgrim's pride; from every mountainside, let freedom ring"—and if America is to be a great nation, this must become true.

So let freedom ring from the prodigious hilltops of New Hampshire.

Let freedom ring from the mighty mountains of New York.

Let freedom ring from the heightening Alleghenies of Pennsylvania.

Let freedom ring from the snow-capped Rockies of Colorado.

Let freedom ring from the curvaceous slopes of California.

But not only that.

Let freedom ring from Stone Mountain of Georgia.

Let freedom ring from Lookout Mountain of Tennessee.

Let freedom ring from every hill and molehill of Mississippi, from every mountainside, let freedom ring.

And when we allow freedom to ring, when we let it ring from every village and hamlet, from every state and city, we will be able to speed up that day when all of God's children, black men and white men, Jews and Gentiles, Catholics and Protestants, will be able to join hands and to sing in the words of the old Negro spiritual, "Free at last, free at last; thank God Almighty, we are free at last."

PART 4

Values That
Relate to Love

# Introduction

Love is something
   If you give it away
   You end up having more.
   Love is like a magic penny
   Hold it tight and you won't have any
   Lend it, spend it, you'll have so many
   They'll roll all over the floor
                        Children's song

The journey to personal and social values begins with love: not least with your love for your children and their love for you. And progress on that journey mirrors how much we extend our love and loving-kindness into the world, even to the neediest among us. Just by being human we have all we need to do just that. Langston Hughes puts it this way,

What is there within this beggar lad
That I can neither hear nor feel nor see,
That I can neither know or understand
And still it calls to me?

James Baldwin, in *Going to Meet the Man*, describes a moment on this momentous journey when familial love ignites in one family member a deep sense of connection within the family and opens him up to the possibility of connectedness with other people—the audience, the world outside:

Then they all gathered around Sonny and Sonny played. Every now and again one of them seemed to say, amen. Sonny's fingers filled the air with life, his life. But that life contained so many others. And Sonny went all the way back, he really began with the spare, flat statement of the opening phrase of the song. Then he began to make it his. It was very beautiful because it wasn't hurried and it was no longer a lament. I seemed to hear with what burning he had made it his, with what burning we had yet to make it ours, how we could cease lamenting. Freedom lurked around us and I understood, at last, that he could help us to be free if we would listen, that he would never be free until we did. Yet, there was no battle in his face now, I heard what he had gone through, and would continue to go through until he came to rest in earth. He had made it his: that long line, of which we knew only Mama and Daddy. And he was giving it back, as everything must be given back, so that, passing through death, it can live forever. I saw my mother's face again, and felt, for the first time, how the stones of the road she had walked on must have bruised her feet.

Baldwin reminds us that we help one another to make true and tender connections and that love—and the ecstasy that can accompany it—brings us closely in touch with our deepest selves as well as with some of the big, big issues in every life: reciprocity, gratitude, and freedom.

How we treat each other is what finally brings personal happiness and affectionate social ties. M. Scott Peck recounts the story of a rabbi and an abbot who become friends. Each tells the other of a great worry: the abbot about his declining monastery, the rabbi about his declining synagogue. On taking his leave the rabbi tells the abbot that even though only a few monks remain in his monastery, "the Messiah is one of you."

In the months that followed, the old monks in the monastery wondered whether the rabbi's words meant anything. If he meant anyone, he probably meant Father Abbot, their leader. But he might have meant Brother Thomas, a truly holy man. It couldn't be crotchty Brother Elred! But come to think of it, despite his temper, Elred is almost always right. It could be Brother Elred. But not Brother Phillip. How could it be Phillip, he is such a nonentity. But Philip does show up when you need him. Perhaps Phillip is the Messiah, they thought. Of course the rabbi couldn't have meant me, the old monk said to himself. But then again, suppose he did. As they considered who the Messiah might be the old monks began to treat each other with a new and deep respect. After all, one of them might be the Messiah.

It is possible to find greater love even for yourself if you embrace the wonderful possibilities in others. Your readiness to love widely returns love to you; your ability to love deeply spreads love like adventurous roots—strengthening you in your own eyes as it extends affection outward.

# Love

The will to do, the soul to dare.
　　　　　　　—Sir Walter Scott

Scott might have said, "The love to dare." The soul, after all, is where we all feel ourselves as part of humanity. In that sense it is another way of talking about love. The experience of connectedness as merging with people and elements beyond ourselves is also the province of love. When we care deeply about another person and about humanity, we are at once *selfless* and *selfish* because each of us is a part of what we love. In this way, love is the source of our ideals, of empathy and compassion, the inner place where we can be entirely ourselves but not for ourselves alone. While our own well-being does not necessarily lie in the hands or in the mind of someone else, it most certainly does lie in our close or not so close relations with other people. In a nutshell, love and the joy that can accompany it bring a sense of trust and safety, softening the harsher aspects of dedication and conviction—allowing us to bring heart to mind.

To bring heart to mind: How easy it can be to look at problems like homelessness, hunger, or unemployment ever so rationally and fail to see the people involved. It's possible, for example, to judge people, to assess whether or not they're worthy of help, and not be moved by their suffering. In that case, if and when the would-be solution doesn't work and people's suffering remains, where will our zeal to help improve life for them come from?

Chaim Potok, in *The Chosen*, pictures the drama involved between parent and child:

> Reuven, I did not want my Daniel to become like my brother, may he rest in peace. Better I should have had no son at all than to have a brilliant son who had no soul. I looked at my Daniel when he was four years old, and I said to myself, How will I teach this mind what it is to

411

have a soul? How will I teach this mind to understand pain? How will I teach it to want to take on another person's suffering?

Gaining and teaching the ability to live in this way is one of the great projects of youth and one of the great responsibilities of parenthood.

——◆◆——

*As* The Velveteen Rabbit *and* The Magic Locket *gently remind us, when we are able to love ourselves, we are also able to love somebody else and become more ourselves. Finding ourselves and getting to know who we are, are sources of inspiration and personal strength as the poems by Walcott and Hikmet show.*

## Margery Williams, *The Velveteen Rabbit*

There was once a velveteen rabbit, and in the beginning he was really splendid. He was fat and bunchy, as a rabbit should be; his coat was spotted brown and white, he had real thread whiskers, and his ears were lined with pink sateen. On Christmas morning, when he sat wedged in the top of the Boy's stocking, with a sprig of holly between his paws, the effect was charming.

There were other things in the stocking, nuts and oranges and a toy engine, and chocolate almonds and a clockwork mouse, but the Rabbit was quite the best of all. For at least two hours the Boy loved him, and then Aunts and Uncles came to dinner, and there was a great rustling of tissue paper and unwrapping of parcels, and in the excitement of looking at all the new presents the Velveteen Rabbit was forgotten.

For a long time he lived in the toy cupboard or on the nursery floor, and no one thought very much about him. He was naturally shy, and being only made of velveteen, some of the more expensive toys quite snubbed him. The mechanical toys were very superior, and looked down upon everyone else; they were full of modern ideas, and pretended they were real. The model boat, who had lived through two seasons and lost most of his paint, caught the tone from them and never missed an opportunity of referring to his rigging in technical terms. The Rabbit could not claim to be a model of anything, for he didn't know that real rabbits existed; he thought they were all stuffed with sawdust like himself, and he understood that sawdust was quite out-of-date and should never be mentioned in modern circles. Even Timothy, the jointed wooden lion, who was made by the disabled soldiers, and should have had broader views, put on airs and pretended he was connected with Government. Between them all the poor little Rabbit was made to feel himself very insignificant and commonplace, and the only person who was kind to him at all was the Skin Horse.

The Skin Horse had lived longer in the nursery than any of the others. He was so old that his brown coat was bald in patches and showed the seams underneath, and most of the hairs in his tail had been pulled out to string bead necklaces. He was wise, for he had seen a long succession of mechanical toys arrive to boast and swagger, and by-and-by break their mainsprings and pass away, and he knew that they were only toys, and would never turn into anything else. For nursery magic is very strang and wonderful, and only those playthings that are old and wise and experienced like the Skin Horse understand all about it.

"What is REAL?" asked the Rabbit one day, when they were lying side by side near the nursery fender, before Nana came to tidy the room. "Does it mean having things that buzz inside you and a stick-out handle?"

"Real isn't how you are made," said the Skin Horse. "It's a thing that happens to you. When a child loves you for a long, long time, not just to play with, but REALLY loves you, then you become Real."

"Does it hurt?" asked the Rabbit.

"Sometimes," said the Skin Horse, for he was always truthful. "When you are Real you don't mind being hurt."

"Does it happen all at once, like being wound up," he asked, "or bit by bit?"

"It doesn't happen all at once," said the Skin Horse. "You become. It takes a long time. That's why it doesn't often happen to people who break easily, or have sharp edges, or who have to be carefully kept. Generally, by the time you are Real, most of your hair has been loved off, and your eyes drop out and you get loose in the joints and very shabby. But these things don't matter at all, because once you are Real you can't be ugly, except to people who don't understand."

"I suppose *you* are Real?" said the Rabbit. And then he wished he had not said it, for he thought the Skin Horse might be sensitive. But the Skin Horse only smiled.

"The Boy's Uncle made me Real," he said. "That was a great many years ago; but once you are Real you can't become unreal again. It lasts for always."

The Rabbit sighed. He thought it would be a long time before this magic called Real happened to him. He longed to become Real, to know what it felt like; and yet the idea of growing shabby and losing his eyes and whiskers was rather sad. He wished that he could become it without these uncomfortable things happening to him.

There was a person called Nana who ruled the nursery. Sometimes she took no notice of the playthings lying about, and sometimes, for no reason whatever, she went swooping about like a great wind and hustled them away in cupboards. She called this "tidying up," and the playthings all hated it, especially the tin ones. The Rabbit didn't mind it so much, for wherever he was thrown he came down soft.

One evening, when the Boy was going to bed, he couldn't find the china dog that always slept with him. Nana was in a hurry, and it was too much trouble to hunt for china dogs at bedtime, so she simply looked about her, and seeing that the toy cupboard door stood open, she made a swoop.

"Here," she said, "take your old Bunny! He'll do to sleep with you!" And she dragged the Rabbit out by one ear, and put him into the Boy's arms.

That night, and for many nights after, the Velveteen Rabbit slept in the Boy's bed. At first he found it rather uncomfortable, for the Boy hugged him very tight, and sometimes he rolled over on him, and sometimes he pushed him so far under the pillow that the Rabbit could scarcely breathe. And he missed, too, those long moonlight hours in the nursery, when all the house was silent, and his talks with the Skin Horse. But very soon he grew to like it, for the Boy used to talk to him, and made nice tunnels for him under the bedclothes that he said were like the burrows the real rabbits lived in. And they had splendid games together, in whispers, when Nana had gone away to her supper and left the night-light burning on the mantelpiece. And when the Boy dropped off to sleep, the Rabbit would snuggle down close under his little warm chin and dream, with the Boy's hands clasped close round him all night long.

And so time went on, and the little Rabbit was very happy—so happy that he never noticed how his beautiful velveteen fur was getting shabbier and shabbier, and his tail coming unsewn, and all the pink rubbed off his nose where the Boy had kissed him.

Spring came, and they had long days in the garden, for wherever the Boy went the Rabbit went too. He had rides in the wheelbarrow, and picnics on the grass, and lovely fairy huts built for him under the raspberry canes behind the flower border. And once, when the Boy was called away suddenly to go out to tea, the Rabbit was left out on the lawn until long after dusk, and Nana had to come and look for him with the candle because the Boy couldn't go to sleep unless he was there. He was wet through with the dew and quite earthy from diving into the burrows the

Boy had made for him in the flower bed, and Nana grumbled as she rubbed him off with a corner of her apron.

"You must have your old Bunny!" she said. "Fancy all that fuss for a toy!"

The Boy sat up in bed and stretched out his hands.

"Give me my Bunny!" he said. "You mustn't say that. He isn't a toy. He's REAL!"

When the little Rabbit heard that, he was happy, for he knew that what the Skin Horse had said was true at last. The nursery magic had happened to him, and he was a toy no longer. He was Real. The Boy himself had said it.

That night he was almost too happy to sleep, and so much love stirred in his little sawdust heart that it almost burst. And into his boot-button eyes, that had long ago lost their polish, there came a look of wisdom and beauty, so that even Nana noticed it next morning when she picked him up, and said, "I declare if that old Bunny hasn't got quite a knowing expression!"

### Elizabeth Koda-Callan, *The Magic Locket*

Soon she began to wonder what made the locket so powerful. It wasn't before she found out.

One morning, when she was putting on the locket, it slipped through her fingers and fell to the floor. When the locket fell, it snapped open. The little girl bent down to pick it up and was very surprised to see what was inside.

Inside the locket was a mirror, and in the mirror was her own reflection.

"Why, it's me!" she thought. "It's really me. *I'm* the magic in the locket."

### Derek Walcott, *Love after Love*

The time will come
when, with elation,
you will greet yourself arriving
at your own door, in your own mirror,
and each will smile at the other's welcome,

and say, sit here. Eat.
You will love again the stranger who was your self.
Give wine. Give bread. Give back your heart
to itself, to the stranger who has loved you

all your life, whom you ignored
for another, who knows you by heart.
Take down the love letters from the bookshelf,

the photographs, the desperate notes,
peel your own image from the mirror.
Sit. Feast on your life.


**Nazim Hikmet,** *Letters from a Man in Solitary,* **translated by Randy Blasing and Mutlu Konuk**

## II

It's spring outside, my dear wife, spring.
Outside on the plain, suddenly the smell
of fresh earth, birds singing, etc.
It's spring, my dear wife, the plain outside sparkles . . .
And inside the bed comes alive with bugs,
                              the water jug no longer freezes.
and in the morning sun floods the concrete . . .
The sun—
every day till noon now
it comes and goes
from me, flashing off
                              and on . . .
And as the day turns to afternoon, shadows climb the walls,
the glass of the barred window catches fire,
                              and it's night outside.
                  a cloudless spring night . . .
And inside this is spring's darkest hour.
In short, the demon called freedom,
with its glittering scales and fiery eyes,
possesses the man inside
                              especially in spring . . .
I know this from experience, my dear wife,
                              from experience . . .


## III

Sunday today.
Today they took me out in the sun for the first time.

And I just stood there, struck for the first time in my life
                              by how far away the sky is,
                              how blue
                              and how wide.
Then I respectfully sat down on the earth.
I leaned back against the wall.
For a moment no trap to fall into,
no struggle, no freedom, no wife.
Only earth, sun, and me . . .
I am happy.

———————

*Becky and her mom in* Splendor *show the wonder of love between parent and child that is always evolving. Sometimes, it is discovered late, as in Louise Glück's* First Memory. *At times, there is a demonstrative expression of love, at other times restraint is necessary, as Tom shows when he preserves his father's dignity in* More Adventures of the Great Brain.

### Lois Lowry, *Splendor*

"Mom?" Becky called later. "Do you think I can get up? I feel better. My throat doesn't hurt at all anymore."

Her mother came to her room and assessed Becky's fever by kissing her forehead. "Okay," she decided. Then she hesitated. She stood beside Becky's bed, her head tilted as if she were thinking about something very far away. Becky watched as her mother, lost in thought, smoothed the folds of her old sweater and fingered the strand of dimestore pearls around her neck. Her mother was smiling.

"Becky," she asked, "would you do something for me? Would you put on your new dress?"

"Mom," Becky groaned, "I'm not sure I ever want to wear that dress!"

"Just this once, Beck. For me, okay? I have a surprise."

"There's nobody here, is there? I don't want anyone but you to see me in it."

"I promise. It's just you and me. I'll meet you in the living room in a few minutes."

"Okay," Becky said, laughing.

After her mother had gone, Becky got out of bed and took the red dress from her closet. Carefully she put it on and zipped it up. She put on stockings, and the delicate sandals she had planned to wear to the Christmas dance. She brushed her hair. Finally she stood in front of the mirror and looked at herself. The dress was still too big, and it bunched awkwardly in the places where her mother had stitched it together to try to make it fit.

But a little of the magic had returned. Suddenly, from downstairs, she could hear music; her mother had turned on the stereo. Becky turned slowly in a circle in front of the mirror, and the skirt full of stars glittered in the dim light of her bedroom. She felt giddy and light-headed—maybe from the day of fever. Or maybe it was just the feeling, once again, that she was beautiful, wearing the dress that was the reddest red any dress had ever been; and that she was safe, here, in a place where no one would laugh.

Becky started down the stairs toward the living room, where the music played softly and she could see that her mother had lighted candles. The familiar room was different now; it flowed in the unaccustomed flickering candlelight, and even the ancient, shabby furniture took on new and unfamiliar shapes as its shadows moved on the walls. The stains in the threadbare rug were blurred and muted in the softened light, and the flowered patterns of the old slipcovers were deepened into subtler shades. Everything seemed changed.

At the bottom of the stairs, Becky stopped in her tracks, and stared.

Waiting in the middle of the living room was Becky's mother, and she was wearing the most hideous dress that Becky had ever seen. It was purple: the most purple of all possible purples, a shiny satin the shade of overripe plums; and it had thin straps which were encrusted with cheap rhinestones. It was too short, well above her mother's knees. And it was too tight; a seam above the waist had begun to rip.

Her mother, who never wore makeup at all, was wearing purple eye-shadow. She had on lipstick and there were dusky smudges of rouge on her cheeks. Her hair, which was always tied back tightly at her neck, was loose, falling around her bare shoulders.

"Where did you get that dress?" Becky finally managed to gasp.

"Do you like it?" her mother asked. She held the edges of the skirt in her fingertips, and turned, posing.

"It's—" Becky said, and stopped. She had been about to say, "trashy." Instead, she bit her lip and suggested, "it's a little young for you, I think."

"Of course it is." Her mother laughed. "It's also too small. You are the only person who's ever seen me wearing it."

"But, Mom, it—well, it doesn't look like you!"

"I know," her mother said, smiling. "Here; have some fake champagne. It's really ginger ale. But the champagne glasses are real crystal. I had to wash the dust off, they've been packed away so long."

Becky sipped from the fragile, long-stemmed glass. She shook her head in wonder. "Where did you get it? When did you get it?"

Her mother sat down on the couch and smoothed the garish purple skirt. "I bought it nine years ago," she said, "and I never told a soul."

"Nine years ago?" Becky said. She calculated in her head. "I was four years old. That was the year that Daddy—"

Her mother nodded. "It was the year your father died."

Becky remembered, though she had been very small. She remembered the sense of confusion and loss, and of the comfort of her mother's quiet voice. She remembered her mother holding her, rocking her in an old chair that creaked rhythmically, mournfully, endlessly, as it moved.

"I don't understand," she said to her mother.

"I'm not sure I do either, Beck," her mother confessed. "It was a few months after he died. By then everyone had stopped feeling sorry for me and paying a lot of attention to me, and all of a sudden I felt all alone— alone with two little girls, and not enough money. I felt—well, scared, I guess. And depressed. I felt as if I would never again be young, or carefree, or pretty. And then one day I walked past a store, and in the window of the store—"

"You saw that dress."

Her mother nodded, smiling, remembering. "I saw this dress. I couldn't afford it, and I certainly didn't need it. And it wasn't a beautiful dress, even then. It was a tawdry, terrible dress. But I wanted it more than I'd ever wanted anything."

"Like me. Like my dress." Becky looked down and touched her own skirt with its cheap golden stars.

"In those first couple of years, every now and then, after you girls were in bed, I would put it on. And a strange thing would happen. One part of me *knew* what an ugly dress it was. But when I put it on, something magic would happen. It made me feel younger—"

"Mine makes me feel older," Becky whispered, almost to herself.

"—and it made me feel beautiful."

"Yes," Becky breathed. "I know. Mine does too."

**Louise Glück, *First Memory***
Long ago, I was wounded, I lived
to revenge myself
against my father, not
for what he was—

for what I was: from the beginning of time,
in childhood, I thought
that pain meant
I was not loved
It meant I loved.


**John D. Fitzgerald, *More Adventures of the Great Brain***
I was scared and felt like crying, and Papa sure didn't help matters after
we'd finished eating.

"I don't want to alarm you, boys," he said as he puffed on his pipe,
"but things look quite serious."

Sweyn doubled up his knees and held them with his hands. "Mom
certainly must have told Uncle Mark to come look for us when we didn't
get back on time," he said.

"Where would he look?" Papa asked. "He had no idea where we were
going except up Beaver Canyon."

"But he could find the tracks of the horses and buckboard," Sweyn
said.

"You are forgetting that cloudburst we had," Papa said. "It certainly
washed out any tracks made by the horses and the buckboard."

I couldn't hold back the tears any longer and began to cry. "We are
going to die," I sobbed.

"We certainly aren't going to die," Papa said. "I read an article one
time about a man who was lost in the Rocky Mountains for five years.
He managed to live on small game, fish, pinenuts, and wild berries until
finally he was rescued by some trappers." Then Papa stood up and
stretched. "I think it is time to bed down now," he said.

. . .

The next morning we found we'd caught two rabbits in our deadfalls
and four trout on our night fishing poles. We ate the trout for breakfast
and saved the rabbits. Papa was very quiet. After we had finished eating,
Papa went back to the boulder and sat staring at that thousand-foot-high
granite cliff as if trying to come to some decision. We had just finished
washing the tin plates and knives and forks when he motioned to us.

"Boys," he said as we stood in front of him. I'd never seen his face so
serious. "I think we should start building a log cabin."

"How are you going to build a cabin without a saw and a hammer
and nails and things?" Sweyn asked

"The same way the early pioneers did," Papa answered. "Using the
bark of aspen trees to bind the logs together and mud from the banks of

the river to chink up the cracks between the logs. And there is a ledge of flat rock over there we can use to build a fireplace. We must prepare for the worst and hope for the best. It may be years before some friendly Indians or some trapper finds us."

Tom shook his head. "Isn't it silly to start building a cabin when Uncle Mark will be riding in here in a few days?" he asked.

"That is impossible," Papa said. "That cloudburst washed away all our tracks."

"No it didn't," Tom said. "I knew when we turned off the logging camp road that we might get lost. I used rocks to make markers that wouldn't wash away, and I cut markers on trees no cloudburst could destroy. That is why I was lagging behind all the time. If my calculations are correct, Uncle Mark should be riding in here in two or three days, if we just stay here. You didn't think my great brain would let us get lost, did you, Papa?"

Papa and Sweyn stared at Tom bug-eyed for a moment, and then they both began to smile happily. Papa got off the boulder and patted Tom on the shoulder.

"I'm proud of you, son," he said. "It was foolish of me to try and find a shortcut out of these mountains without marking our trail."

Then Papa had a second thought about what he had just said. He staggered back to the boulder and sat down. He covered his face with his hands as if he were going to cry.

"What's the matter with him?" Sweyn whispered.

"I don't know," Tom answered. "Suppose we find out."

Tom walked up close to Papa. "What is the matter?" he asked. "I told you we were going to be saved."

Papa raised his head up. "I'll never live this down," he cried as if being tortured. "Your mother will never forgive me for trying to take a shortcut and endangering all our lives. And I can just hear people in town bringing up the subject every time some neighbor's cow wanders away. I'll be the butt of jokes for years."

Then Papa got real dramatic and held his arms out in a hopeless gesture. "That is the only answer," he cried. "I'll stay right here. Better to live out my life in this wilderness than to go back and have people point me out as the town fool. You boys return with your Uncle Mark. I'm staying right here."

'Tom stared at Papa for a moment as his great brain began to click. Then he looked at Sweyn.

"Did you see me mark the trail?" he asked.

Sweyn looked surprised for a second and then smiled. "No," he answered.

Tom looked at me and winked. "Did you see me mark the trail, J.D.?"

"No," I lied.

'Well!" Tom said with a shake of his head, "I sure don't remember marking our trail, and that leaves only Papa."

The look of despair on Papa's face gave way to one of hope. He looked as though he might enjoy the comforts of home more than living like a savage in the wilderness.

"Thank you, boys," he said. "Thank you from the bottom of my heart."

I figured Tom would have liked it better to be thanked from the bottom of Papa's purse but didn't say anything.

We lived for two and a half days on small game we caught in our deadfalls, fish we caught, and roasted pinenuts. On the afternoon of the third day Uncle Mark rode into our camp on his white stallion, leading two pack horses. I was never so glad to see anybody in my life. But Papa folded his arms on his chest and looked positively angry.

"What in the name of Jupiter took you so long?" he demanded. "Leaving me all this time trying to keep up the spirits of my boys?"

I didn't know what spirits Papa was talking about. He sure hadn't kept up my spirits with that story of the man lost for five years in the mountains.

Uncle Mark grinned as he dismounted. Then he looked at Papa. "If you'd just stayed in one place after you knew you were lost," he said, "instead of wandering up and down one blind canyon after another, I would have caught up with you a few days ago. It is a good thing you had sense enough to mark your trail, or I would never have found you."

"What kind of a tenderfoot do you think I am?" Papa asked as if insulted. "You certainly don't think for a moment that I'd try to take a shortcut out of these mountains without marking my trail, do you?"

⤞◆⤝

*Love can simply and profoundly be the feeling of well-being in the wide world of people and of nature. Native American tales are rich with this ideal. Paul Zindel's* The Effect of Gamma Rays on Man-in-the-Moon Marigolds *gives us a contemporary taste of the same possibility.*

### Paul Zindel, *The Effect of Gamma Rays on Man-in-the-Moon Marigolds*

TILLIE:    Today I saw it. Behind the glass a white cloud began to form. He placed a small piece of metal in the center of the chamber and we waited until I saw the first one—a trace of smoke that came from nowhere and then disappeared. And then another . . . and another, until I knew it was coming from the metal. They looked like water sprays from a park fountain, and they went on and on for as long as I watched.

And he told me the fountain of smoke would come forth for a long time, and if I had wanted to, I could have stayed there all my life and it would never have ended—that fountain, so close I could have touched it. In front of my eyes, one part of the world was becoming another. Atoms exploding, flinging off tiny bullets that caused the fountain, atom after atom breaking down into something new. And no one could stop the fountain. It would go on for millions of years—on and on, this fountain from eternity.

TILLIE'S VOICE: He told me to look at my hand, for a part of it came from a star that exploded too long ago to imagine. This part of me was formed from a tongue of fire that screamed through the heavens until there was our sun. And this part of me, this tiny part of me was on the sun when it itself exploded and whirled in a great storm until the planets came to be.

(*Lights start in.*)

And this small part of me was then a whisper of the earth. When there was life, perhaps this part of me got lost in a fern that was crushed and covered until it was coal. And then it was a diamond millions of years later, it must have been a diamond as beautiful as the star from which it had first come.

TILLIE: (*Taking over from recorded voice.*) Or perhaps this part of me became lost in a terrible beast, or became part of a huge bird that flew above the primeval swamps.

And he said this thing was so small, this part of me was so small it couldn't be seen, but it was there from the beginning of the world.

And he called this bit of me an atom. And when he wrote the word, I fell in love with it.
Atom.
*Atom.*
What a beautiful word.

**Octavio Paz,** *A Tree Within*
Words are uncertain
and speak uncertain things.
But speaking this or that,

                         they speak us.

Love is an equivocal word
like all words.
                It's not a word.
said the Founder:
                it is a vision,
base and crown of the ladder of contemplation . . .
To love is to lose oneself in time,
to be a mirror among mirrors.


**Sitting Bull,** *Behold, My Brothers*
Yet, hear me, people,
we have now to deal with another race—
small and feeble when our fathers first met them
but now great and overbearing. Strangely enough
they have a mind to till the soil. And the love
of possession is a disease with them.

These people have made many rules that
the rich may break but the poor may not.
They take tithes from the poor and weak
to support the rich who rule. They claim
this mother of ours, the earth, for their own
and fence their neighbors away; they deface
her with their buildings and their refuse.
This nation is like a spring freshet
that overruns its banks
and destroys all who are in its path.

We cannot dwell side by side. Only
seven years ago we made a treaty
by which we were assured that the buffalo
country should be left to us forever. Now
they threaten to take that away from us.
My brothers, shall we submit or shall we
say to them: "First kill me
before you take possession of my Fatherland . . . "

---

*Love of other people can bring great joy. So too, deep pleasure can come in prized pursuits which can bring the unity of experience that poets call love. These selections show that, with joy, life takes on new meaning and is enhanced.*

### Victor Hugo, *The Hunchback of Notre Dame,* translated by Walter J. Cobb

It would be difficult to appreciate fully his joy on days of the full tolling of the bells. The moment that the archdeacon sent him off with that one word, "Go!" he scrambled up the spiral staircase of the belfry more quickly than another would have descended it. All out of breath, he hurried into the aerial chamber of the great bell, looked at her for a moment intently and lovingly, then talked to her softly, patted her with his hand, like a good horse about to set out on a long journey. He would pity her for the trouble he was going to cause her. After these first caresses, he called out to his assistants, stationed on a lower level of the tower, to begin. They seized the ropes, the capstan creaked, the enormous metal dome began to swing slowly. Quasimodo, panting, followed it with his eye. The first stroke of the clapper against the metal wall shook the wooden scaffolding on which he was standing. Quasimodo vibrated with the bell. "Vah!" he would cry with a burst of mad laughter. Meanwhile the bell swung faster, and as it swung, taking an ever-wider sweep, Quasimodo's eye opened wider and wider, and became more and more phosphorescent and enflamed. At length the full tolling began, and the whole tower trembled—rafters, lead, stone, all groaned at once, from the piles of the foundation to the trifoliations at the summit. Quasimodo was now all wet with perspiration, running to and fro, and shaking with the tower from head to foot. The bell, unleashed and swinging furiously, presented alternately to the two walls of the tower its bronze throat, from whence escaped that tempestuous breath that carried for four leagues around. Quasimodo remained in front of this gaping throat, squatted down, but rose at each return of the bell. He inhaled its boisterous breath, and looked by turns far down at the square swarming with people two hundred feet below him, and at the enormous brazen tongue which came, time after time, to bellow in his ear. It was the only speech he could hear, the only sound that broke the universal silence. He reveled in it like a bird in the sun. All at once, the frenzy of the bell possessed him; his expression became extraordinarily wild. He would wait for the huge bell to pass, as a spider waits for a fly, and then he would fling himself headlong onto it.

Then, suspended over the abyss, carried to and fro by the formidable swinging of the bell, he seized the brazen monster by its ears, gripped it between his knees, spurred it with his two heels, and, with the whole force and weight of his body, he would redouble the fury of the pealing. Meanwhile the tower rocked, while he shouted and gnashed his teeth, his red hair bristling, his chest heaving like the blast of a forge, and his eye flaming, while his monstrous steed neighed, panting under him. Then there was no longer either the great bell of Notre-Dame or Quasimodo; it was a dream, a whirlwind, a tempest, vertigo astride a clamor, a spirit clinging to a flying saddle, a strange centaur, half man, half bell—a sort of horrible Astolfo, carried away on a prodigious hippogriff of living bronze.

The presence of this extraordinary being infused the cathedral with a certain breath of life. There seemed to escape from Quasimodo—at least so said the exaggerating superstitions of the crowd—a mysterious emanation which enlivened all the stones of Notre-Dame, and made the ancient church pulsate to its very entrails. When it was known that he was there, it was enough to make you think you saw life and motion in the thousand statues of the galleries and doorways. And indeed, the cathedral did seem like a creature, docile and obedient in his hands. She waited upon his will to lift up her loud voice; she was possessed by him; she was filled with Quasimodo, as with some familiar spirit.

. . .

Quasimodo did exist. Notre-Dame today is empty, lifeless, dead. They feel that something has gone out of her. That immense body is empty; it is a skeleton; the spirit has quit it. You see the place of its habitation, but that is all. It is like a skull, where the holes for the eyes remain, but there is no sight.

**Langston Hughes, *Song for a Banjo Dance***
Shake your brown feet, honey,
Shake your brown feet, chile,
Shake your brown feet, honey,
Shake 'em swift and wil'—
      Get way back, honey,
      Do that rockin' step.
      Slide on over, darling,
            Now! Come out
            With your left.
Shake your brown feet, honey,
Shake 'em, honey chile.

Sun's going down this evening—
Might never rise no mo'.
The sun's going down this very night—
Might never rise no mo'—
So dance with swift feet, honey,
    (The banjo's sobbing low)
Dance with swift feet, honey—
    Might never dance no mo'.

Shake your brown feet, Liza,
Shake 'em, Liza, chile,
Shake your brown feet, Liza,
    (The music's soft and wil')
Shake your brown feet, Liza,

**Sara Teasdale,** *Barter*
Life has loveliness to sell,
    All beautiful and splendid things,
Blue waves whitened on a cliff,
    Soaring fire that sways and sings,
And children's faces looking up,
Holding wonder like a cup.

Life has loveliness to sell,
    Music like a curve of gold,
Scent of pine trees in the rain,
    Eyes that love you, arms that hold,
And for your spirit's still delight,
Holy thoughts that star the night.

Spend all you have for loveliness,
    Buy it and never count the cost;
For one white singing hour of peace
    Count many a year of strife well lost,
And for a breath of ecstasy
Give all you have been, or could be.

*Love brings demands and responsibilities. The bonds of love can sometimes feel too tight, sometimes not tight enough. Love can easily call us to new heights of courage and resourcefulness. But love can be misused by those who take unfair advantage of it when the idea or name of love replaces the true feeling and the bond. Leigh Hunt takes a look at this experience in* The Glove and the Lions, *and the Jewish sages strongly warn against it.*

## Leigh Hunt, *The Glove and the Lions*
King Francis was a hearty king, and loved a royal sport,
And one day, as his lions fought, sat looking at the court.
The nobles filled the benches, and the ladies in their pride,
And 'mongst them sat the Count de Lorge, with one for whom he
    sighed:
And truly 'twas a gallant thing to see that crowning show,
Valor and love, and a king above, and the royal beasts below.
Ramped and roared the lions, with horrid laughing jaws;
They bit, they glared, gave blows like beams, a wind went with their
    paws;
With wallowing might and stifled roar they rolled on one another,
Till all the pit with sand and mane was in thunderous smother.
The bloody foam above the bars came whisking through the air;
Said Francis then, "Faith, gentlemen, we're better here than there."
De Lorge's love o'erheard the King, a beauteous lively dame,
With smiling lips and sharp bright eyes, which always seemed the same;
She thought, "The Count, my lover, is brave as brave can be;
He surely would do wondrous things to show his love of me;
King, ladies, lovers, all look on; the occasion is divine;
I'll drop my glove, to prove his love; great glory will be mine."
She dropped her glove, to prove his love, then looked at him and smiled;
He bowed, and in a moment leaped among the lions wild;
The leap was quick, return was quick, he has regained his place,
Then threw the glove, but not with love, right in the lady's face.
"By Heaven," said Francis, "rightly done!" and he rose from where he sat;
"No love," quoth he, "but vanity, sets love a task like that."

## *The Wisdom of the Jewish Sages,* translated by Rami Shapiro
Be diligent in study
To learn below your potential
is a betrayal of self
and a betrayal of life

Be careful with words
C-O-W gives no milk
M-A-N-U-R-E has no stench
L-O-V-E knows no passion

If I am not for myself, who will be for me?
If I am for myself alone, what am I?
And if not now, when?
(Hillel)

Receive all people with kindness
(Stammel)

Justice Justice shalt thou praise
Be diligent in study
To learn below your potential
is a betrayal of self
and a betrayal of life

* * *

*Love can occur in the most unexpected places, as the Little Prince discovers. Even Madeleine L'Engle's monsters in* A Wrinkle in Time *show us how great love can come with people we don't expect it from. As* Frankenstein *shows, it can be provoked in us in the strangest circumstances. As the family in* The Patched Pants *discovers, finding love in the oddest of circumstances can produce wondrous results.*

## Antoine de Saint-Exupéry, *The Little Prince*

"Nothing is perfect," sighed the fox.

But he came back to his idea.

"My life is very monotonous," he said. "I hunt chickens; men hunt me. All the chickens are just alike, and all the men are just alike. And, in consequence, I am a little bored. But if you tame me, it will be as if the sun came to shine on my life. I shall know the sound of a step that will be different from all the others. Other steps send me hurrying back underneath the ground. Yours will call me, like music, out of my burrow. And then look: you see the grain-fields down yonder? I do not eat bread. Wheat is of no use to me. The wheat fields have nothing to say to me. And that is sad. But you have hair that is the color of gold. Think how wonderful that will be when you have tamed me! The grain, which is also golden, will bring me back the thought of you. And I shall love to listen to the wind in the wheat . . . ”

The fox gazed at the little prince, for a long time.

“Please—tame me!” he said.

“I want to, very much,” the little prince replied. “But I have not much time. I have friends to discover, and a great many things to understand.”

“One only understands the things that one tames,” said the fox. “Men have no more time to understand anything. They buy things all ready made at the shops. But there is no shop anywhere where one can buy friendship, and so men have no friends any more. If you want a friend, tame me . . . ”

“What must I do, to tame you?” asked the little prince.

“You must be very patient,” replied the fox. “First you will sit down at a little distance from me—like that—in the grass. I shall look at you out of the corner of my eye, and you will say nothing. Words are the source of misunderstandings. But you will sit a little closer to me, every day . . . ”

The next day the little prince came back.

“It would have been better to come back at the same hour,” said the fox. “If, for example, you come at four o’clock in the afternoon, then at three o’clock I shall begin to be happy. I shall feel happier and happier as the hour advances. At four o’clock, I shall already be worrying and jumping about. I shall show you how happy I am! But if you come at just any time, I shall never know at what hour my heart is to be ready to greet you . . . One must observe the proper rites . . . ”

“What is a rite?” asked the little prince.

“Those also are actions too often neglected,” said the fox. “They are what make one day different from other days, one hour from other hours. There is a rite, for example, among my hunters. Every Thursday they dance with the village girls. So Thursday is a wonderful day for me! I can take a walk as far as the vineyards. But if the hunters danced at just any time, every day would be like every other day, and I should never have any vacation at all.”

So the little prince tamed the fox. And when the hour of his departure drew near—

“Ah,” said the fox. “I shall cry.”

“It is your own fault,” said the little prince. “I never wished you any sort of harm; but you wanted me to tame you . . . ”

“Yes, that is so,” said the fox.

"But now you are going to cry!" said the little prince.

"Yes, that is so," said the fox.

"Then it has done you no good at all!"

"It has done me good," said the fox, "because of the color of the wheat fields." And then he added:

"Go and look again at the roses. You will understand now that yours is unique in all the world. Then come back to say good-bye to me, and I will make you a present of a secret."

The little prince went away, to look again at the roses.

"You are not at all like my rose," he said. "As yet you are nothing. No one has tamed you, and you have tamed no one. You are like my fox when I first knew him. He was only a fox like a hundred thousand other foxes. But I have made him my friend, and now he is unique in all the world."

And the roses were very much embarrassed.

"You are beautiful, but you are empty," he went on. "One could not die for you. To be sure, an ordinary passerby would think that my rose looked just like you, the rose that belongs to me. But in herself alone she is more important than all the hundreds of you other roses: because it is she that I have watered; because it is she that I have put under the glass globe; because it is she that I have sheltered behind the screen; because it is for her that I have killed the caterpillars (except the two or three that we saved to become butterflies); because it is she that I have listened to, when she grumbled, or boasted, or even sometimes when she said nothing. Because she is *my* rose."

And he went back to meet the fox.

"Good-bye," he said.

"Good-bye," said the fox. "And now here is my secret, a very simple secret: It is only with the heart that one can see rightly; what is essential is invisible to the eye."

"What is essential is invisible to the eye," the little prince repeated, so that he would be sure to remember.

"It is the time you have wasted for your rose that makes your rose so important."

### Madeleine L'Engle, *A Wrinkle in Time*

The tall one turned back to Mr. Murry, speaking sternly.

"You. The oldest. Man. From where have you come? Now."

Mr. Murry answered steadily. "From a planet called Camazotz." There was a mutter from the three beasts. "We do not belong there," Mr. Murry said, slowly and distinctly. "We were strangers there as we are here. I was a prisoner there, and these children rescued me. My youngest son, my baby, is still there, trapped in the dark mind of IT."

Meg tried to twist around in the beast's arms to glare at her father and Calvin. Why were they being so frank? Weren't they aware of the danger? But again her anger dissolved as the gentle warmth from the tentacles flowed through her. She realized that she could move her fingers and toes with comparative freedom, and the pain was no longer so acute.

"We must take this child back with us," the beast holding her said.

Meg shouted at her father. "Don't leave me the way you left Charles!" With this burst of terror a spasm of pain wracked her body and she gasped.

"Stop fighting," the beast told her. "You make it worse. Relax."

"That's what IT said," Meg cried. "Father! Calvin! Help!"

The beast turned toward Calvin and Mr. Murry. "This child is in danger. You must trust us."

"We have no alternative," Mr. Murry said. "Can you save her?"

"I think so."

"May I stay with her?"

"No. But you will not be far away. We feel that you are hungry, tired, that you would like to bathe and rest. And this little—what is the word?" the beast cocked its tentacles at Calvin.

"Girl," Calvin said.

"This little girl needs prompt and special care. The coldness of the what is it you call it?"

"The Black Thing?"

"The Black Thing. Yes. The Black Thing burns unless it is counteracted properly." The three beasts stood around Meg, and it seemed that they were feeling into her with their softly waving tentacles. The movement of the tentacles was as rhythmic and flowing as the dance of an undersea plant, and lying there, cradled in the four strange arms, Meg, despite herself, felt a sense of security that was deeper than anything she had known since the days when she lay in her mother's arms in the old rocking chair and was sung to sleep. With her father's help she had been able to resist IT. Now she could hold out no longer. She leaned her head against the beast's chest, and realized that the gray body was covered with the softest, most delicate fur imaginable, and the fur had the same beautiful odor as the air.

I hope I don't smell awful to it, she thought. But then she knew with a deep sense of comfort that even if she did smell awful the beasts would forgive her. As the tall figure cradled her she could feel the frigid stiffness of her body relaxing against it. This bliss could not come to her from a thing like IT. IT could only give pain, never relieve it. The beasts must be good. They had to be good. She sighed deeply, like a very small child, and suddenly she was asleep.

When she came to herself again there was in the back of her mind a memory of pain, of agonizing pain. But the pain was over now and her body was lapped in comfort. She was lying on something wonderfully soft in an enclosed chamber. It was dark. All she could see were occasional tall moving shadows which she realized were beasts walking about. She had been stripped of her clothes, and something warm and pungent was gently being rubbed into her body. She sighed and stretched and discovered that she *could* stretch. She could move again, she was no longer paralyzed, and her body was bathed in waves of warmth. Her father had not saved her; the beasts had.

"So you are awake, little one?" The words came gently to her ears. "What a funny little tadpole you are! Is the pain gone now?"

"All gone."

"Are you warm and alive again?"

"Yes, I'm fine." She struggled to sit up.

"No, lie still, small one. You must not exert yourself as yet. We will have a fur garment for you in a moment, and then we will feed you. You must not even try to feed yourself. You must be as an infant again. The Black Thing does not relinquish its victims willingly."

"Where are Father and Calvin? Have they gone back for Charles Wallace?"

. . .

"Charles Wallace!" she cried. "What are they doing about Charles Wallace? We don't know what IT's doing to him or making him do. Please, oh, please, help us!"

"Yes, yes, little one, of course we will help you. A meeting is in session right now to study what is best to do. We have never before been able to talk to anyone who has managed to escape from a dark planet, so although your father is blaming himself for everything that has happened, we feel that he must be quite an extraordinary person to get out of Camazotz with you at all. But the little boy, and I understand that he is a very special, a very important little boy—all, my child, you must accept that this will not be easy. To go *back* through the Black Thing, *back* to Camazotz, I don't know. I don't know."

"But Father left him!" Meg said. "He's got to bring him back! He can't just abandon Charles Wallace!"

The beast's communication suddenly became crisp. "Nobody said anything about abandoning anybody. That is not our way. But we know that just because we want something does not mean that we will get what we want, and we still do not know *what* to do. And we cannot allow you, in your present state, to do anything that would jeopardize us all. I can see that you wish your father to go rushing back to Camazotz, and you could probably make him do this, and then where would we be? No. No. You must wait until you are more calm. Now, my darling, here is a robe for you to keep you warm and comfortable." Meg felt herself being lifted again, and a soft, light garment was slipped about her. "Don't worry about your little brother." The tentacles' musical words were soft against her. "We would *never* leave him behind the shadow. But for now you must relax, you must be happy, you must get well."

The gentle words, the feeling that this beast would he able to love her no matter what she said or did, lapped Meg in warmth and peace. She felt a delicate touch of tentacle to her cheek, as tender as her mother's kiss.

### Mary Shelley, *Frankenstein*

The being finished speaking and fixed his looks upon me in the expectation of a reply. But I was bewildered, perplexed, and unable to arrange my ideas sufficiently to understand the full extent of his proposition. He continued, "You must create a female for me with whom I can live in the interchange of those sympathies necessary for my being. This you alone can do, and I demand it of you as a right which you must not refuse to concede."

The latter part of his tale had kindled anew in me the anger that had died away while he narrated his peaceful life among the cottagers, and as he said this I could no longer suppress the rage that burned within me.

"I do refuse it," I replied; "and no torture shall ever extort a consent from me. You may render me the most miserable of men, but you shall never make me base in my own eyes. Shall I create another like yourself, whose joint wickedness might desolate the world. Begone! I have answered you; you may torture me, but I will never consent."

"You are in the wrong," replied the fiend; "and instead of threatening, I am content to reason with you. I am malicious because I am miserable. Am I not shunned and hated by all mankind? You, my creator, would tear me to pieces and triumph; remember that, and tell me why I should pity man more than he pities me? You would not call it murder if you could precipitate me into one of those ice-rifts and destroy my frame, the work of your own hands. Shall I respect man when he contemns me? Let him live with me in the interchange of kindness, and instead of injury I would bestow every benefit upon him with tears of gratitude at his acceptance. But that cannot be; the human senses are insurmountable barriers to our union. Yet mine shall not be the submission of abject slavery. I will revenge my injuries; if I cannot inspire love, I will cause fear, and chiefly towards you my arch-enemy, because my creator, do I swear inextinguishable hatred. Have a care; I will work at your destruction, nor finish until I desolate your heart, so that you shall curse the hour of your birth."

A fiendish rage animated him as he said this; his face was wrinkled into contortions too horrible for human eyes to behold; but presently he calmed himself and proceeded, "I intended to reason. This passion is detrimental to me, for you do not reflect that you are the cause of its excess. If any being felt emotions of benevolence towards me, I should return them a hundred and a hundredfold; for that one creature's sake I would make peace with the whole kind! But I now indulge in dreams of bliss that cannot be realized. What I ask of you is reasonable and moderate; I demand a creature of another sex, but as hideous as myself; the gratification is small, but it is all that I can receive, and it shall content me. It is true, we shall be monsters, cut off from all the world; but on that account we shall be more attached to one another. Our lives will not be happy, but they will be harmless and free from the misery I now feel. Oh! My creator, make me happy; let me feel gratitude towards you for one benefit! Let me see that I excite the sympathy of some existing thing; do not deny me my request!"

I was moved. I shuddered when I thought of the possible consequences of my consent, but I felt that there was some justice in his argument. His tale and the feelings he now expressed proved him to be a creature of fine sensations, and did I not as his maker owe him all the portion of happiness that it was in my power to bestow? He saw my change of feeling and continued, "If you consent, neither you nor any other human being shall ever see us again; I will go to the vast wilds of South America. My food is not that of man; I do not destroy the lamb and the kid to glut my appetite; acorns and berries afford me sufficient nourishment. My companion will be of the same nature as myself and will be content with the same fare. We shall make our bed of dried leaves; the sun will shine on us as on man and will ripen our food. The picture I present to you is peaceful and human, and you must feel that you could deny it only in the wantonness of power and cruelty.

### Bruno Schönlank, *The Patched Pants*, translated by Jack Zipes

Once upon a time there was a poor widow who worked very hard to support herself and her four sons. Even though she worked the entire day, there was never enough money for everything. She worked as a maid, and she also washed the dirty clothes of other people. Nevertheless, poverty was often an unwelcome guest in her small flat. There's a saying that hunger makes for the best kind of cook. Yet when there is hardly a thing in the home and four hungry mouths to feed, one can gladly do without such a cook. If a child cries, "Mother, I'm hungry," it's often like sweet music to a mother's ears, but only when the cupboard is full, when bread and potatoes are aplenty. However, if the last bread crumb has been eaten and there's no money to buy more bread, the child's hungry cry is enough to break the mother's heart.

Still, she tried to smile. "Soon, children, soon." Yes, that was often the way things were in the widow's home. Whenever it was at all possible, she made sacrifices so that her boys would have something to eat. But that's not all. The boys had to be clothed, and that caused certain problems. The oldest son had the best of the bargain. The youngest, who was six, had the worst, for he had to wear whatever was left over. So anything that wasn't torn into a thousand shreds made its way from Henry down to Johnny and Walter and finally to Frankie, whose suit often appeared to be made out of tiny patches. And his last pair of pants was truly a sort of miraculous patchwork.

Those rips and holes caused by Henry, Johnny, and Walter were repaired, but Frankie added his own, for a fence is a fence and doesn't ask if the pants are strong and durable. And a young boy doesn't pay attention when he romps around and jumps all over the place. "Oh no, the pants!" Frankie's mother could only sigh when the pants came home with new rips and holes in them.

"Oh God, oh God, there's hardly a place for a new patch, and the stuff is already quite worn out!"

You can see that the pants were a sad lot. And Frankie had to suffer a great deal because some stupid children made fun of him and his pants. Sometimes he wished that he had been a girl to see whether his mother could have made a skirt out of the leftover pants. But he only thought about this and would have never said it to his mother.

The boys spent most of their free time on the streets. Every now and then they found ways to earn a little money by moving pushcarts or similar things. Once, when they were running around near a marketplace, they passed a junk store. An old man with a long white beard stood in front of the store. On his right shoulder sat a green parrot, and on the left, a multicolored parrot. The green one screeched:

Come right in,
fat and thin,
come right in!

And the multicolored parrot exclaimed:

Sell your junk!
Buy our junk!
Come right in,
and bargain,
bargain!

Just as little Frankie and his brothers rushed past the store, the two birds began to squeal and jump up and down excitedly on the old man's shoulders. "Come right in, come right in!" The screeching scared the children, and they ran faster. But the old man raced after them; with the parrots flying around his head as he ran. The boys were now more frightened and tried to run even faster. However, the junk dealer came closer and closer. Where could they find a hiding place? Suddenly, they spied an open door in an old abandoned house. The children scampered through the door with the junk dealer on their heels and the parrots crying:

Stay,
Oh, stay!
Just one word.
Don't run away.
Stay.
Don't run away!

The parrots sounded so sad that the boys calmed down. There were tears in the old man's eyes. "Children, children," he called to his parrots, "which one is it?"

The two parrots began to exclaim, "Frankie, Frankie!" Come with me," he said to the boys, and I'll give you whatever you want."

The boys didn't know whether they should laugh or cry out for help. Finally, they summoned up the courage to go with the man. The two parrots flew ahead. The old man walked behind them, and the boys marched in the middle until they reached the store. The old man took his place in front of the door, and the two parrots screeched again. The green one cried,

Come right in,
fat and thin,
Come right in!

And the multicolored parrot added:

Sell your junk!
Buy our junk!
Come right in,
and bargain,
bargain!

The old man waved his hand, and the boys entered the store somewhat hesitantly. The air was stuffy and musty. There were old clothes,
porcelain figures, bed frames, rusted pistols, pictures, watches, chains,
glass pearls. A mess of junk, all mixed up, even shoes that had been
totally worn out. Suddenly all of these things began to babble in confusion. There were so many sad stories to hear. Much trouble, much misery. And yet much love, yes, much love. The pair of shoes that had been
completely worn out had experienced many different things. Up the
stairs, down the stairs, early in the morning. Getting children ready for
school and delivering papers, then cleaning the houses of other people.
Once when it snowed outside, the shoes became soaking wet, and the
poor old woman caught a cold and died. Since every little thing had to
be sold to pay for the funeral, the old shoes went too.

That was only one of the stories. The bed frame told how it had been
exchanged for a small coffin. The dancing porcelain figures that
appeared so graceful with their uplifted skirts had seen better days. The
silver watch had been exchanged for bread because a jobless father did
not have enough money to feed his children. And he had been very
proud of the watch when he received it as a present in his youth. He
must have taken it out of his pocket over a thousand times and had been
happy as a king to tell someone the correct time. And the golden chain in
the junk store blinked sadly. It was difficult to see that it had been spotted by blood. Someone had been murdered because of this golden ornament. But my tale would be endless if I were to tell you all of the stories
behind all of the things in the junk store.

The old man approached the boys and said, "They're all sad stories."
The parrots flapped their wings. "And my story is also very sad. Once I
was rich, but I never thought about anyone else's problems. I hired poor
people to work for me, and I barely gave them enough so that they could
eat. Oh yes, the people called me rich, but now I know just how poor I
really was. Once a frail woman came to me and asked me for money
because her children were starving.

" 'I'll give you this old painting for the money,' she said.

" 'Leave me alone,' I said, for I had very little time and was about to
go to a dance. Then my two daughters cried out.

" 'Come, father, come. We'll be late for the ball. Tell the old woman to go away.'

" 'Sir,' the old woman said. 'Listen. It's for my children's sake. It's for my children!'"

" 'Don't bother me with your junk!' I shouted and shoved the woman aside. Then she touched my shoulders with her bony hands and looked at me with her large, hard eyes.

" 'Well, then learn what junk really is!'

"And I felt myself becoming old, and my daughters were changed into parrots.

"So now I've been buying and selling junk for years. I feel that I'm getting older and older, and there's still no salvation."

And he began to weep so much that his tears fell onto the dusty floor.

"Who knows how long I must keep this up? But I must keep buying and selling until I find the most precious thing in the world. I've learned that the most precious thing is not jewelry or gold. No, it's invisible. The old and miserable things are often more precious than all of the splendors of the world. There's so much love and care, so much suffering and grief tied up with the old things."

The parrots flapped their wings again and called out, "Come, Frankie, give us your pants as a gift."

And Frankie looked at the patched pants, and suddenly the pants began to speak: "Think of how much love has been sewn into me. The gray patch there came from Henry. Do you remember how he slipped and tore a large hole in me? Your mother didn't scold him. She merely sighed, and then late in the evening she sewed the gray patch on me with her weary hands. Yes, you boys ripped many things, but fortunately you've stayed healthy and happy."

Then the patches and stitches began to speak. Stitch, stitch, stitch, stitch on summer evenings. Stitch, stitch, stitch, stitch on cold winter nights. Brrr, brrr, how cold, and yet the mother's hardworking hands toiled for the boys in the evenings, even when they were tired and worn out.

All of the satin and silk, all of the splendors of the earth are not enough to match this. The parrots landed on Frankie's shoulders and begged sadly: "Give us your pants as a gift!"

Frankie had now become fond of his pants, but when he looked at the parrots, he became so sorry for them that he said, "All right, they're yours."

And as he began to take off his pants, he heard wonderful and enchanting music. All of a sudden, two large, beautiful girls appeared and tenderly embraced him and his brothers. And the old man became a strong and healthy man again.

"Come, my boys," he said. "Let's go to your flat."

. . .

The people in the entire building gathered together in the courtyard, and there was a huge celebration. It was really beautiful, so beautiful, that I wish we all could have been there.

# Permissions and
# Acknowledgments

———❖———

"Eleven," from *Woman Hollering Creek.* © 1991 by Sandra Cisneros. By
  permission of Susan Bergholz Literary Services.

*The Endless Steppe: Growing Up in Siberia.* © 1968 by Esther Hautzig. By
  permission of HarperCollins Publishers.

"Everyone Sang," from *Collected Poems, 1908 to 1956.* © 1961 by Siegfried
  Sassoon. By permission of G. T. Sassoon.

"A Fairy Tale About God and Kings" and "The Patched Pants," from *Fairy
  Tales and Fables from Weimar Days,* edited and translated by Jack
  Zipes. © 1989 by Jack Zipes. By permission of University Press of
  New England.

*Farewell to Manzanar.* © 1973 by James D. Houston and Jeanne
  Wakatsuki Houston. By permission of Houghton Mifflin Co.

*Fathers,* compiled and edited by Jon Winokur. © 1993 by Jon Winokur.
  By permission of Dutton Signet, a division of Penguin Books USA
  Inc.

*Fifth Chinese Daughter.* Copyright 1950, renewed © 1989 by Jade Snow
  Wong. By permission of University of Washington Press.

"First Memory," from *Ararat.* © 1990 by Louise Glück. First published by
  the Ecco Press, 1990. By permission of the press.

"Flowers and Freckle Cream," from *Best-Loved Stories Told at the National
  Storytelling Festival.* © 1991 by Elizabeth Ellis. By permission of the
  storyteller.

"For Poets." © 1969 by Al Young. By permission of the author.

*Frederick.* © 1967 by Leo Lionni. By permission of Pantheon Books, a
  division of Random House, Inc.

"The Frog and the Ox," from *Aesop: Five Centuries of Illustrated Fables*
  (retold by William Caxton). © 1964 The Metropolitan Museum of
  Art. By permission of the museum.

"The Genius Child," from *Selected Poems.* Copyright 1947 by Langston
  Hughes. By permission of Alfred A. Knopf, Inc.

"Grandma's Cherries," acceptance speech, Heinz Awards 1995. By permission of Geoffrey Canada.

*The Grapes of Wrath.* Copyright 1939, renewed © 1967 by John Steinbeck.
  By permission of Viking/Penguin, a division of Penguin Books USA
  Inc.

"The Grateful Sparrow" and selections from "Man'Yoshu," from
  *Anthology of Japanese Literature,* edited and translated by Donald
  Keene. Copyright 1955 by Grove Press. By permission of
  Grove/Atlantic, Inc.

"The Growing," from *Poets for the People,* edited by Barry Feinberg.
  Published by Allen & Unwin in 1974; first published in

*Yakhal'inkomo* by Renoster Books, Johannesburg. © 1972 by
Mongane Wally Serote.

"Half the People in the World," from *Selected Poetry of Yehuda Amichai.*
English translation © 1986 by Chana Bloch and Stephen Mitchell. By
permission of HarperCollins Publishers.

"Harriet Tubman Is in My Blood," an oral history from *Talk That Talk:
Anthology of African-American Storytelling.* © 1989 by Mariline
Wilkins. By permission of the author.

*The House at Pooh Corner.* Copyright 1928 by E.P. Dutton, renewed ©
1956 by A. A. Milne. By permission of Dutton Children's Books, a
division of Penguin Books USA Inc.

*How the Children Stopped the Wars.* © 1969 by Jan Wahl. By permission
of Tricycle Press.

"How the Hat Ashes Shovel Helped Snoo Foo," from *Rootabaga Stories.*
Copyright 1923 by Carl Sandburg, 1922 by Harcourt, Brace &
Company, renewed © 1951, 1950 by Carl Sandburg. By permission
of the publisher.

*The Human Cycle.* © 1983 by Colin Turnbull. By permission of Simon &
Schuster, Inc.

*The Hunchback of Notre Dame,* translated by Walter J. Cobb. © 1965 by
Walter J. Cobb. By permission of Dutton Signet, a division of
Penguin Books USA Inc.

*The Hundred Dresses.* Copyright 1944 by Harcourt, Brace & Company,
renewed © 1971 by Eleanor Estes and Louis Slobodkin. By permission of the publisher.

"Hunger," adapted from *The Songs and Stories of Aunt Molly Jackson* in
the Folklife Collection of the Smithsonian Institution. © 1994 by Si
Kahn. By permission of the author.

"I Have a Dream." © 1963 by Martin Luther King Jr., renewed © 1991 by
Coretta Scott King. By permission of the heirs to the Estate of
Martin Luther King, c/o Joan Daves Agency.

*I Have Words to Spend.* © 1991 by Constance Cormier. By permission of
Dell Books, a division of Bantam Doubleday Dell Publishing Group
Inc.

*The Immense Journey.* © 1959 by Loren Eiseley. By permission of
Random House, Inc.

"In Memory of Our Cat, Ralph," from *We Are Still Married: Stories and
Letters.* © 1982, 1983, 1984, 1985, 1986, 1987, 1988, 1989 and 1990
by Garrison Keillor. By permission of Viking/Penguin, a division of
Penguin Books USA Inc.

"In My Craft or Sullen Art," from *Poems of Dylan Thomas.* © 1946 by

New Directions Publishing. By permission of New Directions
Publishing Corp. and David Higham Associates, Ltd.

"Indian Boarding School: The Runaways," from *Jacklight*. First appeared
in *Frontiers*. © 1984 by Louise Erdrich. By permission of Henry Holt
& Company.

*Invisible Man*. Copyright 1947, 1948, 1952 by Ralph Ellison. By permission of Random House, Inc.

"Isabel," from *Adventures of Isabel*. © 1963 by Ogden Nash. By permission
of Little, Brown & Company.

*Izzy, Willy-Nilly*. © 1968 by Cynthia Voigt. By permission of Simon &
Schuster, Inc.

"The Jacket," from *Small Faces*. © 1986 by Gary Soto. By permission of
Bantam Doubleday Dell Books for Young Readers.

*Jaguarandi*. © 1995 by Virginia Hamilton. By permission of Scholastic, Inc.

"Joe Hill." Copyright 1938, renewed by MCA Music Publishing, a division of MCA. By permission of the publisher.

*Just above My Head*. © 1979 by James Baldwin. By permission of
Doubleday.

*Just Like Martin*. © 1992 by Ossie Davis. Published by Simon & Schuster.
By permission of the author.

"Katori Maru, October 1920," from *Crossing the Phantom River*.
Published by Graywolf Press. © 1978 by James Masao Mitsui. By permission of the author.

"The King's Breakfast," from *When We Were Very Young*. Copyright 1924
by E.P. Dutton, renewed 1952 by A. A. Milne. By permission of
Dutton Children's Books, a division of Penguin Books USA Inc.

*Lame Deer: Seeker of Visions*. © 1972 by John Fire/Lame Deer and
Richard Erdoes. By permission of Simon & Schuster, Inc.

"The Laugher," from *The Stories of Heinrich Böll*, translated by Leila
Vennewitz. Translation © 1986 by Leila Vennewitz and the Estate of
Heinrich Böll. By permission of Alfred A. Knopf, Inc.

*Let Us Now Praise Famous Men*. Copyright 1939, 1940 by James Agee.
Copyright 1941 by James Agee and Walker Evans. © renewed 1969 by
Mia Fritsch Agee and Walker Evans. By permission of Houghton
Mifflin Co.

"The Letter 'A,'" from *My Left Foot*. First published in Great Britain by
Martin Secker & Warburg. Copyright 1954 by Christy Brown. By
permission of Reed Consumer Books Ltd.

"Lincoln's Famous Beard," from *Best-Loved Stories Told at the National
Storytelling Festival*. © 1991 by Lucille Breneman. By permission of
the storyteller.

permission of the William Morris Agency, Inc. Inquiries concerning rights should be addressed to William Morris Agency, Inc.: 1324 Avenue of the Americas, New York, NY 10019; Attn: Peter Franklin.

"My Mother's Mother," from *The Common Thread: Writings of Working Class Women.* © by Annette Kennerly. Published by Mandarin Paperbacks.

"A Night in a World," from *Hinge & Sign.* Published by Wesleyan University Press. © 1994 by Heather McHugh. By permission of University Press of New England.

"Not Coming Too Late," from a speech to Clergy & Laity Concerned, Washington, D.C., 1967, in *Abraham Joshua Heschel: Exploring His Life and Thought,* edited by John C. Merkle. © 1976 by Macmillan Publishing. By permission of the Estate of Abraham J. Heschel and Simon & Schuster Macmillan.

"Now That the Water Presses Hard," from *Yehuda Amichai: A Life of Poetry, 1948–94.* © 1994 by HarperCollins Publishers. Hebrew-language version © 1994 by Yehuda Amichai. By permission of HarperCollins Publishers.

*One More River.* © 1973 by Lynn Reid Banks. By permission of Morrow Junior Books, a division of William Morrow Co., Inc.

"Orange Cheeks," from *Best Loved Stories Told at the National Storytelling Festival.* © 1991 by Jay O'Callahan. A version of this story, with the same title, is available as a children's picture book illustrated by Patricia Raine, published by Peachtree Publishers, 1993. By permission of the storyteller.

"O To Be a Dragon," from the *Complete Poems of Marianne Moore.* © 1957 by Marianne Moore, renewed © 1985 by Lawrence E. Brinn and Louise Crane, executors of the Estate of Marianne Moore. By permission of Viking/Penguin, a division of Penguin Books USA Inc.

*Ourika,* translated by John Fowles. © 1977 by John Fowles. By permission of Shiel Land Associates Ltd.

*Papa, Please Get the Moon for Me.* © 1986 by Eric Carle. By permission of Picture Books Studio, an imprint of Simon & Schuster's children's publishing division.

"Pictures of the Gone World," from *A Coney Island of the Mind.* © 1958 by Lawrence Ferlinghetti. By permission of New Directions Publishing Corp.

*Pig Earth.* © 1979 by John Berger. By permission of Pantheon Books, a division of Random House, Inc.

"Pippi Entertains Two Burglars," from *Pippi Longstocking,* translated by Florence Lamborn. Translation copyright 1950 by the Viking Press,

Inc., renewed © 1978 by Viking/Penguin. By permission of Viking/Penguin, a division of Penguin Books USA Inc.

"Poem," from *A Muriel Rukeyser Reader*. Published by W. W. Norton in 1994. © 1994 by William L. Rukeyser. By permission of William L. Rukeyser.

"Prologue from Angelitos Negros: A Salsa Ballet," from *Currents from the Dancing River: Contemporary Latino Fiction, Nonfiction, and Poetry*. © Miguel Algarín. By permission of the author.

"Promised Land," from *Voices from the Fields*. © 1993 by S. Beth Atkins. By permission of Little, Brown & Company.

Psalms 15 and 133, from *A Book of Psalms*. © 1993 by Stephen Mitchell. By permission of HarperCollins Publishers.

"'Race' Politics," from *Cool Salsa*, edited by Lori M. Carlson. Collection © 1994 by Lori M. Carlson. By permission of Henry Holt & Company.

*A Raisin in the Sun*. © 1958 by Robert Nemiroff as an unpublished work. © 1959, 1966, 1984 by Robert Nemiroff. By permission of Random House, Inc.

*Ramona Quimby, Age 8*. © 1982 by Beverly Cleary. By permission of Morrow Junior Books, a division of William Morrow Co., Inc..

*Rascal*. © 1963 by Sterling North, renewed © 1991 by David S. North and Arielle North Olson. By permission of Dutton Children's Books, a division of Penguin Books USA Inc.

"The Republic of Conscience," from *The Haw Lantern*. © 1987 by Seamus Heaney. By permission of Farrar Straus Giroux.

*The Return of the Indian*. © 1986 by Lynn Reid Banks. By permission of Doubleday.

"Running as a Spiritual Experience." © 1977 by Michael Spino. By permission of the author.

"Satisfaction," from *The Art of Writing: Lu Chi's Wen Fu*. © 1991 by Sam Hamill. By permission of Milkweed Editions.

"The School Play," from *Local News*. © 1993 by Gary Soto. By permission of Harcourt, Brace & Company.

"The Scotty Who Knew Too Much," from *Fables for Our Time*. Copyright 1940 by James Thurber, renewed © 1968 by Rosemary A. Thurber. By permission of Thurber Literary Properties.

"The Secret," from *O Taste & See*. © 1964 by Denise Levertov. By permission of New Directions Publishing Corp.

"Shawno." © 1982, 1984 by George Dennison. First published in *St. John's Review*, Winter 1982. Collected in *A Tale of Pierrot and Other Stories*. By permission of the Estate of George Dennison.

"Shooting an Elephant," from *Shooting an Elephant and Other Essays*.

"Unlearning to Not Speak," from *Circles on the Water.* © 1982 by Marge Piercy. By permission of Alfred A. Knopf, Inc.

"Variations on a Theme by Rilke," from *Breathing Water.* © 1984, 1985, 1986, 1987 by Denise Levertov. By permission of New Directions Publishing Corp.

"The War of the Bells," from *Favole al telefono* by Gianno Rodari. Published in Italy by Einaudi in 1962. Translated by Jack Zipes. © 1990 by Jack Zipes. By permission of Julio Einaudi Editore.

*The Way of Life According to Lao Tzu,* edited by Witter Bynner. Copyright 1944 by Witter Bynner, renewed © 1972 by Dorothy Chauvenet and Paul Horgan. By permission of HarperCollins Publishers.

*West with the Night.* Copyright 1942 by Beryl Markham. By permission of Farrar Straus Giroux.

"What I Have Lived For," from *Autobiography.* © 1967 by Bertrand Russell. Published by Allen & Unwin in 1967. By permission of Routledge.

"Who Understands Me, But Me?" from *Poetry Like Bread: Poets of the Political Imagination from Curbstone Press,* edited by Martín Espada. © 1982 by Jimmy Santiago Baca. By permission of Curbstone Press.

"Wilbur's Escape," from *Charlotte's Web.* Copyright 1952 by E. B. White. By permission of HarperCollins Publishers.

*The Wisdom of the Jewish Sages.* © 1995 by Rabbi Rami M. Shapiro. By permission of Crown Publishers, Inc.

*The World Is Round.* © 1939 by Gertrude Stein and renewed by the Estate of Gertrude Stein. By permission of the estate.

*A Wrinkle in Time.* © 1962 by Madeleine L'Engle. By permission of Farrar Straus Giroux.

"You'd Better Believe Him: A Fable," from *Grinning Jack: Selected Poems.* © 1990 by Brian Patten. By permission of HarperCollins Publishers.

While every effort has been made to obtain permission, there may still be cases in which we have failed to trace a copyright holder, and we would like to apologize for any apparent negligence.

# Author Index